EYES FOR THE PHOENIX

Allied Aerial Photo-Reconnaissance Operations
South-East Asia
1941-1945

Geoffrey J. Thomas

HIKOKI
PUBLICATIONS

First published in Great Britain in 1999 by
Hikoki Publications Ltd
16 Newport Road, Aldershot, Hants, GU12 4PB
Tel: 01252 319935 Fax: 01252 655593
E.mail: hikoki@dircon.co.uk
Website: http//www.hikoki.dircon.co.uk/
© 1999 Hikoki Publications

ISBN 0 9519899 4 4

Edited by Barry Ketley
Artwork by Mark Rolfe & David Howley
Maps by Steve Longland
Design by Hikoki Publications
Printed in Great Britain by Alden Press, Oxford

Distribution & Marketing by
Midland Publishing Ltd
24 The Hollow, Earl Shilton, Leicester LE9 7NA
Tel: 01455 233 747 Fax: 01455 233 737

Publisher's Note: Some of the pictures in this book are not of the usual high quality expected from Hikoki Publications. They are included not only on account of their rarity value, but as graphic examples of the conditions in which all members of the photo-reconnaissance units had to live, work and fight—as will become abundantly clear to the reader

Caption to front dust jacket: Grumman Hellcat II(P) JW723, '6G', of 804 NAS aboard HMS Ameer in December 1944. It is finished in Temperate Sea Scheme camouflage with Sky undersides and Eastern Fleet national markings

Caption to rear dust jacket: 'Mercury', a Dakota regularly used by Lord Louis Mountbatten, Supreme Allied Commander South-East Asia, showing the Phoenix symbol adopted by his HQ

Caption to title page: A Mosquito with PRU Blue undersurfaces displays the standard camera positions and the identification lights below the rear fuselage

ALSO AVAILABLE

Courage Alone
The Italian Air Force 1940-1943
by
Chris Dunning
ISBN 1 902109 02 3

The Secret Years
Flight Testing at Boscombe Down 1939-1945
by
Tim Mason
ISBN 0 9519899 9 5

Forever Farnborough
Flying the Limits 1904-1996
by
Peter J. Cooper AMRAeS
ISBN 0 9519899 3 6

Royal Naval Air Service 1912-1918
by
Brad King
ISBN 0 9519899 5 2

Luftwaffe Emblems 1939-1945
by
Barry Ketley & Mark Rolfe
ISBN 0 9519899 7 9

Luftwaffe Fledglings 1935-1945
Luftwaffe Training Units & their Aircraft
by
Barry Ketley & Mark Rolfe
ISBN 0 9519899 2 8

FORTHCOMING

Stormbird
Flying through fire as a Luftwaffe ground-attack
pilot and Me 262 ace
by
Oberst (i. R.) Hermann Buchner
ISBN 1 902109 00 7

Shadows
Airlift and Airwar in Biafra and Nigeria
1967-1970
by
Michael I. Draper
ISBN 1 902109 63 5

Condor
The Luftwaffe in Spain 1936-1939
by
Patrick Laureau
ISBN 1 902109 10 4

CONTENTS

DEDICATION

Above all to my Maureen for her loving care and unfailing patience

ACKNOWLEDGMENTS

The material in this book is derived from a wide variety of sources, published and unpublished. Principal sources are the files of the Air Ministry and Ministry of Aircraft Production, the Operation Record Books of Groups, Wings, Squadrons and PR Units held at the Public Record Office, and the Squadron Historical Data held at the HQ USAF Historical Research Center. Other material is taken from Commanders' Reports published after the war in the *London Gazette*, in some instances here quoted verbatim.

A considerable quantity of additional information has come from personnel who were directly involved in PR operations as do many of the photographs included here. Some of these photographs have an uncertain provenance; copyright is sometimes claimed by 'official' bodies who have acquired prints from individuals.

Others are 'owned' by people who simply had additional prints of photographs which were, technically, Crown Copyright when they were taken. I have therefore not attributed photographs individually, but simply acknowledge a debt of thanks to all those who provided them, where known. These include Group Captain 'Jeff' Jefford MBE, C.A. Jones, Barry Money, Robert Jones, the late John D.R. Rawlings, Alan Barnett, David A. Bearne, Neil Guy, Flight Lieutenant Norman Robertson, Peter Bingham-Wallis, R. Webb, C.H. Kens, S. Hills, R. Crane, A. Latham, R. Wardhaugh, Chaz Bowyer, P. Sweeting, Merton Naydler, Donald McPhail, L.L. Bockford, Pushpindar Singh, AVM Sir Ian Pedder, Barry Ketley and Mervyn Caswell, who also provided some recollections of his time with 681 Squadron.

Affixes to the names of personnel—RAF, RAFVR, RNZAF, RNVR and so on are omitted in most cases, so that the narrative may not be unduly interrupted.

I must acknowledge my thanks to the many friends who have helped in the preparation of this work; in particular to Wing Commander Donald Pearson DFC, Group Captain Derek Thirlwell OBE DFC, Alan Fox DFM and Commander Brian McCaw DSC; to the late Wing Commander Freddie Procter DFC, Wing Commander 'Bunny' Stone DFC and Flight Lieutenant Frank Guy DFC for the loan of photographs and for quotations from their recollections of those stirring times. For encouragement, advice and for documents I am indebted to Peter Arnold, Ian K. Baker, Dana Bell of The National Air and Space Museum, Smithsonian Institution; to Chris Ellis, Commander R.C. Hay DSO, DSC; Dr Jim Kitchens of the Albert F. Simpson Historical Research Center of the USAF, History Center; to Roy C. Nesbit, Gerald Stevens, Ray Sturtivant, Brian Cull, Flight Lieutenant 'Andy' Thomas, Richard L. Ward, Squadron Leader D.W. 'Joe' Warne and to my constant friend Roy Pelham for his support.

I am especially grateful to Dr Ian Douglas and Dr Patrick Trend; without their attention and care this book would not have been completed.

If readers feel that there is a lack of 'balance' in the emphasis on early PR operations, I make no apology. The early activities of the PR units are concealed in a variety of archives here and abroad but anyone requiring further information on the period beginning with the formation of 681 Squadron can easily find it in the Operational Record Books (A.540 and A.541) of the RAF and IAF Squadrons, held at the Public Records Office, Kew. These documents include details of operations and of the activities and movements of aircraft in the squadrons.

The photographic units of the British Pacific Fleet are described in some detail; although the aircraft carriers, aircraft and personnel were no longer under control of South-East Asia Command in 1945, they were the same units continuing operations under US Navy command and are worthy of record here.

Names of places

The anglicised phonetic spelling of place-names is somewhat variable in different histories of Second World War campaigns in the Far East. For instance, the Official Despatches and Reports publicised in the London Gazette describing the campaign in Malaya refer both to Kota Baru and to Kota Bahru (the official spelling of the name). Strictly speaking, both are wrong—the current 'romanised' spelling of the Malay name is Kota Baharu, meaing 'the new fort'.

Here, the names of places in India, Burma and the Malay Peninsula are 'anglicised' but for those in the Netherlands East Indies I have retained the Dutch spelling of the period, with 'oe' for 'u', 'j' for 'y' and 'dj' for 'j'.

In anglicised Burmese, 'Ky' in place-names, as in Kyaiktaw, is pronounced as the English 'Ch-'. Burma (Biruma to the Japanese) was known for some years as Mynamar, and its capital, Rangoon, reverted to the original name of Chunggon. More recently, the familiar names have again been used.

Several versions of names, particularly of places in Siam (Thailand) appeared on wartime maps. These different spellings were usually derived from maps of different origins and dates, some as early as 1889. The alternative names Prachab Ghirikahan or Prachap-khirikhan and Nakhauun Sawan or Nakawn Sawan are typical. In general, I have adopted the late wartime spelling of place names used on the HIND 1050 and 5000 series of military maps (1943-1945) and, where relevant, on the final issue of the Enemy Airfield Serviceability Map (HIND Misc./7225) dated 23 July 1945.

FOREWORD

By
Wing Commander Donald B. Pearson DFC RAF (Retd)

When the Japanese entered the war without declaring their intentions in December 1941 I was flying as Chief Flying Instructor on Harvard aircraft at Kluang in Malaya. From that moment I made attempts to get posted to an operational Fighter Squadron but entirely without success as my rank was that of Acting Squadron Leader. However, I finally contacted Squadron Leader Lewis, CO of No. 4 PRU operating Brewster Buffalos, and by relinquishing my acting rank I was able to join this unit as a Flight Lieutenant. I had already spent three and a half years flying with the RAF in Malaya and was, I suppose, an ideal pilot for PR work as I knew the country so well.

The Far East appeared to be almost totally unprepared for war against Japan, and our knowledge of their Forces practically nil. Reconnaissance was therefore of prime importance, but once again the performance of our reconnaissance aircraft was well below that required for the work.

Any account of the war in the Far East during 1941-1942 must inevitably be a record of disasters due to many reasons; the lack of modern equipment, experience, and Intelligence far outweighed the extreme bravery of the aircrews, some of whom were flying in 100 mph biplanes against modern fighters and bombers. In view of these factors you may

consider when reading this excellent account the value of awards made while fighting a losing battle. Firstly of course, there are fewer awards made, and secondly they are won usually under far more difficult conditions and against far greater odds, and these conditions applied to nearly all the aircrews operating over Malaysia, Indonesia, and Burma.

To many of you who have probably only flown in passenger aircraft it must be difficult to imagine being at 35-40,000ft above the earth, hundreds of miles from your home base over enemy held territory and, in the single-engined Buffalos, Hurricanes and Spitfires, absolutely alone.

I trust that you will enjoy reading this detailed account of an aspect of a war which was fought by so many gallant men of our Allied reconnaissance Forces so long ago, and so far away.

2 Above: Hurricane IIB, BM969, being flown by Flg Off Donald Pearson, 'S' Flight Commander, of No.3 PRU (India) in mid-1942. The weather-beaten special 'royal blue' overall finish was so close to the Dull Blue of the roundels that 2in wide Yellow surrounds have been added to them

3 Right: An unidentified young pilot seated in Spitfire PR.XI PL781, 'F', of 681 Sqn at Kuala Lumpur, Malaya. The 'sighting' mark for oblique photography can be seen marked on the side of the cockpit canopy, port side only

INTRODUCTION

The story of photographic reconnaissance over Europe from bases in the United Kingdom is well known. Less familiar is the record of the units operating in the Mediterranean area, whose activities were vital in keeping watch on the Axis forces during the fast-moving fighting from the Western Desert to Tunisia. Perhaps even more important, in terms of strategy (and mostly unrecorded), was the job of the photographic squadrons in the Far East; to discover Japanese movements and intentions within a vast area, 2,000 miles across and centred on Western Borneo, within which virtually no intelligence could otherwise be obtained after the surrender of the Netherlands East Indies.

Photographic Reconnaissance often brings to mind images of high-flying Spitfires and Mosquitoes against a background of deep blue sky. Here a story is told of a variety of aircraft, some basically unsuited to the task but locally modified for photographic operations, flying often through appalling weather conditions over empty ocean or jungle-covered mountains where interception or simple mechanical failure left small chance of survival.

It may appear unjust to describe some events and operations in detail while ignoring many others that may have been equally dangerous, unfortunately space is limited. Many difficult photographic sorties, in particular between the time of the 1944 monsoon and the end of the war, were, at the time, considered as routine operations and were only briefly described in the squadrons' Operation Record Books; and in the pilots' Flying Log Books. Official recognition of the worth of these operations came with gallantry awards. Cpl Alan Fox, awarded the Distinguished Flying Medal for taking part in 75 photo-reconnaissance sorties may have been too dismissive of the dangers to which he and his fellows were subjected, when he wrote, "Flying high, and alone, and fast, photo-reconnaissance aircraft stood a good chance of getting away with a couple of quick runs over the target followed by a bolt for home—especially since the motivation towards responsible steadiness and prudence was sharpened by the fact that they flew unarmed. Photo-reconnaissance flying therefore suffered less of the emotional tensions and dramas that attended bomber and fighter squadrons."

This was not always true; tactical reconnaissance aircraft usually flew at low-level, and losses occurred from enemy ground fire and, on occasion, from attack by enemy fighters. The success of all aerial reconnaissance was the result of skill and persistence as acknowledged by the award of the decorations listed here. The British Distinguished Flying Cross was awarded to officers and warrant officers, and the Distinguished Flying Medal to other ranks, "for acts of courage, valour or devotion to duty performed while flying on active operations." The less prestigious US Distinguished Flying Cross was awarded to officers and enlisted men distinguished by "heroism or extraordinary achievement while participating in an aerial flight."

Awards to personnel for photographic reconnaissance, tactical reconnaissance and associated duties in South-east Asia, 1941-1945

Sqn Ldr Arjan Singh RIAF	pilot/OC, 1 Sqn RIAF.	DFC
Wt Off W.G. Bannister	navigator, 684 Sqn.	DFC
Lt F.T. Bender USAAF	pilot, 20th TR Sqn USAAF.	DFC
Flg Off D.G. Bhore MBE	pilot, 6 Sqn RIAF.	DFC
Flt Lt J. Bootli	pilot, BVAF, 684 Sqn.	DFC
Flt Lt J. Bradford RCAF	pilot/Flt Cdr, 681 Sqn.	DFC
Flg Off H.N. Bulsara RIAF	pilot, 1 Sqn RIAF.	DFC
Flt Lt I.J.N. Chaterjee RIAF	pilot 1 Sqn RIAF.	DFC
Sqn Ldr G. Craig	Photographic Officer, No.3 PRU; 681 Sqn.	OBE
Flg Off O.A. Dupee DFM	pilot, 684 Sqn	DFC
Cpl A. Fox	Air Photographer, No.3 PRU; 681 Sqn; 684 Sqn	DFM
Flt Lt F.W. Guy	pilot,No.3 PRU; 681 Sqn; 684 Sqn	DFC
Flg Off P.S. Gupta RIAF	pilot, 1 Sqn RIAF.	DFC
Flg Off R. Hawson	navigator, 684 Sqn.	DFC
Lt-Col R.C. Hay RM DSC*	pilot/Wing Leader 47th Naval Fighter Wing; Air Co-ordinator, 1st Aircraft Carrier Sqn.	DSO
S/Sgt H.S. Hinderstein	pilot, 20th TR Sqn USAAF.	DFC
Flt Lt J. Irvine	pilot, 684 Sqn.	DFC
Wt Off M. Johnston	pilot 684 Sqn.	DFC
Sqn Ldr B.S. Jones	pilot/OC, 684 Sqn.	DFC
Maj L.M. Kadell USAAF	pilot, 20th TB Sqn USAAF	DFC
Flg Off K.N. Kak RIAF	pilot, 1 Sqn RIAF.	DFC
Sqn Ldr P.C. Lal RIAF	pilot/OC, 7 Sqn RIAF.	DFC
Sqn Ldr H.G.F. Larsen	pilot/OC, 28 Sqn.	DFC
Wg Cdr W.E.M. Lowry	pilot/OC, 684 Sqn.	DFC
Flg Off P.J. McDonnel	navigator, 684 Sqn.	DFC
Cdr B.A. MacCaw RN	pilot/OC, 888 Sqn.	DSC
Flt Lt F.B. McCulloch	navigator, 684 Sqn.	DFC
Flt Lt K. MacVicar	pilot, 28 Sqn.	DFC
S/Sgt C.P. McGuire USAAF	pilot, 9th PR Sqn USAAF	DFM
Sqn Ldr P.D.F. Mitchell	pilot, 100 Sqn.	DFC
Lt R.G. Mueller USAAF	pilot, 20thTR Sqn USAAF.	DFC
Wg Cdr W.B. Murray RNZAF	pilot/OC, 684 Sqn.	DFC
Wg Cdr K.J. Newman RNZAF	pilot/OC, 684 Sqn.	DFC*
Flt Lt A.C.F. Oldworth	pilot, No.3 PRU; 681 Sqn	DFC
Flt Lt C.D. Pallthorpe	pilot, No.3 PRU; 681 Sqn	DFC
Wg Cdr J. Palmer	Engineer Officer No.3 PRU; 681 Sqn; 684 Sqn.	MBE
Flg Off A.R. Pandit RIAF	pilot, 1 Sqn RIAF.	DFC
Wg Cdr D.B. Pearson	pilot, No.4 PRU; Flt Cdr, No.3 PRU; OC, 681 Sqn.	DFC
Flt Lt A.D. Phillips	pilot, No.4 PRU	DFC
Flt Lt A.J. Picknett	pilot/Flt Cdr, 684 Sqn.	DFC
Wg Cdr F.D. Procter	pilot/Flt Cdr, No.3 PRU; OC, 681 Sqn.	DFC
Flt Lt M.H. Pujji RIAF	pilot, 4 Sqn RIAF.	DFC
Flg Off R. Rajaram RIAF	Pilot/OC 1Sqn RIAF	DFC
Flg Off R. Rao RIAF	pilot, 1 Sqn RIAF	DFC
Sqn Ldr H. Reeves	navigator, No.3 PRU; 681 Sqn.	DFC
Sqn Ldr T.N.Rosser	pilot/Flt Cdr, No.3 PRU; 68l Sqn.	DFC
Lt R.B. Sherman USAAF	pilot, 20th TR Sqn USAAF.	DFC
Flt Sgt R. Smith	navigator, 684 Sqn.	DFC
Flt Lt G. Stevens	navigator 684 Sqn.	DFC
Flg Off B.N. Surendra RIAF	pilot, 4 Sqn RIAF	DFC
Flg Off J.C. Varma RIAF	pilot, 6 Sqn RIAF.	DFC
Sgt C. Wareham RNZAF	pilot, No.4 PRU.	DFM
Flt Lt D.D. Warwick	pilot, 684 Sqn.	DFC
Lt H.H. Welsh USAAF	pilot, 20th TR Sqn USAAF.	DFC
Lt A.R. Williams USAAF	pilot, 20th TR Sqn USAAF.	DFC
Flt Sgt E. Wills	navigator 684 Sqn.	DFM
Flg Off Winship	pilot 684 Sqn.	DFC
Gp Cpt S.G. Wise	pilot/OC No.3 PRU; 681Sqn; 684 Sqn; OC 171Wing; 347 Wing.	OBE,DFC*

Compiled with the assistance of Gerald Stevens of the Ex-RAF South-East Asia Recce Force Old Colleagues Contact Group and Sqn Ldr D.W. Warne

Commanding Officers of US Air Units engaged in Strategic and Tactical Photographic Reconnaissance duties in the Far East

United States Army Air Forces

9th PR Sqn (Light)

Cpt E Kessler	Feb 1942-Aug 1942
Lt-Col JW McCoy	Aug 1942-Jan 1943

9th PR Sqn

Maj DL Swartz	Feb 1943-Dec 1943
Maj HE Miller	Dec 1943-Jun 1944

20th TR Sqn

Cpt/Maj WR Fornof	Sep 1943-Apr 1945

24th Combat Mapping Sqn

Maj JM Hubers	Mar 1943-Jan 1944
Maj HB Allen	Jan 1944-Jul 1945

40th PR Sqn

Lt-Col JW Anderson	Sep 1944-May 1945
Maj WA Bailey DFC	May 1945

US Navy

Sqn VF-12

Lt Cdr RG Dore	Jan 1944-July 1944

Royal Air Force

PR Flight, Far East Command RAF /No.4 PRU

Sqn Ldr CGR Lewis	Nov 1941-Feb 1942

PR Flight, Burma Command /No.3 PRU

direct command of AOC Burma,

AV-M DF Stevenson OBE DSO NC	Jan 1942- Apr 1942

No.5 PRU/No.3 PRU (India)

Sqn Ldr AC Pearson	Apr 1942-May 1942
Wg Cdr SG Wise DFC	May 1942-Jan 1943

No.20 (AC)Sqn

Sqn Ldr HG Fletcher DFC	Jun 1942-Mar 1943

No.28 (AC)Sqn

Sqn Ldr PN Jennings	Jan 1942-Mar 1942
Sqn Ldr ORW Hammerbeck	Mar 1942-May 1942

No.28 (FR)Sqn

Sqn Ldr AS Mann	Jan 1943-Mar 1943
Sqn Ldr TR Pierce	Mar 1943-Aug 1943
San Ldr HGF Larsen	Aug 1943-Jul 1944
FIt Lt AE Guymer	Jul 1944-Oct 1944
Sqn Ldr HGF Larsen	Oct 1944-Feb 1945
Sqn Ldr EG Parnell	Feb 1945-Apr 1945
Sqn Ldr AE Guymer	Apr 1945-Jun 1945
Sqn Ldr J Rhind	Jun 1945-Jul 1945

No.45 (B)Sqn

Wg Cdr CB Wallis DSO	Jan 1942-Feb 1942

No.60 (B)Sqn

Wg Cdr RL Vivian	Dec 1941-Feb 1942

No.67 (F)Sqn

Sqn Ldr A Milward	Jan 1942-Feb 1942

No.113 (B)Sqn

Wg Cdr R Stidolph	Mar 1942-Apr 1942
Wg Cdr JF Grey	Feb 1943-Apr 1943

No.160 (GR)Sqn

Wg Cdr CA Butler	Mar 1943-Jun 1944
Wg Cdr GR Brady	Jun 1944-Nov 1944
Wg Cdr JN Stacey DSO DFC	Nov 1944-May 1945

No.681 (PR)Sqn

Wg Cdr SG Wise DFC*	Jan 1943-Dec 1943
Wg Cdr FD Procter DFC	Dec 1943-Apr 1945
Wg Cdr DB Pearson DFC	Apr 1945-Mar 1946
Sqn Ldr H Roberts	Mar 1946-Aug 1946

became No.34 Sqn

Sqn Ldr H Roberts	Aug 1946-Jul 1949

No.684 (PR)Sqn

Sqn Ldr BS Jones	Sep 1943-Dec 1943
Wg Cdr WB Murray	Dec 1943-Nov 1944
Wg Cdr WEN Lowry DFC	Nov 1944-Nov 1945
Wg Cdr KJ Newman DFC*	Nov 1945-Apr 1946
Wg Cdr JRH Merrifield DFC*	Apr 1946-Sep1946

became No.81 Sqn

Wg Cdr JRH Merrifield DFC*	Sep 1946-Jun 1947
Sqn Ldr BA Fairhurst DFC	Jun 1947-Jan 1949

Indian Air Force/Royal Indian Air Force

No.1 Sqn

Sqn Ldr KK Naumdar DFC	Feb 1942
Sqn Ldr Arjan Singh DFC	Feb 1943-Dec 1944
Sqn Ldr K Rajaram DFC	Dec 1944-Mar 1945

No.2 Sqn

Sqn Ldr HU Khan	Apr 1942
Sqn Ldr Jaswant Singh	Dec 1944-May 1945

No.4 Sqn

Sqn Ldr GS Sharp	Apr 1944-Dec 1944
Sqn Ldr Helsby?	Dec? 1944
Sqn Ldr WB Berry	Dec 1944-Apr 1945

No.6 Sqn

Sqn Ldr Mehar Singh	Nov 1943-May 1945

No.7 Sqn

Sqn Ldr P Chandra Lal DFC	Mar 1945-May 1945

No.9 Sqn

Sqn Ldr DA Adams	Jan 1945-Apr 1945

No.10 Sqn

Sqn Ldr RFD Doe DFC	Dec 1944-Mar 1945

Air Branch, Royal Navy

No.804 Sqn

Lt-Cdr (A) GBC Sangster	Jan 1945-May 1945
Lt-Cdr (A) GB Law	May 1945-Jun 1945

No.807 Sqn

Lt-Cdr(A) DJ Clark	May 1945-Aug 1945

No.880 Sqn

Lt-Cdr(A) RA Crosley DSC*	Jun 1945-Aug 1945

No.888 Sqn

Lt(A) BA McCaw DSC	Jan 1945-Aug 1945

PR Flight, No.5 NFW

Lt-Cdr(A) AM Tritton DSC	Jul 1945-Aug 1945

PR Flight, No.15 NFW

Lt-Cdr(A) AM Tritton DSC	Jun 1944-Jul 1945

Special Flight No.47 NFW/ Air Co-ord, BPF

Maj/Lt-Col RC Hay DSO DSC RM	Jul 1944 - Jul 1945

PR Flight No.1 CAG

Cdr(A) JCH Shrubsole	Jul 1945-Aug 1945

PR/NF Flight No.2 CAG

Maj PP Nelson-Gracie RA	Jul 1945-Oct 1945

PR Flight No.11 CAG

Lt-Cdr(A) TW Harrington	Jul 1945-Aug 1945

THE CAUSES OF THE SECOND WORLD WAR
Japan and China

The origins of the Second World War in Europe are generally understood to have lain in the onerous terms of the 1920 Treaty of Versailles which ended the Great War of 1914-1918. The Treaty imposed humiliating conditions upon an impoverished German Republic which lost control of its former Imperial colonies, while a victorious Italy, aspiring to an African colonial empire, received only some territorial rewards in Europe.

The major consequence of political unrest and weak democratic government in Germany and Italy was the rise to power of the totalitarian Nazi and Fascist Parties and their leaders, Hitler and Mussolini; one committed to creating a 'Greater Germany' with *Lebensraum* (living space), for the German Nation in Eastern Europe, the other seeking "a place in the sun" equal to that of France and the United Kingdom.

By mid-1936 the Italians had overrun Abyssinia and, by supporting the Franco rebellion in Spain, were committed to an alliance with Nazi Germany.

During the 'thirties, with the exception of Alsace, the European territories lost to Germany as a result of the Versailles Treaty were regained. In 1936 the Rhineland was re-occupied and in 1938 Austria and the Sudetenland were incorporated into the 'Third Reich'.

Although politicians in France and the United Kingdom hoped for an accommodation with Hitler, it soon became clear that German expansion would continue. Meanwhile, plans were made to modernise and expand the RAF and new aircraft types began to appear as a re-armament programme progressed.

The causes of war in the Far East can be traced back much further—to the emergence of the Japanese Empire as a major industrial, military and naval power after victory in the Russo-Japanese War of 1904-1905. During the early years of the Twentieth Century resentment grew among Japan's ruling clique against the colonial presence of European Powers in South-east Asia and the Pacific Ocean, the result of exploration and trade. Japan joined the Allies at the beginning of the Great War with nothing to lose and much to gain and, having achieved victory over German forces and occupied Tsingtao in China, became responsible for some of the League of Nations 'mandated' territories in the Pacific. These former German colonies became virtually an extended Japanese Empire.

4 Above: A Mitsubishi G3M bomber, probably of the Mihoro Kokutai *of the Imperial Japanese Navy, in flight over the forbidding mountains of China in August 1938. Aircraft similar to this devastated Hankow, Nanking and Shanghai and, suitably modified, flew reconnaissance sorties over American bases in the Philippines and Guam in mid-1941. Note that in this picture the Japanese censor has removed the two retractable dorsal turrets*

Continuing civil war in China presented opportunities to expand Japanese control in Asia in opposition to the 'open door' policy of the United States of America. The USA sought to encourage stability in China by providing economic aid, which Japanese governments saw as interference in Asian affairs and in conflict with Japan's long-term interests. When the Japanese annexed the north-eastern Provinces of China in 1932, the USA refused to acknowledge the Japanese puppet state of Manchukuo but the American policy of 'isolationism'—strict neutrality in world affairs—prevented any action stronger than a threat of trade sanctions against Japan.

In 1937 the Japanese armies began a drive to detach Northern China from the control of Gen Chiang Kai-Shek's Nationalist Central Government. Chiang was forced to withdraw to Chungking under the threat of attrition but the loss of the ports on the eastern coast to the Japanese did not deter the US Government from its determination to supply Chiang's forces, a resolve strengthened by the news of atrocities such as 'the Rape of Nanking' in which some 140,000 Chinese civilians were killed.

The following year an all-weather road was completed from Lashio in Northern Burma to Kunming in China, enabling materiel landed at Rangoon to be transported up the Irrawaddy Valley, while other supplies were routed via French Indo-China and the British colony of Hong Kong.

When the Germans attacked in the West, Japan applied political pressure and threats against France and Britain to close these supply routes to China. By mid-1940, neither Vichy France nor Britain, which was fully committed to the Battle of the Atlantic and militarily engaged against the Italians in North Africa, dared risk further hostilities. To the Japanese, a military success appeared certain, as did eventual victory for Germany and Italy, considering that the colonial powers (France under a puppet government, the Netherlands occupied and the government in exile and Britain under threat of invasion) would have great difficulty in supporting a defensive war in the Far East. In June, Petain's Vichy Government agreed to Japan's demands to station troops in Indo-China and to pass them through the country to the war in China. On 27 September 1940, Britain's European enemies joined with Japan in a Tripartite Pact of Mutual Assistance but the British Government paid little heed to the implied threat.

In Burma a Volunteer Air Force had been established in June 1940 with a variety of impressed light aircraft and their civilian pilots, their intimate knowledge of the country seeming invaluable for communications and coastal reconnaisance duties. A similar Malayan Volunteer Force was formed in August from the Colony's civilian flying clubs to undertake flying training.

Successive Japanese Governments had become obsessed with the concept of a 'Greater East Asia Co-prosperity Sphere', motivated, of course, by Japan's industrial strength; now it seemed the great obsession could become a reality by military means. With the Army heavily committed in China, any territorial expansion of Japanese political and economic influence could only come from using the dedicated but under-employed Imperial Navy. The Naval Staff prepared plans for *Nampo Sakusen* (Southern Region Operations), a series of thrusts southwards to gain control of Indo-China, the Mandated Pacific Islands, Malaya and the oilfields of Borneo and the Netherlands East Indies. Subsequently planned was *Hawai Sakusen* (Hawaii Operation), a surprise attack on the American bases at Pearl Harbor on Oahu, Hawaiian Islands, to neutralise the American Fleet and allow freedom of operation in the Southern Pacific Ocean. So far, the Japanese had not included Burma in their plans but, with British forces extended in the Middle East, Burma seemed an easy objective where military occupation would cut the Burma Road supply route, open a way to attack the Chinese rear and allow use of the Burmese oilfields.

With southern expansion in mind, on 18 April 1941 the Imperial Navy began clandestine photographic reconnaissance over American bases, using Mitsubishi Type 96 (G3M) bombers of the 3rd *Kokutai* (Air Wing), operating without markings from the Pacific islands of Pelelieu, Truk and Tinian.

Although they flew at 32,000ft, they were sometimes spotted over the Philippines, New Britain and Papua. The US Government protested on 16 June but soon after, having achieved their purpose, the flights ended.

By the end of July the Japanese were established in Saigon, Indo-China, and were openly constructing new airfields in Cochin-China and Cambodia. To assist the US Government in its support for China, at Toungoo in Burma the British provided training and servicing facilities for an American Volunteer Group of some 100 pilots from the US armed forces who were contracted to fly some 100 Curtiss Hawk 81-A3 (export P-40C) fighters, no longer wanted by the RAF, under the command of Chiang Kal-Shek's air adviser, Claire Chennault.

The US Government further reacted to the Japanese moves by freezing assets in America and declaring an embargo on oil supplies, presenting the Japanese Government with a simple choice, to abandon their hopes completely or to begin *Nampo Sakusen* and seize the rich oilfields of the Netherlands Indies. Under pressure from his militarist cabinet, the liberal Prime Minister Prince Konoye resigned and the Emperor appointed General Hideki Tojo in his place on 18 November 1941, pledged to assert Japanese supremacy in Eastern Asia. The US State Department now made belated attempts to reach a settlement but it was too late—the Japanese were committed to *Nampo Sakusen* while, in the Kurile Islands, the Imperial Navy's *Kido Butai* (Mobile Force) was assembling for an attack on Hawaii.

An Intelligence appreciation by the British GHQ Far East of 22 November made clear that the Japanese intended further military action. The position of the Siamese (Thai) Government was doubtful; although expressing friendship for Britain, it had agreed under pressure to the Japanese development and use of Singora and Patani airfields in the south of the country.

A Japanese reply to the US Government's proposals, "crowded with infamous falsehoods and distortions" was delivered on 7 December, while dive-bombers and torpedo aircraft struck at Pearl Harbor. Emperor Hirohito declared, "We, by the grace of Heaven, Emperor of Japan, seated on the throne of a line unbroken in all the ages, proclaim to you, our loyal and brave subjects: We hereby declare war on the United States of America and the British Empire... To ensure the stability of East Asia and to promote world peace is the far-sighted policy...'which We hold always to heart. Eager for the realisation of their inordinate ambitions to dominate the East, both America and Britain, supporting the Chungking regime, have aggravated disturbances in East Asia. The situation being as it is, Our Empire, for its existence and self-protection has no recourse than to take up arms and to crush all obstacles in its path".

5: *Death of the battleships. This view of 'Battleship Row', adjacent to Ford Island in Pearl Harbor, shows the battleships USS* Maryland *(left) and the capsized hull of* Oklahoma *just to the right after being hit by at least three 800kg air-launched torpedoes. Several hundred members of her crew were lost*

6: *'Hawai Sakusen'. The attack on the US Pacific Fleet in Pearl Harbor on 7 December 1941 was accompanied by raids on Army Air Force bases. Here a camouflaged and a natural metal finished B-17D of the 7th Bomb Group at Hickh am Field, Oahu, have escaped unscathed while airfield buildings blaze after the Japanese attacks*

THE PR UNITS

During the twenty-one years between the end of the Great War in 1918 and the start of the Second World War, the Royal Air Force made few advances in the techniques of aerial photography. Although improvement in the resolution of lenses and the manufacture of magazine cameras made accurate high-altitude aerial survey possible throughout the world, operating methods aboard the obsolescent army-co-operation aircraft that equipped the RAF squadrons were little changed.

The development of the RAF Photographic Reconnaissance Units has been set out in some detail in *Eyes of the RAF* by Roy Conyers Nesbit (Alan Sutton Publishing Ltd); here is a short summary of their history.

In 1934, with remarkable foresight, Britain's Chiefs of Staff warned their Planning Staff to be prepared for war in five years' time against Germany. On 1 March 1935 the Reichsluftwaffe was established and its modern aircraft revealed to the world. For some time before the outbreak of war in September 1939, the Germans had

been using high-flying aircraft to take photographs of potential military objectives beyond Germany's frontiers. A *Staffel zur besonderen Verwendung* (Special Duties Flight) was formed in 1934, flying Heinkel He 111 airliners for clandestine photographic reconnaissance. This unit was enlarged in 1939 to become the *Aufklärungsgruppe Ob.d.L* (Reconnaissance Gruppe, C-in-C Luftwaffe), under the direct control of Hermann Goering and flying the Dornier Do 215, a development of the fast Do 17 reconnaissance monoplane.

Unlike the potential adversaries, the British Air Ministry expressed no interest in development of high-speed, high-altitude reconnaissance aircraft such as the German Heinkel He 119 or the Japanese Army Type 100 (Ki-46).

Late in the 'thirties there was no immediate need for aerial survey of the British Isles and photographic Intelligence-gathering was considered a secondary task for Bristol Blenheim bombers or, when Westland Lysanders were fitted with vertical cameras, as one of the varied duties of Army Cooperation Squadrons.

Foreseeing hostilities as inevitable, Sqn Ldr F.W.Winterbotham, Head of AI.1(c), the Air Intelligence Branch of the Secret Intelligence Service (MI.6) in

7 Above: Wg Cdr Sidney Cotton (with glasses) discussing the results of a photographic sortie with Air Marshal Sir Arthur Barratt, who was at the time AOC British Air Forces in France. Barratt had the thankless task of trying to organise a joint air policy with the French at the time of the German invasion in May 1940, which showed the French General Staff to be hopelessly incompetent and divided

13

association with French Military Intelligence, was instrumental in employing Sidney F. Cotton, an Australian businessman. A pilot in the Royal Naval Air Service during the Great War and inventor of the 'Sidcot' heated flying-suit, his task was to obtain photographs of Germany's western defences. In January 1939 Cotton was provided with a Lockheed 12A Electra aircraft, G-AFTL, purchased with Intelligence funds and fitted with additional fuel tanks and concealed cameras warmed by ducted air, providing a range of 1000 miles and the ability to cover an 11.5-mile-wide strip from a height of 20000ft. The Lockheed was to be used for genuine commercial flights, ostensibly to expand the business of a firm called the Aeronautical Research and Sales Corporation, in fact an SIS organisation, at Heston Aerodrome.

The following month Cotton was able to photograph much of the area between Mannheim and the Swiss frontier, then, partly under the direction of French Military Intelligence, in April and June he covered Italian airfields in Africa. In the weeks before the outbreak of war he flew another Lockheed, fitted with 250-exposure magazine cameras, from his base at Heston Aerodrome along the northern extension of the Siegfried Line.

A few days after Britain declared war on Germany on 3 September 1939, Cotton impressed Air Marshal Sir Richard Peirse, Vice-Chief of the Air Staff, by obtaining clear photographs of the North Sea Coast. As a result, Cotton was appointed Wing Commander in charge of the 'Heston Flight' which came under the overall control of No.11 Group, Fighter Command on 1 November with the cover-name of No.2 Camouflage Unit. Whilst the Air Ministry continued to employ bomber aircraft for aerial photography, Cotton insisted that success and a low rate of interception was possible only by using fast, high-flying aircraft and, in October, he was allowed the use of two Spitfire Mk.Is for conversion.

On 17 January 1940 No.2 CU became the Photographic Development Unit; a number of its aircraft detached to a Special Survey Flight based at Lille-Seclin in Northern France, from where clandestine mapping of Belgium was undertaken, then re-numbered as 21 Sqn at Coulommiers until June. Meanwhile a number of Hudsons were delivered, able to operate in North Sea weather conditions that precluded the use of Spitfires. The Hudsons were finished in a non-standard camouflage scheme of Dark Green and Grey devised by Cotton; after one of the Hudsons was shot down in error over Kent, a folder was prepared and distributed to show the colour schemes in use on reconnaissance aircraft. For operations at intermediate height a medium grey-blue, 'PRU Special Blue', was the preferred finish.

During the 'Phoney War' period of the 1939-1940 winter, the USSR, treaty-bound to Nazi Germany, was seen as threatening the Anglo-French Alliance by supplying petroleum products to Germany. On 30 April

and 2 May 1940, a PDU Lockheed Hudson, temporarily re-marked G-AGAR as a civil aircraft, flew from the RAF base at Habbaniya in Iraq to photograph the oil ports of Batu and Bakum in the Soviet Caucasus. An air attack on the oil installations was planned for June but the ill-advised scheme was fortuitously abandoned when the German invasion of Denmark and Norway (*Weserübung*—Operation Weser) began on 9 April 1940.

After *Fall 'Sichelschnitt'* (Sickle-slash), the first German attack in the West, was launched on 10 May, Cotton ignored orders to return the Special Survey Flight to Heston and continued operations for another five weeks. A number of his associates and some senior officers disliked his unorthodox views and the seeming independence of 'Sid Cotton's Air Force'. Partly as a result of his failure to obey orders, on his return to England Cotton was replaced by Wg Cdr G.W. Tuttle. In *The Secret War*, Dr R.V. Jones has written, "his irregular methods were too much for the RAF and he was 'organized out' of his leadership of photographic reconnaissance. He had a raw deal, for his contribution was great." The Unit remained, however, in competent hands.

Soon afterwards, on 8 July, the PDU at Heston was finally renamed as No.1 Photographic Reconnaissance Unit, equipped with 12 modified Spitfire Mk.Is. By October 1940 the Unit was flying Type B (high-altitude), Type C (long-range), Type E (low-altitude), Type F (super-long-range), Type D (extra-super-long-range) and Type G (armed low-level) versions of the Spitfire. Despite losses of several aircraft and equipment from enemy bombing, the Unit continued to operate successfully and at the end of December 1940 was moved to Benson, Oxfordshire, which was to become the base for all photographic reconnaissance in Britain.

Different branches of the Services were eager for the Intelligence that the PRU could gather but facilities were limited. On 16 November 1940 HQ Bomber Command formed its own No.3 PRU (the number 2 being already reserved) equipped with Spitfires and Vickers Wellingtons for raid-assessment. Until Cotton had demonstrated the superiority of the fast single-engined aircraft, the Air Ministry believed that, except for aerial survey, it was simple to use bomber aircraft fitted with cameras as "no special skills were needed."

During the first year of the Second World War the bombers, mainly Blenheims, were too slow and vulnerable to escape interception, as were the Army Co-operation Lysanders but the Air Ministry was loth to accept the superiority of the small, fast aircraft for photo-reconnaissance and called upon the Royal Aircraft Establishment to modify a bomber for efficient PR use. At Staverton, Gloucester a Blenheim Mk.I was used for trials. The glazed nose was replaced by a 'solid' cone similar to that of the Bristol 142 from which the design had been developed, the turret was removed and the wing-plan altered, the whole aircraft then being finely prepared for overall smooth Type 'S' finishes. A 22mph increase in speed was recorded but the project was abandoned when it became clear that there was no remarkable improvement in performance over that of Cotton's smooth-finished standard Blenheims. By the end of 1940 the use of these aircraft was no longer viable for PR over northern Europe —but necessity ensured their continuing use in the Far East.

The Air Ministry had, meanwhile, been considering the formation of a Photographic Reconnaissance Group to direct all photographic operations by Bomber and Coastal Commands. The plan met with opposition from both Commands, such that only limited reorganisation took place; No.1 PRU remained basically unaltered while No.3 PRU retained responsibility for target and post-raid photography, raid-assessment and night photography, principally strike-recording. The development of night reconnaissance was, however, transferred to the Aircraft and Armament Experimental Establishment at Boscombe Down and Nos.1 and 3 PRUs were amalgamated in June 1941.

By September 1941 the Admiralty had approved the formation of its own long-range photographic unit under Cotton's direction and he was initially provided with a Douglas DB-7 attack bomber. His activities were somewhat hampered, it appears, by the Air Ministry and the unit was not developed further. The DB-7 suffered a series of accidents and was struck off charge at the end of the year.

The aircraft of RAF Middle East became immediately involved in action over the Libyan frontier when Italy declared war on 10 June 1940. Reconnaissance over the Italian colonies of Cyrenaica and Tripolitania became the responsibility of an Intelligence Photographic Flight set up at Heliopolis, near Cairo, by Sqn Ldr Hugh Macphail of the Heston Flight.

As the PDU had earlier been renamed No.1 PRU, so the Flight at Heliopolis became No.2 PRU on 17 March 1941. It appears that MacPhail tried to obtain North American B-25 bombers, then the most effective long-range American aircraft provided for use by the RAF, to no avail. When Martin Maryland aircraft were delivered they were rejected but Macphail was allowed the use of three Hurricanes, locally converted by fitting extra wing tankage and two vertical F.24 cameras in the fuselage. Two Beaufighters were soon added and fitted with 20 inch cameras to equip a 'T' (twin-engined) Flight whose commander, Flt Lt J. Walker, called for volunteers from the airman photographers to fly as camera-operators.

Replacements from Britain were difficult to obtain so the repair of damaged aircraft was a priority. No.103 Maintenance Unit at Aboukir completed some 140 reconditioned aircraft each month, many modified for special duties and there, during a twelve-month period, some 70 Hurricanes were converted for photo-reconnaissance and fighter-reconnaissance duties with the Desert Air Force of RAF Middle East. The Mk.I and Mk.II aircraft intended for PR duties were stripped of armament, then fitted with additional 90 gallon internal fuel tanks and mountings for two cameras within a faired housing beneath the fuselage, aft of the cockpit. Two Hurricane Mk.IIs were allocated to No.4 PRU, Seletar, to be flown out later in the year.

During 1941 and 1942 the complement of aircraft and personnel in No.1 PRU was greatly enlarged, with Flights stationed as far away from Benson as northern Scotland and south-west England. The administrative difficulties caused by this dispersion were brought under control by the Air Ministry disbanding and re-forming the Flights into five separate photographic reconnaissance squadrons, numbered 540 to 544, on 19 October 1942.

Early in 1943 the overseas units were brought into line with the organization in Britain. On 25 January No.3 PRU (India) was re-formed as 681 Squadron. A week later No.2 PRU in Egypt became 680 Squadron and a recently formed No.4 PRU at Maison Blanche (Algiers) was re-numbered as 682 Squadron.

8: This Hudson from the PDU was stripped of camouflage and turret and re-marked as a civil aircraft (G-AGAR) and used for clandestine spy flights over the Russian oilfields of Baku and Batum in March and April 1940. Prints from the mission were given to the French High Command which were subsequently captured by the Germans, who condemned the RAF photo-interpreter who had signed the pictures to death in absentia as a gesture to their erstwhile Soviet ally

9: A Blenheim Mk.I, L1348, was modified for use as a dedicated PR aircraft, being lightened, unarmed and generally cleaned up, with clipped wings and a modified nose-cone. Trials showed it to have no appreciable advantages over the Blenheims of the PRU finished in Sky 'Type S'

10: Standard Blenheims Is were not good reconnaissance aircraft. Out of necessity, two Blenheims of 34 Sqn, based at Tengah in Malaya, were fitted with cameras for air survey tasks but proved unsuited for the purpose

11: Spitfire PR.IB, N3117, of the Photographic Development Unit in overall Sky camouflage with 'Type A' roundels in six positions, seen at Seclin in France in 1940, shortly before the German assault in May. At this time a leaflet showing a Spitfire in a finish like the one worn by this machine was circulated by the PDU, Heston, in an attempt to prevent the aircraft being attacked by friendly fighters over Britain. Note the Tiger Moth in the background

12: By 1941 the aircraft of No.2 PRU, including this Spitfire PR.IV, BP935, bore National Marking II (Type B roundel) beneath the wings. Spitfires in factory-applied finish of overall PRU Blue had no under-wing markings

13: This is Armstrong Whitworth XV Atalanta, DG450, formerly G-ABTL, 'Astraea', used on the Indian section of the Far East route as part of the Imperial Airways fleet. The machine is seen here serving with 101 Coastal Defence Flight of the Indian Air Force on reconnaissance duties, still in civilian silver finish, sometime between 7 March 1941, when she was first impressed, and September 1942 when she was withdrawn from service. Oddly, it was not until November 1943 that she was finally struck off charge. Location is probably St. Thomas' Mount, Madras

14: On the North-West Frontier, army co-operation tasks were undertaken by aircraft such as this Hawker Audax, K4839, 'US-L', of 28 Squadron, seen at Kohat late in 1941. The unit was then partly re-equipped with the Lysander Mk.II

15: During late 1941 the Blenheim Is of 60 Squadron were finished in standard Temperate camouflage, exactly as their counterparts back in Britain. L8609 seen here carried the unit's 'MU' code in slightly smaller than prescribed size in Medium Sea Grey

1941-1942
India and Far East Commands

Before 1941 little, if anything, was known of strategic photographic reconnaissance in India and the Far East. Routine photographic cover was obtained by Army Co-operation and Bomber Squadrons during operations on the frontier and during training, and special air survey was carried out for the Survey of India. The resulting photographs were interpreted locally by Air Intelligence Liaison Officers. Although the Japanese menace to India at that time was a distant threat, in the event of a major thrust developing towards India it was appreciated that some strategical reconnaissances of surrounding territories would be required, but unfortunately there were no modern aircraft in the Command capable of any long distance sorties.

On 1 July 1941 a 'target' strength for photographic reconnaissance aircraft at home and overseas was drawn up by the Air Ministry to include six twin-engined aircraft for the Far East. Sqn Ldr P. Ridell from Benson visited India and Far East Commands in August and described the use of fast, single-engined PR aircraft in Britain and the Middle East. It was made clear, however, that no new aircraft could be made available for the Far East for another year and that the Command must meanwhile rely on its own resources.

During the Summer of 1941 one Brewster Buffalo was adapted locally to carry an F24 vertical camera with a 20 inch lens. Successful photographs were taken with this aircraft from 13,000 feet, but it had a range of only 300 miles, and a properly constituted Photographic Reconnaissance Unit was urgently required for P.R. work in the Malay States, Siam and Indo-China. With the move of the Japanese into Indo-China information of enemy movements in the Saigon area could only be obtained by photographic reconnaissance.

In October Far East Command set about the conversion of Blenheim IVs for photographic reconnaissance, but no use could be made of these aircraft as no long-range tanks were available and it was impossible to obtain accurate information of Japanese aircraft on aerodromes in Siam and Indo-China. For such photographs as could be obtained, there was need for trained interpreters. In response to a request made in December, the Air Ministry agreed to the formation of a Far Eastern Interpretation Unit in January 1942, its HQ to be located at Singapore with mobile detachments in other areas as dictated by operational requirements. The few photographic interpreters who embarked for Singapore

16 Above: The Indian Air Force had to make do with a variety of obsolete aircraft during the early days of its existence. This Wapiti Mk.V, JG754, still wears the codes of 27 Squadron, RAF. Probably seen sometime in 1940, while serving with one of the Indian Coastal Defence Flights, the aircraft was later transferred to No.2 Squadron IAF on 5 July 1941, eventually being used as a source of spares

did not reach their destination in February before it fell into Japanese hands. Consequently, they were diverted to India to assist in building up the photographic interpretation work there.

India Command made plans for forming a PR Unit from its own resources, and applied to the Government of India for financial sanction to establish an Interpretation Unit. When this was approved, interpreters were despatched from the United Kingdom to begin the formation of a Central Interpretation Unit for Air Headquarters, India. They arrived in March, 1942 to set up a School of Photographic Interpretation, a Central Interpretation Section, and a Photographic Library.

17: In late 1941 the Japanese began overt reconnaissance sorties over British territory in the Far East with what was probably the finest strategic PR aircraft in the world at the time. This was the Mitsubishi Ki 46 ('Dinah'), an extremely clean aircraft capable of 390 mph and an altitude of 30,000 ft. The RAF had nothing with which to catch it. This example is 'ii' of the Tokorozawa Engineering School

18: Catalina I, Z2144, 'FV-R', of 205 Sqn somewhere over the Johore Strait in late 1941. Camouflage is the standard Coastal Command type of the period. Note the unusual placing of the unit codes on the fin, a style adopted by several Catalina units. A sister aircraft, W8417, 'FV-Y' was the first RAF aircraft to be lost in the war against Japan when it was shot down on 6 December 1941 by four Ki 27s of the 1st Sentai. None of the crew survived

19: According to Australian records, all six of the Beauforts supplied to 100 Sqn RAF returned to Australia. Flt Lt Mitchell's account of the loss of his aircraft (see page 23) clearly shows that one certainly did not. The machine involved is believed to Beaufort Mk.V, T9540, from 100 Sqn, but attached to No.4 PRU. The confusion may arise from a later administrative 'tidying-up' or the fact that the RAAF also had a 100 Sqn equipped with Beauforts

20: *The Brewster Buffalos were factory-finished in Temperate Land Scheme camouflage with light blue undersurfaces, as seen on this aircraft during assembly by 60 Sqn RAF at Minga-ladon in mid-1941*

21: *A typical propaganda picture dating from mid-1941 showing a lineup of Buffalos at Seletar from one of the Commonwealth squadrons equipped with the type.*

22: *Buffalo W8246 being assembled from its packing case by 60 Squadron at Mingaladon, most probably during July 1941. Note how bright the undersurface light blue appears*

Defeat and retreat

The fall of Malaya

Japanese activity in Siam was clearly a threat to Malaya and Burma but despite intelligence reports, the US and British Governments were unwilling to accept that the Japanese intended an offensive, even so a plan to counter any Japanese move against Malaya was made. Known as Operation 'Matador', it involved the seizure of Singora in Southern Siam but was dependent on 24 hours warning and the establishment of British air superiority. For air defence of Malaya and Singapore the Chiefs of Staff proposed to build up a force of twenty-two squadrons, 336 modern aircraft with adequate reserves, and to have sixteen new airfields under construction by the end of the year.

Ironically, while the requests for additional aircraft produced no result, relatively large numbers were being shipped to Russia. Parliament was told on 28 January 1942, "Apart from some raw material, it was only in September that we began to assist Russia with aircraft and tanks, and then obviously only in small quantities. In the time available it is doubtful whether we have sent to Russia much more than 1000 aircraft, 1000 tanks and probably the same number of guns." Of the aircraft, some two hundred were Hurricanes. The Chiefs of Staff protested, "These aircraft would pay a better dividend if sent to the Far East and to the Middle East." They could have changed the course of events in SE Asia.

In Burma, hardly a day passed without Japanese reconnaissance aircraft being plotted by the only radar station in Far Fast Command, 517 Wireless Unit at Moulmein, but the Far Fast Combined Intelligence Unit insisted that the Japanese were not preparing to attack. Work was, however, begun on a chain of eight new airfields as a precautionary measure.

By November it was clear that the Japanese intended further moves. Warships and transports moved into the South China Sea and the number of aircraft in Indo-China increased three-fold. The Japanese 5th and 18th Divisions, trained in landing operations, and the 55th Division from China were identified in Indo-China.

In late October, Japanese air activity became more overt—on the 19th a naval aircraft made an hour-long reconnaissance of Kuching in Sarawak, North Borneo, then on 20 and 22 October high-flying aircraft were reported over Malaya. These were Mitsubishi Ki-46-II Army 100 Model 2 *Shin-Shi-tei* (Headquarters Reconnaissance aircraft) of the Japanese Army's 15th *Dokoritsu Hikotai* (Independent Air Regiment). The first aircraft specifically designed for long-range, high-level photographic duties, their performance was so outstanding that, when they entered service in July 1941, the Germans were negotiating to manufacture them as part of the Japanese-German Technical Exchange Agreement.

Capable of 391 mph at 20,000ft, a ceiling of 36,000ft and a tactical radius of some 700 miles, it was impossible for the RAF's fighters to intercept, and GHQ Far East was unable to retaliate. There was great need for an equivalent aircraft capable of carrying out high-altitude photographic reconnaissance of the airfields in Southern Indo-China and of Camranh Harbour, but there were none. Although a Catalina, of which there were five at Singapore, could have flown the distance, it would have neither the speed nor the ceiling for such a sortie.

The Americans were asked to carry out a reconnaissance with a B-17 from the Philippines but orders from Washington forbade any such operation. The refusal to send aircraft on a reconnissance may have been as much a military as a diplomatic decision, a result of the vulnerability of the early models of the Boeing B-17, shown up by its disastrous record in RAF service.

In 1939 the British Purchasing Commission to the United States had contracted to obtain 170 Brewster B-339 Buffalo Mk.I fighters, then in production for the US Navy as the F2A-2. The first deliveries came in for severe criticism from British test pilots who considered the design outdated. Despite this, and although the A&AEE at Boscombe Down considered the aircraft unsuitable for use in the tropics, the majority were diverted to Far East Command where they were to equip four squadrons at Singapore and one in Burma. The Prime Minister of Australia, R.H. Menzies, pressing for Hurricanes to be sent to the Far Fast, was assured that the Buffalo "appeared to be eminently satisfactory" and his Government was persuaded to buy Buffalos for the Royal Australian Air Force.

Re-equipment of the expanding RAAF in mid-1940 included the diversion of 50 Hudson Mk.I and 50 Hudson Mk.II aircraft from Air Ministry orders. Hudson Mk.IIs of two General Reconnaissance squadrons, Nos.1 and 8 Sqns RAAF, were based at Sembawang on Singapore Island.

As the military situation in the Middle East was, to say the least, difficult for Britain, it was deemed prudent to deploy forces from the Commonwealth rather than the UK to face the Japanese threat to Far East Command. 9 Indian Division was stationed in the west of Malaya, around Kuala Lumpur, capital of the Federated Malay States; 11 Indian Division in the north and 8 Australian Division to defend Johore, the southernmost State, just north of Singapore Island. Although the British Chiefs of Staff had set out the aircraft requirements for Far East Command at the beginning of 1941 as Initial Equipment of 336, with a reserve of 327 aircraft, continual demands for reinforcement of the Middle Fast were given priority.

Two R AF squadrons, Nos.67 and 243, were formed at Kallang, Singapore in March 1941. In October 67 Sqn moved to Rangoon, leaving its aircraft at Kallang for 488

Sqn, Royal New Zealand Air Force. Nos. 21 and 453 Sqns also were equipped with the Buffalo.

As Air Chief Marshal Sir Robert Brooke-Popham, Commander-in-Chief in the Far East, later reported, by early December 1941 there were elements of 16 RAF squadrons with only 122 aircraft (24 of them obsolete Vildebeest torpedo-bombers), three squadrons of the Royal Australian Air Force with 36, and a reserve of 67 serviceable aircraft. Two of the RAF squadrons were 'infiltration' squadrons; No.453 raised in New Zealand and No.488, in Australia. These units are often incorrectly described as 453 Sqn RNZAF and 488 Sqn RAAF but they bore Air Ministry numbers from the series 400-490, reserved for squadrons formed with Commonwealth personnel.

In September 1941, when 21 (General Purpose) Sqn RAAF converted from the Commonwealth CA-3 Wirraway (Australian-built version of the North American Harvard) to the Buffalo, five of the squadron's senior pilots were attached as instructors to a Conversion Training Unit, 'Y' Sqn, of Blenheims and Wirraways at Kluang in southern Malaya. When these RAAF pilots were withdrawn in November, Sqn Ldr D.B. Pearson, 'A' Flight Commander of 36 Sqn (who with his 'No.2', Flt Lt J. Park Thompson, was attending a course at Kluang) was asked to become Chief Flying Instructor to 'W' Flight (Wirraways) of 'Y' Sqn, so he and Park Thompson remained at Kluang, instead of returning to take part in 36 Squadron's disastrous operations a few weeks later.

The decision to send the Buffalos to the Far East was clearly based on a failure to assess accurately the quality of the Japanese air forces. Some writers have implied that the collapse of the air defences of Malaya and Singapore was partly due to the Buffalos' inadequacies. This was not so—the Buffalos were wiped out by attrition and continual attacks on the aerodromes and, perhaps to an extent, by the inexperience of some pilots. Over Burma, the aircraft of 67 Sqn were well handled and achieved greater success. From Peter Bingham-Wallis, "My own comments on the aircraft; comparative tests were carried out by Gordon Williams and Wg Cdr Frank Carey at Alipore between the new Hurricane IIC and a Buffalo with 300+ operational hours. There was no difference in performance up to approximately 16,000ft after which the Hurricane had a far better rate of climb, although at 20,000ft performances were much the same, but the Hurricane was superior from then onwards. All of our fighting in the First Burma Campaign was carried out at heights below 20,000ft. We were pleased with the performance of our Buffalos. Neither in Singapore nor Burma was the Hurricane able to improve our position in the air—we were not 'masters' of the Jap until the Spitfire VIII came onto the scene. Both Hurricane and Buffalo were inferior in many respects, particularly manoeuvrability, to the Japanese Army and Navy fighters against which they were to be tested in battle but the

Buffalo's performance was slightly improved by replacing the 0.5in with .303in machine-guns and reducing the usual load of fuel and ammunition."

Following Sqn Ldr Ridell's visit, Air HQ at Singapore had asked for 'long-range' photographic Hurricanes, as used by No.2 PRU, but with no immediate result. In October six Blenheims of 34 Sqn at Tengah were fitted with cameras for survey. The aircraft were clearly unsuitable for the type of operations undertaken by the converted fighters at Benson and Heliopolis so, when Photographic Reconnaissance Flight was formed at Seletar by the Command Photographic Officer, Sqn Ldr C.G.R. Lewis, two fighters from the reserve pool of Buffalos at Seletar were provided as the 'Initial Equipment' of the Flight, provisionally numbered No.4 PRU by HQ Far East Command in mid-November.

Guns and armour were removed from the aircraft; one Buffalo, with extra fuel tanks to extend its operational radius to 700 miles, was fitted with three F.24/14in cameras* and the other with one F.24, sighted simply through the downward observation panel beneath the Buffalo's cockpit. When Flt Lt A.D. Phillips and Sgt C. Wareham had received instruction in somewhat simplified photographic techniques, No.4 PRU was ready to begin an aerial survey of Malaya for the Army and the civil authorities of the Federated Malay States. Sgt Wareham later described the procedure: "I opened the trap door and had a look down to see what I wanted to photograph and simply pressed the button to take the photograph. Perhaps I would take three photographs at that particular stage, usually from 25,000ft, which was the normal photographing height, then come back and take another run of perhaps a different area. From memory, it was eight or nine seconds between photographs that I had to wait." The Unit was soon enlarged by the addition of a Bristol Beaufort—but events were moving too swiftly for the planned aerial survey to be carried through.

The Government of Australia had decided to make use of the Bristol Beaufort as a dual-purpose bomber/torpedo-bomber for the RAAF and negotiated to build the aircraft under licence at plants established by the Department of Aircraft Production. A Bristol-built Beaufort Mk.I was shipped to Australia to serve as a pattern for DAP production, which was intended to provide aircraft for the RAAF and for RAF units in the Far East. The DAP-built aircraft were designated Beaufort Mk.V, the first batch to be completed being allocated Air Ministry serial numbers.

On 5 December 1941 six of these aircraft were delivered to 100 Sqn RAF at Seletar to reinforce and replace the squadron's Initial Equipment of obsolete Vickers Vildebeest biplanes but the Beauforts' performance under tropical conditions proved disappointing. As they were unarmed and were flown by crews with no previous experience on the type, it was

*The 'F' stood for 'film camera' as distinct from 'P' for 'plate camera'

proposed that they should be returned to Australia but Beaufort T9540 (coded NK-A) was to be retained, fitted with an F.24/14in camera, and attached to Sqn Ldr Lewis's PR Flight for long-range reconnaissance.

The first reconnaissance

On 6 December Japanese convoys left Saigon and headed for the Gulf of Siam. They were spotted by Hudsons of No.1 Sqn RAAF, 180 miles east of the coast of Northern Malaya, then by Catalina W8417, FV-Y, of 205 Sqn flown by Flg Off R.E. Bedell. The Catalina was shot down by four Ki- 27s of th 1st *Sentai*, part of the air-cover for the invasion fleet, without reporting back; this was the first British aircraft to be lost in the war against Japan.

Beaufort T9540 was flown to Kota Bharu in north-eastern Malaya by Flt Lt P.D.F. Mitchell of 100 Sqn and, on the 7th was sent to obtain cover of the anchorage by Ko Kong, off the Siam-Cambodia border.

This reconnaissance failed, due to bad weather that concealed the movement of the Japanese convoys which, by nightfall, were preparing to land assault troops in Siam and Malaya—at Kota Bharu with the intention of capturing the airfield there and at Gong Kedah, Sungei Patani, Butterworth and Alor Star.

At first light on 8 December the Beaufort took off for a reconnaissance of the Tamarat coast, north of Singora in Siam, to discover the extent of the Japanese threat. Mitchell found the landing force some 30 miles off Singora but while taking photographs from 20,000ft, the Beaufort was attacked by a patrol of A6M Zeros of the fighter group attached to the 22nd *Koku Hombu* (Air Flotilla).

Mitchell later wrote, "Believing what we had been told about the slow performance of Japanese aircraft, I thought it would be some time before they got up to our height and we went on taking our photographs. The next thing I knew they were all around us like hornets. I distinctly remember seeing tracers passing my windscreen and the next second they were hitting the side of the aircraft down near my feet. After the first pass I went into a steep turn and then the port engine was hit and the Beaufort rolled on her back and started to spin. We went down to about 10,000 feet before I got her out of it and headed for the nearest cloud.

"A fuel line had been partly severed and we found that by using the wobble-pump we could get enough petrol across the gap to enable us to get back on more or less an even keel. After about ten minutes we popped out of the cloud and, seeing no sign of the Zeros, headed back for the coast which we hit south of Singora and headed back home. During the fight our rear-gunner (Sgt

W.L. Barcroft) was slightly wounded in the leg but hit one Zero which he thought had been shot down." A Zero had been hit and force-landed; the Japanese pilots claimed destruction of a Blenheim. Another crewman (Sgt J.F. Gibson) had suffered a wound in the thigh.

On return to Kota Bharu Mitchell could see enemy aircraft strafing the aerodrome so he flew low over the jungle for a while, then made a swift landing. During a pause in the attack, Mitchell and Plt Off P.J. Gibbs of 1 Sqn RAAF decided to get the Beaufort back to Seletar but, as Mitchell wrote: "Every time we got an engine started the 'drome was strafed. They were doing it about every fifteen minutes as regular as clockwork. We would have to jump out of the aircraft and dive for the nearest slit-trench. This happened about five times and then one of the Japanese pilots saw the engine running and he concentrated on the Beaufort—we had not had time to switch it off—and she caught fire and was burnt out."

The films were processed and printed while the airfield was under attack and the prints were flown to Seletar by a Buffalo of 243 Sqn, one of two detached, rather optimistically, to act as fighter escort for bombers stationed at Kota Bharu.

Sgt Wareham flew from Seletar to cover Singora but no maps of Siam were available; so he took with him a small-scale atlas of the world, flying first to Alor Star to refuel, then across the peninsula to Singora to photograph the landings there. Another 100 Sqn Beaufort, T9544, flown by Flt Lt J. Tillot, carried out a reconnaissance along the Malayan coast the following day.

Shortly after noon on 10 December, 'Force H', the Royal Navy battleship HMS *Prince of Wales* and the battlecruiser HMS *Repulse*, with a destroyer screen but without air protection, was attacked by Japanese bombers and torpedo-bombers 60 miles east of Kuantan, the action being observed by Flt Lt H.C. Plenty and his crew of 8 Sqn RAAF returning from a reconnaissance in Hudson A16-76. Buffalos of 243 Sqn, sent to provide air cover, arrived to find *Prince of Wales* still afloat but listing. Wareham, who accompanied them, took photographs of rescue operations by the destroyers. Two days later Flg Off Phillips accompanied the fighters over northern Malaya and made another sortie to Singora where he was twice attacked by enemy fighters before returning to Seletar via Butterworth.

The four Beauforts remaining with 100 Sqn were to be flown back to Australia on 19 December, one crashing at Soerabaja *en route* and another on arrival. T9544 was flown out by Flt Lt Mitchell three days later.

Singapore now came under frequent air attack. The PR Buffalos operated almost every day throughout the campaign in Malaya, often flying the whole length of the country, and by 5 January 1942 had flown 42 operational sorties.

By the end of the year the Japanese were advancing down the east and west coasts, the northern airfields were abandoned and the runways blown up, but PR flights revealed that they were soon repaired and in use by the enemy. Some eighty bombing sorties were carried out against these targets between 20 December and 15 January and on 27th, when Sungei Patani airfield was attacked. A reconnaissance sortie the following day showed that seven Japanese aircraft had been destroyed, eight more damaged. A sortie by a Buffalo of No.4 PRU on 31 December found 34 supply ships at Singora but no attack could be mounted against them.

By mid January the Federal capital, Kuala Lumpur, had been over-run and on 27 January 1942, with only nine Buffalos still serviceable, it was unfortunately and foolishly decided to withdraw Allied ground forces to Singapore Island, now under frequent air attack. Two reinforcing convoys arrived by sea in January, the second of these, on the 13th, delivered fifty-one crated Hurricane IIs (some intended for Burma) and twenty-four pilots. The Hurricanes were in action almost as soon as they had been test flown. On 20 January, as 232 Sqn, they were in action from Seletar and Kallang, shooting down eight bombers, but the weight of enemy air attack was too great and losses mounted, both in the air and on the ground.

Flg Off N.E.V. Henkel, a flying instructor from Kuala Lumpur, appointed to No.4 PRU, attended Kluang to be checked-out on monoplanes before joining the Unit, possibly to replace Phillips who was tour-expired. Sqn Ldr Pearson recorded, "Squadron Leader Lewis, who was CO of this new unit, I knew quite well, so I 'phoned him up and said I was interested, and he said, 'Oh well I don't think so at the moment but I'll let you know. In any case you're Acting Squadron Leader and we haven't a space for a Squadron Leader—you'd have to drop back to your Flight Lieutenancy'. I said I didn't mind that provided I was getting back to operational flying. A few days after that, he got in touch with me again, ordering me to report to Singapore immediately as Henkel had done a terrible thing; he'd raised the undercarriage of his aeroplane while on the ground which made him rather unpopular with the unit—and with the AOC! They accepted my reversion to Flight Lieutenant and I was flying operationally again on Brewster Buffalos."

It is hardly surprising that, in a situation where every serviceable aircraft was of great value, the Wirraways of 'W' Flt were used briefly in an operational role during the month, led by Flt Lt Park Thompson, before the only surviving five aircraft were flown out to Palembang and on to Batavia in Java.

Phillips had survived uninjured although his aircraft had been several times damaged during operations over Thailand and Malaya. In January he was repatriated, and, having flown more than 50 PR sorties was awarded the DFC, while the unit's other pilot, Sgt C.B. Wareham, with

26 sorties, was awarded the DFM.

On 31 January 1942, Lt-Gen A.E. Percival, GOC Malaya, declared to his troops and to the civilian population of Singapore, "The Battle of Malaya has come to an end and the Battle of Singapore has started. Today we stand beleaguered in our Island fortress. Our task is to hold that fortress until help can come, as it assuredly will come. This we are determined to do."

By the end of January the Japanese were in possession of all the airfields on the Malayan Peninsula, and the Singapore airfields at Seletar, Sembawang and Tengah were all under artillery fire from across the Johore Strait. On 5 February as the Japanese and British prepared respectively for attack and defence of the Island, remaining serviceable aircraft were concentrated at Kallang, to be flown out (with the exception of eight Hurricanes retained for defence) to the Netherlands East Indies. At Seletar Sqn Ldr Lewis told Flt Lt Pearson, "We've got our marching orders. In a couple of days we're going to fly the two aircraft out to Java. I shall be flying one and Wareham and you will have to toss up for who flies the other. Sgt Wareham won the toss but Pearson, unhappy at the prospect of leaving by sea, looked around the airfield and found a Buffalo of 453 Sqn, left behind as unserviceable when the Australians were withdrawn. The aircraft had bullet holes in its propeller and oil-tank, the brakes and flaps were not fully operative and it had no battery. With a battery fitted, the engine gave maximum power so Pearson asked if the CO minded his flying the aircraft. Lewis said, "No, that's fine; you can be our fighter escort!", so the Buffalo was armed and fuelled on the 6th ready for take-off next day.

In his Report on Air Operations, Air Vice-Marshal Sir Paul Maltby, Assistant AOC Far East Command, wrote, "The PR Buffalo Flight, which had functioned almost daily with outstanding success under the command of Squadron Leader Lewis since the beginning of the campaign, finally lost all its aircraft by enemy air attacks on the 7th February. This Flight had carried out over 100 sorties, the majority of which had proceeded as far north as Singora. Aircraft were intercepted by Japanese fighters and hit on numerous occasions, although none was shot down. Throughout, no armour or guns were carried; the pilots had relied entirely upon evasion in order to fulfil their missions. The greatest credit is due to them for the valuable work they did." The fate of the aircraft was not as stated; it was heavy shelling on the night of 6/7 February that destroyed W8166, the Buffalo to be flown by Sgt Wareham. Consequently, when Lewis and Pearson took off for Sumatra, Wareham was left to make his own way from Singapore. He sailed on the cargo vessel *Derrymore* and survived when the ship was torpedoed on 13 February.

The two Buffalos landed at Palembang to re-fuel having been shot at by Dutch gunners. Flt Lt Pearson: "There were two Group Captains and an Air Commodore sitting disconsolately on the steps of flying-control. My CO said 'This looks like a pleasant place—shall we spend the night here?' I said, 'Sir, I've got a feeling that if we do, our aircraft won't be here in the morning. There are three senior officers there; they've all got wings and are all obviously itching to get out of here', so we carried on."

They flew on to Batavia (Djakarta) in Java where Sqn Ldr Lewis overshot the runway in heavy rain and the last of the PR Buffalos turned over. Injured and taken to hospital, he was invalided out to Australia a fortnight later. Pearson was ordered to fly his unserviceable Buffalo fighter to Bandoeng, where it was handed over to the Netherlands Indies Army. Some days later, in charge of some 300 RAF personnel, including Flg Off Henkel, he boarded the cargo steamer *Kota-Gede* which sailed for Colombo. Flt Lt Pearson then travelled by sea to Karachi where he was posted to a new PRU, to become a Flight Commander.

23: One of the first Japanese fighters to be encountered by the RAF in the Far East was the Nakajima Type 97 (Ki 27 'Nate') which despite its fixed undercarriage was an extremely nimble and dangerous opponent. This one wears the early markings of the 64th Sentai, which was just beginning to exchange these aircraft for the later (and even more capable) Nakajima Ki 43 at the end of 1941

24: A good view of the ventral window of a Buffalo Mk.I being assembled in a hangar (probably at Mingaladon) with an Indian Harlow trainer to the right and other Buffalos in the background. Note the size and position of the underwing roundels and the landing light under each wing which was one of the features of the British-specified Buffalos. The glazing to the ventral fuselage window through which the cameras of the PR Buffalos operated has not yet been fitted. Its original purpose was to allow US naval pilots a degree of downward vision when landing on aircraft carrier decks

25: *Making a low pass over Mingaladon airfield for the benefit of the photographer, this is Buffalo I, W8243, 'RD-B', of 67 Sqn RAF in December 1941. The aircraft is finished in standard Temperate Land Scheme uppersurface camouflage. Starboard undersides were sky blue with a standard Type A roundel, while the port side was black with a yellow-outlined roundel. Spinner and fuselage band were Sky, while the codes were Medium Sea Grey*

26: *These are typical Curtiss P-40C Tomahawks from the First Pursuit Squadron ('Adam and Eves') of the American Volunteer Group. Number 7 was usually flown by Sqn Ldr Robert H. Neale, while 33 (serial no. P-8151) was not allocated to any particular pilot, but was the 'property' of Crew Chief George F. Curran. The machine modified for PR use is believed to have been No. 36 (serial P-8123) of the 2nd Pursuit Group and was flown on these type of missions by both Eric Shilling and Ed Rector (JM Bruce/GS Leslie Collection)*

27: *Japanese troops storming over the wreckage of a North American Yale trainer, Z-31, of the Burma Volunteer Air Force at Mergui airfield on 19 January 1942. Note the yellow-outlined roundel on the upperwing surface*

28: 41-2465 was one of several Boeing B-17Es which, supplementing the B-17Ds of the US 19th Bomb Group at Asansol in April 1942, carried material for the American Volunteer Group into Burma and brought out civilians and service personnel to India. The camouflage finish is possibly a field-applied scheme of green and brown

29: For some time it was believed that the aircraft flown by Sqn Ldr Stone was the only Hurricane Trop IIB of No.17 Sqn to carry the 'Type A' roundels above the wings against the Tropical Scheme camouflage. That this was not so can be seen from this picture of BE19?, 'YB-D', at Mingaladon in January-February 1942

30: The barracks adjoining the airfield at Prachaup Khirikand photographed by Flg Off Bingham-Wallis on 19 December 1941 while flying Buffalo W8241 of 67 Sqn RAF. The dark shadows running vertically down the picture are probably an out-of-focus impression of the framing of the ventral window of the aircraft, through which the camera aimed

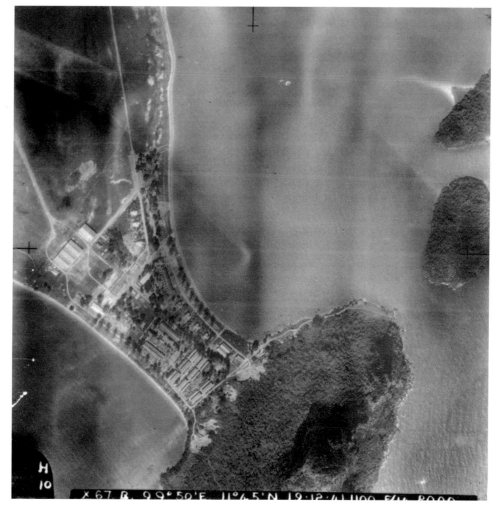

31: *Clearing up operations as the tail of a 77th Sentai Nakajima Ki 27 is removed from the corner of a blast pen housing one of 113 Sqn's Blenheims at Mingaladon, 29 January 1942. The pilot, (probably Sgt Maj Nagashima) had been mortally wounded by the Australian Plt Off Jack Storey of 135 Sqn and had subsequently deliberately tried to ram the Blenheim, only narrowly missing. Sqn Ldr Stone (in peaked cap) "looks after the troops". The nose of the Blenheim IV is just visible on the right*

32: *Hurricane Trop IIB BE171, 'YB-B', of 17 Sqn at Mingaladon in late January 1942. This was Sqn Ldr Stone's aircraft and was one of the few in the theatre to wear desert camouflage. This may be the reason for the 'Type A' roundels above the wings as the colour was so different to other Allied aircraft. BE171 had an eventful career, being used by Sqn Ldr Frank Carey to shoot down a Ki 27 on 29 January over his own airfield, before it was eventually shot down on 26 February while being flown by army co-operation pilot Capt AD Penton, who was unhurt*

33: *A briefing of 17 Sqn pilots at Magwe before the devastating Japanese attacks in March 1942. Sqn Ldr CAC 'Bunny' Stone DFC is on the left, then Flt Lt AW Carvell of 'B' Flight; Sgt JF Gibson, RCAF; Plt Off KG Hemingway*

The long retreat

Through Burma

In Burma, preparations for air defence had been advanced; permission had been given earlier in the year for the three squadrons of Col Claire Chennault's American Volunteer Group to use the RAF airfields at Kadwe, Toungoo and Mingaladon for training and servicing before moving to China in support of Generalissimo Chiang Kai-shek's armies. The AVG was equipped with export versions of the Curtiss P-40C (Hawk 81-A3) fighter (Tomahawk Mk.IIB to the RAF) taken from Lend-Lease allocations when the improved P-40E became available for use by the British. In return for British assistance, it was agreed that the AVG would be available for defence if Burma were attacked. The Group was made up of three fighter (pursuit) squadrons; the 1st, 'Adam and Eve'; the 2nd, known as the 'Panda Bears' and a 3rd, 'Hell's Angels'.

On the outbreak of war the 1st and 2nd Sqns flew to Kunming, Chiang's capital, and on 10 December the 23 fighters of the 3rd Pursuit Sqn were despatched to join 67 Sqn RAF at Mingaladon, near Rangoon, accompanied by three aircraft of the 2nd Sqn. These were flown by Erik Shilling, the Group's photographic officer, and pilots Christman and Rector. Shilling's P-40, unarmed but with a 20in camera fitted within the baggage compartment, was escorted by the other two to Nakorn Sawan and Chiengmai in Thailand. At the same time two 67 Sqn Buffalos provided escort for Flt Sgt Huggard to fly a camera-fitted Blenheim Mk.I, L4915, of 60 Sqn, on a 20,000 ft sortie to Pitsanulok and Sikotai in southern Thailand. The same day Japanese aircraft struck at Tavoy, Mergui and Bokpyin in southern Burma, devastating the airfields and destroying the communications network. When photographs showed more than a hundred enemy aircraft lined up at Don Muang (Bangkok) Chennault asked the US Government for bombers to destroy them but none could be made available.

The need for PR aircraft with fighter performance was clearly understood at Air Headquarters, Burma, well before Air Vice-Marshal D.F. Stevenson DSO OBE MC assumed command at Mingaladon on 1 January 1942. One of 67 Sqn's Buffalo Mk.Is, W8241, was modified for photographic duties by the installation of an F24 14-inch vertical camera beneath the cockpit and on 17 December, with three Buffalos of A Flight (Flg Off D. J. C Pynkney), was ordered to Mergui in readiness for tactical reconnaissance over the Kra Isthmus, where a Japanese invasion seemed imminent. Flg Off P M Bingham-Wallis, flying W8241, recorded, "18th; Mergui to Mingaladon (flew aircraft back with undercarriage problems, returned the same day to Mergui after repairs). 19th escorted by that brilliant pilot Charles Victor Bargh and Colin Pynkney, we carried out three reconnaissances that day as follows:

a) Mergui-Jumborn-Pakcham Victoria Point-Mergui, 2hr 20min
b) Mergui-Girikhan airfield-Mergui, 1hr 45min
c) Mergui-Tavoy-Mesoht-Mingaladon, 2hr 45min.

Our instructions were that neither 8241, which retained two fuselage guns, nor my two escorts were permitted to attack anything during these flights, although we spotted three long passenger trains heading for Malaya which we subsequently learned carried the Jap Guards Regiment!"

Next day the aircraft were replaced by the Buffalos of B Flight which, on the 22nd, with Bingham-Wallis flying W8250, carried out further tactical sorties to Victoria Point and strafed the three troop-trains. 67 Sqn's detachment then returned to Mingaladon.

60 Sqn's Flt Sgt Huggard undertook a further series of recces in L4915, beginning with a sortie over the airfields at Lampang, Chiengmai and Mesarieng on 21 December and, via Moulmein, to Chumphon and the Japanese Army's invasion bases and airfields at Tak, Mesoht and Kamphaeng Phet on the 23rd.

The Burmese capital, Rangoon, was raided for the first time on 23 December and, although the Japanese suffered substantial aircraft losses, such severe damage and casualties were caused that a mass civilian evacuation of the city began and by Christmas Day, when Rangoon suffered another raid, the city was virtually deserted.

On 15 January 1942 the Japanese 55th Division crossed in strength from Siam and advanced on Tavoy, occupying the town on the 19th. Mergui was isolated and the enemy began moving against Moulmein.

On 20 January Plt Off Brewer and Sgt J. Finn of 67 Sqn, detailed to reconnoitre Raheng, were attacked and killed.

Despite an attempt to hold Kyaikmaraw, to the south, the position became untenable and Moulmein was evacuated on the last day of the month, leaving Southern Burma, east and south of the Salween River, in enemy hands. By this time most of 67 Sqn's Buffalos had been destroyed or rendered unserviceable and the PR Buffalo appears to have been lost.

During the last week of January 1942 seven 'long-range' Hurricane IIBs fitted with under-wing tanks were delivered for use by 17 Sqn at Mingaladon, seeming ideal for tactical reconnaissance duties. Fitted with fixed underwing fuel tanks they had the advantage of greater range than the Buffalos and P-40s. In action, however, the tanks put the Hurricane at a great disadvantage as they appreciably reduced speed and manoeuvrability. Of his first action on 23 January against Nakajima Ki 27s, Sqn Ldr C.A.C. Stone DFC, commanding 17 Sqn, recorded, "The three Hurricanes that arrived that day turned out to be IIBs, with twelve machine guns and fitted with their long-range tanks. As they were refuelling the usual air raid alarm sounded and Jimmy, Penny (Sqn Ldr Elsdon, 136 Sqn and Grp Capt Pennington-Leigh, 267 Sqn) and I took off, with myself leading. Shortly after, the AVG and Buffalos were airborne. Climbing to the west to gain height, since the enemy invariably came from their big base in Bangkok from the SE, I found that at full boost we could make only about 1,000 feet a minute, less than half the usual rate of climb. On reaching 10,000 feet we turned back over the Irrawaddy estuary, to find the aerodrome smoking beneath us. The Japs had come and gone. When I landed I told the armourers to remove four of the twelve Brownings from the aircraft and drove over to see Seton. (Grp Capt H. Seton Broughall, OC Mingaladon):

"I told him what had happened and asked if I could have the long-range tanks removed. He immediately rang up Group and after a long conversation with the AOC he replaced the receiver. 'Sorry, Bunny, the old .... said no dice on any account. Guess you'll have to get shot down'. and burst into laughter.

"This is exactly what nearly happened, for the very next day Jimmy, Penny and I, struggling for height, although the rate of climb was slightly faster, were attacked from the sun by about twelve Jap fighters at 15,000 feet. Jimmy and Penny immediately summed up the situation and dived, for the Hurricane could dive much faster than the Nips. For some reason—certainly not bravery, and contrary to my own experience—I decided to have a go. I probably lost my temper—dangerous on the ground, but usually fatal in the air. Naturally the Japs were delighted. The first burst from one of them took the bottom out of my starboard tank—luckily not tracer. Another, approaching at three-quarter head on, at more than full deflection, took away my starboard aileron, causing me by now to move with rudder and port aileron alone. I could not manage to even get my sights on them and boy, could they shoot. With bullets twanging into the aircraft and clanging on the armour plate behind me, for an instant I panicked, when a little heaven-sent voice said 'try the sun'. I climbed up straight into its brilliance and for a brief moment my tormentors lost me, which enabled me to do a stall turn to port, for I dared not spin, and dive straight down at high speed to the estuary, among the shipping, leaving a long white trail of petrol behind me."

Again requests for removal of the tanks by 'Bunny' Stone were met by a firm refusal by Air Vice-Marshal D.T. Stevenson but, having been taken to see the damage suffered by Stone's Z4726, '2', in combat, the AOC was persuaded that they should be removed.

In addition, two Hurricane Mk.IIAs, Z4949 and DG635, from No.2 PRU at Heliopolis, were flown in by F/Os F.D. Procter and K.A. Perkin. The PR aircraft, which arrived on 25 January, had been originally intended for Singapore but were now annexed, (according to 221 Group records) as No.3 PRU, to the headquarters of the AOC, Air Vice-Marshal Stevenson. Tactical reconnaissance was mainly undertaken by the two Army Co-operation squadrons, No.28 RAF and No.1 Indian Air Force, based at Toungoo and both equipped, in accordance with the pre-war concept of army co-operation which assumed the maintenance of air-superiority, with Westland Lysander aircraft. It had become clear, in 1940 in France and later in the Middle East, that these aircraft were unsuitable except in local tribal warfare on the North-West Frontier of India but, although requests were made early in February for re-equipment with Curtiss Mohawks, none were made available and the only aircraft in Burma suitable for tactical reconnaissance under the prevailing conditions were the Hurricanes, although no cameras were fitted.

From Mingaladon, some tactical reconnaissance was carried out by the Mk.IIBs of 17 Sqn, their performance improved by the removal of the two outer Browning guns from each wing and of the underwing fuel tanks. Flying one of these Hurricanes, BE171, 'YB-B', Sqn Ldr Stone shot down a bomber, identified as a Mitsubishi Ki. 21 'Sally', during a raid on the airfield on the night of 27 January. On 2 February he carried out a reconnaissance of Moulmein in the same aircraft.

60 Sqn's last Blenheim Mk.I, L4915, stationed for recon-naissance duties at Bassein, was destroyed in a Japanese raid on the 21 January but the Blenheims of 45 and 113 Sqns also undertook some reconnaissance duties, providing photographs for Intelligence as a supplement to their bombing operations. Photography remained a subsidiary task for the Blenheim and, later, Mosquito and Liberator squadrons, until the end of the war in the Far East.

Before the Army's withdrawal from Rangoon and Prome, two Buffalos of 67 Sqn made a final recon-naissance on 23 January 1942 in search of Japanese re-inforcements from Siam entering over the Three Pagodas Pass, along the route of the later Burma-Siam railway. When the remnants of 67 Sqn were withdrawn to Toun-goo, their duties were taken on by the PR Hurricanes. These two aircraft flew visual recces over the Siamese airfields on alternate days, beginning with a flight to Tak and Mesoht by Flg Off Procter on 1 February. From Zayatkwin, Flg Off Perkin flew the first photographic sorties to Tavoy, Tak and Mesoht on the 8th and to Bangkok the following day, in Z4949. Flg Off Procter flew DG635 to Don Muang airfield, a flight of 4hr 15min, on 10 February. The pilots continued alternate PR sorties, although DG635 was unserviceable with engine trouble by mid-month, seeking out Japanese movement along the Tenasserim coast as far as Heinze Basin on 11 and 13 February and east of the Salween River to Martaban on the 15th and 16th.

28 Sqn was ordered back to India on 17 February,

leaving only a detachment of three Lysanders, their crews and two pilots with flying time on Hurricanes. Flt Lt Mann (later to command the squadron) and Plt Off Dunford-Wood were soon joined by Plt Off D. Harris, from 28 Sqn, to undertake tactical reconnaissance in Hurricanes of 17 Squadron.

On 22 February, during a sortie over the Sittang River, Dunford-Wood was interecepted and shot down into the river but escaped unhurt.Mann encountered a Mitsubishi Ki 15 reconnaissance aircraft of the 8th *Sentai*, riddling it with bullets and wounding the pilot before he escaped. During the next three years, the 'long-range' Hurricanes of the fighter-reconnaissance squadrons were usually accompanied on their sorties by an escorting aircraft, with some degree of success.

On 12 January 1942 Japan had formally declared war on the Netherland East Indies. Two days later, as Japanese airborne troops landed in southern Sumatra, Gen Sir Archibald Wavell arrived at Bandoeng in Java to set up a combined American, British, Dutch and Australian Command, Supreme Allied Headquarters S.W.Pacific (ABDACOM). British (and Allied) strategy for defence of the Far East relied upon the "impregnable fortress" of Singapore and, when the British forces evacuating Malaya were concentrated on Singapore Island, it was still believed that the "fortress" would hold firm long enough for forces to be built up in the Indies. When the inept defence of Malaya and Singapore ended in surrender, the strategy for the whole area collapsed.

As the military situation rapidly became out of control, on 23 February Supreme Allied HQ began leaving Java for Australia. Wavell left two days later and ABDACOM was dissolved, leaving command of Allied forces in the Indies to the Dutch *gen-lt* H.ter Poorten and *vice-admiraal* C.E.M. Helfrich, the Dutch senior commander.

On 21 February the PR Unit in Burma was withdrawn to Magwe, 'John Haig' serving as an advanced landing ground. After a flight to Nakorn Sawan, Tak, and Mesoht on the 26th, Procter was injured in a motor accident and Perkin flew the last sorties from Magwe in Z4919. Under constant air attack, Burma Army was driven back to the Sittang River. There, on 23 February 1942, two spans of the railway bridge were demolished too soon, trapping British and Indian troops on the east bank. Nevertheless, this caused a delay in the Japanese advance that would have been crucial if only the Chinese divisions falling back on Toungoo, 90 miles north, had sought to delay the enemy.

The British fell back to Waw, then to Pegu. Rangoon was still held, for without its port facilities the Army could no longer be supplied or reinforced, but it was clear that the port was not defensible for long.

Capt Penton, the Army Liaison Officer attached to 17 Sqn, was trained as an army co-operation pilot; instructed to make a personal reconnaissance on 26 Februry, he flew Stone's BE171, 'YB-B', unescorted, over the Sittang area. During the sortie he was attacked and shot down by a Japanese fighter but escaped and returned to the British lines concealed in a bullock cart. By the 27th all 17 Sqn's aircraft had been re-located on 'satellite' fields, the tactical recces being flown from the airstrip 'Highland Queen' until the enemy discovered the strip on 6 March, then from 'Park Lane'.

At the end of February Mingaladon was becoming unserviceable due to enemy attacks and the PR Hurricanes, with the fighters, were dispersed to Zayatkwin. From Toungoo the Army Co-operation Lysanders were used principally for close support, fitted with bomb-racks and carrying two 250lb bombs. No.1 Sqn IAF carried out attacks on Japanese airfields in Siam; on 4 February they damaged aircraft and the radio-station at Mehongson. On 12 March No.1 Sqn handed over the few serviceable aircraft to Burma Command Flight and the personnel were flown out to India while 28 Sqn continued to fly in support of the Army retreating northwards.

Late in February the remaining units of USAAF Maj-Gen L.H. Brereton's Far East Air Force, after fighting in the Philippines and the East Indies, were ordered to withdraw and regroup. Most went to Australia but the rest, under Brereton's command, flew out to India. On 27 February Brereton arrived there and was appointed a week later as Commanding General, US Tenth Air Force, setting up his headquarters at Karachi. Meanwhile, he put his only aircraft, a B-17E, two B-24s and two LB-40 transports, at the disposal of the British to carry troops and materiel to Magwe in Burma, on return bringing back civilian evacuees and some service personnel. Flg Off Procter was flown to Calcutta in Capt Kaiser's B-17E on 8 March. On 12 March personnel of the first combat units for the Tenth AF, the 7th Bomb Group and the 51st Fighter Group, arrived in India.

Of the 28 Sqn detachment remaining at Mingaladon, while flying one of the 17 Sqn Hurricanes (Z5473) on tactical reconnaissance over the Sittang on 3 March, Flt Lt A.S. Mann encountered three Nakajima Ki-27 fighters north of Abya. The Hurricane was hit in the coolant tank and Mann was wounded in the foot but he managed to land in a rice paddy when the engine seized. The Japanese fighters machine-gunned his aircraft but Mann escaped and was picked up by a Burmese Rifles patrol and, in course of time, returned to the squadron.

On 6 March all serviceable aircraft on the Rangoon airfields were withdrawn north to Magwe in the Irrawaddy Valley. While the Japanese advanced on Rangoon their motorised columns swept through the Shan States to cut the Burma Road. It was hoped to make a strong point of Magwe, as a base which could be held until the coming of the monsoon rains in April. For three months the Buffalos, P-40s and Hurricanes of the fighter squadrons had been constantly in action, inflicting high losses on the Japanese Army Air Force, and temporarily attaining air-superiority in the Rangoon area, but by March the only all-weather airfields operable by the RAF within striking distance of the enemy were at Akyab, on the Arakan coast, and Magwe, 240 miles north of Rangoon. Two mixed wings were formed, 'A Wing' at Akyab and 'B Wing' at Magwe, the latter incorporating most of the first-line aircraft of the RAF and AVG squadrons.

From Magwe, on 20 March, a reconnaissance Blenheim reported fifty enemy aircraft at Mingaladon and some forty more at the satellite airstrip 'Highland Queen'. An attack was immediately launched, destroying 27 Japanes aircraft without loss. The enemy reacted swiftly— the following day Magwe was raided, the first of a series of attacks by some 230 aircraft over a 25-hour period. The weight of attack made from Mingalaldon and Chiengmei, was greater than any launched by the Germans during the Battle of Britain against a single aerodrome. Flg Off K. Perkin returned from recon-naissance of Zayatkwin airfield in Z4949 while enemy aircraft were strafing Magwe. Plt Off H. Everard of 17 Sqn claimed a Japanese fighter trailing smoke and then attacked "a dark blue aircraft which I incorrectly guessed to be a Navy Zero", which belly landed. This was Perkin's Hurricane, at the time the PR Unit's only serviceable aircraft other than an ex-Burma Volunteer Air Force Tiger Moth. Sqn Ldr Stone observed, "Not a bad day's work, Everard; one of theirs and one of ours!"

The few remaining AVG Hawks were withdrawn to Loiwing in China and twenty surviving RAF aircraft were flown out to Akyab but the PR Hurricane, DG635, which had suffered considerable damage on the ground, crashed during take-off and was written off.

That, day another pilot, Flt Lt J.D. Thirlwell, arrived at Magwe from No.2 PRU in the Middle East. He has written, "The CO at Magwe, Grp Capt H. Seton Broughall (a most cheerful chap) said that since he didn't need PRU pilots any more, I had better arrange some transport and get up to Lashio to find out the possibility of an evacuation by civil air (China National Airways) to Calcutta. I found an abandoned Wolseley car in Magwe and set off that night, not too sure if I was advancing towards or retreating from the Japs. Came the morning, I turned up at Maymyo so I knew I was on the right road. On 26 March 1942 I flew from Lashio to Calcutta in a CNA DC-3, having informed Magwe that there was a chance of evacuation from Lashio." Plt Off Harris, the Lysander pilot from 28 Squadron, was ordered to Toungoo in the BVAF Tiger Moth for a visual reconnaissance.

It seems that attempts were made at Staff level to name Seton Broughall as scapegoat for the disaster at Magwe, but matters were beyond any man's control. In the end no senior officer was held responsible for the Burwing disaster although Lt-Gen William Slim, during an unexpected stop at Magwe on 12 March, thought that "it was a bit rash to leave so many aircraft on a deserted airfield in the midst of a not too reliable population." The only real threat came from the Japanese Army Air Force, but neither effective anti-aircraft defences nor blast pens had been prepared at Magwe before the Japanese assault. The Hurricanes of 17 squadron that escaped destruction were located at the far end of the airfield, away from the crowded bomber dispersal area.

Gp Capt Seton Broughall was briefly replaced as OC Burwing by Gp Capt Singer on 5 April; Air Vice Marshal Stevenson became AOC Bengal after the Army withdrawal from Burma.

On 23 March, Akyab also suffered the first of a series of attacks. When, on the 27th, seven Hurricanes on the airfield and one in the air were destroyed in a surprise attack, the fighter defence of Burma ceased to exist and Akwing was withdrawn to Chittagong on the Bengal coast. 'Burwing' put into operation a scheme suitably called 'Scram', moving personnel and equipment across Central Burma to Lashio and Loiwing to refit but, because of the need to build up the defence of Assam and Bengal, C-in-C India decided that 'Burwing' should not be re-equipped. The organisation remained at Loiwing in control of bomber detachments flying from Lashio and Loiwing.

On returning to Magwe, Harris found evacuation in progress, flyable aircraft going to Akyab, and he flew the Tiger Moth to join the PR Unit at Lashio.

The original intention of the Japanese, the assurance of oil supplies, was achieved with the surrender of the Netherlands East Indies Government in Java on 8 March but practically all the oilfield installations in Burma were seriously damaged as the British retreated.

After the defeat of a combined British-Dutch-American fleet which attempted to destroy enemy invasion convoys in the Battle of the Java Sea, the way into the Indian Ocean lay open to the Japanese Navy. The Nicobar and Andaman Islands, north of Sumatra, were occupied by the enemy late in March and it was feared that Calcutta would be open to surprise naval or air attack. For their part, the Japanese similarly expected naval attacks on the islands, their furthest west outpost, and on their coastal supply route south of Rangoon. The *Toko Kokutai* with their Kawasaki H6K Mavis reconnaissance flying-boats moved to Port Blair in the Andaman Islands at the end of the month, with a defensive force of 18 Mitsubishi G3M 'Nell' bombers and 18 A6M Zero fighters.

'Burwing' operated for a while longer; eight Hurricane IIB's of 17 Sqn were flown in on 6 April but, under constant attack seven were lost during the next four days.

34: *Installation of cameras in Hurricane IIA Z4949 of No.4 PRU at Mingaladon, the enclosing fairing can be seen lying on the ground. A Yellow outer ring was added to the Dull Red and Dull Blue National Marking I ('Type B' roundel)*

35: *A Burma Volunteer Air Force Tiger Moth, probably Z-04, with Blenheims at Magwe, shortly before the Japanese attacks that virtually destroyed the RAF strike force. A Tiger Moth (Z-04 or Z-09) was flown by Flg Off Harris on hazardous local Tac/R sorties throughout the Burma campaign. Just visible on the left is the rear fuselage of the impressed Aeronca Chief, Z-20, (ex-VT-ALN) used by No.221 Group Com. Flt. It was eventually struck off charge on 30 November 1943 after a forced landing earlier in the year*

36: *A Hudson III, AE486, 'N', of the six-strong GR Flight, probably ex-139 Squadron, with other aircraft of 221 Group at Magwe on 27 February 1942, a week before the formation of Burwing. On the left is BVAF Tiger Moth Z-04 which survived the campaign*

37: One of the Douglas DC-2K airliners impressed for service with 31 Sqn. These aircraft took part in the rescue of civilians, wounded and other service personnel, including those of the PR Unit from Shwebo. The location seen here is 'Johnny Walker', a satellite airfield north of Rangoon

38: As the Japanese advanced, the Photographic Section from Rangoon headed northwards. Here they are ploughing through the floodwaters around the Yenangyaung oilfields, which were severely damaged by the retreating Allied forces before the Japanese arrived

39: The Ava bridge, west of Mandalay. When blown up in April 1942, two of the steel trusses dropped into the Irrawaddy, causing a long sandbank to form downstream, as can be clearly seen in this vertical shot

40: *From the end of March 1942 Japanese Navy Kawanishi H6K 'Mavis' long-range reconnaissance flying boats, such as these, were based in the Andaman Islands for long-range reconnaissance before the Japanese attacks on Ceylon. Their activities also created a serious threat to Allied naval movements. Raids by Hudson bombers of 139 (GR) Sqn on 14 and 18 April on the Japanese-held base at Port Blair destroyed a number of these flying boats at their moorings and effectively brought their operations to a halt until June*

41: *Lysander I, P1678, 'BF-M' of 28 Sqn seen from a sister aircraft whose stub wing can just be seen on the lower left of the picture. Aircraft of this and No.1 Sqn, IAF, operated throughout most of the 'long retreat' from Burma. Carrying a 250lb bomb under each stub wing, Lysanders of 1 Sqn IAF carried out over 41 bomber sorties against Japanese airfields and other targets before being evacuated back to India in early March. On occasion the Lysanders were even used as dive-bombers. Sqn Ldr Majumdar, the CO of 1 Sqn, was awarded the DFC for his leadership at this time, the first such award to an Indian pilot of the IAF*

42: *Buffalo AN196, 'WP-W' of 243 Sqn, forlorn and abandoned, being examined by a Japanese soldier. This was one of the first batch of Buffalos, delivered direct to the RAF at Singapore, which is the probable location of this picture. Of interest is the aircraft's unusually pale-coloured instrument panel*

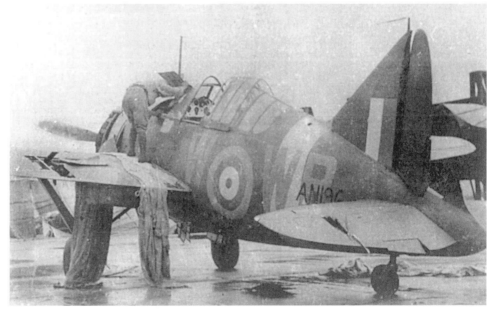

When 17 Sqn's personnel were withdrawn to India, the remaining Hurricane was left at Lashio on 12 April for army co-operation duties and began tactical reconnaissance operations, flying to Magwe on the 15th and 16th, then to Yenangyaung in the Irrawaddy Valley on the 19th, returning via an advanced landing-ground still in British hands at Myittha.

Flg Off Perkin continued flying these longer-range tactical reconnaissance sorties in the 17 Sqn Hurricane, with Plt Off Harris still using the PR Unit's Tiger Moth for short-range reconnaissance from Lashio. Sorties were flown almost every day over Chauk, Loilem and Hopong to observe the progress of the enemy towards Lashio and the Burma Road, the last reconnaissance taking place on 27 April to Loilem and Hsipaw.

Two Hudson aircraft of 139 (General Reconnaissance) Sqn, earlier based at Port Blair, attacked the seaplane base there on 14 and 18 April, destroying five enemy flying-boats and damaging over a dozen more. Thereafter, no Japanese flying-boats appeared on reconnaissance until the following June.

Although one Hudson was shot down, these important operations allowed the passage of seventy or more merchant ships across the Bay of Bengal from Burma to Indian ports without the enemy's knowledge.

43: Smoke rising from fires raging out of control in the Pazundaung district of Rangoon in March 1942 following one of the Japanese air raids shortly before the city fell to the invaders

A new beginning

The B-25 saga

Orders for large numbers of American aircraft for service in the Netherlands East Indies were confirmed by the Dutch Government-in-Exile during 1941 when the Japanese threat to South-east Asia and the Indies oilfields became apparent. Among the aircraft ordered by *major* E.J.C. Te Roller's Aviation Department of the Netherlands Purchasing Commission in New York were North American B-25C bombers, replacements for obsolete Martin 139WH aircraft in service with the *Wapen der Militaire Luchtvaart, Koninklijk Nederlands-Indisch Leger* (Military Aviation Arm; Royal Netherlands Indies Army).

In June 1941 a contract was placed with North American Aviation Inc for 162 B-25s, to be given the ML-KNIL registration numbers N5-122 to N5-283, the prefix 'N' denoting North American Aviation and '5' signifying the bomber role, for delivery from November 1942 to February 1943.

Immediately after the Japanese attacks on Malaya and the Philippines in December 1941, the Dutch Government asked for earlier delivery and the US Government agreed to release 60 B-25Cs from a current USAAC Contract. They were assigned to the Purchasing Commission at Hamilton Field of Embarkation, San Francisco, and the first of the B-25Cs was handed over on 18 February 1942 as part of the Netherlands East Indies Defense Aid Program. The aircraft were to be ferried by civil airline crews to Australia via Hawaii and by RAF crews to India via the Atlantic/trans-Africa route. On 2 March *kapitein* R.Wittert van Hoogland, arriving from Bandoeng,

44 Above: The B-25Cs allocated to the Militaire Luchtvaart *were finished in USAAC 'Basic Camouflage' and marked on the fuselage sides and upper surfaces with the Dutch national insignia of a black-outlined orange triangle. N5-126 was re-allocated to the US 3rd Bomb Group*

established a detachment of six three-man ML-KNIL ferry crews at Bangalore, Mysore State, expecting to take over and deliver a total of 20 aircraft to Java. The first three were intended to arrive at Bangalore on 5 March and three more the following day but, of the first eight despatched, two remained at Palm Beach with damage and another, 41-12468, crashed at Accra, Gold Coast (Ghana). Because of the rapidly deteriorating military situation, on 5 March *gen-maj* L.H. van Oyen, *Commandant Militaire Luchtvaart*, signalled to India, '*Captain Wittert must return as soon as possible stop Ferry stopped after sixth plane stop CML stop.*'

During the past thirty years, a number of otherwise reliable researchers and authors in the Netherlands and the United States have repeated wholly false tales of the provenance of the B-25Cs, seven in all, which were in service between 1942 and 1945 with the RAF in India.

The history of the B-25Cs used for photographic reconnaissance, as set out here, is taken from the Operation Record Books of HQ No.221 Group and of No.3 PRU(India), 681 Sqn and 684 Sqn RAF, held at the Public Record Office, Kew; from documents held at the *Central Archievendepot* of the Netherlands Ministry of Defence, The Hague, and the HQ USAF Historical Research Center, Maxwell Air Force Base, Alabama. It should be noted that the Operation Record Book of 684 Sqn contains a story, written three and a half years after the events described: "The squadron's Mitchells were originally supplied to the Netherlands Air Force prior to the outbreak of war and took part in the evacuation of the NEI. Finally they were flown to Ceylon and taken over by the RAF...." This story is not correct.

When the Dutch armed forces in the East Indies capitulated to the Japanese on 8 March, *maj* Te Roller asked the US Air Staff to hold the B-25Cs at Hamilton Field but 20 had already been despatched to Brisbane and eight to

India, the first arriving at Bangalore that day. Learning that *vice-adm* C.E.L. Helfrich, former C-in-C of the Netherlands-Indies Navy, had been sent to establish a headquarters for the Dutch armed forces at Colombo and had been appointed *Bevelhebber Strijdkrachten Oost* (Commander, Armed Forces, East), Wittert proposed combining his detachment with a group of *Marine Luchtvaart Dienst* (Naval Aviation Service) personnel with Y-boats (Catalinas) under Helfrich's command at Koggala, Ceylon.

Another B-25C arrived on 9 March and three more by the 17th. The following day all Wittert's pilots, supervised by *lt* P.L. de la Porte, had flown solo on their new aircraft. On 19 March, Air HQ India proposed to 222 Group AF, Colombo, that the Dutch pilots and their aircraft remain at Bangalore until 222 Grp could employ them.

On the 21st *kapt* Wittert and *lt* André de la Porte flew B-25C, N5-145, on a 1,100 mile flight-test to Karachi, to check fuel consumption and the system of fuel transfer from the additional internal fuel-tank fitted for the ferry flight to India. Two days later they flew on to New Delhi and sought spares and technical assistance from Maj-Gen L.H. Brereton's HQ Tenth Air Force.

Brig-Gen F.M. Brady, Brereton's deputy, and Air Marshal Sir Richard Peirse, Air Officer Commanding Air Forces in India, were both eager to have use of the B-25Cs. On 24 March Wittert invited the Air Marshal to a test flight in his aircraft; Peirse, who had been actively promoting the formation of a new PR Unit, was greatly impressed and promptly signalled the Air Ministry in London about the possibility of forming a new PR Unit. He proposed that the

```
IMMEDIATE
Air Ministry Whitehall   (R) 222 Group
From - Air H.Q. India,
A 1071 24/3

Have now inspected and flight tested B-25. My views are:-
(A)The aircraft is of no use for transport purposes.
(B) In view of its performance it should be able to operate over enemy territory by
day unsupported.
(C) Either be used as a light bomber (radius of action under 400 miles) or
(D) for reconnaissance, with radius of action approximately 900 miles by use of
extra fuel tanks in the bomb bays. These tanks are now fitted.
(E) The small number of aircraft available does not recommend itself for development
as a small unit for day bombing but
(F) A few aircraft can fill a very pressing need for long distance photographic
recconnaissance, We have been enormously handicapped by lack of knowledge of enemy's
rearward movements.
These B-25's should by virtue of their performance make good PRU aircraft and if
operating from Burma could cover Malacca Straits, Bankok, Saigon and Hanoi. Long sea
reconnaissance from Ceylon can stil be done safely by Catalinas whereas reconnaissance
of enemy air and land bases requires a well armed aircraft of high performance to
evade enemy defences.
I propose therefore to form the five serviceable B-25's into a flight under the
command of senior Dutch Officier available.
When operational shall move unit into Calcutta Area. Have already asked in my A 1070
22/3 for urgent despatch to India of first class photographic Wing Commander, with
preferably PRU experience to command PRU Squadron. He should be flown out bringing
with him at least one photographic outfit.
Further details of spares required for B-25 and photographic equipment follows.

PEIRSE
A.O.C.-in-C., Air Forces in India,
New Delhi
```

B-25s should become a Reconnaissance Flight under Wittert's command:

A series of signals sent by Air Marshal Peirse set in motion urgent and rapid negotiations between the Air Ministry and the exiled Dutch Government in London. Thus began the development of successful photographic reconnaissance in India.

Helfrich was still hoping to maintain control of the B-25Cs, using them for long-range maritime reconnaissance with his Y-boats. He instructed Wittert, *"B-25 to be prepared at once to be flown to Racecourse aerodrome Ceylon for sea reconnaissance duties x Naval observers will be provided here x Signal numbers of trained pilots you have available at Bangalore."* Wittert and two Naval officers prepared a report for the admiral on 29 March, suggesting merging Army and Navy air units, but Helfrich awaited a decision on policy from his Government in London. The Dutch Navy Ministry refused to consider incorporating ML personnel into the Naval Air Service and, having been made aware of the content of Peirse's signal of the 24th, the Dutch Foreign Ministry informed Helfrich that the five B-25Cs were to he placed under RAF control and flown by RAF crews.

At the end of March 1942 the US Air Staff decided to repossess the B-25Cs for American use, excepting only those on their way to Australia where they would be manned by crews from the ML-KNIL and the *Marine Luchtvaart Dienst* who had been transferred or had escaped from Sumatra and Java. It was first intended that the five aircraft arriving in India would be allocated to the Commanding General, US Forces in India, for use by the 7th Bomb Group of the US Tenth Air Force; then it was proposed that two B-25Cs be handed over to the RAF and the USAAC Materiel Command charge the Netherlands Purchasing Commission only for 18 aircraft delivered to Australia and for the one that had crashed at Accra. The US 3rd Bomb Group, however, appropriated 15 of the B-25Cs on arrival in Brisbane; the consequent financial wrangle was but the first in a series of disagreements that soured relations between the US Government and its Dutch allies.

Helfrich was right to stress the need for more fast, long-range aircraft to supplement his 'Y-boats' and the Catalinas of 413 Sqn RAF at Koggala. Reconnaissance along the eastern coast of India was the responsibility of the Coastal Defence Flights of the Indian Air Force Volunteer Reserve, flying the only available aircraft, obsolete Wapiti and Hart biplanes and impressed Atalanta airliners from Vizagapatam and Madras. Air HQ India, however, saw a greater need for reconnaissance over the Andaman Sea and Southern Burma when, as seemed certain, that country was lost to the Japanese. When the General Reconnaissance Flight of Hudsons were no longer able to operate from Akyab, the Allied commanders would have no knowledge of enemy naval movements.

In March, Intelligence warned of an imminent attack on Ceylon on, or about, 1 April and the ports of Calcutta and Madras in India, Colombo and Trincomalee in Ceylon, were ordered to be cleared of shipping. The purpose of the impending raid was twofold: to cripple Vice-Adm Sir James Somerville's Eastern Fleet (although this had been withdrawn to a new, secret base at Addu Atoll in the Maldive Islands, far to the south-west) removing a source of danger to the Japanese supply routes from the south to Rangoon, and to disrupt supply from the sea to British forces in Burma.

On 4 April the Japanese Imperial Navy's 'Malaya Force' under Adm Ozawa, including the aircraft carrier *Ryujo*, began a series of attacks on shipping, sinking 23 freighters in the Bay of Bengal. At the same time Vice-Adm Nagumo's Strike Force, including four battleships, five carriers and two heavy cruisers, was sailing towards Ceylon, the route reconnoitred by H6K flying-boats of the *Toko Kokutai*. 'Nagumo Force' was found by a Catalina of 413 Sqn from Koggala (pilot Sqn Ldr L.J. Birchall RCAF) who signalled Ceylon before being shot down. Shipping at Colombo and Trincomalee was immediately ordered to leave and to scatter.

The next morning carrier-borne aircraft from Nagumo's 1st Air Fleet attacked Colombo, then sank the cruisers HMS *Cornwall* and HMS *Dorsetshire* heading for the Maldives. Ozawa's force was discovered by Plt Off Barkar IAF, flying a Wapiti of No.6 CDF from Vizagapatam. His aircraft was not seen by the fighter cover of the Japanese fleet but Vizagapatam and the coastal town of Coconada were bombed by *Ryujo's* aircraft. Three days later further strikes were launched from Nagumo's carriers against the naval base at Trincomalee and its airfield at China Bay. Further east they sank the carrier HMS *Hermes* and escorting vessels before retiring towards the Strait of Malacca.

By this time a new bomber force was being assembled at Asanaol, 120 miles north-west of Calcutta, to support the Army retreating northwards though Burma. A new photographic unit was formed at Calcutta as No.1 PRU (India) at the beginning of April under the command of Sqn Ldr A.C. ('Fatty') Pearson, who had served with No.2 PRU early in 1941 and was familiar with the efforts made in the Middle East to achieve effective results. Coming from the Aircraft Delivery Unit to Air HQ India on 29 March, he was given wide authority to organise No.1 PRU (India) as quickly as possible. To avoid confusion with No.1 PRU in England, within days the unit was re-numbered as No.5 PRU, reforming at Asansol on 11 April 1942, still without aircraft.

Technical personnel with a mobile darkroom and equipment for No.3 PRU had earlier been established at Rangoon although the photographic section at Mingaladon carried out processing. All were withdrawn by road to Magwe then to Mandalay and Lashio, from where the photographers were ordered back to Mandalay and across the Ava Bridge to Shwebo.

Meanwhile, Flt Lt Thirlwell records, "On 9 April, I flew from Calcutta to Shwebo in a DC-2 of 31 Sqn and thence by road to Maymyo. I picked up some F.24(?) cameras and took them to Lashio to send on to Calcutta, then I returned to Maymyo and on 12 April to Shwebo." There he, with the photographers and their gear and cameras, were loaded into aircraft of 31 Sqn and flown out to Dum Dum, where Flt Lts Thirlwell and Procter and some Blenheim aircrew of 45 Sqn. were absorbed into No.5 PRU.

On 9 April Wittert flew to Colombo Racecourse aerodrome, where he had arranged for the clearance of trees to allow B-25s to land and take off. There he was told that there could be no integration of the Army and Navy air units, although Helfrich saw no problem in a combined unit, and was instructed to hand over the five B-25Cs to the RAF, to co-operate fully with the British and to 'liquidate' the 'patrouille Bangalore'.

There is no truth in the suggestion that has been made, that the Dutch crews were unwilling to fly the unarmed aircraft on operations. Indeed, they were eager to fly with the RAF, as Air Marshal Peirse had earlier proposed. The need for long-range reconnaissance was so desperate that Air HQ India instructed: "Aircraft B-25 at Bangalore this aircraft to proceed Calcutta taking Squadron Leader Vallins and photographers. Employ this aircraft for PRU purposes with single camera only if possible CRO will make turrets serviceable if possible. Remaining B-25 aircraft proceed Karachi for turrets servicing. Ask help from Fortresses' personnel if needed. These aircraft then proceed Calcutta. Arrangements conversion all B-25 to PRU aircraft to be made between Squadron Leader Pearson and CRO immediately."

There followed a series of signals between Helfrich and the Dutch Government, Helfrich and van Oyen's HQ at Brisbane, Helfrich and Wittert, and between London and Air HQ India. One read: "Reference yours T 145 8th April Captain Wittert conferred yesterday with Helfrich. Latest orders cabled from Dutch Government in London that Dutch personnel return to units in Australia and U.S.A. as early as possible after instructing RAF crews for B-25's. Wittert suggests that all repeat all B-25's proceed immediately to Karachi for servicing and training. Immediate instructions required."

While arrangements were being made for flying out personnel and materiel from Shwebo, on 12 April Sqn Ldr Pearson was flown to Bangalore with new orders from Air Marshal Peirse, confirming to kapt Wittert van Hoogland that all the B-25Cs were to be flown to Karachi and placed under Pearson's command. Wittert had already begun making arrangements for the move—the first aircraft, N5-148, was intended to be flown to Karachi that day but the flight was postponed until the following

day, and the others over the next few days. Immediately, in the Karachi workshops, the work of conversion was begun under Pearson's supervision. To save weight the gun turrets were removed and the upper turret openings panelled over, then the USAAC 'Basic camouflage' was stripped off and the aircraft refinished in a dull dark blue, similar to the 'royal blue' of the Hurricanes, with National Marking 1 applied only to the upper surface of the wings. Wittert expressed surprise at the colour of the aircraft, with what appeared to be only a Dull Red marking, but he was told that the RAF did not expect the aircraft to be intercepted at high altitude and that blue was the usual camouflage colour for reconnaissance aircraft.

The kapitein was not the only one to express reservations about the refinishing; camera-operator LAC Alan Fox recalls, "I remember a few uneasy jokes to the effect that the red circles might be taken by our own fighters to stand for the Japanese rising sun, the blue being invisible." The colour was, of course, chosen by Sqn Ldr Pearson who had experience with both No.103 Maintenance Unit and with No.2 PRU in Egypt. The B-25Cs were ideal for long-range reconnaissance. 2,000 gal fuel tanks installed within the bomb-bays extended the operating radius to about 1,000 miles. Three cameras, F.8 or F.24, were mounted above the ventral turret opening aft of the bomb-bay, the side cameras set at a slight angle to overlap the coverage of the vertical central camera, and an F.52/20 inch camera was mounted within the rear of the fuselage. Because the centre of gravity had been shifted forwards by the conversion, ballast was added within the rear fuselage.

Each aircraft was flight-tested in turn by the kapitein, with RAF technical personnel aboard—and not without incident; Wittert wrote, "During one of these test flights when I was in charge as pilot, being on 15,000 feet the cockpit filled up with blue smoke and somewhere fire broke out because of too heavy a current in an electrical wire. I switched off all electrical currents and we managed to extinguish the fire, very lucky, nobody had a parachute with him so we (sic) could not bail out if we had not mastered the fire." On 19 April Air Vice Marshal Peirse expressed his satisfaction with the progress so rapidly made in converting the B-25Cs, which were allocated to a 'T' (twin-engined) Flight of No.5 PRU.

Throughout their service with the RAF, all five aircraft retained their ML serial numbers, N5-139, N5-143, N5-144, N5-145 and N5-148. There has since been some misunderstanding in a number of publications because these serial numbers were re-used on aircraft of No.18 (Netherlands East Indies) Sqn of the Militaire Luchtvaart in Australia later in the year. There is no Air Ministry record of the B-25Cs being transferred to the RAF. Although the US Air Staff had intended repossessing the five B-25Cs, the Dutch Government, with knowledge of what had happened in Australia, clearly believed the aircraft to be Dutch property. No.18 (NEI) Sqn received 18

45: *A Lysander, 'HN-F', of 'B' Flight of 20 Squadron, well concealed among trees during a detachment to Tezpur in Assam during 1942 for operations with IV Army Corps in north-west Burma. Tasks carried out included personnel transport, mail flights and PR of Allied airfields in the area. The canopy has been covered over by a tarpaulinn to both protect the glazing and prevent giveaway glare*

46: *The dark tone of the blue camouflage applied to the B-25Cs can be clearly seen on N5-145, about to take off from Pandaveswar with Lt JH Van Rooyan of the SAAF at the controls*

47: *When first in service with No.3 PRU (india), the B-25Cs were finished dark blue overall, with National Marking I (the Type B roundel) only on the upper wing surfaces. Yellow surrounds were soon added to these markings*

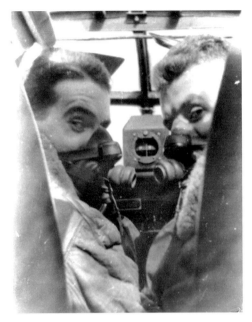

48 Far left: *Sqn Ldr Alec Pearson was responsible for the establishment of No.5/ No.3 PRU (India); later as Wg Cdr Pearson, he commanded 194 Sqn*

49 Left: *In the cabin of a B-25C in April 1942 sit Flg Off Procter (left) and Cadet Air-Observer Fridjof Olsen of the* ML *'Patrouille Bangalore'*

50: *Aircrew of No.3 PRU at Pandaveswar in May 1942; from left to right: unknown, Flg Offs Pailthorpe and Procter, Plt Off Pannifer, lt Van Rooyan and Flt Lt Frostick, OC 'T' Flight. The Japanese invasion not only effectively finished the British Empire in the Far East, it also saw the demise of the, until then, ubiquitous pith helmets*

51: *Mitchell N5-145, 'C', of No.3 PRU (India) during a pre-flight check in June 1942. Note the clear dome covering the extremity of the tail. Crews of these early model B-25s often placed dummy guns in this position to scare off attacking Japanese fighters*

B-25s in August 1942 and the matter of ownership and payment appear then to have been settled between the Netherlands Purchasing Commission and Materiel Command USAAC. *Maj* Te Roller understood that the six aircraft that left Palm Beach for India would be classed as Lend-Lease deliveries to the RAF. Two B-25Cs allocated to the UK Government awaited despatch from Palm Beach by the end of the month and were later held in reserve by US Tenth Air Force in India for more than a year but none of the ML-KNIL aircraft were transferred under Lend-lease. In mid-1942 elements of Maj Gen Brereton's command were transferred from the CBI Theatre of Operations to the Middle East; it appears that the dispute about 'ownership' of those B-25Cs ended and it is likely that Materiel Command then lost track of their whereabouts.

Flt Lt Thirlwell was one of the few pilots sent to Karachi to convert to the B-25Cs, instructed by *kapt* Wittert van Hoogland and *lt* P.C. André de la Porte. On 25 April, André and Flt Lt Thirlwell left Karachi to flight-test N5-l39, the first converted aircraft. Their flight took them to Dum Dum, from where No.5 PRU was intended to operate. Thirlwell later wrote, "I will always remember flying from Karachi to Calcutta with André de la Porte and on arrival overhead Dum Dum he feathered one engine and then proceeded to beat up the airfield. I found Wittert and de la Porte friendly and charming people, albeit rather surprised at the inexperience of the pilots they were handing over to. De la Porte's surprise, on our flight from Karachi to Calcutta, when I confessed that I did not know exactly where we were, had to be seen to be believed."

The next trial flight by André and Thirlwell was to be a high-altitude test. For this, oxygen masks were designed and made in Calcutta. In a subsequent report to *gen-maj* van Oyen, Wittert gave some details: "A look at the map showed that Calcutta was only 400 miles away from Mount Everest in the Himalaya and so he decided to take his test flight in that direction. The plane climbed higher and higher to reach its ceiling; Mount Everest is something between 29,000 and 30,000 feet and the plane was hovering around the high peaks and the crew took some fine photos of the perpetual snow shower that is blowing from the top, and then suddenly one engine gave a bang, boost pressure dropped several inches lower than the other engine, ceiling was losing rapidly and a forced landing on the other side of the Himalayas in Tibet was nearly unavoidable, but the engine kept enough power to hop over the mountain chain and the descent in the Ganges plain was possible. Before landing the crew discovered that one carburettor-handle had moved by itself on full position 'hot' instead of 'cold' and André landed safely in Calcutta as if nothing unusual had happened. Some years ago they made twelve months preparation before they started an expedition to the Himalayas!" Meanwhile Wittert had flown B-25C N5-145 to Pandaveswar, then to Dum Dum on 30 April. When all five aircraft were available, No.5 PRU was declared 'ready

for operations' and on 4 May two B-25Cs were flown to Dum Dum to begin photo-reconnaissance for 221 Group.

On the 5th a visual reconnaissance was made of Heho, Namsang and Lashio, followed by flights to the Andaman Islands and to Mingaladon where two Ki.43 *Hayabusa* fighters of the 5th *Hiko Shidan* (Air Division) attempted an interception on the 7th.

The American fighter aircraft found most satisfactory for conversion to PR use was the Lockheed P-38. This was developed into the F-4, the only USAAF photo-reconnaissance aircraft to fly unarmed, like the British PR aircraft, relying on speed and altitude to avoid interception. With the guns removed from the nose compartment, considerable space was available for different camera combinations. By the beginning of 1942, 100 F-4s were on order, 20 to be delivered each month to the Army Air Forces.

On 29 April 1942, while the RAF's No.5 PRU prepared for operations, HQ US Tenth Air Force signalled Gen H.H. Arnold requesting that "*a photographic squadron of P-38 planes be sent here immediately... since without these planes, long-range missions do not produce to the fullest extent, thus making a high-speed and high-altitude reconnaissance squadron muchly needed in this locality.*" An immediate result was the allocation of the 9th PR Sqn to India in July, although the first of the squadron's crated F-4s did not arrive by sea until September.

At Dum Dum, Sqn Ldr Pearson followed the highly satisfactory example set by No.2 PRU and invited technical personnel to act as camera operators in the B-25Cs. Like their counterparts in the Middle East, the three volunteers who were accepted were not made up to air-crew rank of sergeant as there was no aircrew classification of camera-operator, but they were allowed flying pay!

Late in April, with the Chinese armies withdrawing from eastern Burma into Yunnan province, the only course open to the British was to extricate what remained of Burma Army and retreat into Assam before the monsoon rains made withdrawal impossible. On the last day of the month a final stand was made at Kyaukse, south of Mandalay, then the Army withdrew across the Irrawaddy bridge at Ava and headed north across the plain for the Chindwin River and India.

The bridge at Ava was cut, denying the Japanese rail or direct road access across the Irrawaddy. Next day, the single ex-17 Sqn Hurricane was flown north to Myitkyina, its duties completed.

52: The accommodation for the aircrew and ground staff of No.3 PRU at Pandaves-war was somewhat less agreeable than they had experienced in Calcutta

*53 **Far left:** View forward from the tail compartment of a B-25C of 681 Sqn. Beyond the 'sanitary can' is the aft F.52 camera position and, through the bulkhead doorway, the middle compartment for 2 or 3 F.24s, lit by the astrodome that replaced the upper gun turret. Further forward can be seen the bomb-bay fuel tank and 'tunnel' to the pilots' cabin*

*54 **Left:** Flt Lt Freddie Procter stands unhappily beside mud-spattered N5-148. On 6 September 1942 he taxied around a pothole only to drop the starboard wheel into a slit-trench and was given the job of recovering the aircraft*

55: No.3 PRU's B-25C, N5-139, with its rear fuselage demolished after an accident on 22 June 1942. Without a replacement tyre available after a puncture, the aircraft was left in place with warning lights around it. Even so, a Hurricane IIC, BG873 of 67 Sqn, collided with the B-25C during night-flying training, cutting into the fuselage at the mid-turret position so that it collapsed with the tail unit to the ground

56: The mangled rear fuselage and tail unit of N5-139 under inspection. Astonishingly, the forward part of the aircraft was completely undamaged (RAF News)

57 Right: Wg Cdr SG (Bill) Wise soon after taking comand of No.3 PRU (India)

58 Far right: Much of the Imperial Japanese Army Air Force opposition to the RAF in Burma was provided by Nakajima Ki 43 ('Oscar') fighters, flown by men such as this anonymous pilot of the 59th Sentai. At the time they were probably some of the most combat experienced aircrew in the world, many having served on operations since the start of the war against China in the early 1930's. Note the archaic telescopic gunsight

59: Mechanics shelter from the sun under the wing of an early model Nakajima Ki 43-I of the 64th Sentai, shortly after the unit arrived at Sungei Patani in Malaya from Java in mid-March 1942. There the unit had claimed 18 victories in two weeks. The dark green and brown camouflage pattern is similar to that of the RAF fighters and was used by the Japanese primarily in the Malaya and Burma campaigns. Clearly visible are the red and white spinner and similarly coloured arrow marking of the 2nd Chutai on the tail, while the white band indicates that the aircraft was a front-line type

60: *A fine overhead shot of Hurricane IIB, BM969, being flown by Flg Off Donald Pearson, 'S' Flight Commander, of No.3 PRU (India) in mid-1942. Some views of this aircraft, taken against the glare of the sun, appear to show much wider yellow surrounds to the upperwing markings than was the case. Here it can be clearly seen that 2in wide Yellow surrounds (the same dimension as those on the fuselage) have been added. Note, though, how the sun has already begun to fade the red of the wing roundels*

Respite

The Monsoon begins

Despite considerable losses of men and materiel, the British and Indian position now had some advantages. While Japanese lines of supply and communication were extended the length of Burma, the routes to Lt-Gen William Slim's Burma Corps were shortened, through the passes from the Brahmaputra Valley and via the port of Chittagong in East Bengal.

On 12 May the monsoon began and the enemy was left in possession of all Burma except for the jungle-covered mountains west of the Chindwin, along a broken 'front' stretching from China to the Bay of Bengal, greater in length than the Russian Front. That day the first photographic sorties were flown by the B-25Cs, de la Porte and Procter flew to Port Blair, Wittert to cover Moulmein and the Rangoon airfields. Braking the B-25Cs on the short runway at Dum Dum caused heavy tyre wear which was partly made good by vulcanising patches onto the rubber. As no spare tyres were available a longer landing

run was needed so the aircraft were flown to Pandaveswar, some miles north-east of Asansol, on 13 April. There was no aerodrome with a metalled or stabilised runway, simply a long strip of levelled ground. The other RAF photographic reconnaissance units were No.1 PRU at Benson and No.2 PRU at Heliopolis, so No.5 PRU was re-numbered in sequence as No.3 PRU (India). The unit's three Hurricanes were flown to Pandaveswar on 13 May so that, for the first time, all the aircraft were stationed in one place.

At "unspeakable" Pandaveswar the personnel were accommodated under canvas; the aircrew exchanging the luxury of the Great Eastern Hotel in Calcutta for primitive conditions they shared with the ground crews, with temperatures up to 115°F (46°C).

Although a few PR pilots had been posted to the unit, there were too few aircrew to make full use of the available aircraft so the complement had been already enlarged by the transfer of seven pilots and navigators from 45 Sqn. Although based at Dum Dum, the squadron's rapidly decreasing number of Blenheim IV aircraft had been continually on the move, from the Rangoon airfields to Magwe and on to Loiwing, and from Dum Dum 45 Sqn was unable to undertake operations.

Meanwhile a Photographic Intelligence Unit had been set up at Calcutta under the command of Sqn Ldr J.D. Braithwaite who had carried out aerial surveys of the Burma oilfields while serving with the Burma Volunteer Air Force before the Japanese invasion. It was decided that all the aircraft should fly out on operations from their base but return via Dum Dum so that the camera magazines could be changed and the films processed and printed at nearby Barrackpore.

In response to Air Marshal Peirse's request for an experienced senior officer, Wg Cdr Wise, who had served with the PRU at Benson and whose 248 Sqn of Beaufighters was undergoing a re-organisation, was posted to New Delhi and took over No.3 PRU. Sqn Ldr Pearson was posted to 31 Sqn and later took command of 194 Sqn. Rumours persisted that Alec Pearson, in order to 'commandeer' the B-25Cs for the RAF, had anticipated promotion from Flight Lieutenant by arriving at Karachi already wearing Squadron Leader's badges of rank. This story was untrue; he had been appointed Squadron Leader in September 1940.

Reconnaissance continued, one sortie being made almost every day despite deteriorating weather; down the Arakan coast, to Myitkyina and Lashio and to the Andamans. Approaching Port Blair on 18 May, Flg Off Thirlwell's B-25C encountered two enemy fighters. He recalled, "the first indication I had that a Japanese fighter was after us was a boiled egg (part of our flight ration) smashing against the instrument panel, having been thrown by the camera operator to attract my attention" —presumably the intercom was not connected. The camera operator was almost isolated in the rear of the fuselage by the bomb-bay fuel tank, only a cramped crawl-space giving him access to the pilots' cabin. Although the speed and operating altitude of the aircraft was considered usually sufficient to prevent interception, an essential duty of the camera operator was to keep a look-out for enemy aircraft.

Wt Off Huggard of 60 Sqn, who had carried out early photographic sorties, became well-known when on 22 May, of one formation of Blenheims, only Huggard's Z9808 reached the objective—Akyab airfield. He attacked at low-level but was chased out to sea by five Ki-43 *Hayabusa* fighters of the 64th *Sentai*. Two were hit by fire from the Blenheim's gunner, Flt Sgt Mc Luckie, and turned back, then the *Sentai* commander, the fighter 'ace' *Chusa* (Lt-Col) Tateo Kato attacked the Blenheim but his aircraft also was hit, to catch fire and dive into the sea. The Blenheim's crew received congratulations from Air Vice-Marshal Stevenson.

By the end of the month the 'T' (twin-engined) Flight of No.5 PRU was commanded by Flt Lt D.R. Frostick and the 'S' (single-engined) Flight was established at Dum Dum under the command of Flt Lt D.B. Pearson.

By this time PR Spitfires were arriving in the Middle East to replace the Hurricanes, now completely outmoded there. The AOC-in-C, Middle East, was therefore requested to send on to India the photographic Hurricanes as soon as they were replaced by Spitfires.

A camera-equipped Hurricane Mk.IIB, Z5594, was flown from No.2 PRU, Heliopolis, to Pandaveswar by Pearson on 26 May and flown on to Agartala, 200 miles further east, on the 29th. Another Hurricane was delivered that day, then BM992 was flown in by Sgt Kirvan on 20 May; this aircraft, fitted with guns was later handed over to 28 Sqn for tactical reconnaissance duties. Flt Lt Pearson began operations by obtaining good cover of Magwe and Oyster Island during a 4hr 20min flight the next day, returning to Dum Dum. Sgt Kirvan also flew to Magwe on 6 June but ran out of fuel on the return flight and crash-landed near Kanchrapara; although his Hurricane was damaged, the films were recovered and successfully processed.

The Air Ministry advised Air Headquarters, India, that formation of a Photographic Reconnaissance Unit had been approved and was to be established with twelve aircraft. Owing to the general shortage of photographic reconnaissance aircraft, however, the number required to bring the strength up to the newly established figure had to be supplied from within India Command. As India already had five B-25s and three Hurricanes modified to the PR role in May 1942, the official establishment was optimistically issued as two Mobile Flights, one of six B-25s, the other of six Hurricanes.

The monsoon rains, at first a relief at sun-baked Pandaveswar, made operations increasingly hazardous as the landing-ground became flooded. Early in June several operations had to be aborted and on the 10th No.3 PRU began moving to Dum Dum. All the aircraft were intended to be based there from 28 June but the unit's long-range capability was halved within a week.

On 22 June N5-139, 'E', suffered a punctured tyre while landing. As noted earlier, there were no replacement tyres available so the B-25C was left at the side of the runway. Although warning lamps were set around the aircraft, a Hurricane IIC, BG873 of 67 Sqn, collided with the B-25C during night-flying training, cutting into the fuselage at the mid-turret position so that it collapsed with the tail unit to the ground.

A few days later an engine of N5-143, 'D', flown by Flt Lt Frostick caught fire immediately after take-off from Pandaveswar. Flt Lt Thirlwell, second pilot, writes, "We were fully laden with petrol to fly to the Andaman Islnds.

I think that since we were really a flying fuel bowser at take-off decided Frostick to ditch a.s.a.p.". The fire was extinguished when the B-25C was set down in the 3ft-deep mid-channel of the nearby Ajay River, a tributary of the Ganges, forlornly awaiting a ground party to strip out equipment and consider salvage.

Apart from the incursion by their fleet into the Indian Ocean, culminating in raids on Ceylon in April, the Japanese made no attempt to widen their perimeter of expansion. After their defeat at Midway in June, the danger of their invading India so diminished that Gen Sir Archibald Wavell, C-in-C in India, began planning limited post-monsoon operations for the Chindwin and Arakan Fronts, to be followed by Operation 'Anakim', a seaborne assault aimed at Rangoon. Disaster in the Western Desert, civil disorder in India, the diversion of troops to Iraq and difficulties in obtaining shipping and

equipment caused 'Anakim' to be postponed and eventually abandoned. Operations by No.3 PRU began again with a Hurricane sortie by Flt Lt D. B. Pearson to Mandalay on 23 July and to Prome on the 28th. The following week B-25C operations recommenced; on 7 August Flg Off Edmonds flew to the Andaman Islands, followed by Lt Van Rooyan SAAF on the 8th—on this occasion two Nakajima Ki.27 fighters attacked his B-25C and inflicted damage before Van Rooyan was able to escape.

It was later reported that "by the end of July all the B-25s had been put out of action by Japanese fighter interception. This left only the Hurricanes..." but the records show that this was a 'managed untruth'.

61: Under a rain-laden sky, B-25C, N5-143, lies ditched and abandoned in the flooded Ajay River after the aircraft caught fire on 28 June 1942

62: Hurricane IIB BH125, 'U', was delivered to No.3 PRU in September 1942. It is finished overall in the unit's special 'Royal Blue' paint, with no National markings on the fuselage sides and 4in wide Yellow outlines to its wing markings. The fairing for the camera is clearly visible under the rear of the fuselage. An undercarriage failure led to the aircraft crashing at Chittagong in August 1943 while with 631 Sqn

63: Hurricane PR IIBs, BH125 and BM969, on a test flight from Agartala in November 1942

64: 20 Sqn sent a detachment to assist the Army in Northern Burma. This Lysander IV, DG445, was at Bairagarh in June 1942, its heavily weathered camouflage carrying Dull Red unit codes

65: BP911, a Spitfire PR.IV(Trop) on arrival at Karachi from Egypt on 10 October 1942

1942-1943
The first Spitfires for India

Another Hurricane PR Mk.II, BH251, was delivered from No.2 PRU on 7 September and made a recce of Akyab on the 12th, when two more Hurricanes, BH125 and BN124, were flown in. Next day Flg Off Procter flew a B-25C on a successful recce of Mingaladon, Zayatkwin, Insein, Toungoo and Magwe. By the end of the month No.3 PRU had on its strength the full complement of six Hurricane Mk.IIBs fitted with three cameras, F.24 14 inch or 20 inch, in the rear fuselage; of these the forward pair were 'split' so that overlapping vertical photographs could be taken simultaneously. Additional internal fuel tanks enabled the operational range to be increased to more than 550 miles.

Weather conditions throughout September seriously hampered attempts by the serviceable B-25Cs to obtain cover of the Andaman Islands and the Rangoon area, and it was feared that more Japanese naval operations against Eastern India or Ceylon could be mounted with out warning. The AOC-in-C India therefore made a personal appeal to the Vice-Chief of the Air Staff for "*even two PR aircraft with an adequate supply of spares, which would be worth their weight in gold*"—meaning Spitfires.

The Hurricanes of No.2 PRU were supplemented and eventually replaced by Spitfire PR IVs. The first were delivered to Heliopolis in April 1942, making additional Hurricanes available for delivery to India. HQ RAF India signalled Middle East, "*In view of our present heavy reconnaissance commitments I suggest that you despatch two PRU Spitfires to India as soon as you can spare them and subsequently two more each month beginning in October.*"

As Middle East Command had a reasonable supply of PR Spitfires by this time, a request was made to assist India Command whose "*Hurricanes were insufficient for the operations planned after the end of the monsoon period.*"

On 6 September Flt Lt Procter, swerving N5-184 to avoid a pot-hole in the perimeter track, dropped a wheel into a slit-trench unseen by him and his co-pilot; damage was minimal but a sortie was cancelled. When Flt Lt Frostick landed on return from a sortie to the Rangoon airfields on October, the port tyre of N5-144 burst, causing damage to the hub.

Only two B-25Cs remained serviceable by mid-October and more aircraft were urgently needed. The AOC-in-C Middle East at last agreed to release two Spitfires; at the end of September Wg Cdr Wise and Sgt

66 Above: Unidentified groundcrew pose by Spitfire PR.IV (Trop) BP911, which shows signs, by its scarred paintwork, of its earlier service with No.2 PRU. It was flown in by Wg Cdr Wise for No.3 PRU on 29 September 1942. The first Spitfire sortie was on 10 October

Cusak were flown to the Canal Zone to collect two already well-used Spitfire PR. Mk.IVs, BP9ll and BP935, which they ferried back to India on 10 October.

It was intended that a Spitfire Flight be formed to take the place of the B-25Cs. The nominal establishment of No.3 PRU was accordingly amended in October to "twelve Spitfire/Hurricanes."

Sgt Cusack, one of the first pilots of No.5 PRU, survived the dangers of operations but, as a unit member recalled, "Towards the end of the war, when he'd completed his 4-year tour, he went on a binge the night before beginning the journey home. Coming back to his bamboo 'basha' (hut) he flopped into bed, lit a cigarette and then passed out. The cigarette set fire to the bed and burned down the basha and him with it."

Flt Lt Norman Roberson has written of continuing tactical reconnaissance operations by the Lysanders of 20 Sqn: "From July to September 1942, 20 Squadron found itself busy with internal security operations in connection with the disturbances that were occurring in various parts of India. Mahatma Ghandi's Congress Party was attempting to subvert the Government by practising 'Civil Disobedience', and in Bihar and Bengal his followers had been disrupting communications by damaging railway lines and so on. As a consequence, the Squadron was called upon to carry out recce flights in the Bihar and Bengal areas, particularly along roads and railway lines. This kind of flying and the various associated PR tasks, served a dual purpose in providing good training for the newer crews. The use of the aircraft on this work also gave the Army some insight into the capabilities of the Lysander.

"On 19 July, A and B flights were detached to Tezpur in Assam, to relieve No.113 Squadron and No.5 Squadron, who were there flying Audaxes. The Squadron was assigned man pick-up (MPU) tasks, carrying Army personnel, practice AA co-operation flights; mail carrying to and from Calcutta and PR of Allied airfields in the area. A sub-detachment also operated from Dinjan, further forward in eastern Assam. Some worthwhile sorties were flown from Dinjan, towards the extreme northern zone of Burma, to contact remnants of British Forces and civilians who were endeavouring to get through the jungle-clad mountains to India. These sorties were probably the first made in an area into which the Japanese were advancing.

The detachment at Tezpur came to an end on 1 October and the crews and aircraft, bar one, returned to Jamshedpur on 21 October. However, the one aircraft remaining at Dinjan for AA calibration tasks was destroyed on 25 October, when the airfield was attacked by low-flying Japanese bombers.

"Meanwhile, Brigadier Orde Wingate had arrived in India and with the backing of Winston Churchill and Field Marshal Wavell, he commenced training a Special Force for operations against the Japanese. For this he had selected a large area of typical country near Bhopal, and by the end of June 1942 had established his training camps there. By mid-September he was sufficiently confident in his force to hold a major exercise and manoeuvres, to which four Lysanders were invited; two each from Nos. 20 and 28 Squadrons.

"This exercise undoubtedly had a lot to do with forging close bonds between the Army and Air Force. Wingate's force, which became known as the Chindits, completed its training towards the end of 1942 and began to move forwards towards bases in the Imphal valley, prior to venturing into Burma early in 1943."

When operation 'Anakim' was postponed, Gen Chiang Kai Shek refused to permit the use of Chinese forces for Wavell's proposed offensive in northern Burma. Nevertheless, Wavell continued with associated plans for log range penetration and for a limited offensive on the Arakan coast.

As the 1942 monsoon eased the first moves against the Japanese were made, with the intention of re-capturing Akyab and establishing a base there. On 21 September an advance began down the Mayu Penninsular over difficult terrain and in atrocious weather. The enemy brought forces up to Buthedaung and Maungdaw at the head of the Peninsular, then, as the British advanced, retired across the Mayu River to Rathedaung. Maungdaw was taken on 17 December and the advance continued to Donbaik where the Japanese had established an elaborate series of bunkers across the coastal strip.

On 17 October Flt Lt Procter took over command of 'S' Flt from Flt Lt Pearson who, tour-expired, was soon to leave for the UK. The first Spitfire reconnaissance was flown by Wg Cdr Wise over Shwebo, Mandalay, Maymyo and Monywa on 19 October. Four Mk.IV Spitfire's were on the unit's strength by the end of the month. These production aircraft were developed, following a series of Spitfire PR variants from the Spitfire Mk.V, but with a 66.5 gallon fuel tank in the leading edge of each wing, instead of armament. Alternative mountings for cameras in tandem could be installed in the rear of the fuselage; those normally used by No.3 PRU were 'S' fitting (two vertical F.24/20 inch cameras) or 'Y'-fitting (two F.52/36 inch cameras). There was also provision for an F.8/13 inch oblique camera, rarely used. Most of the aircraft received from the Middle East were 'tropicalised', with an air-filter mounted beneath the nose-cowling, as fitted to the Spitfire Mk.V (Trop).

Flt Lt Frostick and Flg Off Reeves proceeded by air to Karachi to collect a 'reconditioned' B-25C from 30 MU which they flew to Dum Dum on 14 November. Flg Off Reeves has noted only 'B-25C' in his log book but this was certainly N5-139, rebuilt perhaps by replacing the wrecked rear fuselage and tail-unit with the equivalent undamaged parts from N5-143. By the end of November the unit once again had four B-25Cs serviceable.

Typical of the longer sorties, for which the B-25Cs were used, was one on 24 November with Flg Off F.W. Guy as pilot of N5-148, 'A': "Airborne 10:20 hours, set course for Pakokku, climbing steadily to 20,000 ft. Photographed aerodrome and set course for Namsang. Sighted Meiktila to starboard and photographed two satellites and Meiktila airfield. Sighted Heho airfield to starboard and made run over aerodrome. Camera operator and co-pilot reported 12 fighters below. Flew south for approximately ten minutes. Set course for Namsang, two runs made over aerodrome. Set course for Maymyo, made one run over aerodrome and town. Second run made over Anisakan aerodrome. Set course for Mandalay and photographed reported position of aerodrome and railway sidings. Set course for base. Landed at 16:30."

For the next two months the B-25Cs maintained their distant operations over Central and Southern Burma while the Hurricanes and Spitfires continued short-range sorties over the Arakan battle area and the coast as far south as Ramree Island.

After its long absence, N5-139 was again available for operations and was in use from 2 December until the end of January 1943. A sortie by Flg Off A.G.F. Oldworth in N5-139 over the docks and the Rangoon River on 14 December was interrupted by intense anti-aircraft fire, but the operation was to continue with runs over Mingaladon and Zayatkwin airfields. The aircraft flew on towards Toungoo but was intercepted by a Japanese fighter and chased for twenty-five minutes before the enemy aircraft turned away. In addition a series of air survey flights was made by the B-25Cs to the Andaman Islands and completed early in January 1943.

Earlier, the 9th PR Sqn of the USAAF had arrived in India and the unit's aircraft, thirteen crated Lockheed F-4s, were delivered in September. The F-4 was a photographic reconnaissance version of the Lockheed P-38E Lightning fighter (two 1375 hp Allison V-1710-F-17 engines) without armament but with provision for four K.17 cameras mounted in place of the guns and magazines within the nose of the fuselage.

67: Lt Van Rooyan of the SAAF poses with one of No.3 PRU's first Spitfire PR.IVs (BP911) in October 1942. The interesting wheel chocks appear to be made out of corrugated iron sheet

68: *BP935 was one of the first two Spitfire PR.IVs for No.3 PRU and had earlier been flown by No.1 PRU at Benson before transfer to No.2 PRU at Heliopolis in Egypt. There it was refinished in the dark blue finish seen here and the fin flash was eliminated*

69 Right: *The Gokteik Viaduct photographed on 13 March 1943 before the proposed Chindit attack. This prime rail target was 2,260ft long, supported on 17 trestles up to 320ft in height*

70 Below: *A few F-4As were painted with Olive Drab uppersurfaces and under-sides a field-applied light blue, although it is possible that 'Foto-Jo' of the US 9th PR Sqn at Barrackpore was in poorly applied Synthetic Haze, the uppersurfaces appearing as a dark Flight Blue, the undersides pale Sky Base Blue. Unusually, nose guns are still retained*

Disappointment in Arakan

When the British Eastern Army began an offensive down the coast of Burma in December, supported by 224 Grp RAF, its purpose was to re-occupy the 90-mile long Mayu Peninsula and the Island of Akyab. By the end of 1942 much of the peninsula had been retaken. Delays came when the British and Indian force came upon Japanese bunker 'fortresses' and unseasonal storms disrupted the lines of supply, then enemy reinforcements, brought in by sea, crossed the mountainous spine of the peninsula to cut off the forward brigades. By the beginning of the south-west monsoon in May 1943, Eastern Army had withdrawn the survivors to the positions in East Bengal where they had stood a year before. It was admitted that the main cause of failure in this First Arakan Campaign was lack of Intelligence as to Japanese plans and movements. Far to the north-east, however, the First Chindit Expedition had proved that ordinary British troops could cause disruption and survive far within enemy-occupied territory.

With the end of the monsoon rains, 9th PR Sqn had moved to Chakulia, 80 miles west of Calcutta, at the end of November and the first sorties were flown on 13 December by the Squadron Commander, Col McCoy, and Capt H. Miller. Two days later the Squadron suffered its first battle casualty when an F-4 was damaged by anti-aircraft fire and crash-landed at Dum Dum. The pilot, Capt C.P. Webster, was slightly injured. Apart from the Arakan offensive, no attempt was made by either army to undertake ground operations of any extent and a Flight of 9th Sqn was detached for operations in China throughout the dry monsoon period. The demand for high-level medium range photo-reconnaissance meant that the aircraft of No.3 PRU were fully employed when serviceable.

The increasing needs of the ground forces were met by moving four Lysanders of 20 Sqn to Imphal for tactical and photographic reconnaissance for 14 Division. Then four Hurricanes from A Flight, 28 (Fighter Reconnaissance) Sqn were moved from Ranchi to Chittagong on 8 January and thence to begin operations from a forward bare-earth, unpaved, 'kachcha' airstrip at Maungdaw South ('Hatchetts') for operations in support of IV Corps.

The first sortie, on 10 January, was a reconnaissance of Rathedaung by Flg Off Dunford Wood in HB485, the first Hurricane IIB of 28 Sqn modified for camera installation and with the two outer guns removed from each wing. On the 19th, both Sqn Ldr Mann in BW938 and Dunford Wood in BW928 were intercepted by two 'Zero' (sic) aircraft while on their way to a reconnaissance in the Donbaik area, but they returned undamaged. Three days later Flt Sgt Hilton in JS223, escorted by Flt Lt Scott in BW938, was 'jumped' on returning from a photographic reconnaissance sortie over Rathedaung by two Nakajima

Ki.43 *Hayabusa* fighters (at the time code-named 'Jim', later 'Oscar'). JS223 was shot down and Flt Sgt Hilton killed but Flt Lt Scott escaped with his screen and gunsight damaged and landed safely at Bawli Bazar. By the end of the month, the detachment had received another four Hurricane IIBs, all modified for camera installation at 308 MU Allahabad.

Initially, sorties were flown by single aircraft, seeking out and attacking concentrations of enemy troops and small craft on the Mayu River. Single-aircraft sorties over the Kaladan River were continued, but over the Mayu peninsula, as the battle for Donbaik developed, the Army asked for complete photographs of the enemy positions every five days. These sorties were undertaken by Hurricanes of 28 Sqn flying at various heights, from 2,000 to 8,000ft with a fighter escort of one or two sections. Except at dawn or dusk, the low-level tactical-reconnaissance sorties were each accompanied by a single Hurricane escort or 'weaver'; the leading aircraft would beat up any suitable target and then act as protective cover while the weaver followed up the attack. After the loss of JS223, one or two sections of fighters on 'cab rank' patrol, under the direction of Air Support Control Units with the Army, acted as top cover for tactical recce and as escort for the high-level photographic sorties by Hurricanes of 28 Sqn and No.3 PRU (India). To conform with administrative pracrice in Britain, the Air Ministry required Photographic Reconnaissance Units overseas to be nominally disbanded and re-formed as squadrons. No.3 PRU (India) at Dum Dum was consequently re-numbered as 681 Sqn with effect from 25 January 1943.

By the end of the month only three B-25Cs; 'A', 'B', and 'C' were still in operational use but the crew flying N5-148, 'A', had an engine problem on 25 January. On the 28th Flg Off Barnett reported the port engine 'ropey' at altitude. On 1 February Plt Off Tapp, on return from Rangoon in 'A', reported "A fire developed on the way out in the port wing, just off the Burma coast, sparks and smoke coming into the cabin; fortunately it went out in a few seconds. Covered the docks, saw several fires burning from bombing by USAAF twenty minutes before. Went on to Mingaladon, Zayatkwin, Hlengu and 'Cascade'. Intercepted N. of Bassein at 22,000 ft by two enemy aircraft (probably Naki 05), they attacked from either beam separately, saw six guns firing from one aircraft. Avoiding action taken by weaving and diving, the speed reaching 400 IAS at 2,000 ft. No strikes by enemy aircraft which were eventually lost over the Burma Coast Line. A little inaccurate AA encountered over Rangoon Docks. 4/10-5/10 Cumulus over the Rangoon area. Bay of Bengal 8/10-9/10 St-cumulus at 12,000 ft."

Flg Off Barnett and his crew in N5-148 were lost on a sortie to Rangoon on 13 February. It was feared that the cause was engine failure and the next day Sqn Ldr Frostick searched along the coast for signs of wreckage. The Japanese later claimed the B-25 was shot down by

Gunsô (Sgt) Satoshi Anabuki, the most successful Army pilot, of the 30th *Hiko Sentai* at Mingaladon. 28 Sqn's Tac/R operations over Northern Arakan continued throughout February but, by the end of the month, the enemy's Mitsubishi Dinahs were no longer flying overland further north than the Maungdaw-Buthidaung area for fear of the RAF's fighter defences. Over the sea, however, their reconnaissance flights continued to seek the launches and small supply craft supporting XV Corps on the coast. Even there the Japanese rarely ventured far, and only one was intercepted and destroyed by RAF fighters, although on the last day of 1942 a formation of launches was located off the Naf Peninsular by a Dinah and was later attacked by bombers. Considerable air-support was given to the developing Japanese counter-offensive, mainly by Oscar fighters.

During January 1943, 20 Sqn was partly re-equipped with Hurricane Mk.IIBs for tactical reconnaissance but a few weeks later the squadron was re-designated a fighter/ground attack unit.

By early March 1943, the benefits to the ground forces of tactical reconnaissance resulted in greater demands for sorties to be made by fighter-reconnaissance Hurricanes but it was made clear that there were insufficient aircraft and pilots trained in army co-operation to meet all the army's needs. For the artillery, no specifically Arty/R (artillery recce) sorties were possible but the vertical PR photography proved of great value in Arakan. Obliques, which could be easily and economically taken by a single Hurricane, appeared ideally suitable when the 'Merton' method of printing grids onto the photographs was used. The system, attributed to Lt-Col Merton of the Army Photographic Research Branch, was used to make a panorama of gridded obliques which enabled the location of targets to be fixed with an accuracy equivalent to that obtained from a 1:2500 map. On receiving a demand, a liaison officer with a fighter-reconnaissance detachment established the start and finish of the photographic run, normally parallel with, but just behind the forward ground troops and out of range of the enemy ground fire. Runs were usually made at heights of up to 3,000 ft and obliques were thus often obtainable when weather conditions were unsuitable for taking verticals, which required greater altitude and several parallel runs over enemy-held territory. The Merton method required cameras to be mounted, preferably, at an angle of 12° to 14° below the horizontal; the installations now fitted to Hurricane IIBs closely approached this criterion, allowing several alternative fields of view. The A (forward) position took a vertical F.24 camera with either 5 inch or 8 inch focal length lens, with a mirror attachment for rearward oblique photography; the B (rear) position took a similar camera for 'split' vertical photography, or an oblique F.24 camera at 16° depression from the horizontal with an 8-inch lens or at 11° depression with a 14-inch lens.

As new aircraft were gradually made available, No.151 Operational Training Unit, Risalpur, was allocated a number of Hurricanes. One of the first units to convert to the Hurricane IIB was No.1 Sqn Indian Air Force in mid-1942, to be followed in September by 2 Sqn IAF and in December by 6 Sqn IAF, equipped with Hurricane IICs.

By January 1943 camera installations were being manufactured in India for the Hurricanes of No.2 Sqn and No.151 OCU, and additional production was put in hand for mountings to be fitted to aircraft of Nos. 1 and 6 Sqns IAF.

With increasing operational demands, 28 Sqn had great difficulty in maintaining its aircraft; the squadron still had a flight of Lysanders at its base at Ranchi and, with a total of only twelve Hurricanes as Initial Equipment, it was impossible to keep ten, in two detachments, serviceable at all times.

Early in February 1943 Maj-Gen O.C. Wingate's '77th Bde' (the 'Chindits') crossed the Chindwin River to disrupt enemy communications and, if possible, cut the Madalay-Lashio railway. On 24 March, orders were given to demolish the viaduct across the Gokteik Gorge, regarded as the most important railway target in Burma and kept under constant observation by PR squadrons. The plan was thwarted by difficulties of air supply. Proposals were made for an attack by USAF bombers but it later became clear that the railway was of less strategic importance to the Japanese than it could later be to the Allies.

On 24 February 1943 another detachment, this time of four Hurricanes from No.1 (FR) Sqn, Indian Air Force, moved to Imphal under control of 170 (Army Co-operation) Wing for tactical recce duties with HQ IV Corps and was joined on the 27th by four aircraft from 28 Sqn. It was soon apparent that, without long-range fuel tanks, these Hurricanes did not have sufficient range for the operations required and they returned to Ranchi for the tanks to be fitted, returning to Imphal on 7 March.

The first operation flown from Imphal was a high-level PR sortie over the KaIewa-Kalemyo area on 9 March by Flt Lt H.G.F. Larsen. His Hurricane, escorted by Mohawks of 155 Sqn, was met by intense and accurate anti-aircraft fire but the reconnaissance was successfully completed. The next day a similar sortie to obtain a mosaic of Wuntho again had an escort of two Mohawks.

As Japanese fighter activity intensified it became increasingly important to keep track of enemy aircraft movements so 28 Sqn's detachment was supplied with fighter-frequency crystals for their sets, allowing intercommunication between the Tac/R Hurricanes, their 'weavers', the fighter units and the Fighter Operations Controller at Maungdaw. Although this meant that 28 Sqn's pilots had no direct link with ASC units on the ground, it enabled them to take advantage of RAF fighter sweeps and escorted bomber strikes as cover for 'deep-in' reconnaissance. From March, oblique and vertical cameras were carried on all Tac/R sortie and detailed information was brought back about enemy positions, types of gun etc. The 'split-8' camera modification installed in the fighter-reconnaissance Hurricanes enabled PR vertical cover to be obtained in fewer runs over the target; as time spent over the area was reduced, only a 'weaver' escort was needed.

Wavell's intended assault on Akyab soon had to be abandoned—priorities elsewhere meant that no landing-craft could be made available while a promised additional brigade could not be spared in sufficient time. Moreover, the Japanese brought up their 55th Division from the Irrawaddy Valley to encircle the British troops facing Rathedaung. A final assault was made on Donbaik in the hope of securing the peninsula but, when this failed, the troops in the Mayu River, with constant air support, were withdrawn to join the main British force on the coast.

When, on 3 April, the Japanese blocked the road north of Indin and cut the British line of communication, 28 Sqn's Hurricanes flew 'contact recces' for several days to establish the exact location of the trapped forces so that they could be re-supplied by sea at low tide and enabled to break out.

With the approach of the monsoon and with no port facilities available, the British supply situation was becoming dangerous and retreat inevitable. By 7 April the situation at Indin was critical and 28 Sqn's aircraft were withdrawn leaving only a servicing party at 'Hatchetts' where two Hurricanes were sent for operations during daylight hours. On the 15th the remaining ground staff moved north to 'Ritz' (Maungdaw 1) another fair-weather strip used by fighters on 'stand-by'. The following day 28 Sqn's B Flt left Imphal and returned to Ranchi.

On 26 April two aircraft on a tactical reconnaissance to Donbaik and Foul Point came under machine-gun fire; Plt Off Carmichael was shot down into the Mayu River and, although his companion, Plt Off J.L.R. Flynn in BK117, circled, there was no sign of life.

It was considered essential for army co-operation that the aircraft should be close to the controlling Army formation so, when the Army HQ retired at the beginning of May, 28 Sqn's forward detachment moved also, to 'Sybil' (Chhota Maunghnama), B Flt taking over from A Flt on the 4th. Operations were curtailed because of deteriorating weather, a foretaste of the monsoon, but on 14 May Flt Lt Larsen discovered fifty or so Japanese troops whom he strafed before returning to base, later leading a fighter sweep onto the same target.

By the end of the month operations were so hindered by the weather that three Hurricanes were sent to the all-weather airfield at Chittagong for a few days while the rest of the detachment moved to Cox's Bazar. The detachment was astounded at a report that one of their aircraft had machine-gunned a Burmese Navy launch on the Kalapanzin River but it was later announced that a Hurricane in Japanese hands had made low-level attacks at times when 28 Sqn aircraft were not flying. Three Hurricane IIB (Trop), including BD778, had been captured in Malaya and allocated to the 64th *Sentai*. These were test-flown in Thailand by several Japanese pilots of the unit, including Kato. One was lost in an accident, the others may have been destroyed or damaged on the ground during a strafing raid on the 64th's base at Chiengmai in Thailand on 24 March 1942 by the AVG. Three fighters were claimed destroyed and ten damaged for the loss of two AVG aircraft and the death of the 2nd Sqn's commander, Jack Newkirk.

From the Feni satellite strip 'Manston' when the surface was not waterlogged, or from Chandina, the Blenheim Mk.Vs of 113 Sqn were raiding Japanese communications and bases from February 1943. The leading aircraft of each formation usually carried automatically-operated cine-cameras to record the bombing. Several Blenheims were fitted with F.24 cameras for photographic operations; BA611 (Flt Sgt D.K. Campbell), escorted by four Mohawks of 146 Sqn, flew to Kanpetlet and on 4 April Sgt B. Kitchen flew BA677 on the first 'offensive PR' sortie, combining cover of the enemy supply route to Kaladan with low-level strafing of 'targets of opportunity'.

Similar successful operations were made along the Myohaung-Taungup road by Flt Sgt Campbell in BA675 on the 9th and by Flg Off N. F. Fallon, flying BA592, on 24 April.

In April 1943 overall responsibility for operations in Arakan fell upon XV Corps, now commanded by Lt Gen W.J. Slim. A series of fierce actions was fought in the jungle-covered hills overlooking the Maungdaw-Buthidaung road where the Japanese at last broke through. Slim realised that the main British line of communication, the road frm Maungdaw to Cox's Bazar, was dangerously exposed and he withdrew his forces to positions in the open terrain of the Ramu area, where they could not be easily outflanked. Here he proposed to hold a line on the Burma-East Bengal frontier when the monsoon again brought operations to a halt. Although the Japanese 55th Division was constantly harassed by aircraft of 224 Group during the later stages of the campaign, the air effort (some 5,000 sorties) was unable to alter the course of the battle. At the time, the outcome seemed depressingly reminiscent of the disasters of early 1942 but it later became clear that the campaign drew off essential enemy strength intended for an offensive in Assam.

On 16 April 28 Sqn's pilots left Imphal, handing over

71: *Hurricane HV418 on arrival at Cox's Bazar for 28 Squadron at the height of the monsoon rain of July 1943. The ground crew struggle to keep the aircraft on the Somerfeld Track as they slither their way to the dispersal area*

72: *BN168 was one of the first camera-fitted Hurricane IIs of 28 Sqn, seen here in difficulties at Imphal in March 1943. Like many other Hurricanes, although this aircraft carried post-April 1942 fuselage and tail markings, those underwing were earlier 'Type A' on Sky finish*

73: *B-25C, N5-148, 'A', of No.3 PRU displays its only markings, the roundels above the wings and the identification letter. This aircraft was shot down near Rangoon on 13 February 1943*

74: *A later Hurricane IIB, Z4573 of No.2 Sqn IAF, had Medium Sea Grey undersurfaces and Type C1 underwing roundels. The 'fixed' wing fuel tanks of the 'long-range' Hurricanes of the type which had earlier caused Sqn Ldr Stone so much aggravation are clearly seen*

75 Left: *Liberator GR.IIIA FL936, 'V' of 160 Sqn in Temperate Sea Scheme with White undersides which flew PR sorties over Sumatra and Malaya from Sigiriya in 1943. Note the bulldog emblem on the nose*

76 Below: *A Lockheed F-4 of the first series, 41-2159 of the 9th PR Sqn, taxies in at Dum Dum on 4 March 1943. This aircraft is finished in the Haze camouflage scheme with natty patterned wheel hubs*

Tac/R duties to a detachment of No.2 Sqn IAF which had been operating on the North-West Frontier of India. The Indian squadron's Commanding Officer, Sqn Ldr H.U. Khan was, however, killed in a forced-landing on 21st. From Imphal the Indian pilots operated in support of Wingate's 'Long Range Penetration' expedition behind enemy lines. The 'Chindit' columns split into small groups for their return at the end of the operation and the Hurricanes of No.2 Sqn carried out 'contact recces' to locate the scattered troops and identify supply-dropping areas, besides strafing enemy positions along the Chindwin River, attacking river-craft on the Upper Irrawaddy and transport in the Kabaw Valley. By mid May the detachment had lost three pilots as a result of accidents at Imphal and only three of their Hurricanes IIBs remained operational. Four pilots of 28 Sqn's A Flt were flown in from Ranchi to relieve the Indian detachment, taking over No.2 Sqn's aircraft on 26 May.

All the Hurricanes of 28 Sqn were now modified to carry 'split-vertical' cameras although the oblique mounting was most often used. A Flight moved to Cox's Bazar on 1 June and the servicing section at last moved forward from Ranchi to Alipore. From Cox's Bazar, a tactical reconnaissance sorties continued with only 'weaver' escorts as Japanese fighter activity decreased but ground fire was consistently heavy and accurate over all targets in Arakan, and the Hurricanes were frequently hit. An additional hazard was the firing of parachute projectiles up to a height of 1,000 ft. Sorties were now flown primarily to provide target-maps and mosaics for 26 Division, taken from various height as the deteriorating weather permitted. Prints were usually delivered to Div HQ within two hours of landing.

The photographic reconnaissance organisation in India had "a lone furrow to plough"—they were not fighting a common enemy like the PR Units in the United Kingdom and the Mediterranean and so could not benefit from any exchange of Intelligence between the various theatres of war. They had to start almost from scratch in compiling details of Japanese military objectives, naval units, and aircraft, but by the spring of 1943 they had succeeded in issuing over a hundred reports and intelligence summaries on Japanese activities, and in May, 1943 issued their first edition of *Evidence in Camera (India Command)*, a booklet giving examples of outstanding photographic work, based on lines similar to those of the Home edition.

During May and June, B-25s of the US 1st Photo Charting Sqn based at Gura, Ethiopia, flew a strip from Aden, across India to Kunming in China, to prepare maps of the route for future deliveries of heavy bombers. The B-25s were modified for photographic use, retaining armament but having fuel-tanks within the bomb-bays.

After losing 2nd Lt Humphrey (believed taken prisoner) on 5 May, the US 9th PR Sqn received the first

three of a number of B-25Cs modified for photographic use and early in June two more B-25Cs and three Lockheed F-5As were delivered to the squadron. B-25C operations began with a sortie to Sagaing and Indaw by Lt G.J. Schmeisser on the 10th, and on 27 June Lt M.L. Bates flew the first F-5A sortie. The Lockheed F-4 had insufficient speed to be safe from interception, so it was supplemented and eventually replaced by the F-5A, the P-38G conversion. This had a speed of 430 mph and a range, when fitted with under-wing fuel tanks, of 3,000 miles. K.17/6-inch 'trimetrogon' cameras or K22 cameras with lenses of up to 40-inch focal length were installed according to need.

Early in 1943 it had been proposed that the responsibility for surveillance of the Andaman Islands be taken by 222 Gp at Ratmalana in Ceylon, this formation having, on some occasions, more aircraft available than were necessary for duties on convoy patrol and anti-submarine reconnaissance over the Bay of Bengal. At the beginning of the Pacific war, the Consolidated B-24 had been considered by the Americans as suitable for long-range photographic reconnaissance but the resulting conversion, the F-7, with mountings for eleven cameras, did not appear until July 1941. The RAF had used B-24 Liberators for maritime reconnaissance and, in April, camera tests were carried out in a Liberator GR.IIIA of 160 Sqn's detachment at Sigiriya. Already, HQ 222 Gp had acknowledged the arrival of these Liberators of 160 Sqn and anticipated the delivery of three more filled with ASV radar for anti-submarine duties. Their estimated range when modified to carry cameras was some 3,000 miles and the AOC suggested that they might be used for photo-reconnaissance as far east as Sumatra and Malaya, following up with bombing attacks on selected targets. When it was proposed that aircraft should attack a Japanese cruiser in Sabang Harbour, however, he chose not to take action because of the greater importance he attached to the Liberators being employed on photographic reconnaissance.

By May three Liberators had been fitted with camera mounting within their bomb-bays. Initially, it was proposed that the Liberators of 160 Sqn should undertake photographic reconnaissance of Sumatra and Malaya, following up with bombing attacks on strategically selected targets, but the plan suffered a series of unexpected set-backs; the only cameras available for installation were F.24s with 14-inch focal-length lenses—an attempt was made to obtain 20-inch lenses from 681 Sqn but none could be made available—and during trials, the Liberators' fuel-consumption was found to be greater than had been estimated. This reduced the safe range from 3,000 miles to 2,400 miles, too short a distance for cover of Malaya and Java but still sufficient for sorties to the Andaman and Nicobar Islands and Northern Sumatra.

It was intended that three aircraft be employed

simultaneously to complete all the sorties in a minimum of time. As the aircraft were fitted with neither nose nor belly guns, it was thought prudent to cover all the most distant targets before the Japanese could re-dispose their fighter aircraft to intercept the Liberators. The first sortie was flown on 24 May but only one aircraft, FK239 (Flt Sgt Hill) reached the target of Sabang on We Island, off the northern tip of Sumatra. One Liberator was unable to take off because of faulty brakes and another returned with engine trouble. After this unpromising start, two successful sorties were flown on the 27th, by Wg Cdr G.C.A. Butler, OC 160 Sqn, in FL936; and by Flt Sgt Cross in FL945, 'H', over the ports of Bireuen and Lhok-seumawe in northern Sumatra.

Operations were undertaken by 681 Sqn whenever the weather conditions permitted. With cloud cover extending over most of Burma the squadron often stood down for several days; when sorties were flown they were not enjoyable, for the air currents within a monsoon cloud-front are freakish and violent. Camera operator LAC A. Fox recalled, "Often we would bump, jerk and lurch through thick black cloud for hours, flying blind, never able to fly straight and steady and never seeing the ground. Arriving over the target in ten tenths cloud, we would simply have to turn round and bump and jerk all the way back. On one occasion I looked through the bomb-bay tunnel and saw both pilots with their booted feet raised high and braced against the upper instrument panel as they dragged back on their control columns, struggling against a downward pressure that forced us to within a few hundred feet of the sea." On 8 June 1943, Spitfire PR.IV AB318, returning from a sortie to Lashio and Loiwing at 25,000 ft, flew into an intense storm over the Ganges Delta. The aircraft was thrown into a spin and the pilot, Wt Off Brown, was knocked unconscious as the Spitfire disintegrated. He regained consciousness above a small island and managed to pull his rip-cord, having fallen 20,000ft. 681 Sqn lost another aircraft, AB319, 'J', when Sgt P.S. Marman, on a sortie to Meiktila, force-landed in Japanese-occupied territory near Alethangwin. Although injured, he escaped and eventually returned to the squadron. It was impossible to recover the Spitfire so Vengeance dive-bombers of 45 Sqn were briefed to destroy it on 9 July.

Meanwhile the 20th TR Sqn was under pressure in Northern Burma, its missions a mixture of photographic-reconnaissance and close-support dive-bombing; on 19 June Lt H.A. Lawler was missing in action and on 28th Lt D.W. Baker also failed to return.

Bad weather halted operations by 160 Sqn until 10 June, when FL945 (Plt Off Rees) flew to Meulaboh and FL239 (Flg Off Campbell) made the first recce of Nancowry Island in the Nicobars. On 13th FL936 (Plt Off Hill) reached Phuket Island at the southern end of the Kra Isthmus, while FL945 (Sqn Ldr Paisey) photographed Koetaradja and the Sumatran ports. In July 160 Sqn's

Liberators were repeatedly flying to Sabang, Lho'nga and Bireuen on the north-eastern coast of Sumatra but reconnaissance over the Andamans was hampered by monsoon clouds until well into the next month. The problems of co-ordinating operations by different formations, based 1,000 miles apart, were highlighted on 29 July when USAAF aircraft from India bombed Port Blair while Liberator FL911, 'K' (Plt Off Moody) was making a run over the target and the Dutch submarine O.23, diverted from a clandestine operation to Malaya, was on patrol just outside the harbour. It was made clear that no further PR sorties should be flown from Ceylon and no offensive action taken against the Andaman Islands without a full exchange of information between the various headquarters.

By the end of June the Imphal strip was breaking up under constant use in monsoon conditions so 28 Sqn's Hurricanes were withdrawn on 4 July to Agartala, 230 miles to the west, and operated from there until the Imphal strip was re-surfaced. 28 Sqn's sorties continued from Cox's Bazar and Agartala until late July when, for three weeks, the weather brought operations almost to a halt. Vertical photographic-reconnaissance was impossible; low cloud and heavy rain storms often prevented the Hurricanes gaining enough height so oblique photographs were usually taken instead.

Although the US 21st PR Sqn arrived in India during July, the unit was not yet operational. In 681 Sqn, despite a reduction in the number of sorties caused by the weather, the serviceability of aircraft was becoming critical and no new aircraft suitable for long-range sorties had been provided.

Mosquitos for India Command

The success throughout 1942 of the de Havilland Mosquito in the PR role over Europe was viewed with envy in India, where it was hoped that Mosquitos would eventually be provided for long-range reconnaissance. In the event, the entry of the Mosquitos into service in the East caused almost as much controversy as did the introduction of B-25Cs twelve months before.

In February 1943 the Air Ministry agreed with De Havilland that six Mosquitos would be delivered to India fir trials under the supervision of Messers Myers, de Havilland' representative and Waterhouse of Rolls-Royce. None of the aircraft were then intended for operational use as the manufacturer's were doubtful of the durability under extreme heat and humidity of the casein adhesive bonding the wooden airframes, yet Air HQ India signalled Air HQ Bengal, the operational headquarters, on 2 April, "*Six Mosquito aircraft, of which the first has arrived, are being delivered India near future. The first four will be Mk.II, the day intruder version, for general trials and familiarisation, the other two will be Mk.VI, the fighter-bomber version. These aircraft are having weathering protective treatment incorporated and special weathering trials will be carried out on these two aircraft. The aircraft are being allotted to 27 Squadron additional to establishment for long-range daylight intruder duties".* 27 Sqn, flying Beaufighters, was stationed at Agartala near Jessore in East Bengal where the temperature could reach 130°F and the humidity 90%. The "protective treatment" was the use of formaldehyde glue, intended to prevent deterioration of the airframes, thought possible when casein was employed in the Mosquito F.IIs.

Mosquito F Mk.II DZ695 was delivered by Flt Lts McCulloch and Young on 11 April; DZ696 a week later by Flg Off Fielding and Flt Sgt Steer, and DZ697 on 2 May by Flg Offs O.A. Dupee DFM and J.P. McDonnell.

Meanwhile, at Air HQ, the opportunity to employ the aircraft operationally could not be ignored and on 17 April it was announced, *"In order to release Beaufighters and facilitate formation of 177 Sqn, it has been decided that the Mosquitos will be included as Initial Equipment of 27 Squadron instead of being held additional to establishment."*

It was reported that Maj Hereward de Havilland, the firm's liaison with the RAF, while visiting Agartala, was appalled to discover that the aircraft were intended for intruder operations and demanded that the Mk.IIs be grounded as unsafe because of his fears about the casein adhesive being unable to withstand insect damage and the rigours of the climate. It was rumoured that he attempted to damage the wing of one aircraft to prevent it being flown but this was to no effect.

The first sorties against the Japanese were on 19 and 29 May, the second of them (by Dupee and McDonnell) a reconnaissance of the Meiktila airfields. They encountered a Nakajima *Hayabusa* over He-Ho but outpaced the fighter at low level. DZ695 crashed at Agartala on 30 May while making an emergency landing. Both the crew, Fielding and Steer, were injured, the latter fracturing his spine. The other Mk.IIs attacked Kangaung on 5 June; on return DZ696 developed a coolant leak and made a single-engined landing at Cox's Bazar. There a tyre burst and the Mosquito's undercarriage collapsed. Dupee and McCulloch escaped injury but the aircraft remained at the advanced landing ground for three weeks awaiting repair.

Although AHQ India had agreed to Wg Cdr Wise's requests for a Mosquito to be fitted with cameras and to be allotted to 681 Sqn, no action was taken until the end of July 1943.

On 16 May Wg Cdr Wise proposed that one of the Mosquito Mk.IIs from Agartala be delivered to 1 CMU Kanchrapara for conversion as a PR aircraft but he was told that it would be unsafe to undertake modifications without Air Ministry technical advice. The aircraft situation on the squadron was causing great concern; the two serviceable B-25Cs had been in constant operational use for over twelve months and there were no alternate aircraft in the Command with the range to reach the Andaman Islands or southern Burma. With the wet monsoon period about to begin, it appeared that no further cover of these areas could be obtained.

Apart from the limited Intelligence obtained from reports by Allied submarines, little was known of enemy air or naval activity in S.E. Asia beyond the Andaman Islands; there always remained the possibility of a Japanese raid on Ceylon, the eastern coast of India, or an attack on convoys in the Bay of Bengal. Air HQ India requested assistance from HQ Tenth Air Force which provided two B-25Cs on 14 June. These aircraft, 41-12659 and 41-12666, had been allocated to the UK Government in April 1942 but were retained in India by the USAAF. Designated Mitchell II, they were officially "diverted from Army Air Forces to Britain" on 25 June and 5 July and, unlike the NL-KNIL aircraft, they were given Air Ministry serials, MA957 and MA956 respectively from a block of numbers otherwise applied to civilian aircraft impressed into service by Air HQ India. Flg Offs Reeves and Rothwell of 681 Sqn were sent to Agra on the 25th to collect one of the new aircraft for it to be fully modified for photographic reconnaissance operations.

The Americans had already converted a number of B-25Cs and Ds to carry cameras. These aircraft retained their armament and were in operation early in 1942. A later variant was the conversion from the B-25D to the F-10, intended for use by US Photo Charting squadrons. It had a 'chin' fairing to contain 'trimetrogon' cameras and, like 681 Sqn's aircraft, was stripped of armament. The Fairchild T.5 camera, developed in the USA at the beginning of the war, introduced a valuable innovation in the form of a low-distortion 6-inch focal-length 'metrogon' lens that had a receiving angle of 90-degrees; this covered a wide band of ground for which multiple cameras had previously been required. By the end of 1943 these lenses were in use on American K.17 cameras. Still wider coverage was obtained by operating three of these cameras in unison in 'trimetrogon' (triple-fan) formation. Long-focus lenses in triple assemblies enabled aircraft to obtain large-scale photographs from greater height. Cameras were often angled to give greater than 180-degree (horizon-to-horizon) coverage. Of whatever lens type or size triple assemblies in US aircraft became generally known as 'trimetrogon' or 'trimet' installations.

In reply to the requests from 681 Sqn, on 7 August 1943 HQ India Command signalled, *"Mosquitos allotted to 27 Squadron are PRU type fitted with cameras and camouflaged for PR work"*, but there appears to have been some misunderstanding at Air HQ as to what was required. The Mosquitos transferred to 681 Sqn were, indeed, each fitted with a camera but not the four cameras of the 'PRU type', nor did they have installed the additional internal fuel tanks of PR Mosquitos, or, in the case of the Mk.IIs, the provision for fitting external wing tanks.

Despite de Havilland's concern for the aircraft having been exposed to high temperature and humidity, the feared deterioration of the adhesive had not occurred and the Mosquitos were obviously serviceable. Two more crews flew in Mosquito FB.VI Series 1 aircraft, HJ759 and HJ760, to Agartala on 28 July; they were posted to 681 Sqn on 8 August and the two remaining Mk.IIs, followed by a third Mk.IV, HJ730, which had been delivered to Karachi on 1 August. The two ex-10th Air Force Mitchells were soon put to use; MA957, 'K', beginning ops on the 17th and MA956, 'E', a week later, flown by Flg Off Sutcliffe to Pyu and Toungup.

On 20 August the last PR Hurricane, 'U' flown by Wt Off Carpenter, crashed at Chittagong when the undercarriage failed. The squadron's first Mosquito operations were then flown by Flg Off Dupee DFM and Flg Off McDonnell in DZ697, 'J', over Mandalay, Shwebo, Ye-U, Monywa and Wuntho on 23 August and, the following day, by Flt Lt Picknett and Sgt Townsend in HJ760, 'Y' to Akyab Island. With these new aircraft, the operational potential of 681 Sqn was considerably extended, although the squadron lost Spitfire PR.IV AB316, 'D', (Flg Off Gordon White) on a sortie to Mandalay; it was later reported that he had been captured by the Japanese, tortured and mutilated, then burned to death.

Advised of the need for close-support, on 1 July Maj Fornof sent a detachment of three P-40Ns of the 20th TR Sqn and a photo-lab section to Myitkyina airfield which was subjected to mortar fire and raids by Japanese fighters and bombers. The P-40s were in close touch with forward ground units, the results of their visual reconnaissance missions being reported within 15 minutes.

On 10 August Brig-Gen T.F. Wessels, commander of NCAC's Myitkyina Task Force, commended the accuracy of the air operations; "Without this efficient support, the capture of Myitkina would have been considerably delayed, and our casualty lists would have been much larger. The effectiveness of the air attacks would not be possible without efficient co-ordination of the air staff in deciding priorities of targets, preparing excellent photographs, taken by the 20th Tactical Reconnaissance Squadron, and advising and co-operating at all times with the staff of this Headquarters. I doubt if any more perfect co-ordination of ground and air attack can be found in this war. S/T.F. Wessels, Brigadier General USA, Commanding."

Following the allocation of the two replacement B-25Cs to the RAF, in a Daily Report dated 7 August 1943 the USAAF 'condemned' (ie 'struck off charge') the five aircraft originally taken over by No.3 PRU (India), although two remained still in service with 681 Sqn.

The pressure on the RAF and IAF squadrons during the later stages of the Arakan campaign appears to have resulted in adverse criticism of the fighter-reconnaissance detachments' independent operations. Subsequently, Air

HQ India issued Operational Directive No.9 (12 July 1943) 'Fighter-Reconnaissance Squadrons' defining the role and employment of the PR squadrons. It stated: "*There appears to be an impression that these are fighter squadrons used for reconnaissance. In fact, they are Tactical Recce squadrons forming part of a Tactical Air Force*" and added that, although "*it was decided that the squadrons should be equipped with fighter types so that they could carry out their tasks where there was enemy air opposition, ...this did not imply any change in the role of the squadrons. It is no part of the duty of Tac/R pilots to become involved in air fighting. They have received special training in military subjects and in co-operation with ground forces and are not, therefore, interchangeable with fighter pilots.*"

Of reconnaissance in Arakan, Command HQ noted, "*Very little information is forthcoming from pilots engaged in ground-strafing operations... In this type of country, the only height at which anything can be seen is in the region of 50ft. The country normally allows the pilot to make a covered approach to his recce area, therefore hoping to achieve some element of surprise. It has also been found that more can be got from a pilot if he has a 'weaver', even at 50ft.*"

77 Left: *The first Mosquito F Mk.IIs delivered to India for trials were finished in 'nightfighter' camouflage. DZ695 was used on operations but crashed at Agartala on 30 May after an emergency landing*

78 Right: *Mosquito FB.VI Series I aircraft, HJ770, bound for 27 Sqn late in 1943, carried the word 'SNAKE' above the serial indicaing that it was not to be retained by any other formation en route to India*

79 Below: *Mosquito DZ695 while with 27 Sqn after its crash at Agartala on 30 May 1943. Both crew members were injured*

80: *113 Squadron's Blenheim Mk.VD, BA952, taxies out for take-off at Feni satellite 'Manston' in April 1943*

81 Left: *Blenheim VDs of 113 Sqn from Feni undertook escorted PR sorties in April 1943. The crews must have been exceptionally courageous men*

82 Below: *HJ759, one of the Mosquito FR.VI Series I aircraft delivered to 27 Sqn at Agartala on 28 July 1943 and transferred a week later to 681 Sqn. As seen here it is finished in PRU Blue*

1943-1944 NEW COMMANDS
The formation of SEAC

At the Washington Conference ('Trident') in May 1943, the US and British Governments decided that the American and British forces in India and Burma and the British Eastern Fleet, previously under separate commands, should be combined under a single headquarters. At the subsequent Quebec Conference ('Quadrant') in August Vice-Admiral Lord Louis Mountbatten was appointed Supreme Allied Commander, South-East Asia (SACSEA) to control all Allied military, air and naval forces throughout an area covering Burma, Malaya, Sumatra, Ceylon (Sri Lanka), Siam (Thailand) and some in Assam and French Indo-China (now Vietnam and Cambodia).

When formed, the Command was intended to become an increasingly offensive theatre but the Allied Governments soon decided that the defeat of Germany must remain the primary objective. Equipment intended for SEAC was diverted to the Mediterranean and the landing ships which SEAC intended to use for one or other of a number of proposed combined operations were used in the landings at Anzio and later in Normandy. SEAC was left to make do with whatever it could gather together for less ambitious operations. Immediate operations were

83 Above: The Supreme Allied Commander's 'personal' Dakota, 'Mercury' with his chosen badge, the Phoenix, painted on the nose. Barely visible on the access door just behind the cockpit glazing is a list of names of the personnel responsible for flying and maintaining the aircraft

to be confined to the capture of Mogaung and Myitkyina with their airfields and an area southwards down the Irrawaddy to protect them against recapture.

The AOC-in-C India described the development of the photographic reconnaissance organisation as a "notable feature of the period", and stated that No. 681 Squadron "operated magnificently during the whole of the 1943 Monsoon period." The 1943 PR Expansion Programme for India was for two squadrons of twenty aircraft, including a PR Mosquito Squadron which it was intended would be equipped in 1944. Nevertheless, in August 1943 authority was given to increase the establishment of No.681 Squadron to twenty Spitfires and to form a new squadron—No.684—to re-equip wholly with PR Mosquitos by April 1944.

Three Photographic Interpretation Sections were formed to under-take interpretation for Bengal; 160 Sqn in Ceylon and No.225 Group, Bangalore, by detaching interpreters from the main Interpretation Unit at Delhi, while tactical reconnaissance carried out for the Army, mainly by Hurricanes, was handled and interpreted by Army Photographic Interpretation Sections.

A review of PR requirements was made in August by Air Ministry so that they might arrange the distribution of the latest marks of Mosquitos and Spitfires in accordance with future strategy, and it was agreed that

India should have high priority both for Mosquito IXs and Spitfire XIs, the flow of the latest mark of Spitfire being planned to commence in September, 1943.

Before the end of August, however, it became important for India to obtain early photographic cover of Sumatra and Malaya to assist in making plans for the defeat of Japan. These areas were outside the range of any PR Spitfires based on India or Ceylon. Five of the Liberators in Ceylon being used for PR work were modified to give them an extended range, but they were not suitable for reconnaissance work in the face of enemy air opposition. It was even suggested at this early stage that an aircraft-carrier should be transferred from the Mediterranean to act as a mobile base for photographic reconnaissance aircraft, but the Admiralty would not even consider such a suggestion until the invasion of Italy was well launched.

During September a detachment of 9th PR Sqn was stationed at Dinjan, 30 miles from Ledo and far up the Brahmaputra Valley in northern Assam, with B-25Cs, F-4s and F-5s. The squadron was allocated long-range sorties over central and southern Burma, losing two pilots over the Rangoon area; Capt Webster on 10 September and Lt F.H. Tilcock three days later, both flying F-5s. On 1 September A Flight of 28 Sqn returned to Imphal but the strip was still too rough for the aircraft's tyres and there were no further operational flights until the 20th. By this time most of the roads and tracks in the battle-area were impassable but an improvement in the monsoon weather during September brought a renewal of patrol activity on the Central Front. Tactical recces often revealed potential targets for strikes by the Vengeance dive-bombers of the light-bomber squadrons. The 1943 monsoon period passed without major action, but the Japanese, faced with problems of reinforcement and supply to their Burma Area Army, set about linking the railway systems of Siam and Burma.

Continuous reconnaissance over their most westerly outposts was of sufficient concern to the Japanese to cause them again to station a dozen or so A6M Zero fighters of the 331st *Kokutai* at Port Blair and Sabang to intercept the aircraft of 160 and 681 Sqns. Bad weather over the Indian Ocean prevented successful operations by 160 Sqn until 21 September when Flt Sgt Riley flew FL790, 'P', to Mancowry. The following day, however, FL939, 'M' failed to return from a sortie to the Nicobar Islands; the Japanese-controlled Saigon Radio announced that a B-24 had been shot down by Navy Zero fighters, one of which was destroyed during the engagement.

Wg Cdr Wise pointed out that the B-25Cs were still the only aircraft able to carry out routine surveillance of the Andaman Islands but that such operations did not justify the risk of losing the aircraft and their experienced crews. Mosquitos could carry out much the same tasks as the B-25Cs but with a crew of two, pilot and navigator/

camera-operator. The B-25C crews were made up of first and second pilots, navigator and camera-operator. For much of the time, during sorties of seven or eight hours' duration, the operator was isolated from the rest of the crew by the 2,000 gallon fuel-tank in the bomb-bay. At operational height, 26,000 to 30,000 ft, the air was bitterly cold and the aircraft, with camera openings in the fuselage floors, was extremely draughty.

The small navigational astrodome above the rear of the cabin and, later, an astrodome in the turret position and the side windows in the rear fuselage compartment provided the only rear view for the B-25C crews.

The camera operator's other function, apart from fitting his electrically operated battery of cameras, changing film-magazines and rectifying faults, was to keep a look-out from the astrodome while over enemy territory.

On 1 October 1943 Mitchell MA957, 'K' was intercepted over Port Blair by a Kawasaki Ki.45 *Toryu* fighter, one of a small number on detachment from 21st Air Regt, recently equipped with the new aircraft and based at Mergui. The enemy was spotted by the B-25's camera-operator, LAC A. Fox, who reported, "I had been many times to Port Blair, and its grim wheel-shaped penitentiary of Imperial days had become a familiar sight. I found myself staring through the astrodome at a black dot in the distant sky that grew rapidly in size to become an enemy fighter. Nobody else had yet seen it, so there was some brisk activity in the front cockpit as I delivered this news over the intercom. As he closed in on our tail to within a hundred yards and opened fire, I was the only member of the crew to have him in vision and so had to deliver a running commentary. He was a poor shot but, even so, Flg Off Rothwell gave him no second chance. Since the B-25 had the gliding angle of a brick, the usual technique in such encounters was to go into a steep and prolonged dive—one of the amiable qualities of the B-25 being that, even when pulling out of the steepest plunge, one could always rely on the wings staying on. As it happened, cloud helped us to get out of sight. I, who was not seated, was forced almost to the floor.

But there, just below us, were the palm trees and the tropical sea breaking on a golden shore and the fighter had lost us. It was not long, however, before I discovered the one small fly in this otherwise soothing ointment, dressed for the bitter cold of 26,000ft, I was now in the tropical temperature of 500ft. True, clothing that had been put on could be taken off; this involved first removing my parachute harness. In the circumstances this seemed injudicious. I bathed in my own sweat until we regained height and started all over again. We got the pictures and a view of our pursuer as he weaved in and out of the clouds still searching for us."

The same day 160 Sqn's FL936 (Plt Off C. Wall), returning from a successful flight to Sabang, was intercepted 100 miles out from the target by a Zeke fighter and a running fight followed; the enemy fighter broke off the engage-ment after 25 minutes and the Liberator returned to Sigiriya with tail-plane and fuselage damaged by cannon and machine-gun fire, with the tanks holed and a member of the crew slightly injured.

On 11 October Mosquito FB.VI HJ759, 'W', (Flg Off McCulloch and Plt Off Burridge) was forced to abandon a sortie over Rangoon when attacked by three Oscar fighters. Typical of operations was a sortie by Flg Off Fielding and Sgt Wells in the same aircraft on the 16th; "Set Course for Sittang. Covered Minhla aerodromes N and S. Both Bridges across Sittang fully covered. Ran down railway on east bank of Sittang River and covered Mokpalin station. Visual rec. of river, no shipping to report. Proceeded to Rangoon. Town covered by heavy cu. Managed to get a run on Ahlone Dock area. Covered Mingaladon, Zayatkwin, John Haig and Pabst. The Rangoon-Prome railway covered between Oku and Tharawaddy. Weather 7/10 cloud."

The Japanese had enlarged radar network along the western perimeter of their conquests, from the Andaman Islands to Western Sumatra. HQ 222 Group signalled on 12 October, "*Following action was taken when second Liberator was reported missing on 22.9.43. It was decided to vary the time of sorties, improve look out while photographs are being taken, and order aircraft on PR sorties to report by W/T when AA fire is encountered as well as enemy aircraft.*"

For reinforcement and supply to Burma Area Army, the enemy now had available, in addition to the ports of Nergui, Tavoy, Moulmein and Rangoon, a railway linking Bangkok with Moulmein, built almost entirely by Allied prisoners of war and completed by mid-October 1943. Preparations for new offensives were now begun by the Japanese; supplies could be transported from Siam directly to Moulmein, thence across the Salween by ferry to Martaban, by rail to Mokpalin and ferried again across the Sittang River and on by train to Rangoon and all parts of Burma. The bridge across the river at Sittang, near Mokpalin, blown-up during the British retreat, was slowly rebuilt by the Japanese; this work and traffic between the riverside ferry quays were kept under surveillance by Photographic Reconnaissance Force but the rail link from Siam was beyond the range of the early Mosquitos.

Although Air HQ India had informed 681 Sqn, "*Mosquitos allotted 27 Sqn are PRU type fitted with cameras...*" the F.II and FB.VIs transferred to 681 Sqn, each fitted with only one camera and with no provision for additional fuel tanks, were unable to reach targets further south than the Gulf of Martaban. Fortunately, the first Mosquito PR.IXs, flown out to India in September, were awaiting delivery at Allahabad. On 9 August, Air Ministry had promised a flight of PR Mosquitos for additional air-survey work, to be used by Air HQ India

sparately from the PR squadrons, but a brisk exchange of signals between HQ and the OC 681 Sqn resulted in their allocation for immediate use on reconnaissance. On 29 September Dum Dum, in effect the 'twin-engined' Flight of 681 Sqn was to be expanded by the provision of more Mosquitos, while 681 Sqn would continue flying the single-engined aircraft. Given the alternative option of joining 684 Sqn as a Flight Commander, Sqn Ldr Procter chose to take command of the reduced 681 Sqn flying Spitfires and a small number of Hurricanes. Nothing changed until 16 October when the division began, 684 Sqn, under command of Sqn Ldr B.S. Jones, taking over the four B-25Cs and the Mosquitos and the crews and ground-staff experienced on the aircraft. The first Mosquitos specifically converted for photographic reconnaissance were B. Mk.IVs, modified by the install-ation of camera-mountings instead of bomb-carriers within the bomb-bay, but none of these aircraft were delivered to India. When the high-altitude bomber Mk.IX was produced, another PR variant was developed during the early months of 1943.

The Mosquito PR.IX had 1,650hp Merlin 72/73 engines with two-speed, two-stage superchargers, enabling the aircraft to operate up to 30,000ft. Three additional fuel-tanks in the bomb-bay and two 100 gallon under-wing drop tanks allowed the operational radius, under temperate conditions, to be extended to about 800 miles.

Four cameras could be mounted within the bomb-bay. Of the ninety Mosquito PR.IXs built, nine were supplied for use by 684 Sqn between late 1943 and mid-1944. The first of these to be delivered was LR440 on 18 October but a second, LR441, crashed at Ranchi before joining the squadron and the crew were killed. Another Mk.IX, LR463, was delivered on the 23rd.

From 1 to 15 October 28 Sqn's A Flight was engaged on photo-reconnaissance over the Japanese forward positions along the Central Front, from the Kale Valley westwards, and carried out a full survey of the enemy's lines of supply forward of the Shwebo-Myitkyina railway line. On 13 October B Flight's HV489 was badly damaged by ground fire during a sortie from Cox's Bazar but re-turned safely.

The first operational sortie in a Mosquito PR.IX was by Flt Lt McCulloch and Sgt Vigers, in PR440, 'V', to Rangoon and Magwe on 21 October. Three days later, in the same aircraft, Flt Lt McCulloch with Flt Lt Reeves flew to the Andamans. Enemy fighters were seen on Port Blair airfield and three aircraft, identified by the crew as Oscars, climbed in an attempt to intercept but were unable to catch the Mosquito. The same day, Flt Sgt Johnston and Sgt Willis in DZ696 flew to Rangoon and reported, "Set course from Chittagong to Zayatkwin. Two runs 'drome. Set course for Mingaladon, one run over 'drome. Did two runs over dock area. Weather 5-6/10ths cloud. A/A encountered at 27,500 ft. Two Zeros attempted interception." Again the Mosquito evaded the enemy fighters but other PR aircraft were less able; two days later, 160 Sqn lost another Liberator, FL926, 'J', (Flg Off W.A. Wallace). The aircraft signalled to indicate that the target, Car Nicobar, had been reached but nothing further was heard of the Liberator. The Japanese Navy had already established a radar station on Mount Augusta near Port Blair and, it was believed, others on Car Nicobar and Sabang. The improvement in the enemy air defences led HQ 222 Group to question the use of the lightly-armed and relatively slow Liberators of 160 Sqn for further photographic use and Wg Cdr C. Butler, OC 160 Sqn, proposed to send three Liberators in formation, for mutual defence, on future sorties whenever possible.

Meanwhile, it had been intended that No. 3 Sqn IAF should share in tactical reconnaissance duties and training had begun to that end; late in October, however, the squadron was re-equipped with Hurricane IICs and was designated a fighter-bomber unit on 1 November. The same day, 28 Sqn's HQ moved to Imphal to join A Flight but B Flight, detached to Cox's Bazar, remained there for a further five weeks. 28 Sqn's duties were taken over by No.6 Sqn IAF whose fighter-reconnaissance Hurricane Mk.IIBs, each fitted with a two-camera mounting, began operations with a tactical recce on the last day of the month, when F/Os G.C. Babra and Jagjit Singh, in BG852 and BE291, surprised a party of some 150 Japanese troops near Indin. Later, six Hurricanes of the squadron put in an attack on the enemy force.

During June it had been decided that 20 more 'long-range' Hurricane Mk.IIs should be modified for fighter-reconnaissance (army co-operation) duties. These aircraft were fitted with additional 50gal fuel tanks within the wings and mountings for three cameras, the first three being ready for delivery to the squadrons in November.

Spitfire sorties continued despite appalling weather conditions over the mountains of northern Burma, resulting in a gradual reduction of serviceable aircraft. On the 28th 681 Sqn lost Flt Sgt Hain on a sortie to the Indaw area in Spitfire PR.IV AA793, 'F'. Meanwhile, at the beginning of October, two Spitfire PR.XIs, EN679 and MB889, were delivered to Dum Dum and Wg Cdr Wise made the first test flight in the new type on the 7th. The PR Mk.XI was a development of the Spitfire F.IX, combining the experience gained from earlier photo-recce Spitfires with the advantages of the Merlin 70 Series engine fitted with a four-blade Rotol airscrew. The late production aircraft issued to 681 Sqn had the same rear fuselage as the later F.Mk.VIII, with retractable tail-wheel and pointed rudder. Like the PR.IV, the PR.XI had leading edge tanks of 133 gal capacity instead of armament, besides provision for an external jettisonable tank. The introduction of the Vokes 1945 Aero-Vee air filter on the Mk.VIII and later Spitfires allowed the aircraft to be 'tropicalised' without the need for the large filter housing of earlier Marks. The Mk.XI, however, had

a deeper nose cowling to enclose a larger-capacity oil tank. A 'universal installation' provided for the mounting of either two F.52 or F.8 vertical cameras or one oblique F.24 and two vertical F.24 cameras in the rear fuselage.

At the beginning of October US 9th PR Sqn began a move to Barrackpore but, on the 5th, 1/Lt Bates was killed when his aircraft crashed on take-off. Another pilot parachuted to safety when an engine failed over the jungle but he returned on foot three days later.

When the 1943 monsoon began, the Japanese had intended to stand on the defensive along the Burma Front, from the Naf River to the Chindwin and on to the Upper Irrawaddy. The continuing build-up of Allied forces in Assam and the realisation, after the incursion of the Chindits from February to May 1943, that the jungle and mountains of northern Burma were no barrier against enemy operations, forced a change of plan. The Japanese therefore decided to forestall a possible Allied offensive on the Central Front by occupying the main British bases on the Imphal Plain in Manipur and by holding the passes giving access to it from the north and west.

In October 1943 the Combined Chiefs of Staff considered alternative strategies for defeating Japan. The US Chiefs of Staff proposed an 'island hopping' offensive in the Pacific, to provide bases for air-attacks against the Japanese islands—the British advocated an 'Indian Ocean Strategy' with a number of options directed against Japan's 'Indian Ocean Front'; capture of the Andaman Islands (Operation 'Buccaneer', abandoned at the end of the year), a sea-borne invasion of southern Burma aimed at the recapture of Rangoon (Operation 'Dracula') or the preferred alternative, an assault on north Sumatra (Operation 'Culverin') at the end of 1944. 'Culverin' was aimed at the eventual recapture of Singapore and disruption of the enemy's raw materials supplies from the East Indies. A major problem in detail planning for all these operations was the lack of accurate maps and of knowledge of Japanese dispositions.

In mid-1943 the Fleet Air Arm allocated and trained its squadrons for Army co-operation duties only when they were not required for service aboard aircraft carriers. No consideration had yet been given to any such future requirements in the Far East so it was decided to include training in ground support for all Royal Navy fighter pilots under Maj R.C. Hay RM who, after achieving great success in North Africa with photographic and tactical reconnaissance when commanding 809 Sqn, had recently qualified on an RAF Wing Leader's Course. In November he was posted to Ceylon to organise training facilities for Naval squadrons in the Far East.

On 26 October FL926, 'T' of 160 Sqn (Flg Off W.A. Wallace) failed to return from a PR sortie to Car Nicobar. The aircraft was due over target at 1100 and at 1109 transmitted its call-sign, a 30-second 'dash'. It was then attacked by a fighter from a detachment based at Car Nicobar landing ground, adjacent to the radar station on the island, which had a range of 100 miles and had already observed the Liberator's approach. The AOC 222 Gp wired AHQ India, "*Seriously worried about continuing use of Liberator for the PR work within the enemy's RDF* cover I have asked for a Mosquito to cover the NIcobars. The last Liberator shot down by Japanese after a chase of 40 miles. Good chance of interception in prevailing good weather conditions.*" He added the seemingly cynical but pragmatic comment, "*A PR sortie is not like a bombing sortie. The aircraft must be able to return to base.*" 160 Sqn now had only two cameras left and it was clearly necessary to restrict PR flights to the period when cloud cover could be used to conceal the aircraft.

Although reconnaissance by day was virtually abandoned except to a few negligibly defended areas where large areas were surveyed and shipping in the ports reported. The especial value to the strategic minelaying planners for their Liberator operations was soon realised.

No.222 Gp's Quarterly Review recorded, "*The most charts of enemy-controlled waters in the Eastern Bay of Bengal and Malacca Straits area available were at least three years old. The majority were more venerable and the areas close inshore inaccurate. The approaches to anchorages and harbours (which were often affected by silt, forming bars, through which deep water channels had to be dredged) were unknown until photographed... Study of photographs of ports enabled estimates of shipping to be made and, coupled with the results of seagoing convoy photographs, a fairly full picture of the enemy's sea supply system emerged... The various moves of the Japanese from port to port and changes in the type of vessels used showed up clearly when this information was most needed, laying open the way to strikes by surface ships or carrier-borne aircraft or a shift of emphasis in minelaying.*"

An improvement in the weather as the south-west monsoon abated brought an increase in air activity on both sides.

84: This photograph, taken during the enemy aircraft counts of late 1943, shows a formation of Mitsubishi Ki-21 'Sally' bombers waiting to take off from Toungoo

85: A Mosquito PR.IX of 684 Sqn taxies out for take-off from Dum Dum late in 1943. Three other Mosquitos can be seen in the background

"Keep China in the War"

Reorganisation and forward planning

As the 1943 monsoon clouds broke up, the Japanese began regular reconnaissance sorties over the American airfields in Assam and the British supply bases in Bengal with the Mitsubishi Ki.46s of 81st *Sentai* based at Hlegu and 8th *Sentai* from Toungoo. Unlike Allied photo-reconnaissance, which was intended primarily to provide a constant up-dating of the Japanese military situation the enemy used his Ki-46 Dinahs largely for tactical intelligence, the appearance of a *Shin-Shitei* invariably signalling enemy intentions to launch ground or air attacks. These aircraft had a performance still superior to that of the Hurricanes sent out to intercept them and were able to reconnoitre the British positions with impunity. They kept constant watch on the movement and con-centration of shipping along the coast of Bengal and at Calcutta. In September, however, 607 and 615 Sqns were re-equipped with the Spitfire Mk.VC at Alipore and, moving forward to Arakan, were able to intercept and destroy four Dinahs by the end of November. Operations by the PR squadrons continued into November but F/Os R. A. Fielding and R. A. Turton were lost on 2 November, shot down in Mosquito FB.II DZ697, 'J', during a sortie to the Rangoon area. The reconnaissance task was repeated two days later, when Flt Lt McCulloch and Sgt Vigers in HJ759, 'W', covered the Japanese supply-route from Moulmein to the Sittang bridge and on, westwards, to Bassein.

On 4 October a Dinah was plotted approaching Cal-cutta at 30,000ft. For the first time a Hurricane of l36 Sqn was able to intercept and damage the reconnaissance aircraft and on the 19th a P-40K of the 26th Fighter Sqn from Dinjan achieved the first confirmed victory over a Ki- 46. Another Dinah appeared over Cox's Bazar on 24 October, heralding an attack on 28 Sqn's base the following day.

The Japanese achieved a measure of air-superiority over the forward areas during November, refuelling and re-arming at advanced landing grounds and mounting a series of raids on the RAF's principal airfields at Chitta-gong, Agartala, Feni, Tiddim, Khumbirgram and Palel. With the end of the monsoon, the Japanese Army Air Force began a series of attacks on airfields: on 9 November Imphal Main airfield was raided by seven-teen Kawasaki Ki.48 'Lily' bombers escorted by Oscars. Three of 28 Sqn's Hurricanes were burnt out after two direct hits on a dispersal pen but two other aircraft were 'scrambled' with 155 Sqn's Mohawks and 28 Sqn claimed an Oscar destroyed by Flg Off Dunford Wood.

Although often scrambled, the Hurricane fighters were unable to intercept the Ki- 46s but the move of 615 Sqn, re-equipped with the Spitfire VC, to Chittagong in November changed the situation. On the 8th, Flt Lt P. Louis and Flg Off S.L. Wiggery destroyed a Dinah over

Chiringa; two days later Flt Sgt A.R. Hyde sent another into the sea in flames off Chittagong and another was destroyed near Feni on 16 November.

681 Sqn continued operations over north and central Burma and the Arakan coast. Flg Off Parry, flying Spitfire PR.VI BR66l, 'G', was lucky to escape disaster on 18 November when he flew into a flock of sea-birds while making a low-level run along the coast of Akyab Island. His airscrew hit the sea but he pulled the aircraft away, out to sea, and managed to climb to 800ft by the time he had flown the hundred miles north to Cox's Bazar.

By this time it was apparent that full coverage of Burma and the Andaman Islands could be achieved only if British and American PR resources were co-ordinated and additional Mosquito PR.IXs delivered from the UK. 684 Sqn still had only one Flight of six Mosquitos of various marks and one Flight of four B-25Cs but Air Ministry agreed to supply another twenty PR. Mk.IXs over the three months to March 1944. At Mountbatten's HQ, on 16 November, it was made clear that, even with additional aircraft, there was no hope of obtaining cover of the Kra Isthmus, Malaya or Sumatra. It was suggested that the Americans might provide technically suitable aircraft with a range of 1,500 miles (no type was specifically mentioned) but there were no aircraft available other than Liberators, of which improvised use had already been made; these were thought unsuitable because of their vulnerability to fighter attack and difficulty of maintenance. Alternatively, it was suggested, the Andamans might be re-captured to serve as a base for Mosquito operations. Air Ministry had no alternative proposals and it was concluded that Intelligence requirements for photographic reconnaissance over Japanese rear areas could not be met until a forward base could be occupied.

The policy of the Anglo-American Combined Chief of Staff was to 'keep China in the war': of Japan's 51 army divisions, 27 were in China, their maintenance being a constant drain on dwindling Japanese resources. Any 'understanding' reached between the Japanese and Chinese Government would have allowed the release of up to a million enemy troops and would have made a complete change to Japanese resistance in the Pacific. By mid-1943, it had become clear to the Japanese High Com-mand that eventual defeat could be avoided only by a victory that would cut the line of supply from India to China, causing that country's surrender and a revolt in India against the British. A great offensive, planned by Tarauchi, the Japanese Supreme Commander, and Kawabe, C-in-C Burma, was code-named '*U-Gô*' with a subsidiary offensive, '*Ha-Gô*'.

No. 6 Sqn IAF moved to Cox's Bazar late in November to undertake tactical reconnaissance. The squadron's paired Hurricanes became a familiar sight to the forward troops and were variously called 'the Maungdaw Twins' by 5 Inf Div, 'the Arakan Twins' by HQ, XV Corps and 'the Kaladan Twins' by the West Africans. The squadron lost Hurricane HV436, flown by Plt Off Daniel, over Indin on 5 December. Another pilot, Flt Lt Reporter, was lost when he force-landed and his aircraft turned over; when help arrived the Hurricane had sunk into deep mud. By the end of the month No 6 Sqn had completed 350 hours of operational flying in twenty-five days.

Two DFCs were awarded to 684 Sqn—to Flg Off Dupee DFM and to Flg Off McDonnell—and a DFM to LAC Fox for his work as a camera operator on numerous B-25C sorties over an eighteen-month period but the year ended on a tragic note when on 10 December the last of the Mosquito Mk.IIs DZ696, 'S', (Sgts G.M. Bools and E. A. Wilkins) was shot down during a sortie to Rangoon. Additionally, on the 25th, HJ760, 'Y', one of the Mk.VIs out on a training flight, seemingly struck a bird and crashed some twenty miles south of Feni killing the crew, Flg Off A. Orr and Sgt F. Johnston. The crash was provisionally attributed to the aircraft hitting a large bird but, in retrospect, it seems likely that this was the first instance of the structural failures that were to be evident the following year.

Early on 16 December, as a prelude to a midday attack by some fifty enemy aircraft, a Dinah overflew Chittagong. Flt Sgt R.O. Patterson of 615 Sqn, now equipped with Spitfire VIIIs, intercepted at 23,000ft and set it on fire.

The possibility was considered of fitting more aircraft of 160 Sqn with cameras and of similarly equipping a Flight of Liberators from 354 Sqn as neither squadron was fully engaged in general reconnaissance. Lack of equipment was a problem; K17 cameras from USAAF 'trimetrogen' assemblies were sought, but arrangements had to be made to obtain them from the UK, to be flown to India in reinforcing Mosquito PR.IXs or PR.XVIs. 160 Sqn had only two sets of cameras remaining—but attempted sorties to Meulaboh on the Sumatran coast and to Simaloer Island—100 miles to the south but the cloud-cover in November was too extensive. On 18 December FL936, 'V' (Plt Off G.L. Boyle), FL940, 'P', (Plt Off R.A. Servos) and FL945, 'H', (Plt Off L.E. Hill) obtained successful cover of both targets before the aircraft were returned to anti-submarine patrols.

The formation by the Allies of South East Asia Command in November 1943 resulted in an extensive re-organisation of the command structure. British and Indian ground forces were brought into a new formation. 14th Army under Maj-Gen Slim, comprising IV and XXXIII Corps on the Central Front, while XV Corps in Arakan became a separate command under Lt-Gen A.F.P. Christison. The Supreme Commander, Admiral The Lord Louis Mountbatten, chose as a badge for his Headquarters the phoenix, the mythical bird rising from its own ashes, to signify renewed life.

Until this time the American air effort had been under the command of Lt Gen 'Vinegar Joe' Stilwell but the Supreme Commander enforced integration of British and American air forces under Air Chief Marshal Sir R.E.C. Peirse, as Allied Air Commander-in-Chief, S.E.Asia. US Lt Gen C.E. Stratemeyer was given control of a new Eastern Air Command based at Barrackpore, Calcutta, with three subordinate formations: Strategic Air Force, Troop Carrier Command and Third Tactical Air Force. This last, commanded by Air Marshal Sir John Baldwin, disposed tactical units to provide support to the three areas of land operations—a USAAF Northern Air Sector Force (Brig Gen E.F. Egan) to support the Chinese and American forces of Stilwell's Northern Combat Area Command, 221 Grp RAF (AVM S.F. Vincent) at Imphal for 4 Corps on the Central Burma front, 224 Grp RAF (AVM the Earl of Bandon) at Chittagong to support 15 Corps on the Arakan front, and Photographic Reconnaissance Force (Grp Cpt S.C.Wise).

HQ Fourteenth Army was established at Comilla in the Eastern States, 150 miles east of Calcutta, and at a series of conferences plans were proposed for:

(1) occupation of the Mayu Peninsula in Arakan
(2) an advance across the Chindwin to draw Japanese forces away from
(3) a drive southwards by the Chinese to take Myitkyina and
(4) a diversionary long-range penetration behind the Japanese front

While these plans were finalised, Flt Lt Guy of 684 Sqn was detailed to transport Maj Gen Slim, Air Marshal Baldwin and members of their Staffs between Comilla, Dum Dum and HQ India Command in the B-25Cs, the fastest RAF aircraft available in India. These transport flights, carrying personnel, continued as HQ PR Force also was set up at Comilla.

It was first proposed that the staff of 171 (Tac/R) Wing from Southern India should take over control of 681 and 684 Sqns until they were incorporated into Strategic Air Force. 684 Sqn moved to Comilla in East Bengal on 10 December and 681 Sqn to nearby Chandina, with a combined operations room under Wg Cdr Wise at Comilla, where 171 Wing was established on 9 December. No truly long-range reconnaissance had yet been carried out, aircrews were still gaining flying experience on the Mosquito and its operational potential under tropical conditions was not yet appreciated. The effective range of PR cover was under 700 miles, apart from regular twice-weekly sorties by the B-25Cs to the Andaman Islands as a precautionary check on Japanese shipping and reconnaissance flying-boats. The US 9th PR Sqn flying B25Cs and Lockheed F-4s and F-5As was stationed at Barrackpore under control of 10th USAAF. On 5 December, 684 Sqn's Mosquito PR.IX LR463, 'A' (Flg Off O.A. Dupee DFM and Flg Off P.J. McDonnell) obtained cover of part of the Burma-Siam railway and, on the 15th, LR445, 'F', reached Bangkok for the first time. The crew, Sqn Ldr B.C. Jones and Flg Off R. Dawson, were each awarded the DFC for the operation which revealed Japanese reserve positions and their use of 'lay-back' airfields. In the same month this crew flew to Mount Everest in a Mk.IX aircraft and took some fine obliques, the first photographic cover obtained of the mountain since the Houston Expedition in 1924. By the end of the year the Mk.II and Mk.VI Mosquitos were withdrawn from operations. Another record flight was made by Maj J.F. Baffin who flew an F-5A of US 9th Sqn to Kunming in China and on to obtain cover of Bangkok. The task of the reconnaissance squadrons was now to provide material for aircraft-counts, to cover communication routes and potential targets for attack.

At the Cairo Conference in December 1943 the Joint Chiefs of Staff approved the formation of a strategic bombing force to be employed against Japanese industry in Formosa (Taiwan), Manchuria and the Japanese Home lslands, equipped with the Boeing B-29 Superfortresses that had been so far delivered to the USAAF. The plan proposed the enlargement of airfields in India as bases for the bombers, and the construction in China of advanced airfields within reach of Japan. It was also planned later to capture the Marianas Islands in the Pacific to provide closer bases.

Adm Mountbatten then took up the fight for further photographic reconnaissance assistance. He pointed out to the Chiefs of Staff that since the previous request made in October by the Commander-in-Chief, there had been further losses of PR Liberators over the Andaman Islands, and in any event the South Andamans could only be covered by the Mosquito Mk.IX, four of which were at that time operational in the Command. Full pressure was placed accordingly upon the provision of Mosquito IXs for India as being the only suitable aircraft both for long-range and survey photography. At the same time the establishment of No.684 Squadron was altered to twenty Mosquitos Mark IX. Air Ministry could not hold out any hopes of being able to complete this establishment before February 1944, however, as there were calls upon this type of aircraft from all theatres.

86: Three cameras fitted with protective muffs and film magazines about to be loaded into Liberator GR. III FL935, 'S', of 160 Sqn. The roundel was of non-standard proportions and the aircraft letter was Night instead of the more usual Light Slate Grey

87: *An Isuzu starter truck fires up the engines of a Kawasaki Ki 45-II Toryu heavy fighter of the 21st Sentai. This particular example is seen at Palembang in Sumatra, but detachments from the unit made life difficult for the B-25s of No.3 PRU during sorties over the Andaman Islands. Note the unit emblem painted on the truck door, a most unusual practice in the IJAAF*

88 Right: *LAC Alan Fox DFM about to install an F.24 camera in a Mosquito of 684 Sqn at Dum Dum*

89 Far right: *At the same time Japanese photo-interpreters were assessing the results of the sorties by their own reconnaissance aircraft. Once the limits of Japanese expansion had been reached most reconnaissance was tactical in nature, often acquired by simple hand-held cameras used by the observers of small aircraft such as the Mitsubishi Ki 51 ('Sonia')*

90: *Scourge of Allied aircraft until well into 1943 was the Nakajima Ki 43, a group of which from the 50th Sentai are seen here. These* Hayabusas *(Peregrine Falcons) are from the 3rd* Chutai*, as indicated by the white lightning stripe and are lined up for the benefit of the press on an airfield in Burma during November-December 1942. The Ki 43's close similarity to the Japanese Navy's better-known 'Zero' meant that Allied pilots were claiming victories over the latter type even when the Japanese Navy was hundreds of miles away*

91: A Hurricane FR.IIC of 28 Squadron's Imphal detachment early in 1944 shows the usual armament, with the two inboard cannons removed, of the fighter-reconnaissance variant

92 Left: LAC GE Smith holding an F.24 camera. Behind him is ex-Tenth Air Force B-25C MA956 wearing 24 June 1943 markings. Eddie Smith died when MA957 was lost at sea on 5 November 1944

94 Top right: Installing and removing the Spitfire's cameras was an awkward operation. This is BS503, 'A' of 681 Sqn, marked with 30in roundels, at Chandina

93 Left: A B-25C of the US 9th PR Sqn, the crew wearing conspicuous American flags on their jackets. By mid-1944 these aircraft were rarely used for reconnaissance, remaining based at Barrackpore as the 8th Photo Group's courier flight

95 Right: 'The Flying Scotsman', alias BP880 of 681 Sqn, at Chandina, a Comilla satellite strip laid out in the paddy fields in 1943. Chandina, like other kachcha *airfields, was simply of rolled earth and became unusable when the monsoon rains began in 1944*

96: *Grp Capt SG Wise with Air Marshal Sir REC Peirse, AOC-in-C and Lt Gen GE Stratemayer, Air Commander Eastern Air Command, SE Asia*

97: *A PR pilot's view of the ground from 29,000ft, with the first clouds of the southwest monsoon casting shadows across East Bengal*

98: *Spitfire PR.IV BP880, 'S', at Chandina dispersal in February 1944. The lens cone of the rear F.52/36-inch camera projects beneath the fuselage*

Second Arakan and 'The March on Delhi'

In December 1943 the Chinese began their advance from Ledo and units of XV Corps moved forward from their positions protecting Cox's Bazar southwards again into the Mayu Peninsula. On 9 December they occupied Maungdaw and pressed over the Ngakyedauk Pass towards Buthidaung. By the end of December they faced the enemy's main defensive position, their 'Golden Fortress' on the Maungdaw-Buthidaung road. The offensive was planned for 4 February, but on the 1st the Japanese launched their first drive towards India, '*Ha-Gô*', intended to destroy the two divisions facing them, to capture Chittagong and so embroil 14th Army's reserves in Bengal that they would be unable to assist on the Central Front when a major Japanese offensive opened a month later. Almost the whole strength of their 5th *Hiko Shidan* (Air Division) was committed to provide air support for '*Ha-Gô*' from 3 February and during the Imphal offensive, to maintain air-superiority on the Central Front, attacking Allied air fields and major tactical objectives from main bases at Meiktila and Kalaw in central Burma.

In January 1944 No. 6 Sqn IAF and 28 Sqn were still engaged in photographic and tactical reconnaissance from Cox's Bazar and Imphal. On 15 January, another Hurricane of No.6 Sqn, HL881, was shot down during a PR sortie to Razabil and Bauthidaung but the pilot, Flg Off Bhullar, escaped and returned to the squadron, unlike R.L. DeVliey of US 9th PR Sqn whose F-5 failed to return from ops on 18th. On 27 January the unfortunate Bhullar was shot down again and killed.

Operational experience with high-flying Mosquitos over Europe showed that crews suffered fatigue and discomfort from prolonged exposure to low air-pressure. A constant danger was an attack of 'bends' caused by release of nitrogen within the body as bubbles in the bloodstream. The introduction of a pressurized cabin in the Mk.XVI, supercharged by a Marshall blower located on the port Merlin 76 engine to 21 lb/sq in above external pressure, now made long flights bearable. The construction of the Mosquito made pressurization simple, the only modifications entailed sealing off the cabin at the bulkhead forward of the bomb-bay (which in all these Mosquitos contained fuel tanks and camera mountings) and sealing thirty-six junctions—hatches, windows, cables and control tubes—and the wing-to-fuselage joints. An inner crew door formed an air-lock. By the end of 1943, 684 Sqn had received nine Mosquito PR.XVIs and over the next eighteen months operated some fifty of this most widely-used reconnaissance aircraft.

A member of the squadron wrote, "Our fleet of B-25s, once our pride and joy, had dwindled—one now pock-marked with metal patches over bullet-holes—and was being replaced with the new, sleek, wonder machine, the Mosquito. There was now no role for the airborne photographer."

In the new year 681 Sqn, now under the command of Sqn Ldr F.D. Procter, was up to full complement with six Spitfire PR.IVs and ten PR.XIs, moving to begin operations from Dum Dum with 684 Sqn on 31 January 1944. The following day survey photography was begun by 684 Sqn as far as Martaban, to provide material for new maps of Burma, the immediate battle areas having priority. Accurate maps of the country did not yet exist, earlier maps having being based on ground-surveys made thirty years before, often with major errors.

Altogether, the two RAF squadrons flew 162 sorties during January; on the 25th they obtained cover of eighty enemy-held airfields.

On 16 January in advance of an enemy fighter sweep over Bengal, a Ki-46 appeared. The 615 Sqn team of Louis and Wiggery were again successful in their interception, shooting down the Dinah in flames 35 miles south-east of Chittagong. The Spitfires continued hunting the Dinahs but the enemy reconnaissance aircraft rarely ventured further north than the Mayu Peninsula until the beginning of February. The Japanese offensive began on the 4th and the following morning a Ki-46 was plotted west of Bawli Bazar. Flg Off L.G. Coons and Sgt J.B. Neville of 607 Sqn, flying Spitfire VIIIs, sent the Dinah into the sea off Elephant Point.

Gen Slim was alerted to the likelihood of a Japanese counter-attack in the Ngakyedauk area of Arakan by the increased enemy air operations. In mid-January, he spent several days visiting the Arakan Front, noting that Japanese fighter-bombers were coming over in formations of up to a hundred at a time. He wrote, "Our Spitfires, much inferior in numbers, fairly laced into the Zeros and began most effectively to knock them out of the sky. While these whirlwind dogfights streaked about high in the clear air, our reconnaissance Hurricanes kept up their steady patrols. I was impressed by the conduct of a reconnaissance squadron of the Indian Air Force. Flying in pairs, the Indian pilots in their outmoded Hurricanes went out, time and again, in the face of overwhelming enemy fighter superiority. I looked in on the squadron just at a time when news had come in that the last patrol had run into a bunch of Zeros and been shot down. The Sikh squadron leader, an old friend of mine, at once took out the next patrol himself and completed the mission. His methods, rumour had it, were a little unorthodox. It was said that if any of his young officers made a bad landing he would take them behind a *basha* and beat them. Whatever he did, it was effective; they were a happy, efficient and very gallant squadron."

Four Allied operations were planned for early 1944: an advance by Stilwell's NCAC (Northern Combined Area Command) forces, a limited advance across the Chindwin by 14th Army to link up with the Chinese, an advance by XV Corps to secure Akyab, and harassment of the enemy's communications by Maj Gen Wingate's Special Force.

On 1 February 28 Sqn was joined at Imphal by No 1 Sqn IAF, also flying Hurricane IIBs and fresh from tactical reconnaissance operations on the North West Frontier of India. On the 4th No 6 Sqn moved south to Ratnap, at the head of the Naf Peninsula, and, engaged in constant support for the Army, suffered more casualties, Plt Off Gracious, on a tactical sortie, was bounced by enemy fighters and Gracious was shot down and killed. On 8 February twelve Oscars were reported over their area of operations but only one attempted an attack before the enemy fighters were driven off by Spitfires. Later in the day, however, Flg Offs Delima and Reddy, in AP892 and BG868, were caught and shot down while on a Tac/R sortie over Taung Bazar. 28 Sqn's B Flt was hurriedly moved to Ratnap in support the following day but returned to Imphal a week later when No 1 Sqn IAF began operations with reconnaissance over the Uyu River on 14 February. On the 15th another of No.6 Sqn's Tac/Rs was intercepted by Zekes. HW428 (Plt Off Battacharji) was shot down but Flg Off Varnia in BG852 damaged one of the enemy fighters during a fifteen-minute running battle at low-level along the coast and the enemy aircraft was later reported shot down. Sweeps by fifty or more Japanese aircraft were mounted daily to intercept the Hurricanes and Vengeances of the RAF and IAF on close-support duties.

As before, the enemy struck back, moving 8,000 men by forced march to cut off the base of 7 Div at Sinzweya where a similar number of mostly administrative Allied troops were gathered, and Tokyo radio declared, "The March on Delhi has begun!"

The headquarters of 7 Indian Div was soon isolated in what became known as the 'Admin Box' and the communications of 5 Indian Div were in peril; once again the Japanese had achieved surprise and, despite the efforts of the Spitfire squadrons, which destroyed or damaged some sixty enemy aircraft during the campaign, the Japanese retained air-superiority and carried out over 300 sorties against the aircraft dropping supplies by day to beleaguered Sinzweya. Attempts to air-drop supplies by day were mostly abandoned and night-drops became usual.

By mid-February Japanese air activity diminished as aircraft were withdrawn to prepare for 'U-Gô', 300 miles to the north-east, as planned. In Arakan the enemy, unprepared for 7 Indian Division's prolonged resistance, was unable to make further progress and on 24 February, with 26 Indian Div approaching from the north and the 'Box' relieved by 123 Bde; 'Ha-Gô' was called off. For the Japanese, this was a disaster—of 8,000 troops engaged in the first advances, 5,000 perished. Even more serious was the resulting delay in the main offensive which was put back until 15 March for, by that time, two British divisions held in reserve in Bengal for the Arakan battle, became available to be air lifted to the Central Front later in the month. For the first time a Japanese offensive had failed. By 4 March they had fallen back to their original line; a week later Butbidaung was in British hands and the battle was over. On the Central Front. there was, as yet, little activity although 28 Sqn lost a pilot on 22 February. Flg Off D.S. Thomson, on an offensive recce from Imphal, crashed in AG342 during an attack on a Japanese post and was taken prisoner.

On 3 March the Japanese Army aircraft made one of their rare appearances over the British rear areas; ten Ki-44 Tojos attacked Akyab airfield and damaged five Hurricanes of No.2 Sqn IAF.

Although the Japanese Army's 5th Hiko Shidan was con-centrated on the airfields of central Burma for operations over Arakan, Naval air detachments remained on the islands in the Bay of Bengal. On 7 February 1944 Mosquito PR.IX, LR440, 'V', (Sdn Ldr B.S. Jones DFC and Flg Off R.C. Hawson DFC) found a Zeke waiting over Port Blair—the same day NS497, 'J', was forced to

99: *P-40s of the US 20th Tac/R Sqn provided reconnaissance for Gen Stilwell's NCAC in Northern Burma. The camera port can be seen as a vertical rectangular panel breaking into the star marking on the fuselage of 'Stardust'*

abandon its sortie to the Bangkok area when intercepted. On 25 February Flt Lt F.B. McCulloch and Flt Sgt T.S. Viggers in LR493, 'P', flew to Mergui, then south down the coastal road to Tavoy; there they were met by five Zekes at 22,000 ft but climbed away and were not attacked. On a reconnaissance of the Andaman Islands in LR445 on 29 February, Flg Offs J.J. Winship and B.C. Haynes, covered Port Blair, Stewart Sound, and Port Bonington before they encountered a Zeke which was unable to catch the Mosquito. By the end of February 684 Sqn was having great difficulty in maintaining enough

Mosquitos to fulfil its tasks, due to a shortage of spares, and operated a modified 'Christmas Tree' system of borrowing spares from aircraft being serviced in order to keep others flying.

100: *Hurricane FR.IIB HL857 of 28 Sqn's 'A' Flight detachment at Imphal in February 1944. Note how small the fuselage roundel appears*

101: *The Nakajima Ki 44 Shoki (named after the legendary Chinese god Zhong-Kui—the 'Demon Queller')was one of the most potent Japanese fighters, albeit regarded as something of a 'hot ship' by its pilots. This is the eighth pre-production example, being flown by Capt Kuroe Yasuhiko, commander of the 3rd flight of the newly-named 47th Sentai, during operational trials in Malaya in January 1942*

102: *42-68298, a US 9th PR Sqn F-5B-1-LO probably in Synthetic Haze finish, within the shelter of a hangar built from packing-cases at Tingkawk Sakan*

103: *44-41680 is a Consolidated F-7B from the 24th Combat Mapping Sqn during a stopover at Agra in India on 1 August 1945. The rather plain finish in which it left the factory is only enlivened by the Squadron emblem on the fin*

104: *An Olive Drab finished Consolidated F-7A of the 24th Combat Mapping Squadron undergoing overhaul at Gushkara*

105: *A Dodge ambulance on 'stand-by' as a Lockheed F-5 of the 9th PR Sqn taxies in on the 'bit-hess' runway at Barrackpore*

Operation 'Thursday'

PR and the Chindits

The only further major operation by 14th Army before the 1944 monsoon began was Operation 'Thursday', a long-range penetration of Japanese-occupied territory in Northern Burma by Maj Gen Wingate's Special Force, the Chindits, supported by a USAAF task force, 1st Air Commando, based at Hailakandi. On 5 February one LRP brigade began making its way overland towards Katha, another two brigades were to be landed in two jungle-clearings, 'Broadway' and 'Piccadilly', on 6 and 10 March, with two more brigades to a third clearing, 'Aberdeen', on 24 March and on 5 April. The initial lift, by glider from Lalaghat, was to be of covering infantry and engineers to improvise airstrips for the flying-in of the main force of infantry. Beginning on 2 February, Flt Sgt. Ross of 681 Sqn reconnoitred Wuntho and Pyawbwe in HP880, 'S'. The PR squadrons then undertook a series of sorties during the following six weeks over all the enemy airfields and landing grounds in northern Burma, at Bhamo, Lashio, Loiwing, Kawlin and many others to assess the likely air support for an expected Japanese offensive on the Central Front. At the same time they covered the 'Special Areas' where Special Force would land and operate, within the Wuntho-Mogaung-Bhama triangle.

Four of 684 Sqn's Mosquitos were allocated for trial survey flights for the preparation of new maps of the areas of intended operations by '3 Indian Div' (the cover-name for Special Force), Stilwell's forces (officially Northern Combat Area Command from 1 February 1944) and IV Corps. Other 'Special Area' sorties were flown by 681 Sqn's Spitfires to photograph ground signals laid out and landing-areas used for clandestine operations by detachments of Force 136 (Special Operations Executive units organising resistance forces) in Eastern Burma and Arakan.

The US 20th Tactical Reconnaissance Sqn, newly arrived in India, was stationed at Gushkara on 5 January 1944. By the end of the month the unit had 19 Curtiss P-40s on the strength and immediately began, with great ingenuity, to improve the aircraft's performance. By sanding the entire surface of the aircraft, removing unnecessary lights and modifying the radio antenna to reduce drag an increase in cruising speed of 10 to 15mph was achieved and manoeuvrability was improved.

From 31 January to 3 February Lts C.A. Kramer and L.C. Posey and, the next week, the squadron commander Cpt W.R. Fornof and three other pilots flew 21 photographic missions at the request of Col P.Cochran, commanding the 1st Air Commando Group at Haila-kandi. The prints were used in a final selection of sites for Operation 'Thursday', the airborne landing by Wingate's Special Force.

February and March were notable also for the many sorties flown to obtain airfield information and to assess the damage to enemy communications by the Third Tactical Air Force and First Air Commando. Survey work was also carried out together with regular flights to the Andamans and the vast area bounded by the line Kengtung, Sittang, Mergui, Goh-Sichang, the latter south-east of Bangkok. Small countrycraft were now being used by the enemy and the waterways of Arakan and central Burma were frequently photographed to assess the density of traffic and activity at staging points. On 27 March the longest flight so far, 1,860 miles, was achieved when a large stretch of the Bangkok-Singapore railway was photographed.

US 9th PR Sqn was still operating independently under the control of HQ 10th USAAF but there was some duplication of effort as a result of poor communication between that headquarters and 171 Wing, RAF. Co-ordination was considered essential so, at the end of January 1944, preparations were made for a combined Photographic Reconnaissance Force with a new ops room at Bally Seaplane Base, Calcutta. Control was provisionally taken by 171 Wing ops room at Dum Dum until the official formation of PR Force on 23 February, staffed largely by 171 Wing staff and commanded by Wg Cdr S.G. Wise DFC and Bar. The Force was still made up of 681 and 684 Sqns and, for only a week, 9th PR Sqn; all directly under Eastern Air Command.

684 Sqn lost two aircraft during the month from similar causes: 'L', returning from a 'Special Areas' sortie on 23 February, and LR463, 'N' during an outward flight on February 29. Both developed engine-trouble so damaging that, when inspected after landing, they were struck off charge.

During the last week of the month 160 Sqn despatched two daytime sorties to Simaloer Island off Sumatra, both abortive because of cloud over the target area. The squadron had carried out several night-photography trials with FL936, 'V'. Now a series of experimental sorties began with a first attempt by Flg Off R.C. Hall on the night of 29/30 March—this sortie also was abandoned because of the weather conditions.

After preparatory reconnaissance of the 'Special Areas' had been completed with a sortie by BR415, 'T', (Flt Lt A.J. Brookes) of 681 Sqn to Hsipaw on 27 February, Wingate ordered that the landing areas were not to be over-flown again but Col C. Russhon of 1st Air Commando proposed a final, secret reconnaissance as a reasonable precaution. Although the unit's aircraft were not fitted with camera-mountings, hand-held cameras were usually carried and used on most operations. On the morning of 5 March, the day for the launching of 'Thursday', a B-25H of 1st Air Commando (pilot Col R.T. Smith, ex-AVG ace) made a sortie over the landing areas and found that logs had been dragged across the clearing at 'Piccadilly'. The aircraft returned to Hailakandi and prints were flown to Lalaghat from where the first gliders were due to leave at 17.40. The photographs were in the hands of the operations commanders at 17.15 and caused consternation. The previous year a C-47 had landed at the 'Piccadilly' clearing to pick up wounded from the first Chindit expedition and just two weeks before the planned operation, a photo of 'Piccadilly' had appeared in *Life* magazine. It was feared, therefore, that the Japanese might be prepared for another landing so, after some indecision, it was decided to divert the gliders intended for 'Piccadilly' to 'Broadway' and the first were lifted-off at 18.12. In fact, the obstructions on the ground were just part of a logging clearance.

77 Brigade troops under Brigadier Calvert landed at 'Broadway' so rapidly that some of the gliders collided, causing 61 casualties and the next night 11 Brigade landed at 'Chowringhee'. Within 24 hours the engineers at 'Broadway' had levelled a runway using the bulldozers that had been flown-in, making it possible to fly out the wounded by Vultee L-1 Vigilant aircraft. By Sunday, 12 March, over a period of six nights, C-47 Dakotas of the RAF and the 1st Air Commando had flown 9,052 men, 1,458 animals and 242 tons of materiel into 'Broadway'. That same day, six Spitfire F.VIIIs of 81 Sqn landed on the strip. The presence of the RAF fighters caused some annoyance at 1st ACG, which regarded all air operations for Special Force as its own task but the 81 Sqn Spitfires were essential for the escort of RAF Dakotas ferrying into the strip. They soon became involved in local defence with but a few minutes of radar warning.

Several days passed before the Japanese discovered the location but within a week Oscar fighter-bombers mounted a series of attacks which caused the loss of aircraft and pilots, including 81 Sqn's commander, Sqn Ldr W.M. Whitamore DFC, who was killed on 17 March. The surviving remnant of the detachment was joined by P-51B Mustangs of the 1st ACG but was soon withdrawn to Tulihal.

On the last day of March the US 8th Photo Reconnaissance Group was established at Bally as the American component of P.R Force, which included the 20th TR Sqn equipped with P-40N aircraft, the 24th CM Sqn with Consolidated F-7As and the 9th PR Sqn with F-5s. The detachment of the 9th Sqn was recalled from Dinjan to Barrackpore and a Flight of the F-5s was sent to Tingkawk Sakan for operations in support of NCAC.

The F-7A was a photographic-reconnaissance and survey adaptation of the B-24J Liberator, fitted with a 'trimetrogon' mounting in the nose and 'split vertical' mountings in the rear bomb-compartment. The forward bomb-bay was permanently closed, housing additional fuel-tanks. The later F-7B had no nose-mounted cameras but carried six in the aft bomb-bay.

Late in the month 681 and 9th US PR Sqns were again committed to photographing road communications in the battle-areas around Imphal and Myitkyina and to covering the waterways and ports of the Arakan coast and the Irrawaddy River, where the Japanese were again making use of small craft. In Arakan No.6 Sqn IAF was still engaged in unspectacular but essential Tac/R sorties along the Kaladan River. Flg Off Hall of 160 Sqn again attempted a night sortie on 5 April this time to Car Nicobar, and obtained a degree of success, fifteen out of his twenty flash exposures on two runs over the target producing results. Further attempts at night reconnaissance during April were abandoned because of thick cloud over Sumatra.

With the B-25Cs, the 9th Sqn had undertaken a mapping survey programme over the Brahmaputra Valley and the 'Hump' air routes to China. This survey was extended to cover the areas around Chengtu in Szechuan Province where airfields were to be constructed for Project 'Matterhorn', (the planned raids on Formosa).

The 20th Sqn was then attached to the 5320th Defense Wing (Provisional) at Maingkwan and increasingly undertook ground-attack, escort missions and interceptions in addition to its Tac/R duties. Lt Posey recounted:

"On March 27, 1944 about 1100 hours, Lt. McGuire and I were sitting on the ground at Maingkwan, when a twin engine Jap bomber came in from the north and strafed the field. After he had passed, I got in my ship and started to chase the bomber south toward Kamaing. I caught the bomber about 5 miles north of Shadazup and noted that the right engine was smoking heavily. As I opened fire on the bomber a Zero fighter, Oscar type, came up from in front and below. The fighter flew through my tracers, and I pulled up trying to lead him. The fighter was a very new-looking shiny ship; had a yellow leading edge and the large dots in the usual place. As soon as I had completed my 180° turn I applied evasive tactics and headed for Maingkwan. When last seen the fighter was heading south-west. I believe hits were scored on the fighter, but I observed no evidence of damage".

In early May an Oscar was discovered by Chinese troops north-west of Shaduzup, damaged by belly-landing; this aircraft was presumed to be that attacked by Lt Posey.

Despite the failure of 'Ha-Gô', enemy preparations for the offensive on the Central Front continued and air reconnaissance showed that the Japanese intended a series of crossings of the Chindwin River directed against Imphal. The beginning of Operation 'U-Gô' was signalled by the usual pre-attack reconnaissance by the 81st *Sentai* and Spitfires of 81 Sqn scrambled from Imphal to intercept them. On 4 March Flt Lt I.R. Krohn shot down the first 'Dinah' near Kangla, and two days later Flg Off L.F.M. Cronin destroyed another, repeating the mission, near Palel. The offensive opened with attacks on airfields as, on 7 March, the Japanese 33rd Division struck at British positions around the 9,000 ft Kennedy Peak near Tiddim, captured Fort White and cut the Tiddim-Imphal road to block the withdrawal of 17 Indian Divsion. 20 Division, guarding the direct route into India, the Sittang-Palel road, withdrew slowly towards Imphal, fighting all 160 miles of the way.

The Japanese offensive was aimed at Imphal and Kohima, sixty-five miles to the north, on the only all-weather road through the Naga Hills from 14th Army's railhead at Dimapur. Three enemy divisions were employed, with lines of communication through Kalewa, Wuntho, and Indaw. 'Special Force' set about cutting both these latter routes and disrupting the lines of supply to Myitkyina and Komaing where the Japanese were faced by Stilwell's Chinese-American forces. The enemy had long feared a seaborne assoult in the south, as indeed was proposed by SEAC, and had stationed troops in the areas of Bassein and Moulmein against such an attack: now part of this force, with reinforcements intended for '*U-Gô*', was moved north to deal with the Chindits.

In early March the PR squadrons again concentrated on airfield cover and sorties to assess the damage to the railway system resulting from air attack by 3rd TAF and No 1 Air Commando Force. During the month 681 Sqn lost two Spitfires: Flt Lt C.B.P. Davies baled out over the Bay of Bengal on 5 March and was not recovered. Flg Off V.E. Cross failed to return from a sortie on the 27th. 684 Sqn returned to air-survey operations but still continued the regular flights to the Andamans, with a few long-range sorties over south-eastern Burma and beyond.

Cover was now being demanded of targets over 1,000 miles from the forward landing ground and the 766 gallons of fuel carried by the Mosquito was insufficient for this range, a request was made to ACSEA for the fitting of a 90 gal drop tank beneath the bomb bay. After a great deal of discussion an aircraft was alloted to the RDU at Cawnpore (Kanpur) for a tank to be fitted and trials carried out by Flg Offs J.J. Winchip and P.C. Haines flying PR.IX, MM254. This modification proved successful and several of the aircraft were thus fitted and used for all long range targets.

On 22 March, NS688, 'Q', (Flt Lt Sinclair and Flg Off Stocks), briefed to cover the Bangkok-Singapore railway from Chumphon southwards as far as they could go, reached Northern Malaya. NS688 was the first RAF aircraft to fly over Malaya since the fall of Singapore.

On 27 March Flt Lt K.J. Newman and Flt Sgt R.K. Smith, in Mosquito PR.XVI MM295, 'C', carried out the squadron's longest flight so far, 1,860 miles, when they covered a 170 mile stretch of the railway, Bangkok and Hua Hin airfield, while Sqn Ldr J.A. Johnston flew MM296, 'M', to the Nicobars to photograph Port Blair and Mount Augusta radar station. Four days later Flg Offs

Dupee and McDonnell, in the same aircraft, obtained the first daylight photographic cover of Car Nicobar Island.

By the end of March enemy forces were firmly established on the Imphal Plain and investing Kohima where on 4 April they cut off the defenders within a tight perimeter. Once again the garrison stood their ground until relieved on 20 April. On the the evening of 29 March Sqn Ldr Arjan Singh DFC, OC No 1 Sqn IAF reported a battalion of Japanese a mere ten miles from the airfield. Thirty-three aircraft from four squadrons scrambled, including several of 28 Sqn whose pilots were relaxing after flying a total of twenty-five sorties during the day. With landing lights on the Hurricanes strafed the enemy troops, inflicting heavy casualties, and returned to land in the dark.

In April the Army's requirements entailed a considerable increase in the number of sorties flown over the battle-areas beyond the range of the reconnaissance Hurricanes. 684 Sqn was still experimenting with long-range flights to determine the range of the Mosquito and to discover whether it was feasible to fly over the monsoon weather to cover Japanese rear areas. Despite the loss of MM296, which crashed on take-off from Dum Dum on 10 April, these experiments produced some notable flights.

Flg Offs G. E. Winship and Haines carried out a sortie over Siam on 5 April. After passing over their objective at Loey, the port engine of the Mosquito PR.IX, MM294, 'H', failed. Jack Winship wrote, "This prevented us from transferring the fuel from our 50 gallon drop tanks to our main tank and we had to jettison 100 gallons of our very precious fuel. Things were pretty shaky for the first hour or so of our 780 mile return trip. We did a gradual descent to around 12,000 ft and, after some tuning, the good old Mossie settled down and purred along beautifully. we made the trip back to the landing ground at Ramu in a little over an hour." The crew received a Commendation from the Air Commander EAC Lt Gen G.E. Stratemayer. US 9th PR Sqn continued sorties to southern Burma where enemy air reinforcements were encountered. On 2 April an F-5 was intercepted by enemy fighters over Monywa and forced to abandon the sortie and on 5 April another aircraft of the squadron was damaged during an encounter with a 64th *Sentai* Tojo over the satellite 'Highland Queen' airstrip at Hmawbi, north of Rangoon.

On 7 April plans were made for emergency evacuation of up to two-hundred Chindit casualties by flying boat from Indawgyi Lake, should the monsoon break before contact could be made with the forces of NCAC. A secret briefing was undertaken by HQ PR Force at Bally.

The most important target on the Burmese railway system was, at this time, the Sittang Bridge. On 4 April Sgt T. Cocks and Flt Sgt G. Smith of 684 Sqn, in NS497, 'J', on a sortie to Mergui, found the Tenasserim coast covered in cloud and photography impossible, but they photographed the Mokpalin area and the bridge on the return journey. It was clear that repairs had been completed and that there was again a direct railway route from Martaban to Rangoon and to the Japanese bases in central and northern Burma. The bridge was bombed by USAAF B24s of Strategic Air Force on 8 April and again wrecked; photographs taken on 10 April from LR445, 'F', of 684 Sqn (Wt Off J.A. Johnson and Flt Sgt F. Wells) showed the two western spans of the bridge destroyed. Thereafter the bridge was not again repaired.

From 14 April, because of the necessity of reaching long-range targets early in the day before cloud could build up, it was decided to send the Mosquitos south to Ramu in the evening before their sorties so that they could take off at first light.

Throughout April No.1 Sqn IAF was engaged on tactical recce over the forward enemy positions although a few PR sorties were flown. Near Palel, twenty-five miles south of Imphal, the Japanese continued to attack in an effort to capture the airstrip there and to control the road to Ramu before the monsoon. Further west, the heaviest fighting took place in the Bishenpur area where the Indian squadron maintained standing patrols over Potsangbam. Here on 4 April Flg Off Murcott's Hurricane was hit by ground fire and crashed while strafing an enemy tank.

Ten days later, two No.1 Sqn aircraft were damaged when Imphal was raided—Japanese aircraft made a series of sweeps over the Plain, and Plt Offs Cheema and Masih, on a Tac/R sortie near Bishenpur, were attacked by six Oscars of the 50th *Sentai*. Masih, the 'weaver' was shot down and Cheema's Hurricane was hit in the wing. The long-range petrol tank caught fire but Cheema was able to jettison it and took evasive action to escape; the enemy presumably believing his Hurricane was destroyed.

By the middle of March 1944 some 12,000 men of Special Force were established behind the Japanese front; 77 Bde and 11 Bde had been landed at 'Broadway' and at 'Chowringhee' a hundred miles to the south. 14 Bde had been flown in to 'Aberdeen', near Manhton, and were joined there by 16 Bde at the end of their march from the Chindwin. Later in the month 681 Sqn flew further sorties over these 'Special Areas', providing regular Intelligence about the position in the Chindit brigades' areas of operations.

On 24 March, Wingate was killed in an air crash but operations by Special Force continued under the command of Maj Gen W.D.A. Lentaigne. On 8 April Flt Sgt M. George in Spitfire PR.XI MB896, 'V', covered the area around Aberdeen and, ten days later Flt Sgt D.E. Kemp, in MB900, 'Z', reconnoitered the 'Chowringhee'-Katha area. 77 Brigade set up a stronghold, named 'White City' because of the great number of supply parachutes caught in the trees, near Mawlu on the railway between Mandalay and Myitkyina.

At the beginning of April B Flight of 28 Sqn moved to Jorhat and returned to operations on 9 April. Many of the Hurricane IIBs had meanwhile been replaced by Mk.IICs. These were modified for tactical reconnaissance operations by the removal of both inboard 20mm cannon and the installation of a camera in the leading-edge of the inboard section of the starboard outer wind assembly. Several of these new aircraft were soon lost—HV978 (Flg Off J. Perry) crashed on return from a sortie on 27 March, HV737 suffered wing damage during a low-level attack on 7 April and the pilot, Flt Sgt Draycott, baled out.

On 19 April Flg Off D.A.B. Macpherson crashed near Tetzumi in LD300 but escaped with only slight injuries; he was hidden by Naga tribesmen for several days and eventually returned to the squadron. 16 Bde attempted the capture of the supply centre and airfield at Indaw but were held off by strong Japanese resistance—the Brigade was then flown out from 'Aberdeen' by returning supply aircraft, early in May leaving the enemy free to concentrate against 'White City'. This stronghold was abandoned and 77 Bde established another block, 'Blackpool', north of Hopin, to cut the enemy's main line of communication. The Chindits movements were constantly under surveillance by 681 Sqn Spitfires; although the squadron moved base from Dum Dum on 5 May to Alipore, south of Calcutta, a detachment of two aircraft was maintained at Imphal despite the onset of the monsoon, to continue reconnaissance of the Hopin area where 77 Chindit Bde was in action and over Mawlu and Pinlebu where 111 Bde was operating. In April Kamaing and Mogaung had fallen to Stilwell's Chinese and 77 Chindit Bde; on 18 May Myitikyina airfield was captured and the main purpose of 'Special Force' operations was completed. Scattered groups of Chindits making their way back overland were kept under observation and were provided with supplies by pilots of No.2 Sqn IAF.

Meanwhile, the 20th TR Sqn's capability was increased by fitting to two P-40Ns K.17 cameras, able to produce 9in square negatives. The cameras were installed vertically in the baggage compartment below the usual K.24s. Earlier difficulties of oil and mud accumulating on the camera lens were avoided by the installation of a sliding panel, operated by the pilot only while the camera was in use. These cameras were mainly used between 5,000 and 10,000ft for reconnaissance strips of roads and for pinpoint airfield targets.

Most of the 20th Sqn operations were in the area of Myitkyina and the Mogaung and Hukawng valleys but these missions were often made impossible by the need to fly through the Ledo Pass, where weather conditions were hazardous so, on 21 May, Flight 'B' aircraft were detached to Tingkawk Sakan. The missions flown by the B-25s were mostly for the Forward Echelon of NCAC, the film magazines being dropped by parachute for processing and printing at Shaduzup instead of by the photo-laboratory at Dinjan.

Chinese-American forces and 36 Division, a Flight of P-40Ns of US 20th Tactical Reconnaissance Sqn was detached to operate alongside 9th PR Sqn's F-5s at Tingkawk Sakan in support of NCAC. It was normal practice for troops requiring air-support to lay out a directional panel indicating enemy positions but this was often impossible in thick jungle. Here smoke-bombs were usually mortared onto the target in a pre-arranged pattern so that the bursts formed a triangle or rectangle in plan view. With NCAC a preferred third method employed a

variation of the 'Merton method', using a transparent grid overlay on plastic sheet superimposed on aerial photographs. An appropriate print could thereby be divided into grid squares and only the co-ordinates needed to be signalled when a strike was required.

Although Myitkyina airfield had been retaken, the Japanese continued a stubborn defence of the town. Often under fire from the enemy positions, a detachment of three P-40Ns from 20th Sqn was based on the west airstrip with a small processing plant nearby to produce prints in minimum time. Here the detachment remained until the town was captured on 3 August, after a siege lasting two and a half months.

106: Flying a B-25H of the 1st Air Commando Group, Col RT Smith, the ex-AVG ace, photographed landing ground 'Piccadilly' on 5 March 1944 and brought about a change in the Chindits' plans. This was 43-4329, 'Sweet Sue'. The striking diagonal white bands were a unit identity device which was applied to all the different types of aircraft in use by the Air Commandos

107: B-25s of the US 20th PR Sqn began reconn-aissance for NCAC late in May 1944 and in order to speed up the Intelligence, dropped the film maga-zines by parachute to be processed and printed at Shadzup, close to the for-ward headquarters

108: With the aid of a map prepared from 684 Sqn's and 20th TR Sqn's 'Special Areas' final reconnaissance photographs, Col Philip Cochran, commanding the 1st Air Commando Group, briefs his transport and glider pilots for the intended landing by Special Forces at 'Piccadilly'

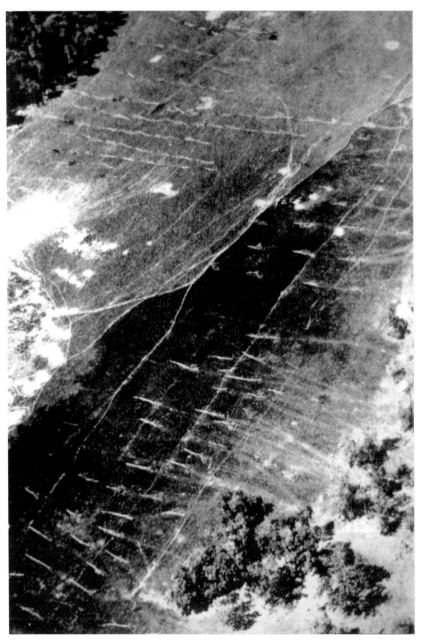

109: One of the photographs that almost caused cancellation of the Chindit Operation 'Thursday', showing the scars left by logs being dragged across the clearing at 'Piccadilly'. At the time it was feared that this was the result of Japanese fore-knowledge of the impending landing, but in the event was discovered to have been caused by innocent forestry work by local Burmese

110 Right: *Less than an hour before take-off for operation 'Thursday', Col John Alison, deputy commander of the 1st Air Commando Group, shows photographs of the logging obstructions at 'Piccadilly' to Maj Gen Orde Wingate and Staff officers at Lalaghat*

111 Far right: *Heavily-laden Chindits about to board one of the 68 Waco CG-4A gliders of the 1st Air Commando Group employed during Operation 'Thursday'. 31 gliders made it to Broadway; 31 men were killed in the landings, 30 more were seriously injured*

112: *After the night landing on 5 March 1944: the wreckage of two CG-4As that collided after the diversion from 'Piccadilly' to 'Broadway'. The men are American glider pilots and engineers engaged in clearing the debris and creating a useable jungle airstrip by the afternoon of the 6th March*

113: *6 March 1944. Chindits clear scrub at 'Broadway' while a US Army bulldozer, brought in by glider, grades the airstrip ready for C-47s and more gliders to carry in the main body of troops. By this stage of the war, probably the only member of the entire Chindit force still to wear a pith helmet was Orde-Wingate himself*

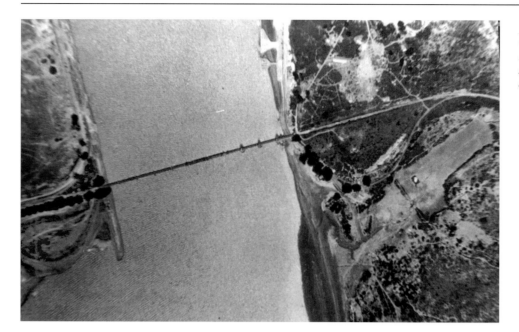

114: *Mosquito NS497's view of the Sittang rail bridge on 4 April 1944, the middle spans repaired after destruction in 1942*

115: *Another 684 Sqn picture of 10 April 1944 shows the two western spans destroyed by bombing. Between the bridge and the pagoda (at right) are anti-aircraft gun emplacements*

116: *USS* Saratoga *(CV-3) had a long and eventful career with the USN, being one of the few pre-war carriers to survive the war, only to be used as an atom bomb target at Bikini Atoll. This view reveals her distinctively shaped island structure and dark blue camouflage while moored at Pearl Harbor in spring 1942, probably soon after her return following repairs after being torpedoed on 11 January*

The US Navy shows the way

After the Japanese carrier attacks in the Indian Ocean in April 1942, the British Eastern Fleet remained on the defensive. With the surrender of the Italian Navy late in 1943, additional heavy and supporting units were promised for operations in the Bay of Bengal. While the US Navy was pressing for offensive action to be taken against the enemy's western perimeter in the Netherlands East Indies, American fast carriers in the Pacific, by striking at the Japanese anchorages, had forced the enemy to withdraw capital ships to their home ports and to Singapore, close to the oil fields of the Indies.

The lack of aircraft capable of obtaining information about Japanese activities in the East Indies was a continuing cause for concern at HQ SE Asia Command. Before the USA entered the War, the US Navy had fitted experimental camera installations in several fighters before Grumman developed the long-range recon-naissance version of the F4F-3 Wildcat at the end of 1941. These aircraft were not used aboard ship but Wildcats were used during Operation 'Torch', the invasion of French North Africa, late in 1942. The first PR aircraft operational aboard carriers were 'Navy-yard modified' F6F-3 Hellcats, fitted with various oblique and vertical camera installations remotely-operated from the cockpit.

These aircraft were usually fitted with Fairchild K.17/6-in and K18/24-in cameras. Maximum speed was 391mph, cruising speed 200mph and range 850 miles. The service ceiling was 39,400 ft. Camera-fitted F6F-3s of US Navy SquadronVF-12 were operational with Air Group 42 aboard the 'fast carrier' USS Saratoga (CV-3) by the end of January 1944.

In March the American carrier and three destroyers

were sent to supplement the British Eastern Fleet based at Trincomalee (China Bay) for operations against the enemy's shore installations in the Netherlands Indies and, by the threat of further action, to compel the Japanese to maintain strong naval and air forces on their south-western perimeter at a time when US forces were landing at Hollandia, New Guinea. The first of these operations 'Cockpit', was an attack by Task Force 70 (*Saratoga, Illustrious* and supporting vessels) upon the harbour and airfield at Sabang, We Island, on 19 April, when Adm Somerville, commanding the combined Allied Force 70, hoped "to catch the Japs with their kimonos up".

There were substantial differences in the practices of the US and Royal Navies in operating carrier aircraft, mainly related to anti-aircraft defence, combat air patrols and signals. With a view to future joint naval operations, the Eastern Fleet began adapting to US Navy methods.

The commander of *Saratoga*'s Carrier Air Group 12, Cdr J.C. Clifton USN, was appointed tactical controller of all air units in Force 70. He accompanied the strike aircraft and directed the attack, flying a F6F-3. The attack was successful and the results were spectacular; oil spilled from a damaged oil storage tank spilled into the sea and was ignited. By midday almost half of the harbour was ablaze.

The Hellcats of the fighter squadron VF-12 attacked Sabang airstrip and the airfield at Lho'nga, 25 miles away, and claimed twenty-four enemy aircraft destroyed. Although there was no Japanese fighter opposition, anti-aircraft fire was accurate and one of the F6F-3 was hit and set on fire while photographing the damage caused by the strike from *Illustrious*. The pilot. Lt D.C. Klahn, baled out at low level. The commander of VF-12, Lt-Cdr R.G. Dore, detached four Hellcats to patrol the airstrip and detailed four more to protect the pilot in his dinghy, then directed HM Submarine *Tactician* twelve miles to the scene to rescue him under fire from a shore battery. As Klahn was taken aboard, a last shell burst some fifteen yards away and the submarine crash-dived.

Saratoga's daily news bulletin *Plane Talk* noted that "the fires started by *Saratoga* and *Illustrious'* flyers increased in fury twelve hours after our strike".

The Allied force returned to Ceylon, where it was decided that another attack, Operation 'Transom', should be made, this time against the Wonokromo refinery, the only oil-refinery in Java, and the harbour and aircraft factory at Soerabaja, beyond the range of land-based bombers. The strike on 17 May was eminently successful. Again, no Japanese fighters were encountered. Only two enemy aircraft were seen in the air and one of these, a Betty, was shot down by Lt Klahn. Once more, high quality obliques were obtained by the Hellcats. The ships then withdrew southwards to Exmouth Gulf, Western Australia, where they separated and returned to their bases at China Bay and Pearl Harbour.

On 15 May 160 Sqn's FL945, 'H', (Flg Off Servos) at last obtained rewarding PR cover of Simaloer by day, but bad weather prevented any further success until the 22nd and 23rd, when good results were again obtained. On 21 May Plt Off J.J. Jackson flew the same aircraft to Tapaktoean on the coast of Sumatra, 100 miles east of Simaloer, and discovered a new and unknown enemy airfield nearing completion at Troemon, forty miles further south. Some twenty minutes after leaving the area, a Japanese fighter, identified as a Kawasaki Ki.61 *Hien*, (Swallow) code-named Tony, supposedly from 71st *Dokuritsu Chutai* (Independent Air Company), intercepted the Liberator. Jackson took evasive action and escaped into cloud before the fighter could close to attack.

Sorties by Liberators FL935, 'S' and FL945, 'H', continued despite generally poor results due to cloudy weather; only one sortie was made by night, this on 17 June by Flg Off J.C. Rowley flying FL936, 'V', but the flash system failed on this occasion.

During April 1944, 274 sorties were flown by 684 Sqn, 16 being rendered abortive by a period of cloudy weather, and the area of aerial survey cover was increased by 76,000 sq miles. Among long-range targets photographed by 681 Sqn were the airfields and bases at Khon Khaen in Central Siam and Luang Prabang, Lai Chau and Vientiane in Northern Indo-China. On 6 May PR Mk.IX PR445, 'R', made the first sortie by a Mosquito to Great Nicobar Island.

Operational difficulties of many kinds were caused by the south-west monsoon. From May to October the sea swell created by high winds would prevent landing operations on any exposed shore and, apart from the

inability to use *kachcha* or 'fair-weather' airstrips, air operations would be made hazardous by cumulo-nimbus clouds rising, often from only 300ft in an unbroken mass to 15,000ft, occasionally to 30,000ft. Mountbatten found that military opinion considered no operations possible through the monsoon but, believing that the Japanese also thought the monsoon season to be a time for merely localised operations, he was determined that fighting must continue as hard through the south-west monsoon, with materiel supplied wherever possible from the air.

By the end of April the major Japanese offensive, 'U-Gô': had progressed as the 14th Army commander, Lt-Gen Slim, had anticipated, yet there had been no large-scale deployment of enemy forces beyond Imphal where, supplied by air, 60,000 British and Indian troops were still besieged. As over the 'Admin Box', Japanese Army aircraft were unable to maintain superiority over the Imphal Plain, while attacks on their airfields in Northern Burma by P-38 Lightnings of the US 459th Fighter Sqn (under 224 Grp, Chittagong) forced the enemy to operate from beyond the Irrawaddy River.

On 26 April a 'Dinah' ventured over the Imphal valley and was shot down by Flt Lt Day and Lt Copeland of 81 Sqn. The repeated sortie two days later also was intercepted and the Japanese aircraft (another Ki-46) damaged by Plt Off Curnock and Flt Sgt Townsend flying Spitfires of 607 Sqn.

Increasingly bad weather, a foretaste of the monsoon, restricted the two RAF PR Squadrons to only 195 sorties during the month, priority being given to photographing only the most essential targets in the areas of clear sky and only three of the survey sorties were completely successful.

When the monsoon rains began in May there was little reduction in Allied air activity despite increasingly hazardous weather conditions; as the Japanese air strength diminished, operations by 3rd Tactical Air Force increased in scale to achieve virtual air superiority.

The short-range squadrons, No.681 and 9th US Sqn, undertook operations only when the weather prospect appeared to be good but the monsoon, characterised by enormous cloud banks, stretching unbroken for hundreds of miles and producing air currents and storms which made flying hazardous caused a reduction in the area which could be safely covered. The monsoon weather badly affected 81 of the 140 sorties made in June although the aircraft were operational on all but two days.

The Hurricane FR.IIBs of No.6 Sqn IAF were still flying regular tactical reconnaissance sorties over the 'Tunnels' Japanese stronghold area between Buthidaung and Maungdaw while XV Corps withdrew from Buthidaung to hold a line from Taung Bazar to Maungdaw, there to 'sit out' the monsoon period. On 31

May, 6 Sqn flew its last operations of the season and withdrew to Dohazari on 6 June.

Such importance was attached to the survey of Burma and Malaya that when the new Mark 34 PR Mosquito commenced delivery in March, 1944 the first four were immediately allocated to Air Command, South East Asia. The long distances and great areas involved required the employment of every available PR Mosquito, but as ACSEA became more familiar with the potentialities and performance of the aircraft under tropical conditions during the spring of 1944, tremendous strides were made in the photographic survey work.

681 Sqn's Flt Lt Newman and Flt Sgt Smith in Mosquito P.IX LR445, 'R', improved upon all previous records by obtaining almost total cover of the Nicobar Group and Port Blair in the Andamans, observing twelve small ships at Nancowry and, at Port Blair, three vessels entering the harbour and eight aircraft on the airfield. One fighter was seen airborne 1,000ft below the Mosquito but was unable to intercept. The total distance flown was 2,256 miles in 7hr 20min. After this sortie, only one of the many pioneering flights, the crew were awarded the DFC and DFM. A number of new Mosquito PR.XVIs were delivered to the squadron during May and June, compensating for the loss of LR463, 'N', which crashed on 9 June and an accident to B-25C N5-145, 'Z', when the nose wheel failed to lock down. With great skill the pilot, Flg Odd Duke landed the aircraft with the damage done only to the front panels of the fuselage, to the Perspex and the propeller tips when the nose finally dropped.

By the end of June the weather had so deteriorated that it had become impossible to detail sorties with any real chance of success, so only freelance reconnaissance continued as opportunities appeared. Only 50 sorties were flown in July and fewer than half were even partly successful, and 681 Sqn lost another Spitfire PR.XI,

PA848, 'P', flown by Flt Sgt Cooper during a flight from Alipore to Cox's Bazar on 2 July. Another Mosquito, MM343, 'W', crashed on take-off on 6 July, when the undercarriage collapsed and the starboard engine caught fire; the whole aircraft was aflame before it came to rest on the edge of the runway, but the crew escaped with only slight injuries.

The Army lacked information about the enemy rear but PR Force had not previously been permitted to operate from strips in forward areas, nor had authority been given for two or three PR Spitfires to be attached, as requested, to each of the fighter reconnaissance squadrons. On 10 July, however, it was decided that small detachments of 681 Sqn's aircraft should be located at forward bases approved by 3rd Tactical Air Force, to provide reconnaissance when local weather conditions were suitable.

Weather conditions obviated any survey sorties and 684 Sqn was unable to keep aircrews in practice, so a detachment of Mosquitos was sent to Yelahanka, near Bangalore, where 1672 (Mosquito) Conversion Unit could maintain the aircraft, to provide aerial survey facilities in southern India under the control of HQ 225 Group, Bangalore.

On the Central Front, because of the danger from Japanese fighter sweeps and following the loss of several Hurricanes, the range of the fighter-reconnaissance squadrons was officially restricted to one hundred miles from Imphal and it was decided that because of the reduction in performance they caused external tanks should be carried only on specially-authorised long-distance sorties when a fighter escort could be provided. By this time 6,000 British and Indian troops were besieged at Imphal under constant enemy pressure and the beginning of the monsoon was hindering the air-supply upon which the defence relied. However, the Japanese

118: The first successful photographic operation from an aircraft carrier in the Indian Ocean occurred on 19 April 1944. One of USS Saratoga's F6F-3 Hellcats took this oblique while recording Operation 'Cockpit'. Sabang harbour lies to the right, the airfield to the left. Numerous fires can be seen burning on the airfield, while a much larger conflagration burns among the harbour buildings

gamble with time was lost for the second time. Supplies of ammunition and food could not be replaced, lines of communication were continually under air attack and the monsoon rains turned every jungle track from the Japanese advance supply dumps into a morass as the enemy began to withdraw from Kohima.

War correspondent Shizuo Maruyaina recorded, "We had no ammunition, no clothes, no food, no guns... the men were barefoot and ragged, and threw away everything but canes to help them walk...all they had to keep them going was grass and water. At Kohima we were starved and then crushed ." While the starving survivors of the enemy's 15th and 31st Divisions struggled back in retreat from Kohima and Imphal, the Hurricanes searched for their jungle camps. The Japanese 33rd Division, however, continued their attempts to capture Bishenpur and Palel but early in July a general enemy withdrawal began. A Japanese officer wrote, "I have fought three times in my life; in the battle of the Shanghai line, in North China and in Burma. Each time there was heavy fighting... but the heaviest was at Kohima. It will go down as one of the greatest battles in history."

Allied PR operations began to tail off but in support of the Chindits, Plt Off A.E. Dowling in Spitfire PR.IV BP937, 'N', covered Hopin on 14 May and Plt Off A.W. Dick in PR.XI PA848, 'P', covered the Indaw River and Magaung on 22 and 24 May. Air support and supply for 'Blackpool' were brought to a stand-still by the monsoon weather and, on the 25th 77 Brigade abandoned the block and joined the other Chindit columns around Indawgyi Lake, fifteen miles to the west. On 30 and 31 May, Flt Sgt R.K. Brown in MB891, 'A', despite the weather, obtained cover of the area for the briefing of an air-lift of Special Force casualties, Operation 'River'. By this time, the number to be flown out had reached almost four hundred. A final, secret briefing was given to crews of 130 Sqn and two Sunderlands were sent to an anchorage at Dibrugarh on the Brahmaputra in the Assam Valley. On 22 June the first flying-boats ('Gert' and 'Daisy') landed on the lake and began the task of flying out more than five hundred sick and wounded before the weather forced the last Sunderland to withdraw on 4 July. Later that day, Japanese fighters strafed the anchorages.

119: The B-25Ds of the 9th PR Sqn carried only single-number tail markings on their tail fins. Here is B-25D-15 41-30440, '1', stripped of all guns for extra speed. The black checker-tailed P-51Cs in the background are from the 25th FS of the US 14th Air Force

120 Left: During 'Cockpit' Saratoga's CVAG-12 and Royal Navy aircraft destroyed 21 Japanese aircraft on the airfield at Sabang, Sumatra, seen here during the attack

121 Top right: Spitfire PR.XI FL773 of 681 Sqn's forward detachment at Imphal late in 1944. The serial number and code letter are White on what is almost certainly the standard RAF High-Flying Day-Fighter camouflage scheme of Medium Sea Grey uppersurfaces and PRU Blue below, the demarcation line between which can be just made out on the rear fuselage

122 Right: A Tac/R Hurricane Mk.IIB of 'B' Flt, 28 Sqn, at Cox's Bazar late in 1943. The locally made windsock (or 'eff-ell') on a bamboo pole gives an idea of the primitive conditions under which forward detachments operated

123 Below: Spitfire PR.XI PA934 of 681 Sqn seen on take-off from Alipore late in 1944. Note how spilled fuel has faded the paintwork on the fuselage forward of the canopy

124 Above: *Operation 'Banquet'; Hellcat Is of 1844 Sqn being guided into position for take-off from HMS* Indomitable *on 14 August 1944. The aircraft were finished in Temperate Sea Scheme camouflage above and Sky beneath. They carried part-serial numbers roughly sprayed on their cowlings; nearest is FN430, '6-R', being guided by P/O Hannay*

125 Left: *Hellcats of 1839 Sqn, also on* Indomitable, *after 'Banquet' on 14 August. Markings are those authorised on 24 July*

126: *By mid-1944, replacement F-5Es were no longer camouflaged. This is F5E-10-LO 42-67877, 'K', a machine of the 9th PR Sqn, at Tingkawk Sekan in June, wearing the later unit marking of three red(?) bands around the tail booms*

127: Corsairs of 1833 Sqn aboard HMS Illustrious *returned after Operation 'Crimson' in June 1944, the strike on Pangkalan Brandon, all marked with the squadron symbol '6'. All wear weathered Temperate Sea Scheme camouflage with the National Markings approved in June 1943 and what appear to be White squadron markings. Nearest aircraft with flak damage to the tailplane is JT324, '6C'*

128: Operation 'Crimson'; an oblique of the naval bombardment taken by Maj RC Hay showing shells ranging-in on a small Japanese vessel. According to crew members aboard HMS Illustrious *at the time, her captain, Admiral Sir Philip Vian of* Altmark *fame, found it difficult to shake off his destroyer background and insisted on taking his ship in close enough to be able to bombard the Japanese positions with the aircraft carrier's 4-inch guns. This is the result—one of the rare times in which an aircraft carrier has engaged surface targets with gunfire*

The Eastern Fleet strikes back

South-East Asia Command was still handicapped by lack of very long-range aircraft for photographing areas 1500 miles away, and there was still no operational base nearer than Ceylon from which photographic reconnaissance aircraft could operate over the Dutch East Indies and Indo-China. Again the suggestion was put forward by the AOC-in-C, ACSEA, that a mobile base might be used for this purpose in the form of an aircraft-carrier. None of the British Fleet Air Arm aircraft were suitable for such a task, and it was therefore suggested that Washington might be asked to provide Corsairs suitably modified for photographic reconnaissance. At the beginning of May the United States Navy offered Hellcats in lieu of Corsairs, and the Admiralty announced their intention of forming a Unit of six PR Hellcats as soon as the aircraft were modified, to ensure the provision of a long-range PR Unit for the Command as early as possible.

With a view to future operations, the Supreme Commander, who had been blamed for the disaster of the Dieppe Raid which failed partly through a lack of Intelligence concerning enemy dispositions, had become a keen supporter of photo-reconnaissance. He made a personal request to the Admiralty for the formation of a naval PR Unit to provide preliminary intelligence and post-raid photography following bombardments and air-strikes. In consequence, No.888 Sqn of the Fleet Air Arm was re-formed as a PR squadron in the UK on 10 June 1944.

These first Hellcat Mk.1(P) aircraft (JV-serials), modified by the Blackburn Aircraft Co in the United States, each had the facility for mounting an oblique camera in the lower fuselage with a window aft of the port wing, as required for tactical reconnaissance. As 888 Sqn later recorded, they had no provision for mounting vertical or 'split-vertical' cameras and, as delivered, were unsuitable for PR work although they differed internally from the fighter Hellcats in having trimming-tab and arrester-hook handles positioned high, clear of the required camera mounting positions.

They were soon further modified for 888 Sqn's PR role; 'Type I' mountings in the fuselages of these aircraft were able to carry all types of American and British cameras and any two in combinations. Each of 888 Sqn's aircraft was thus able to carry a K.16-7in vertical and a K.18-24in vertical camera, two F.24-20in split vertical or one F.52-30in camera within the large rear fuselage.

Meanwhile in Burma, the Hurricanes of 28 Sqn's A Flight continued their sorties from Imphal; on 8 June Plt Off Muff in LH336 and Wt Off Baker in HV784 were attacked by some twenty Japanese fighters. Muff was shot

*129 **Above:** The evening of 23 August 1944 aboard HMS* Indomitable; *the PR Flight of Hellcats ranged in readiness for early take-off for the beginning of Operation 'Banquet', attacks on Padang and Emmahaven on the west coast of Sumatra with extensive airfield PR cover. Behind the Hellcats are four Barracudas*

down and injured but Baker escaped with his Hurricane badly damaged.

On 22 June relief forces of 2 Div made contact with the defenders of Imphal and the road was opened for reinforcement. The enemy had now exhausted their available supplies and, unable to capture material from the stores on the Plain, began to fall back, leaving over 60,000 dead in Assam. The loss to Burma Area Army was never made good; by September only 4,000 replacements had been sent to northern Burma—thereafter no more arrived.

By 26 June 28 Sqn had moved to Dalbumgarh in India—there A Flight from Imphal rejoined the squadron, which became non-operational on 3 July. No.1 Sqn IAF, however, continued to operate from Imphal throughout the monsoon with Hurricane IIBs and the first Hurrcane IIC replacements which were delivered to the squadron in June, these aircraft each fitted with a forward-facing camera in place of the starboard cannon, for low-level high-speed reconnaissance.

The US 24th Combat Mapping Squadron, subordinate to the Tenth Air Force, undertook no significant operations over South-East Asia at this time, a detachment at Liuchow in China moving later in the year to Chanyi.

A clearing of the weather over the Indian Ocean at the beginning of July 1944 had enabled 160 Sqn's Liberator crews to obtain excellent results from night flash photography. As a preliminary to naval bombardment of Sabang and air-strikes on nearby airfields in Sumatra (Operation 'Crimson'), on 8/9 July Flg Off Rowley in FL936, 'V', obtained cover of Sabang and Lho'nga although his aircraft was twice hit by anti-aircraft fire; on the 12th he flew a daylight sortie to Pangkalan Brandan on the Malacca Strait coast of Sumatra.

During the monsoon period, the operational radius for a Mosquito PR.IX or PR.XVI with full fuel load, was found to be approximately 2,000 miles, and this was only when flown by an experienced crew. This meant that, allowing a safety margin for diversion due to adverse weather, no aircraft of Photographic Reconnaissance Force had sufficient range to fly beyond the area of monsoon clouds. An attempt was made to extend the range by fitting supports and connections for a jettisonable fuel-tank beneath the fuselages of the newer aircraft and although weather conditions were poor, Flg Offs L.A. Tapp and R. Fletcher flew to the Andamans and Nicobars on 22 July for cover of the three airfields in MM392, 'K', with a 90-gallon ventral tank.

The Corsairs of 1837 Naval Fighter Sqn embarked in HMS *Illustrious* on attachment to No.15 Naval Fighter Wing, and those of 1838 Sqn were attached to No.47 NFW aboard HMS *Victorious*. It was intended that four sections, each of two Corsairs from *Illustrious*, should operate as spotting aircraft for the guns of the Fleet.

In readiness for this Operation 'Crimson', Corsair II JT427 (the 'personal' aircraft of No.47 Wing Leader Maj R.C. Hay DSO RM) was fitted with an F.24 oblique camera, and three Corsairs of 1833 Sqn were modified, two fitted with vertical cameras, as No.15 NFW's PR Flight.

During the strike on 25 July, 1833 Sqn's PR aircraft, with an escort of two fighter Corsairs, made runs across the target area at heights between 5,500 and 6,000 ft. On the third run one of the photographic Corsairs was shot down by anti-aircraft fire but the pilot, Sub-Lt L.H.E. Retallick, was recovered from the sea by a destroyer of the attacking force. A number of 'verticals' were taken by the leader of the PR Flight, Lt-Cdr A.M. Tritton, DSC, but no useful record was obtained of the target damage. When the operation was over it was agreed that future PR 'vertical' sorties should not be flown below 10,000ft because of the high risk of anti-aircraft fire. There was also some criticism from *Victorious* about the lack of adequate maps and briefing photographs, confirming the need for extensive survey photography.

After a flight to Sabang by Flg Off Boyle in FL935 on 29th to record the results of 'Crimson', 160 Sqn's PR operations again ceased. Meanwhile, in Northern Burma, Stilwell's NCAC forces cleared Myitkyina and entered the town on 3 August. Two US squadrons, 9th and 20th moved there from Barrackpore and Dinjan to occupy the main airfield, leaving only 9th Sqn's B-25s at Barrackpore. These aircraft were now little used for photo-reconnaissance and were attached to US 8th Grp (the US component of PR Force) as a 'courier flight'. The 9th Sqn detachment was withdrawn from Chittagong and its place was taken by four aircraft of 40th Sqn stationed at Cox's Bazar.

The problem of obtaining photographic cover during the monsoon period remained; it was proposed by HQ 171 Wing that two or three PR Spitfires should be allotted to each of the fighter-reconnaissance squadrons but the suggestion continually met with disapproval by HQ 3 Tactical Air Force. In July, however, it was decided that detachments from 681 Sqn should be located in the forward areas at bases selected by 3 TAF. The first of these detachments of Spitfires began operations from Comilla on 9 August.

The day after, Sqn Ldr J.S. Sharp, whose No.4 Sqn IAF had been engaged since July on Tac/R for 25 Div in the Arakan, carried out his squadron's first photographic reconnaissance sortie for HQ XV Corps.

On 11 August a detachment of Mosquitos from 684 Sqn at Alipore was sent to China Bay in Ceylon to operate under the control of HQ 222 Gp in providing the first large-scale survey cover of Northern Sumatra and the offshore islands and for economy of effort in processing and maintenance they were joined by the detachment from Yelahanka on 16 August. Operations by the China

Bay detachment began on the 15th with a sortie by LR467, 'R', fitted with an additional ventral drop tank, to Nancowry and Sabang, and to Car Nicobar and Sabang on the 23rd. Two days later MM228, 'D', flew to obtain further cover of Sabang harbour, Koetaradja, and then down the western coast of Sumatra to Sibolga harbour, 340 miles away, in a total flying time of 8hr 43 min, the longest Mosquito flight yet made. On the 26th LR467, 'R', was detailed to cover the Nicobars but, meeting bad weather, diverted to North Sumatra and discovered a hitherto unknown enemy airfield at Padang Tidji, eight miles west of Sigli. While returning from a sortie Wg Cdr Murray had both his engines cut at 30,000ft while still 100 miles from the airfield. An SOS was sent and acknowledged but by good fortune the engines picked up again at 13,000ft and the aircraft made a safe return.

HMS *Indomitable* sailed from Trincomalee to launch an air strike, Operation 'Banquet', against the port of Emmahaven and a cement works at Padang on the west coast of Sumatra on 24th August. With the intention of emulating USS *Saratoga*'s photographic success, Hellcat Mk.Is of *Indomitable*'s No.5 Fighter Wing (1839 and 1844 Sqns) were modified to carry internal vertical cameras before the attack, as an interim measure before the arrival of 888 Sqn.

Major R.C.Hay from *Victorious* flew Corsair JT427 to record 'Banquet'. At the same time, Lt L.V.Godfrey of *Indomitable*'s 1844 Sqn in Hellcat Mk.I JV143 with K.I7/6in and F24/14in cameras, covered both the Pagai aand Sipoera Islands. Sun Lt A.G. Valentine of 1839 Sqn flew FN433, fitted with K.17/6in and K.8/24in cameras over an area north and ease of Emmahaven. The air strikes occupied the attention of the fighter defences and the high-level PR Hellcats met no enemy opposition—these simultaneous operations proved equally successful during the Navy's later reconnaissance operations. Sub-Lt Valentine's sortie disclosed three more unknown enemy airfields; Pariaman 1 and 2, and Padang.

The Burma-Siam railway was also covered by 684 Sqn. By 24 August 1944 no reconnaissance had been possible for some time because of the monsoon and cover was urgently required of the railway. Sqn Ldr K.J. Newman and Flt Sgt R.K. Smith took off from Cox's Bazar for the purpose of obtaining both vertical and low level oblique pictures. Very bad weather was encountered as the aircraft flew southwards towards Bassein and most of this part of the trip was made at a height of less than 200 feet. At Bassein conditions improved a little and the aircraft climbed to 6,000 feet, but at Thanbuzayat, which is at the northern end of the railway, the cloud base was 500 feet decreasing to 200 feet southwards. The aircraft flew down the railway straight and level at an altitude of 400 feet in the face of accurate anti-aircraft fire. One bullet passed through the air intake of the port engine, through the nose of the aircraftsmashing the pilot's oxygen economiser and ricocheting off the starboard propeller. The crew returned to base at 23,000

feet sharing what oxygen they had left and making many deviations of course to avoid towering cumulo-nimbus clouds which lay everywhere across their route.

The tactical requirements of Lt-Gen 'Vinegar Joe' Stilwell's forces caused some concern, the Americans having earlier insisted that all US Army formations in the China-Burma-India theatre be under his command. Differences were temporarily overcome by the appointment of Gen H.H. Arnold to oversee the strategic use of the new Twentieth Air Force. For Project 'Matterhorn', the destruction of Japanese industry, in April 1944 he assigned the 58th Bombardment Wing (Very Heavy) of XX Bomber Command to bases on the plains west of Calcutta. The four Groups of the 58th Wing were at first used in May to transport materiel from these bases at Chakulia, Charra, Piardoba and Kharagpur over 'the Hump' to the forward airfields in Szechuan Province of China but their first 'shake-down' bombing missions, to Bangkok on 5 June and to Yawata, Honshu on the 15th, left their targets disappointingly intact.

An assessment of the enemy's economic situation made in mid-1944 showed that two-thirds of all Japanese aviation spirit and a quarter of all Japan's fuel oil was produced by the Pladjoe refinery at Palembang in Sumatra, far beyond the range of the B-29s in India. The nearest airfields in Allied hands were in southern India and Ceylon (Sri Lanka). For the night of 10/11 August a major attack on the refinery by 45 B-29s was planned, using China Bay on the eastern coast of Ceylon for arming and refuelling. This Operation 'Boomerang' was a complete failure—no damage was done to the refinery for all the effort in mounting the longest B-29 mission of the war, a round trip of 3,950 miles. One small advantage for 681 Sqn arose from the presence of the B-29s; in the squadron workshops spare 'blister' windows from the huge bombers were fixed to the upper turret positions of the B-25Cs as over-sized astrodomes for all-round observation.

At HQ ACSEA it was realised that difficulties of communication and control still existed in Photographic Reconnaissance Force where there was, as yet, no provision for a Headquarters organisation. The Force was still commanded by Wing Commander Wise but he was also operationally responsible for 171 Wing, the RAF component of PR Force. It was proposed to form a new Force HQ, combining the operations personnel of US 8th PR Gp and 171 Wing, but a protracted series of proposals and disagreements about the command structure left the matter unresolved for several months. Meanwhile the PR squadrons continued operations, hindered less by the problems of command than by the monsoon.

On 26 August Flg Off Duke flew MM341, 'B', from Alipore, bound for China Bay, but failed to arrive; he was later reported to have crashed in the sea, just offshore, a hundred miles south of Madras. He was recovered, injured, and the aircraft was successfully salvaged but struck off charge at the end of the month. 681 Sqn lost another Spitfire when, due to engine-trouble, Flg Off Mahoney was forced to bale-out from MB981, 'A', on 30 August, returning to the squadron four days later.

In August 1944, 8th PR Group was joined by 40th PR Sqn stationed at Alipore with Lockheed F-5Es, modified P-38Js and P-38-Ls with increased speed and operational range, but the squadron's activities were confined to familiarisation flights over non-operational areas until 6 September when the first mission was flown by Lt-Col J.W. Anderson, the Commanding Officer. By the end of September the squadron had completed 18 photo-yielding sorties.

After further reconnaissance of the Andamans and Western Sumatra at the end of the month, 684 Sqn's China Bay operations also came to a halt due to continuously bad weather until 13 September when LR467, 'R',

obtained more photographs of Sigli and Padang Tidji airfield, then covered the coastal road from Salamanga to Bireuen where three bridges had been shelled by a submarine of the Eastern Fleet.

160 Sqn's Liberators moved from Sigiriya to Kankesanturai at the northern tip of Ceylon late in August 1944. With the move, photographic operations ceased apart from the detachment of FL935, 'S', to China Bay for air survey of Simaloer and Nias Islands, off the coast of Sumatra.

130: The northern dispersal area of Lho'nga airfield photographed on 10 October 1944 by Flt Lts Guy and Stevens. Five enemy aircraft can be seen

131: In front of one of their B-25Cs, the 'twin-engined' Flight of 681 Sqn at Dum Dum on the occasion of the award in July 1943 of the DFC to Flt Lt Oldworth (seated, sixth from left). To his left are Sqn Ldr Frostick, Flight Commander, and Flt Lt Guy, later commanding the China Bay Detachment of 684 Sqn

1944-1945
The turn of the tide

By the end of August, five months after the beginning of 'U-Gô', the Japanese drive to control the passes leading to the Brahmaputra Valley had failed and the last enemy formations had withdrawn in disarray from Assam. After the relief of Imphal, 14th Army moved slowly forwards despite the continuing storms; 5 Indian Div harried the Japanese for distances of 50 miles along the Manipur River to Tiddim, while 11 East African Div pushed down the road to Tamu and Sittaung where they forced a crossing of the Chindwin River and turned south for Kalewa.

The Imphal Plain, enclosed by hills up to 7,000 ft high, was completely cut off from India by the surrounding Japanese, except by air. To Imphal Main airfield in the valley, regular transport flights were organised of Dakotas flying in supplies every day from bases in India some 200 miles away and returning with casualties, about 300 transport aircraft arriving and leaving each day throughout the monsoon period.

132 Above: A Hurricane FR.IIC of 28 Sqn is fitted with a vertical F.25 camera while armourers reload the 20mm cannon magazines

Based on satellite strips at Imphal were two squadrons of Spitfires. So effectively did they protect the transport aircraft that only twenty were lost to enemy action. Kohima was in a far worse position because it had no airstrip and so was supplied by air-drops until the Imphal-Kohima road was cleared. During these two battles 30,000 non-combatants and 30,000 casualties were flown out of Imphal while two and a half Divisions and their equipment, replacement troops and 50,000 tons of supplies were flown in.

In a Despatch summarising operations by PR Force from its formation on 1 June until 16 November, Wg Cdr Wise reported, "Very Long Range Photographic Reconnaissance had to be abandoned for a period of just over four months... Banks of cloud stretching for hundreds of miles and extending from almost sea-level to anything up to 35,000 feet often made photography impossible. From the beginning of June to the end of September these conditions were being encountered almost every day and it was not until October that any real results were achieved."

"Flying out of Alipore we were horribly and

dangerously blasé. Japs no worry, only the weather. I ask you—that milk run to Viccie Point. Same time, same height, almost every day of the month." wrote Max Howland of 684 Sqn, "But what weather! Watching narrow strips of fabric peeling back off the wing in the rain. Being told on arrival that wouldn't be able to tell the difference between blue sky and black cloud—oh yeah!—till it happened. And those other storms, the one we saw dead on track as we crossed the Sunderbans—a brown storm—the daddy of them all. And flying past a cu-nim at 33,000 feet and not even halfway up!"

For the fighter-reconnaissance squadrons the monsoon brought no end to their operations, merely a reduction in the number of sorties as low-level tactical reconnaissance became very dangerous in heavy rain and low cloud among the mountains. No.1 IAF even managed to undertake further PR sorties—on 12 September Sqn Ldr Arjan Singh DFC, flying LE804, with Flg Offs Rao and Kak in LD830 and LE861 carried out an extensive and valuable reconnaissance over the enemy's bases in the Kalemyo area, escorted by six Spitfires of 152 Sqn. Five days later Flt Lt Chatterjee in LE861, with fighter escort, covered Kalemyo and the Japanese advanced landing-ground at Taukkyan, twenty miles further south.

Despite bad weather conditions 354 sorties were made during August, sixty-two of these entailing photography, along the Tiddim road and the Chindwin River. These tactical recces in support off the XXXIII Corps were carried through into September, to Sittaung. In addition to providing tactical reconnaissance for the ground forces on the Central Front, No.1 Sqn IAF operated in support of the Chindit columns whose regular supply drops were dependent on accurate forecasting of the troops' positions by the Hurricanes.

From Barrackpore 9th PR Sqn sent a detachment to Tingkawk Sakan in the north and four aircraft to Chittagong for operations when the weather cleared sufficiently to enable sorties down the coast to be made.

On 1 September the greater part of the 9th PR Sqn was detached to operate under HQ 10th USAAF, from Tingkawk Sakan in North-west Burma. The 20 Tac/R Sqn also moved base to Tingkawk Sakan, but as a component of PR Force, co-ordinating its operations with those of the 9th PR Sqn. Only 381 sorties were flown by the PR Squadrons during the month, 168 of these being wholly successful and a further 100 partially so. On the last day of the month another alteration was made to the organisation when 171 Wing was disbanded, to become the RAF element of PR Force at Alipore. The 24th Combat Mapping Sqn meanwhile was partly responsible to PR Force and undertook only nine sorties; the squadron's flights were mostly controlled by its other master, HQ 14th Air Force, for transport of petrol into China in the bomb-bay tanks of the F-7s.

Operations by other American PR squadrons came to halt as the demand for photographic cover on the Northern Front temporarily ceased while Stilwell's forces stopped all offensive operations, awaiting the outcome of the battle on the Central Front.

During 'U-Gô' the Imperial Japanese Army had no need of aerial reconnaissance but, as the headquarters lost touch with their forward troops and with the movement of British and Indian forces, a Dinah was sent out over Imphal on 24 September. It was followed by a Spitfire Mk.VIII and destroyed near Pinlebu. The anticipated repeat operation came the following day when another Dinah was chased through cloud by Spitfires of 155 Sqn. 'Pink One' (Plt Off A. Witteridge) scored hits then pulled up to allow his No.2, Flt Sgt Lunnon-Wood, to attack. "It blew up! Just like the films—little bits—poof!" the Flt Sgt reported on landing.

Early in 1944, Mountbatten had proposed two plans; an advance across the Chindwin to recapture Northern Burma as far as the line Pakokku-Mandalay-Lashio (Operation 'Capital') and an amphibious attack on Rangoon (Operation 'Dracula'), to be followed by an advance northwards. The Chiefs of Staff, however, preferred operations in the north to be confined to a holding operation until 'Dracula' could be mounted early in 1945 as a step towards an assault on Sumatra or Malaya.

As part of the preparations for later operations, 160 Sqn increased the air survey flights from 16 September and, by the end of the month, completed the cover of Simaloer Island. On 1 October a survey of Nias was begun despite bad weather along the Sumatran coast, further delayed after FL935 developed engine-trouble on the 9th and returned on two engines.

Early in October the airfield surface at China Bay began breaking uo under the monsoon rains; on the 10th FL936 was again available but became bogged down while taxiing and the intended sortie to Sumatra was carried out by 684 Sqn's MM228, 'D'. Efforts were made to obtain PSP (pierced steel plank) to surface the hardstanding areas but it was not supplied. The reason became clear at the end of the month when 222 Group gave up res-ponsibility for the airfield which was then taken over by the Royal Navy as Royal Naval Air Station Trincomalee. 160 Sqn's Liberators were withdrawn to Kankesanturai and 684 Sqn's detachment was instructed to move to Minneriya. Flt Lt Guy DFC, the Detachment Commander, observed that this would add eighty miles flying to each sortie and advised that the detachment should return to Alipore; so authority was promptly given for the Mosquitos to remain at China Bay. On the Central Front, 14th Army continued its pressure against the retreating Japanese and No.1 Sqn IAF was constantly on tactical reconnaissance, despite the bad weather, as 161 Bde advanced, fighting their way along the Tiddim-Kalewa road and through enemy blocks in the 'Stockades' area east of Fort White.

While US forces in the South West Pacific Area were preparing to assault Pelelieu and Morotai in the Moluccas, the British Eastern Fleet, based at Trincomalee, began a series of operations in the Indian Ocean as a diversion to deter the Japanese from reinforcing their Pacific Ocean garrisons. The first operation ('Light A') was intended for 17 September as a strike against enemy airfields in Sumatra, accompanied by PR of Pangkalan Soesoe, but the weather was so bad that aircraft could not be flown off the carriers. Operation 'Light B' the following day, was an attack by aircraft from the fleet carriers *Victorious* and *Indomitable* against the Sumatran port of Sigli. After the PR Flight's success over Padang in August, a total of eight Hellcats of No.5 Naval Fighter Wing had been fitted with camera mountings. Four were flown off *Indomitable* on the morning of 18 September. From 1839 Sqn, Lt N.G. Mitchell in FN433 covered Pangkalan Soesoe, Tandjoengpoera and Medan while Sub-Lt F.J. Rankin flew FN396, 'J', to Koetaradja and Sabang. From 1844 Sqn Sub-Lts J.C. Ruffin and A.R. Anderson obtained cover of the Nicobar Islands, Sigli and Meulaboh successfully in FN434 and JV143.

A second Eastern Fleet diversionary attack (Operation 'Millet') was made on 17 October when a force bombarded the Nicobar Islands. Oblique photographs were taken during the action by Maj Hay in his Corsair and, again, high-level verticals were taken by the Hellcats of *Indomitable*'s PR Flight. Two days later, a Dinah located the Fleet and twelve Oscars were later detected and intercepted by the carrier's fighters. Seven Oscars were claimed destroyed for the loss of two Corsairs and a Hellcat. At Command HQ it was hoped that an advance base for reconnaissance of the Netherlands-Indies and Malaya would become available in March 1945, following a decision by the British Chiefs of Staff to develop an airfield in the Cocos-Keeling Islands early in the coming year. Meanwhile, only the Fleet's PR aircraft were available, supplemented by the Hellcats of 888 Sqn in Ceylon.

The squadron had embarked for Ceylon in HMS *Rajah* and the Hellcats were launched from the carrier on 11 October to work-up on photographic operations at Minneriya.

In Assam, where the monsoon rains were decreasing, two Spitfires of 681 Sqn were detached to begin operations from Imphal on 6 October and, four days later, the remaining aircraft of 9th PR Sqn were moved to Chittagong to meet Army demands for reconnaissance along the Arakan coast. The weather rapidly improved and a total of 781 sorties was flown by PR Force in October.

A despatch on operations by PR Force between June and November 1944 recorded, "Two sorties which should have met the strongest opposition of all, according to the state of the enemy's defences and the height at which the aircraft flew, did not have a shot fired at them. These were

two low-level oblique recces of the Akyab waterfront, flown by Spitfires of 681 Sqn at heights between 50 and 200ft. Specially speeded-up cameras were used for these sorties and excellent results were obtained". The Photographic Section's Sgt D.E. Fuller reduced the time interval of the F.24/14in. cameras mounted in the aircraft to give overlapping large-scale prints; the sorties were flown by 681 Sqn's Flight Commanders, Flg Offs A.K. Hadingham and J.W.(Brick) Bradford.

These were but two of a series of low-level sorties, such as those of 25 October when Sqn Ldr Procter (awarded the DFC in September) in Spitfire PR.XI MB776, 'Y', his 'personal' aircraft, led a formation of five Spitfires to Cheduba Island to take simultaneous low-level photographs of possible landing beaches at low tide. A final operation in the series was recorded simply in Sqn Ldr Procter's Pilot's Flying Log Book; "Nov.13. Spitfire XI, Y. (Pilot-) Self. (Duty-) PR Obliques 100ft Akyab waterfront. 2hr 55".

'Brick' Bradford, based at No.21 Ferry Control at Karachi, ferried Spitfires until April 1944, then was posted to 681 Sqn. He summarised the squadron's operations during the year following, "During 1944 and 1945 and my association with the squadron, we did all types of photography over all Burma and as far east as the Chinese border and south-east to the Siamese border. We covered airports, bridges, railways, roads, towns, harbours etc. A certain amount of mapping was done and also old-fashioned reconnaissance, ie, go down and take a look visually. We also did before and after shots when the bombers were out. We had two detachments working up at the front line supplying close support for the army. These were the Detachments from Imphal and Akyab to Kalemyo, Monywa, Meiktila and eventually to Mingaladon".

By late November, No.1 Sqn IAF was fully re-equipped with Hurricane IICs, fitted with the two-camera 'universal installation'. On the 22nd Flt Lt Chatterjee in HW557 and Flg Off Kapur in LD240 were on reconnaissance over Wetkauk when LD240 developed a coolant leak. Kapur found that his long-range tanks could not be released and when he crash-landed, the Hurricane turned over and caught fire with the pilot trapped, the Squadron's Operations Record Book noted. "The entire ruddy mechanism had gone on strike. He took out his revolver, took aim—and then a strange thing happened. The revolver worked; the hinges of the emergency release panel gave way and, jabbing at the Perspex with his jungle knife, Kapur dashed out and threw himself to the ground. He was given up for dead by his fellow. After this, Kapur walked some thirty miles through the jungle before meeting a Punjabi patrol three days later". The following week, on a Tac/R sortie to Shwegyin, Flg Off Eduijee DFC crashed and was killed while making an attack in LE804. During the month the Indian squadron made 524 sorties with a total flying time of 1,000hr 30min.

133 Above: *This B-25C of 684 Sqn, probably MA956, was relegated to courier duties at Comilla in 1944. A large astrodome was fitted in place of the upper turret and the aircraft refinished PRU Blue*

134 Right: *Hurricanes delivered to India in the Tropical Land Scheme were required to be refinished. This IIC, BP704, of 28 Sqn was unusual in having the colours of the Temperate Scheme pattern interchanged before new markings (as of September 1943) were applied*

135: *Between January 1944 and May 1945, Spitfire PR.XI MB776, marked with his initials, was flown regularly by Wg Cdr Procter. It is unclear whether the light patches on the wings are abbreviated White identity bands or evidence of repair work*

136: *An overall PRU Blue Mosquito PR .XVI rolling at take-off*

137: *Wt Off Davison, a navigator with 684 Sqn, about to board Mosquito PR.IX MM295, 'C', on the brick-paved dispersal area at Alipore during a lull in the monsoon rains of 1944. Note the warning notice, 'Beware of Airscrews', inside the access door and Davison's very neat back parachute. Also of note are the special canvas-topped flying boots for use in tropical areas*

The Mosquito fiasco

So effective and reassuring was 684 Sqn's experience of the Mosquitos that in January 1944 the Air Ministry planned to equip no fewer than twenty-two bomber and strike squadrons in Air Command South-East Asia with the Mosquito, the first to be squadrons already in the Command, equipped with the Vengeance and Beaufighter and De Havilland were instructed to arrange for the manufacture of replacement airframe components at Karachi.

At Yelahanka, near Bangalore, No.1672 (Mosquito) Conversion Unit was established to implement a programme of conversion to the Mosquito FB.VI, beginning with 45 Sqn in March. In July 82 Sqn began conversion at Kolar, 35 miles to the east. Each squadron moved, in turn, to Ranchi, 45 Sqn flying its first Mosquito operation on 1 October. The programme began to gain momentum as 47 Sqn moved to Yelahanka on 7 October, followed by 110 Sqn three weeks later and 84 a week after that.

It seemed likely that 681 Sqn's effort would produce a record photographic coverage in November but all Mosquito operations came to an abrupt halt when on 10 November a signal was released to units requiring all Mosquitos to be grounded pending inspection; it had been rumoured that many Mosquitos had broken up in the air during violent manoeuvres and a series of accidents now brought matters to a head.

138 Above: In April 1944, Mosquito PR.XVI MM332, 'A', of 681 Sqn flew in factory finish of overall PRU Blue with 'Medium' India Command markings and aircraft letters in Sky

The crew of HP886, a Mosquito FB.VI of 82 Sqn, died when the aircraft crashed during training on 13 September, apparently due to wing or tail failure. On 4 October, the wing leading edge of a 45 Sqn Mk.VI buckled in flight but the pilot was able to land safely. On the 20th two more Mosquitos crashed; HP919 of 82 Sqn lost a wing during bombing practice and HP921 of 45 Sqn broke up when about to land at Kumbhirgram in Assam—all four aircrew were killed. A few days later it was explained that the faults were a result of aircraft standing for long periods in the open; extreme heat had caused the glue to crack and the upper surfaces to lift from the spars.

Major de Havilland had been dismayed at the operational use in India of the first Mosquitos delivered the year before, in which casein glue was employed—supposedly unsuited to the heat and humidity of the monsoon season—and the glue failure was immediately suggested as the cause of the structural failures. It soon became clear, however, that the adhesive was not the principal or only cause of trouble.

In March 1944, production of the first batch of Mosquitos in Australia had been disrupted when it was discovered that components failed to 'mate' and gaps occurred in the glue joints between the main spar and the plywood skin of the wings. Under stress, the wing surface could become detached and the box-section spar assembly collapse.

In the United Kingdom, a series of fatal flying accidents among Mosquitos of various Marks (at the rate of two to four per month from January to June 1944) was attributed to the failure of the wings and HQ No.8 Gp reported alarm over nine accidents in the ten weeks from

27 June to 16 September, some caused by wing failure.

An investigation by Sqn Ldr C.J. Chabot of HQ Base Air Forces, S.E. Asia, a Headquarters formed in October 1944 to administer maintenance and supply for RAF units in ACSEA, and Mr P.G. Myers, De Havilland's representative in India, attributed the accidents definitely to faulty manufacture. Myers signalled, *"Defects not due to climate conditions. The standard of gluing... leaves much to be desired"*. The structural findings threw some light on the structural failure of 684 Sqn's HJ760 in December 1943, earlier ascribed to a 'bird strike'. Meanwhile, uncertain if the cause of failure was the heat and humidity, BAFSEA required the operational squadrons to fly-in to No.1 CMU Kanchrapara all Mosquitos that had been in the Command for more than three months—or one month if received from the Middle East. A method of opening up part of the wing for internal inspection with mirrors was devised and, when a split spar was found in an aircraft with only 52 flying hours, all Mosquitos were grounded on 1 November. Most of the Mk.VI aircraft in the Command were declared unserviceable and struck off charge (SOC) during the following weeks.

On 26 November 1944 HQ BAFSEA signalled, *"There have three been serious accidents attributable to faults in the wing-spar manufacture. It cannot be definitely stated that these are due to faulty manufacture or to glue deterioration but the evidence goes to show that there are errors in the shaping of the wood making up the spar assembly. A common fault running through one series of Mosquitos coming mainly from one factory is that the pieces of wood are so shaped that, when assembled, essential elements do not make surface contact and no adhesion takes place"*.

Wg Cdr Jefford has commented, "shortly after the war ended, Nos 47, 82, 84 and 110 Sqns carried out some attacks on Indonesian nationalists in the Dutch East Indies but operations were hampered by the discovery of more faulty wing structures. Plagued as it was by periodic groundings and flying restrictions, the Mosquito was of doubtful value and the type was withdrawn from service in the attack role in the Far East before the end of 1946.

"Although De Havilland were reluctant to acknowledge that their construction techniques were faulty there seems little doubt that this was the case in 1944, although it was more a question of quality control than a fault in the Mosquito's design. With hindsight, however, two additional factors become apparent. First, it seems probable that the evident weakness of the Mosquito's wing was exacerbated by the stresses imposed by attack operations. This conclusion is based on the fact that, although inspection of 684 Sqn's aircraft revealed that they suffered from the same defects as the fighter-bombers, the squadron did not suffer any catastrophic failures. Furthermore, despite the early post-war

withdrawal of Mosquitos from the attack squadrons in the Far East, the type continued to give safe and relatively trouble-free service with 81 Sqn which flew Mosquitos from Singapore on high-level PR and survey work, until as late as 1955.

"Second, there must have been some basis for the manufacturer's contention that the glue broke down under tropical conditions. Mosquitos issued to squadrons in the Far East from mid-1945 onwards came from later production batches with RF and TE serials. Most of these aircraft were built after De Havilland had tightened up on quality control. Despite this, the type continued to suffer from faulty structures and Mosquitos were still being grounded for defective glued joints in Singapore in 1954, eg VT628 of No.45 Sqn. It must be concluded that regardless of the type of glue employed none was really able to stand up to the high ambient temperature and humidity of the tropics".

The effects of the discovery were far-reaching; de Havillands ordered the destruction of components not made with formaldehyde glue, the intended manufacture of airframe parts at Karachi was abandoned and the re-equipping of additional squadrons in India was delayed. It first seemed that the defects were in the Mk.VI aircraft built by Standard Motors Co. at Coventry. Of twenty-four various Mosquitos inspected by 8 November, 23 had defects adjacent to rib No.12, 6ft from the wing-tips, but within a few days similar faults had been found in four PR.IXs, five PRXVIs and seven FB.VIs, all built by De Havilland at Hatfield.

684 Squadron's aircraft at China Bay were flown back to Alipore and by 20 November the squadron was left with only four Mosquito PR.IXs passed as airworthy. Of the PR.XIVs, NS501, 'G', fitted with a fuselage drop-tank, was given clearance for a priority sortie to Victoria Point on the 20th but a drop in oil pressure forced the aircraft to return on one engine to Cox's Bazar. Priority emergency landing permission was given by flying control and the pilot, Flg Off R.W.E. Duke made a low approach. As he came into land on the one engine, a Hurricane cut in front and landed in spite of warning flares fired by the controller. Duke attempted another circuit but the aircraft crashed beside the runway; both pilot and the navigator, Flg Off A.O. Rhodes, escaped unhurt.

An investigating team led by Maj de Havilland from Farnborough and the manufacturers arrived in India on 26 November. A week later it was reported that the accidents were "not caused by deterioration of glue but excessive shrinkage of aircraft in India during the monsoon" but Air HQ India recorded the principal causes of the accidents as (1) defective scarf joints between the main spar and edge boom at ribs Nos.11 and 12, (2) failure of the fixing between spar and the plywood surface of the wing—as found in Mosquitos in England.

De Havilland introduced a modification (Mod.638) on the production lines, an additional cover strip to the plywood joints along the front wing spar, and provided additional sets for fitting to Mosquitos already in service.

The method of opening the wings for inspection, followed by repair by the application of an external patch, was abandoned and replaced by a simple test for lifting of the plywood skin along the spar. The joint cover strips were applied to the serviceable aircraft.

On return to England, Maj de Havilland told an MAP meeting on 1 January 1945 that the wing failures could be attributed to water-penetration, differential shrinkage and to defective glue joints. In addition to the intended application of joint cover strips, it was suggested that, as Air Command SE Asia was already prepared to accept un-camouflaged aircraft, heat-reflective aluminium finish be applied to Mosquitos in the Far East.

Although records showed that accidents classified as due to 'loss of control' were three times more frequent on Mosquitos than other types of aircraft and six Mosquitos of the MAP's Telecommunication Research Establishment also were found to have wing defects, the Ministry forestalled possible loss of confidence among the fifty Mosquito squadrons by stating that the accidents in India were caused by "faults largely due to climate".

The PR Force had no medium-sized transport aircraft of its own and until September 1944 had been able to borrow aircraft from either an American or an RAF squadron but, when detachments were attached to advanced Army headquarters, it became impossible to keep them adequately supplied. During the first six months of 1944 each of the B-25Cs of B Flt 684 Sqn was frequently used for the fast transport of senior officers, including the Fourteenth Army Commander Lt-Gen William Slim and members of his Staff between Calcutta and the forward headquarters. Requests for transport aircraft met with no response so in October PR Force had to organize its own courier service using the B-25Cs for the supply of materials, transport of senior officers and squadron personnel, and the delivery of photographic prints to forward areas.

On 25 October 1944 Wg Cdr W.E. Lowry DFC, took over command of 684 Sqn from Wg Cdr W.B. Murray, with only six serviceable Mosquitos. By the end of the month seven aircraft had been despatched to No.1 CMU Kanchrapara for inspection and possible repair; all were expected to be off the squadron strength for at least a month and other aircraft were to follow. The few Mosquitos cleared for operations were used for survey of the Victoria Point area, PR Force HQ instructing that no other targets were to be allocated until the survey had been completed. Apart from a single sortie to the Nicobar Islands by N5-145, 'Z', on 21 October, the B-25Cs remained on courier duties.

On 5 November MA957, 'X', flown by Flt Lt N. Robison, was sent out on an emergency rescue search from China Bay. A Walrus Air-Sea Rescue aircraft of 292 sqn's Detachment in Ceylon was also employed but was forced to alight on the sea by extreme weather and poor visibility. Camera operator Alan Fox recalls, "One of the Superfortress crews had seen a fellow crew ditch their aircraft, damaged by Jap fighters, in the sea some distance out in the Bay of Bengal. They had got an approximate fix, but this needed to be made more precise so that air-sea rescue launches could make their way to the ditched crew. Useful supplies and equipment also needed to be dropped as soon as possible. Even as we vaulted out of our lorry, preparations were afoot for a search by the B-25 which had accompanied the Mosquitos on our detachment. Since additional pairs of eyes were always useful for a job like this, several of us offered to join the official crew and the offer was accepted. I found myself behind Bob Holroyd, one of the ground crew, as he climbed up the ladder of the rear hatch.

"I was just about to follow him when there came a shout from the cockpit. Our lorry was in their taxiing path and had to be moved. I looked around but there was now nobody else at hand to do this short stretch of driving. Though unqualified as a driver I knew enough of the essentials to have driven lorries loaded with cameras from the Section to aircraft dispersal when necessary, so I had no hesitation in undertaking this chore. But such was their haste to get away that, even as I got the lorry moving, the rear hatch was pulled up and they were taxiing off. Rather disappointed, I made my way back to the Section.

"Several hours later, feeling slightly uneasy, I wandered across to the mechanics' hut and found the small group there even more so. The B-25 had only fuel for four hours but this should have been more than enough for the fix given them. As darkness fell we stopped bothering to look and listen. The flare path was lit in a quite irrational hope, but the flames, guttering in the wind off the sea, now seemed forlorn.

"Next morning it all turned out to have been a mistake. The aircraft thought to have ditched was in fact limping home on two of its four engines, skimming the waves but managing to stay airborne. It had landed at another airfield after the B-25 had taken off. Our own crew, searching for an aircraft that was not there, had fatally reached their point of no return. Among those lost was LAC Smith, the other camera operator remaining from the early days of No.3 PRU(India)".

To make matters worse, MA956, 'E', was damaged by fire during routine inspection on 15 December. Although prompt action saved the aircraft from destruction, the nose section was distorted beyond the repair capability of the squadron and only the veteran N5-145, 'Z', was left serviceable.

The 40th PR Sqn flew 113 successful missions during November but suffered a first loss on the 27th, when 2/Lt T.U. Permain failed to return from a sortie over Central Burma. The following day the squadron recorded a total operational flying time of 2,068 hours.

At the end of November HQ 3 TAF was disbanded and changes were made in PR squadron detachments, 681 Sqn's Comilla Detachment was withdrawn and the Imphal Detachment increased in strength. The half-dozen F-5As of 9th PR Sqn at Chittagong were sent to Tingkawk Sakan for a brief period before the whole squadron moved to a new base at Myitkyina, and a new Arakan Detachment from 40th PR Sqn, re-equipped with Lockheed F-5Es, was stationed at Cox's Bazar for medium-range reconnaissance.

681 Sqn's Spitfires were thus committed to medium-range targets and the F-5Es of US 40th PR Sqn to longer-range sorties over western Siam and south-eastern Burma.

To make up for the lack of operational aircraft occasioned by the grounding of 684 Sqn's Mosquitos the US 24th Combat Mapping Sqn's F-7s (photographic reconnaissance B-24s) were temporarily placed under the control of PR Force. Ten survey sorties were flown by Superfortresses of XX Bomber Command and some short-range tasks were allocated to the F-5Es of US 40th PR Sqn.

It was anticipated that, when the overland route for supplies from Assam to China was re-opened and secured against further enemy attack. USAAF elements in the India-Burma Theatre would be re-deployed in the Central Pacific Area. Already, the B-29s of 58th US Bomber Wing, after flying twenty missions from their Chengtu airfields, were being withdrawn to bases near Kharagpur and made temporarily available to SEAC for bombing raids and reconnaissance.

Pending delivery of the projected 'Very Long Range' Mosquito PR.34 or the planned military occupation of an advanced base, the only means of obtaining the required cover of distant areas would be by calling upon the services of the camera-equipped B-29s or by employing naval aircraft within the limitations of aircraft carrier availability.

XX Bomber Command of the USAAF, intended to operate from forward airfields in China, had no photographic reconnaissance component but, as most of the targets for the Command's Superfortresses were far beyond the reach of other aircraft, a few B-29s had been field-modified for PR use. Meanwhile Boeing developed a reconnaissance version of the aircraft although the Americans had earlier concluded that 'due to size and weight and operational altitude the B-29 is not considered to be a suitable type for conversion'. Nevertheless, Superfortresses were so converted and designated F-13, with mountings for 'trimetrogon' K.17Bs, two K.22 and one K. 18 camera. This conversion was soon followed by an improved model, F-13A, developed from the B-29A, with fuel-tanks in the bomb-compartment and mountings for K.18 and K.22 vertical and oblique cameras. A Photographic Reconnaissance Detachment was formed by XX Bomber Command in October 1944, initially equipped with converted B-29s of 468th Bombardment Gp's 794th Sqn. When F-13As began arriving in November, the Command established 'C' Flight of the 1st PR Sqn at Hsinching in China and 'A' Flight with four aircraft based at Chakulia, 100 miles west of Calcutta, from where ten 'shake-down' survey sorties were flown for HQ SEAC in December 1944, to Penang, Bangkok and Saigon.

139: Hurricane FR.IIC LB835, 'L', of No.4 Sqn Indian Air Force, being fitted with vertical cameras at Cox's Bazar in January 1945. Note the aperture for the oblique camera in the fuselage side, and how exposure to the weather has heightened the contrast between the two upper-surface camouflage colours

Beyond the Chindwin River

Operation 'Capital'

In October 1944 Stilwell was recalled to the USA and changes were made in the SEAC command structure, followed in November by the formation of ALFSEA (Allied Land Forces SE Asia). By this time Slim's plans for the recapture of Northern Burma and the destruction of the Japanese Army between the Chindwin and Irrawaddy (Operation 'Capital') were in progress. On the coast XV Corps were moving to clear northern Arakan in Operation 'Romulus', prior to assaulting Akyab. By late November, 14th Army had reached the Chindwin and had secured bridge-heads, ready to advance for the decisive battle in the Ye-U—Shwebo Plain where mobile columns and armour could operate to best advantage.

As 14th Army began probing across the Chindwin and the possibility developed of a widespread and rapid advance to the Irrawaddy, it became clear that the need for tactical reconnaissance as practised in Arakan was somewhat reduced. The Army now needed more large-scale cover of distant areas than the fighter-reconnaissance squadrons could manage. Early in December Sqn Ldr Rajaram replaced Sqn Ldr Arjan Singh as OC No.1 Sqn but on the 15th the squadron was withdrawn following a decision that all 14th Army tactical reconnaissance should be taken over by 28 Sqn, with one Flight attached to IV Corps and one to XXXIII Corps. From this time on, the IAF fighter-reconnaissance squadrons became responsible for operations in Arakan. On 9 October, 28 Sqn commanded by Sqn Ldr H.G.F. Larsen DFC, moved forward to Tamu, just within the Burma frontier, partly re-equipped with fighter-reconnaissance Hurricane IICs. These aircraft were modified by having their inboard cannon removed; some had a forward-facing camera in the starboard wing in place of one cannon but most later aircraft were fitted with fuselage camera-mountings similar to those of the Mk.IIB. Several aircraft of No.1 Sqn remained at Imphal until late in the month and took part in a few more sorties in company with pilots of 28 Sqn until 21 November.

During the monsoon period, nine Hurricane squadrons had been re-equipped with Republic Thunderbolts in India and no further Hurricane IICs were due for delivery. On 15 November an instruction was issued for all units to bring their non-operational Hurricanes up to operational standard; some had been stored for long periods and the fabric covering, particularly of the tail units needed replacement. The fabric of Hurricanes was often so rotted beneath the coats of dope that it tore away from the airframe and it was normal practice, unknown to the Air Ministry, to completely recover and refinish Hurricanes after twelve months in the Command. All replacement Hurricanes for the fighter-bomber and fighter-reconnaissance squadrons would now have to be provided from Command resources, although this entailed the re-issue of old aircraft by MUs, those not fitted with bomb-racks to be used in the reconnaissance role.

On the 27th Flt Lt K. MacVicar, DFC, in LD299 of 28 Sqn, a hundred miles further south near Ye-U, came under fire and struck a tree while taking evasive action. The Hurricane's radiator was damaged but the pilot force-landed safely and, after destroying the aircraft, headed north. He was twice fired upon by Japanese patrols, but made his way through their forward positions under artillery fire and made contact with advancing British troops five days later.

After a period of Tac/R operations on the North-West Frontier No 2 Sqn IAF, also flying Hurricane IICs, moved to Cox's Bazar then south to Mambur at the end of November and flew PR sorties to Thaungdaw and Maungdaw for XV Corps on I December. Two aircraft were lost on the following successive days; Flg Off Sharma crashed on the 2nd and Flt Off Nair crashed LA316 on the 3rd but returned safely to the squadron.

After the debacle at Imphal, Gen Kimura was made Commander of Burma Area Army. He believed that he could only hold the country by maintaining a defensive line from Lashio through Mandalay and Yenangyaung to Kangaw on the Arakan coast, thereby protecting the Burmese oilfields and the essential rice-growing areas of the Lower Sittang and the Irrawaddy Delta. In December 1944 he disposed Honda's 33rd Army between Lashio and the Upper Irrawaddy to oppose the forces of the Chinese-American Northern Combat Area Command and British 36 Div. Katamura's 15th Army was deployed along the Irrawaddy from Mandalay to Pakokku, and Sakuari's 28th Army to the west and south in Arakan.

By now 28 Sqn was providing support for IV Corps' advance from Sittaung where 19 Div had gained a bridgehead across the Chindwin. Earlier in the month, however, the Japanese had begun to withdraw their forces to hold the defensive line from the Northern Shan States to the coast at Akyab. The light opposition offered by the enemy east of the Chindwin alerted Slim to the withdrawal of the Japanese 15th Army but he was determined to fight them in open country and formulated a new and audacious plan, 'Extended Capital', aimed at cutting the main enemy line of communication in Central Burma and destroying the Japanese army between Meiktila and Mandalay in terrain where 14th Army's armour would be most effective. Preparations were also made for following the capture of Meiktila with a drive southwards to Rangoon, a plan unofficially called 'Sob' ('Sea or Bust'). No.10 Sqn IAF, based at Ramu since early December, was equipped with Hurricane IICs, several of which were fitted with the 'universal mounting' and K.20 cameras. The squadron's operations began on the 23rd but, apart from a few offensive recces, No.10 Sqn was employed until the end of March 1945 in the ground-attack role and undertook no tactical reconnaissance.

In spite of difficulties, most sorties flown by the PR squadrons were successful. Two, in particular, which were expected to meet strong opposition, produced no enemy reaction; these resulted from an urgent demand from the Army for large-scale details of the Japanese defences on the north-west coast of Akyab Island where a landing, planned for 20 January, was brought forward to be launched on the 3rd. On 30 December, while Wg Cdr F.D. Procter, OC 681 Sqn, made twelve runs at 6,000 ft in PL769, 'A', to obtain vertical photographs using, for the first time, an F.53/36in-lens cine camera, Flt Lt R.E. Ford in MB985, 'R' and Flt Lt R.F. Death in PA946, 'E', made high-speed runs at 200ft along the coastline to obtain low-level obliques.

Wg Cdr Butler and the crews of 160 Sqn were unwilling to give up opportunities for photographic sorties, although HQ 222 Gp had made it clear that, because of the Liberator Mk.III's lack of defensive fire-power, there was no compulsion to continue photographic reconnaissance. However, C Flight (three Liberators and four crews) was allocated to PR duties on 4 December to undertake flights from Kankesanturai for the PR Board of the Supreme Commander's HQ at Kandy, co-ordinated with Fleet operations.

140 Below: *A typical 28 Sqn oblique picture, reproduced slightly larger than life-size, showing an ineffectually camouflaged river steamer on the Irrawaddy near Sagaing on 16 January 1945. The appalling condition of most of the roads in Burma, and the constant threat of air attack on them, meant that the Japanese were obliged to make much use of river traffic to supply their garrisons*

141: *Indian troops of the 4/ 7 Rajput Rifles occupied Kalemyo on 16 November 1944. There, some 250 miles from the Chindwin, they found this wreck of a Mitsubishi Ki 46 'Dinah' on the perimeter of the airfield. The aircraft was one of a just a few of this type to reach the 8th* Sentai *(as indicated by the winged '8' emblem on the fin) which was primarily a bomber unit*

142: *In conditions of exposure to strong sunlight and humidity the fabric covering of aircraft deteriorated within a few months. Here a Hurricane awaits recovering of its fuselage*

143: *A camera-equipped Boeing B-29 of XX Bomber Command. 'Shanghai Lil' of the 676th Bomb Sqn at Piardoba displays mission markers for eight 'Hump' transport flights, 16 bombing missions and three photo-reconnaissance missions*

144 Left: 'Bengal Lancer', a Boeing B-29-30-BW, 42-24487, of the 794th BS, showing the bright red tail bands of the unit

145 Below: A Liberator of 159 Sqn over Kaungh-mudyai in Burma. Japanese positions below are receiving a severe bombing, (note the dust clouds) but in deference to Burmese sensibilities, the pagoda has been left untouched

146: *Hellcat PR.Is of 888 Sqn being refuelled on Colombo racecourse in Ceylon during their period of training there in October-November 1944. It was proposed that the aircraft be repainted PRU Blue over the Temperate Sea Scheme camouflage in which they had arrived, but no such paint was available. Consequently, they were all painted in a specially mixed dark blue, similar to that used on 684 Sqn's B-25s, which were a common sight at China Bay at that time*

147: *An unarmed Hellcat of 888 Sqn undergoing maintenance, probably on the escort carrier HMS* Rajah *in September 1944 during the voyage out from Belfast to their new operational base at China Bay/Colombo racecourse*

148: *Hellcat FR.II, JW370, 'A', of 804 Sqn taking-off from HMS* Ameer *during Operation 'Stacey' in March 1944. As was usual during flying operations, crowds of 'goofers' are sitting around watching the fun*

149: *Aboard* Indefatigable *during preparations for Operation 'Lentil', the strikes on Pangkalan Brandan on 4 January 1945, the Hellcat PR.Is of 888 Sqn merely had the red of their roundels over-painted white. The Firefly of 1770 Sqn further forward on the deck wore standard Eastern Fleet markings*

150: *This Nakajima Ki-44-II-koo (s/n 1134) of the 85th Sentai, seen at Nanking in China, was flown by 20-victory ace Koki Wakamatsu, leader of the 2nd Chutai, in defence of the Palembang oil refineries. Wakamatsu, nicknamed 'Red Daruma', was the top ace of the 85th, but was killed in action on 18 December 1944. The characteristic bulbous engine cowling and short fuselage and wingspan of the 'Tojo' are clearly shown in this picture. On the fin leading edge is the red unit emblem, while the red fuselage band denotes the Chutai leader*

151: *Major, later Lt Col, RC Hay DSC, RM, (on right) the Wing Leader of 47 Naval Fighter Wing, poses with bearded Commander TWB Shaw, DSC, RN, the Commander Operations aboard HMS* Illustrious. *They are seen here at China Bay in March 1944 in front of a Corsair*

152: *Lt Knight flying Corsair JT422, 'T8-B', of 1836 Sqn. Finished in faded Temperate Sea Scheme camouflage the aircraft carries 36in Dull Blue/White fusealge roundels, with the newly-introduced Wing symbol, 'T', hastily chalked in place*

153 Right: *Corsair 'T7L' of 1834 Sqn from HMS* Victorious *being ferried, probably to save aviation fuel, on a lighter in Colombo harbour. The squadron took part in the raids on Palembang in January 1945*

154 Below: *11 September 1944. The Corsairs of 1834 and 1836 Sqns (parts of the 47th Fighter Wing) taxying out from the racecourse strip at Colombo in order to join HMS* Victorious *for an attack on Sigli. All wear recently modified national markings. The Defiant target tug was used by 797 Fleet Requirements Unit*

155: *A low-level oblique taken by Maj Hay, as Air Co-ordinator, of camouflaged oil storage tanks at the refinery at Pladjoe bursting into flames during Operation 'Meridian I', 24 January 1945*

156: *'Meridian I'; the first strike against the Pladjoe refinery created such dense smoke that Maj Hay was unable to take vertical pictures of the damage*

Fleet re-organisation

Pacific Fleet operations

At the 'Octagon' Conference of September 1944, Churchill, who unlike the US State Department, believed it essential that the Asian nations should see Britain taking an active part in the final offensive against Japan, offered President Roosevelt the services of a British naval force in the Pacific. Despite the opposition of Adm Ernest King, US Chief of Naval Operations, Roosevelt accepted the offer.

Although American concern was justified by the Royal Navy's insufficient replenishment facilities and a shortage of supply vessels, the Allied Combined Chiefs of Staff approved the deployment of British air and naval forces to the Pacific Ocean, provided only that a totally independent 'fleet train' of oilers and supply vessels could be maintained.

At Trincomalee, the British Eastern Fleet was divided on 22 November 1944 into two. An East Indies Fleet was formed, including five battleships and an Escort Carrier Squadron; to embark on its five carriers were several squadrons of Hellcats and, later, one of Seafires for photographic reconnaissance, air cover and spotting for the Fleet along the coasts of Burma, Sumatra and Malaya. A British Pacific Fleet included four battleships and the 1st Aircraft Carrier Squadron of four armoured fleet carriers.

By this time the Japanese were unable to maintain a naval force in the Indian Ocean and it was clear that the main purpose of the East Indies Fleet would be support for the Army's operations; it was therefore decided that each fighter squadron of the Fleet Air Arm should have a quarter of its aircraft equipped with camera-mountings, enabling them to operate in the fighter-reconnaissance role.

Only 804 Sqn's pilots had received any degree of army co-operation training and the camera-equipped aircraft of the other Naval fighter squadrons were almost entirely employed on CAP (Combat Air Patrol) and strafing operations. Because of the massive sinkings of their tanker fleet by US submarines, the Japanese forces were becoming desperately short of oil. To deny them further stocks of aviation fuel, it was decided that, before they left for the Pacific, the carriers of the British Pacific Fleet should mount attacks on Palembang as Operation 'Boomerang' the previous August had left the refinery undamaged.

The US Navy had developed a system whereby an 'Air Co-ordinator' controlled operations from the air, a system similar to that adopted by the RAF in Burma, where a 'Master-Bomber' directed strikes onto their targets as required in a developing situation, in accord with the military axiom, "No plan can last longer than the first

alteration". The US Navy summarised the technique (with particular reference to support of ground operations): the Air Co-ordinator "is an experienced and senior officer, usually a Group Commander. He patrols the battle area in his own aircraft, usually a single-seater fighter... The value of the Air Co-ordinator is evidenced particularly during the most fluid stages of the assault. He can readjust the planned air support, and divert an attack to a different target when necessary... the Air Co-ordinator is often called upon to co-operate or divert the actual support mission, as he is in the best position to see how the battle is developing".

Maj R.C. Hay, Wing Leader of No.47 Naval Fighter Wing in HMS *Victorious*, was appointed Air Co-ordinator of Adm Vian's 1st Aircraft Carrier Squadron and was soon promoted to the rank of Lieutenant-Colonel, RM.

Before making the attacks, preliminary 'rehearsal' strikes were made against the Pangkalan Brandan refineries in Northern Sumatra, the series of operations being code-named 'Outflank'. The first strike was to he made by aircraft from the carriers *Illustrious* and *Indomitable* on Pangkalan Brandan (Operation 'Robson') on 20 December but persistent dense cloud along the coast, the cause of failure on so many PR sorties, compelled diversion to a secondary target, the oil-port and railway yards at Belawan, north of Medan. Here, visibility was poor and the strike aircraft caused little serious damage.

Daylight sorties to observe the results of the attack were made by 160 Sqn on 23 December by Flg Off R. Jones and on the 26th by Wt Off F.A. Hughes, each flying FL935, 'S', but were unsuccessful because of cloud cover. A second attack in the series was made on 4 January 1945 against Pangkalan Brandan by aircraft from *Victorious* and *Indefatigable* (Operation 'Lentil'). While supporting strikes were made against the airfields at Tandjoeng Poera and Medan. Avengers attacked the oil installations but were engaged by enemy fighters as they left the target. Maj Hay, in his Corsair JT427 with a fighter escort from 1836 Sqn, circled the target at heights between 5,000ft and 7,000ft to take oblique photographs. He had proposed to remain in the area until the fires had died down but there was so much smoke that vertical photography was impossible. Two of the Corsairs stayed to take additional photographs while Maj Hay made a photographic run over the oil installations at Pangkalan Soesoe, some ten miles further north, before returning to *Victorious*.

While the attacks diverted the attention of the Japanese, five Hellcat Mk.I(P)s of 888 Sqn carried by *Indefatigable* flew the squadron's first photographic reconnaissance sorties, two over the target area and along the east coast between Medan and Idi, and one over Nias Island, the others along the west coast of Sumatra from Niew Singkel harbour to Sibolga and on a route from Troemon, inland over the mountains to Parapat on the shore of the great volcanic lake, Toba Meer, to Rantauparapat airfield on the eastern plain and back to the coast near Sibolga. The unit commander, Lt B.A. MacCaw, flying the unarmed Hellcat JV230 at 30,000ft, was surprisingly confronted by the Nakajima Ki 44 'Tojo' of the enemy fighter co-ordinator from the 87th *Sentai*, who did not attack but retired at high speed.

Having gained valuable experience from the 'rehearsals' of Operations 'Robson' and 'Lentil', the British Pacific Fleet, including the carriers *Indomitable*, *Victorious*, *Illustrious* and *Indefatigable*, mounted major strikes against the Palembang oil refineries in January 1945. An essential adjunct to these attacks was high-level photographic reconnaissance of the airfields in south-eastern Sumatra by *Indomitable*'s Hellcats. Two F.52 cameras with 36in lenses were made available at Trincomalee just before the fleet carriers sailed to carry out the operation *en route* to Australia before joining the US 5th Fleet in the Pacific. The new camera/lens combination was longer than the cameras with 14in lenses previously mounted in the Hellcats so special fairings were hurriedly designed and fitted to protect the lens cones which projected beneath the fuselages.

On 16 January the operational component of the British Pacific Fleet sailed from Trincomalee to make the first attack, 'Meridian I' on the Pladjoe oil refinery from a flying-off position at the extreme eastern limit of the SEAC area, some sixty miles from the southern coast of Sumatra. The attack necessitated a flight to the target of 160miles overland, crossing the 6,000ft high coastal range and the plain beyond, by the Avengers of the strike force.

Maj Hay, Air Co-ordinator for the operation, directed the Pladjoe strike and photographed the resulting damage while Corsairs from *Illustrious* and *Victorious* provided escort and attacked the two principal fighter airfields of Lombak and Talangbetoetoe. The strike was considered 60% successful as the targets were spread over a wide area. Fourteen enemy fighters were destroyed for the loss of eleven Royal Navy aircraft.

Maj Hay recorded, "The escort was engaged by an estimated twenty-five Tojo fighters although I myself only counted about twelve at the time. Their initial height was 13,000-15,000 feet. Throughout the attack the enemy had just sufficient fighters to saturate the escort. Enemy pilots showed as much contempt for Japanese heavy AA fire as we did and fights were raging all over the target area. It was almost funny to see the aircraft scrapping and all the while the AA bursting at all heights up to 15,000 feet. When not engaged with enemy fighters or occupied in avoiding predicted flak, I was able to secure a series of oblique photographs".

Ki-44 Tojo interceptor fighters of the 87th *Sentai* were stationed at Soengei Gerong and Talangbetoetoe in the Palembang airfield group to defend the vital Sumatran

oil-installations, with support from several other units flying Ki-43 Oscars and Ki-84 Franks.

Maj Hay and his flight of Corsairs joined the fray. The Wing Leader shot down one enemy aircraft and shared the destruction of a Tojo with 'Sheepdog 3', Sub-Lt D.J. Sheppard in JT410, 'T8H', over Tandjoeng Radja.

The PR Hellcats flew meanwhile over the 9,000ft Barisan Range, one to photograph the airfield at Lahat, then north-east to Lembak, Palembang and Tandjoeng Radja, then to Teloek Betoeng at the southern tip of the island and back via Mana; the other aircraft flew in the opposite direction. Lt N.G. Mitchell and Sub-Lt F.R. Rankin flew the two sorties, covering the target and eight airfields at Pendopo, Martapoera and the Palembang group where the enemy's fighter defences were concentrated. A subsidiary attack was made on Mana airfield on the coast, from where the Dinahs of the 74th *Dokoritsu Chutai* (Independent Air Company) flew periodic reconnaissance over the Indian Ocean to the Cocos-Keeling Islands, 600 miles to the south. At Cocos the British Chiefs of Staff had decided an air staging post should be established early in 1945.

'Meridian II' was another attack on 29 January against the oil refinery at Songei Gerong, during which Maj Hay observed that the fires at Pladjoe had been extinguished. At 0840 the target was in sight, then heavy anti-aircraft fire opened up as the Avenger bombers began their attack and Maj Hay began taking photographs as the first bombs were released. He reported, "From visual observation some targets were severely hit and the photographs have confirmed this. Bombing by No.1 Wing" (Avengers from *Indomitable* and *Victorious*) "was truly impressive. By the time No.2 Wing" (*Illustrious* and *Indefatigable*) "commenced bombing, it was getting a bit difficult to see. The first squadron of that Wing set off some oil tanks in the vicinity and certainly were very close to their target. It seemed a pity that so many aircraft were put onto one small target while Pladjoe was completely clear and could have been bombed accurately.

"About three minutes after the last aircraft bombed I finished photographing. I then climbed from 6,000 feet to 10,000 in order to take some vertical line overlap photographs as the flak had died down. I soon had to change my mind as a Tojo was coming at us. In shooting this one down we descended to zero feet and, attracted by the gunfire, an Oscar came along and by 0905 he too was dead". Maj Hay's No.4, Sub-Lt H. Griffin in Corsair 'T8U' accounted for another Tojo. Meanwhile the Hellcats of *Indomitable*'s PR Flight returned from high-level reconnaissance with photographs of the airfields in the vicinity, including a newly-constructed airfield at Paja Raman.

Although it was becoming apparent to most Japanese in positions of authority that their forces no longer held the initiative, the people as a whole were allowed no knowledge of Allied successes. Since the end of Japanese expansion in 1942 all operations were presented by their Government as victories while Allied losses were greatly exaggerated and Japanese losses minimised.

The attacks on the installations in Sumatra so reduced the supply of oil fuel that the Imperial Navy was no longer effective and the air forces were faced with an imminent shortage of aviation spirit. During Operation 'Lentil' only one British aircraft was lost and the pilot recovered, yet the Fleet fighters shot down a dozen or more enemy aircraft and damaged another twenty on the airfields at Medan and Tandjoeng Poera. 'Meridian I' caught the Tojos of the 87th *Hiko-Sentai* on their airfield at Soengei Gerong; although four British aircraft were shot down by the Tojos that managed to take off, twelve of which were claimed destroyed, Japanese reports claimed eighteen 'kills' (fifteen confirmed!) for the loss of eight pilots. During 'Meridian II', when the Palembang airfields were again attacked, Japanese fighters were on standing patrol but the Fleet losses were small; two Avenger

bombers hit barrage-balloon cables and were destroyed and five Naval fighters were lost. In all, twenty-five Fleet aircraft were shot down or lost when 'ditched', for a claimed thirty Japanese aircraft shot down and thirty-eight destroyed on their airfields, but the enemy claimed fourteen 'kills' by fighters and fifty more shot down by anti-aircraft fire.

After 'Meridian II' Japanese aircraft shadowed the Force throughout the day, CAP Seafires from *Indefatigable* making an early interception and 'splashing' a Ki-46 Dinah. Later, seven Ki-21 Sally bombers attempted suicide attacks on *Illustrious* and *Indefatigable* but all were destroyed by the Seafire patrols. After this operation, the carriers of the British Pacific Fleet left the area of South-East Asia Command, taking with them the Photographic Reconnaissance Flight of Hellcats aboard Indomitable and the Air Co-ordinator's camera-fitted Flight of Corsairs aboard *Victorious*. The Fleet reached Fremantle, Western Australia, on 4 February and sailed on to its main base at Sydney, New South Wales.

157: Smoke billows thousands of feet into the air from the flames of a massive oil fire at the refinery at Soengei Gerong during the attacks of 'Meridian II' on 29 January 1945. Bombing by the Avengers from the four Royal Navy fleet aircraft carriers which took part in the raids was "truly impressive"

Into Burma

Operations by the PR squadrons of the RAF continued through January. On the 2nd Spitfire PL858, 'R', returning to Imphal from a sortie in advance of the troops moving towards Mandalay developed engine trouble and caught fire. The pilot, Wt Off F.V. Entwistle parachuted into dense jungle 40 miles east of the Chindwin River. The importance attached to operations by Fig Off Lehman's 681 Sqn Detachment at Imphal by the Army and by HQ 221 Grp may be judged by the exchange of messages that followed. On 4 January Air Vice Marshal Vincent CB DFC AFC, commanding 221 Grp, signalled to 681 Sqn:

"Please accept my sympathy for the loss of Entwistle the other day. It is, of course, to be hoped most sincerely that he will yet walk in, which does appear to be more than a chance. In the meantime he is a loss to the Detachment up here, which has been doing such excellent work. In the event of his non-return due to some unknown reason, I close with sympathy, and wishing the Squadron the best of luck in the future".

Wt Off Entwistle survived to walk out of the jungle to reach Mawlaik on the 6th and Sqn Ldr Procter later signalled HQ 221 Grp,

"I have the honour to thank you on behalf of myself and the Squadron for your letter of sympathy when Wt Off Entwistle was missing on Operations at the beginning of this month.

Since receiving your letter this pilot has returned to the Squadron after walking out through the jungle. I am happy to tell you that he suffered no ill effects and after a week on leave has now returned to operational duties".

684 Sqn was now able to operate twelve new or renovated Mosquitos and NS622, 'X', flown by Sqn Ldr K J. Newman with Flt Sgt G. W. Williams, obtained complete cover of Phuket Island on 5 January, making a round trip of 2,286 miles.

On 3 January No 4 Sqn IAF began operating from 'Hove', a landing strip on the beach at Mardhaibunia thirty miles south of Cox's Bazar, where take-off and landing had to be made at low tide.

On 8 January, the weather appearing favourable, C Flight of 160 Sqn sent out two Liberators. Flg Off J.I. Jackson flew FL936, 'V', to recce the west coast of Sumatra and Flt Lt J.F. Leeper in BZ900, 'C', obtained cover of Penang, off the north-west coast of Malaya. Both aircraft dropped Nickels (leaflets) over inhabited areas before returning to base. The next two days, further sorties were attempted but the weather prevented any cover being obtained and, apart from one successful sortie over Simaloer by FL935, 'S' (Flg Off L.R. Jones) on the

27th, operations ceased until the weather cleared. At the beginning of the year heavy rain made the fair-weather strip at Mambur unserviceable but by mid-January No.2 Sqn IAF had a detachment operating from Akyab. On the 22nd Flg Off Kumar failed to return from an offensive recce along the coast. The next day Flg Off Harbans Singh crashed and was killed on return from a sortie over the Lemro River. Despite difficulties caused by the weather, the squadron flew 746 operational hours during the month and produced 11,000 photographic prints.

No.1 Sqn IAF remained based at Imphal, beginning the New Year with short-range 'vertical' photographic reconnaissance sorties, each camera-equipped aircraft being escorted by a 'weaver'.

No. 28 Sqn was constantly on Tac/R operations in support of 'Capital'; on the 4th Flt Lt Johnson's Hurricane was shot down by anti-aircraft fire from Pagan on the east bank of the river. He baled out but could not be seen by his 'weaver' and was given up for lost; on 6 February he returned to the squadron. On 30 January a single Japanese aircraft bombed Tamu airfield and slightly damaged one of 28 Sqn's aircraft at dispersal. Later that day the other Hurricanes were flown to Ye-U North, a hundred miles south-east and only forty miles from the Irrawaddy. The squadron was now fully occupied with Tac/R operations for XXXIII Corps' advance towards the Irrawaddy bend and by the end of the month was flying offensive recces along the river from Singu forty miles north of Mandalay to the south-western limit of XXXIII Corps' front at Ngazun.

For future operational planning, cover of the west coast of Malaya was considered the most urgent requirement. The Planning Staff warned that, unless Fleet and F-13A aircraft were used primarily for this reconnaissance during February and March, operations would be delayed for lack of information. It was recommended that the PR capabilities of the East Indies Fleet and of XX Bomber Command be used to the full, and that when Mosquito PR.34s were delivered they should operate from Cocos Island until some nearer base became available.

When formed Photographic Reconnaissance Force had been intended to be a combined Anglo-American formation under the control of Eastern Air Command but no provision was made for a Headquarters organisation. Direct operational control remained with 171 Wing staff who had taken over PR duties at Dum Dum. After several months of inter-Allied disagreement Gen Stratemeyer resolved the problem by appointing Col M.W. Kaye, USAAF, to command PR Force on 9 January 1945, with Wg Cdr Wise as his deputy and OC 171 Wing, which was re-formed to co-ordinate RAF reconnaissance.

The appointment of Col Kaye was a 'political' rather than an 'operational' matter, reflecting the major part being taken by the United States in providing men and machines to the Command. The film and print processing facilities supplied by the US Army were superior in many ways to those provided by the RAF, although their overall efficiency was no greater. The brunt of the task of covering the tactical and immediate strategic targets was still taken by the squadrons of the RAF and IAF. In September 1944 for instance, the mobile processing section attached to No.1 Sqn IAF had turned out no fewer than 9,555 prints for the Army and HQ XXXIII Corps praised "the skill and speed with which air photographs have been produced and dropped on the forward troops".

Throughout the period of political wrangling, the squadrons' operations continued, as shown by the number of sorties:

	681	684	9th	20th	24th	40th
Nov 1944	132	40	176	260	15	119
Dec l944	158	33	188	367	29	109

The 20th Tactical Reconnaissance Sqn, although under command of HQ PR Force, was almost entirely involved in tactical flights for NCAC. North American P-51 Mustang 1As, fitted with cameras for low-level reconnaissance, were in use in mid-1942 by the RAF's

Army Cooperation Command: subsequent models were modified for the USAAF as the F-6 series of reconnaissance fighters. In January the 20th TR Sqn received ten F-6Cs. Their K.22 cameras and the squadron's existing K.24s could not be installed together so one-third of the aircraft were fitted with K.24 oblique, the others with K.22 vertical cameras. During the next few weeks the squadron became increasingly engaged in photographic reconnaissance—267 sorties in March—rather than 'bomb and strafe' missions.

During January 1945, No.2 Sqn IAF put in 746 operational hours, producing 10,000 photographic prints of good quality. On the last day of the month the aircraft were moved from Akyab for a period of ten days to the nearby strip of Dabaing, but the Indian squadron lost another pilot, Pt Off D'Souza, who crashed while making a print delivery drop to the Army. No.1 Sqn also was fully engaged on Tac/R, averaging eighteen sorties per day throughout February, mostly by a detachment which followed IV Corps south to Kan, fifteen miles north of Gangaw in the Myittha Valley.

In February 1945 Mountbatten's Joint Planning Staff outlined the requirements for future air survey and photo-recce cover. With the possibility of Rangoon being re-captured before the onset of the south-west monsoon, the next objective would be to clear the Strait of Malacca

158: 42-105940, aka 'Pistol Packing Pete' was a long-fuselage Curtiss P-40L-5—or should be. It has somehow acquired an extra digit in its serial number while in service with the US 20th Tac Recon Squadron, sometime in 1944. Apart from the white spinner, the unit wore no special markings on their Olive Drab/ Neutral Grey aircraft

159: 20th Tac Recon Squadron F-6Cs were almost as anonymous as the unit's P-40s. 43-25148 is in all-silver finish enlivened only by the addition of Insignia Blue identification bands on the wings and tailplane, as required from February 1945. Myitkyina, Burma

and to re-occupy Malaya. New, accurate maps of most of Burma had been prepared following air-survey by PR Force, but those of Sumatra were inadequate for operational planning; most had not been revised since the original surveys in 1900 and there were considerable gaps in some essential areas. Photographic intelligence of Japanese activities and development in the occupied countries of SE Asia, other than Burma and Siam, was scanty—for most of Malaya and Sumatra it was non-existent. No information of airfield development, port facilities, communications or the condition of possible landing beaches could be obtained, as only the northern part of Sumatra was within reach of the available PR aircraft. It was estimated that the survey cover of Malaya alone would require about sixty sorties, each $1\frac{1}{2}$ hours photographic flying, and a total of ninety sorties would be needed to meet all survey and PR requirements.

During the October-May period the weather over Burma and Siam is generally ideal for high-altitude reconnaissance.

In Malaya and Sumatra, however, there is no 'dry season' but, for most of the year, a gradual build-up of cloud which frequently culminates in rain late in the day and clears at nightfall; the months of least rainfall being February and March. In such weather conditions, aircraft flying PR sorties from distant bases would have to take off before dawn in order to be over their objectives early in the day. The Mosquitos of 681 Sqn were usually flown from Alipore to Cox's Bazar the evening before a sortie, taking off at first light to reach the target while the sky was still clear.

The first aircraft for the long-promised additional squadron of the new Mosquito PR.34s were expected to arrive soon in the Command and it was tentatively proposed that an all-weather airstrip, to be constructed as soon as Ramree Island could be cleared of the enemy, would provide operational facilities for these aircraft more conveniently than Cocos Islands. At the beginning of February work began to construct an all-weather airfield at Kyaukpyu on Ramree Island.

160: Boeing F-13A-55-BW, 'Double Exposure', serial no. 42-24877, was one of the first photo-reconnaissance aircraft operational with the 3rd PR Sqn. It was one of many American aircraft in the Theatre to wear artwork inspired by Alberto Varga's pinups. As seen here the aircraft carries nine black 'camera lens' mission symbols; the next four took place while the machine was on loan to the 13th AF and were painted red. As they were over Java, a small white coffee pot symbol was added over the top

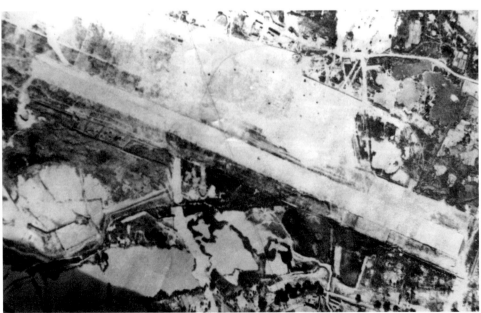

161: A Japanese fighter, probably a Ki-44, is seen here taking-off from Kuala Lumpur airfield in a vain interception attempt while being overflown by an F-13A of the 1st PR Sqn

162 Above: A vertical of Mingaladon taken by an F-5 of the 9th PR Sqn early in 1945

163 Right: The Liberators usually carried both hand-held and fixed cameras for strike recording. This picture shows B.VI, 'S', of 356 Sqn turning away after a success-ful raid on the rail yards at Amarapura, by the Irra-waddy Bend, south of Man-dalay on 25 January 1945. The heavily weathered cam-ouflage appears to be basic US Olive Drab, with later areas of repainting. Note the distinctive unit tail markings

Crossing the Irrawaddy

Operation 'Extended Capital'

At the eastern end of the Central Front 2 Div of XXXIII Corps had pressed on to Shwebo and linked-up with 19 Div of IV Corps on the Upper Irrawaddy where, after several days of skirmishing, a crossing was made 60 miles north of Mandalay at Thabeikkyin and another at Singu. Believing this crossing to be the beginning of a drive on Mandalay, Kimura moved tanks and artillery to contain these beach-heads in the north.

By early February 14th Army was up to the river along a front of 200 miles and the only intact Japanese force on the west bank was at Sagaing, opposite Mandalay. There the enemy was contained while 20 Div crossed at nearby Myinmu. As the Army advanced, the lines of supply from Bengal and Assam became seriously over-loaded and it was clearly necessary to seize a coastal base for air-supply to the advance and for the proposed assault on Rangoon.

Seafires of No.4 Naval Fighter Wing had been employed on tactical reconnaissance and gunnery-spotting duties during the Normandy D-Day landings, Operation 'Overlord' in June 1944. They and fighter-reconnaissance Hellcats were equally successful during and after the 'Dragoon' landings in southern France in mid-August. Towards the end of the year the Admiralty had decided that the equipment of all Hellcat squadrons should include four aircraft fitted with cameras for beach-head reconnaissance and for support landing operations, and that a number of pilots should be trained in Tac/R duties. The escort carrier HMS *Ameer*, the first 'assault carrier' to join the Eastern Fleet, carried such F6F-3(P) reconnaissance Hellcats.

Ports and air-supply bases were needed on Akyab and Ramree Islands. Akyab, abandoned by the enemy, was occupied three weeks earlier than expected and Operation 'Matador', an attack on Ramree, was mounted on 21 January. Here, at Kyaukpyu, a site was prepared for an all-weather airfield. For 'Matador', a strong Naval force was assembled, including the escort carrier *Ameer* with No.804 Sqn of the Fleet Air Arm aboard. This squadron, having undergone army co-operation training in South Africa before embarking for Ceylon in December 1944, was equipped with Grumman Hellcats, including a Section of armed Hellcat Mk.II(P)s with provision for K.17/6in vertical and F24/20in oblique cameras. 804 Sqn was the only Naval Air Squadron in the East Indies Fleet specifically trained for tactical recce and Arty/R duties. The Hellcats spotted for the guns of the warships and flew Combat Air Patrols but the only contacts were the B-29s of 58th Bomber Wing on mining operations. *Ameer* retired temporarily to Akyab before accompanying a cruiser force which landed Royal Marines on Cheduba Island (Operation 'Sankey') on 26 January; here 804 Sqn flew cover for the landings but there was no opposition and they were again spotting for a

Naval bombardment of the Ramree defences on the 30th and carrying out their first Tac/R sorties for the Army, returning to cover further landings in the south-west of the island on 12 February.

By this time IV Corps had reached Pauk on the Irrawaddy and XXXIII Corps was closing up on to the river between the beach-heads across the river at Thabeikkyin, seventy miles north of Mandalay, to Myinmu, 100 miles further south-west. The Japanese suffered heavy losses during concentrated attacks on the beach-heads and on 10 February 19 Div broke out and headed south towards Mandalay.

While a series of diversionary crossings of the Irrawaddy were being planned, the ever-changing channels in the river-bed were photographed daily so that information was always available on the position of the sand-banks and obstacles which might affect the operations. No.28 Sqn (now under the command of Sqn Ldr E.G. Parnell) continued photographic reconnaissance from heights varying between 3,000 and 7,000ft, north and west of Mandalay, over Singu, Madaya, Sagaing and Ngzun, uninterrupted by a squadron move on 13 February to Sadaung, only fifteen miles from the river.

By February, while 681 Sqn's Spitfires continued to cover the battle-area and airfields and communications, in southern Burma, 684 Sqn's Mosquitos had returned from No 1 CMU and the detachment at China Bay was again equipped with serviceable aircraft to complete its survey commitment in Southern India. Although central Burma was clear of cloud, 'chhota monsoon' storms persisted until 10 February when Flt Lt H.C. Lowcock and Flt Sgt D. Lewin in NS298, 'K', flying from China Bay, found the sky cloud-free over northern Sumatra and obtained cover of the airfields at Lho'nga, Padang-Tidji, Samalanga and Koetaradja.

The Japanese conquests of early 1942 produced enormous short-term benefits but faced the Japanese Army with a potential logistical problem if the Allies should mount counter-offensives. The Imperial Navy was unable to provide the convoy protection needed for reinforcement and supply of forces throughout the newly-occupied territories. It thus became necessary to improve land communications wherever possible, the immediate need being a line of supply between from Malaya and Siam into Burma.

Well-maintained railways already existed from Singapore to Bangkok, and from Ye, south of Moulmein to Rangoon. Between these lines, the Japanese Army in November 1942 began construction of the 259-mile Burma-Siam railway employing 70,000 *Romusha* (forced labourers) from Siam, Burma and Malaya, a third of whom died, and 55,000 Allied prisoners-of-war of whom 12,000 also died in dreadful conditions. 300 miles of Malayan Railways permanent way was lifted and transported north to be re-laid.

The line followed the valley of the Mekong River and its tributary the Menam Kwae Noi ('River Kwai') from Bon Pong near Kanchanaburi in Siam northwards via the Three Pagodas Pass to Thanbuzayat, south of Moulmein. Bridge-building was a feature of the enterprise—690 bridges along the line, ranging from simple wooden trestle structures to a 14-span steel bridge over the Mekong at Tamarkand, near the southern junction. 100yd away from this, a timber 'by-pass' bridge was built to carry traffic while the steel bridge was erected and to carry light traffic. Weather conditions and the character of the country through which the railway passed caused delay in completion of the line until late October 1943, in time for the movement of troops and stores for the forthcoming Operations 'Ha-Gô' and 'U-Gô', but the operation of the railway was not considered of great importance by 14th Army or by Eastern Air Command, Allied air action in Central Burma seeming sufficient to disrupt Japanese logistical plans. During the first six months of operation, only two trains (400 tons) per day made the journey north but by December 1944 five trains a day were getting through. Air attacks by the US 7th Bomb Group on rail yards, workshops and bridges along the line caused an average three-day delay before normal traffic could be restored. At the end of 1944 the 493rd Sqn began attacks on rail bridges with 1000lb AZON (AZimuth ONly) bombs which could be accurately guided to their targets by radio control. The 493rd Sqn's precision bombing was soon to be directed against the Tamarkand bridges, the first being a 14-hour mission on 13 December which inflicted only superficial damage. On 4 February 1945 the timber bridge received serious damage, and on the 13th an attack by a B-24 at 300ft placed four 1,000lb GP bombs on the steel bridge (known to the 7th Bomb Group as Bridge No.277 and to 224 Group RAF as Q.654), dropping two spans into the Mekong.

On 14 February Wg Cdr Lowry and Flt Lt G. Stevens tried out a new, locally-designed camera rig fitted to NS622 for the first of a series of sorties to obtain low-level cover of the Burma-Siam railway. Mosquito low-level reconnaissance had first been developed at Benson in August 1944 when a forward-facing camera was installed in dummy drop-tanks beneath each wing of a Mosquito PR.IX.

No 684 Sqn's installation was similar in principle; it comprised one F.24/5inch forward-facing oblique camera in the nose, at 30° depression, one side-facing oblique camera and two F.24/14inch cameras mounted in adapted drop tanks to give forward-facing stereoscopic pairs. As the railway was believed to be well-protected by anti-aircraft guns, the first exposures were made in short runs, breaking off into cover of the hills beside the line. As no enemy opposition was encountered, Wg Cdr Lowry decided to make continuous runs along the line and to cover the bridges broadside-on. Only a few people were seen running for cover or hiding in trucks but it was not possible to see whether they were Japanese or Allied PoWs.

However, the fuselage-mounted drop-tanks fitted to the Mosquito PR.XVIs to extend their range were not proving entirely satisfactory; LR464, 'R' was forced to abandon a sortie and return to Cox's Bazar on 20 February, when the tank failed to release. Two days later, when NS524, 'V' was taking off from Cox's Bazar, the tank became detached from its forward bracket and scraped along the runway before breaking free without damage to the aircraft, although the tank burst into flames.

The crew of NS499, 'N', returning to China Bay from a partially successful sortie to the Nicobar Islands, almost met with disaster when the dinghy suddenly inflated. The pilot, Flg Off J.J. Bannister, was thrust against the roof escape panel with his Sutton harness and parachute-straps broken but the panel held. The dinghy forced the control column against the instrument panel and the Mosquito went into an uncontrolled dive. The navigator, Wt Off G. G. Hoppit, with great presence of mind, managed to puncture the dinghy with a pencil and the pilot regained control although the cockpit was completely fogged with the carbon-dioxide gas from the deflated dinghy.

By the end of the month 684 Sqn again had a full complement of twenty-two Mosquitos, three of which were at China Bay; the B-25Cs were still in use as a Courier Flight ferrying between China Bay and Alipore.

In February demands for increased cover of distant targets were received but an increase in the operational range of the US 40th PR Sqn to 500 miles from their forward base at Akyab, and the assumption of some survey tasks by US 24th Combat Mapping Sqn, reduced the pressure on 684 Sqn.

When forward units of XX Bomber Command began withdrawing from the Chengtu airfields to India in January, to await transfer to new airfields under construction in the Marianas, 1st PR Sqn's 'C' Flight remained to continue an extensive survey of northern China, Korea and Manchuria. 'A' Flight, stationed at Chakulia in India, had already begun a limited programme of 'training' operations in conjunction with attacks on port and rail installations in Burma and Siam. From November the Japanese defence of Malaya and Singapore was entrusted principally to the Ki-44 *Shoki* of the 1st *Yasen Hojyu Hikotai* (Field Reserve Sqn) based at Tengah and detachments from the 87th *Sentai* in Eastern Sumatra.

The Superfortresses were now of great importance to the 58th Wing's last operations, for which HQ SEAC had prepared a list of target priorities in Malaya, namely, the rail workshops and marshalling yards outside Kuala Lumpur, Singapore Naval Base and the port facilities at Georgetown, Penang. All these targets were covered by US 1st PR Sqn over a period of several weeks. In all, nineteen sorties were flown during January. The B-29s of

58th Bomber Wing attacked Sattahib Naval Base and targets in Indo-China on 25 January, while an F-13A flew to Penang and Singapore, providing valuable information about the location of Japanese cruisers and smaller naval units. This sortie resulted, on night of 1 February, in an attack by 88 Superfortresses on Singapore Naval Base, causing considerable damage to the port installations and great concern to HQ SEAC, whose plans envisaged future use of the base. The following day Mountbatten directed that there should be no further attacks against naval installations at Singapore or Penang.

By late January 1945 it seemed probable that the 14th Army would soon inflict a major defeat on the Japanese in Central Burma and open up an opportunity for a thrust down the Irrawaddy to Rangoon, 350 miles away, before the south-west monsoon in mid-May. The British Chiefs of Staff proposed that the immediate purpose in SEAC should be the liberation of Burma and Malaya. Although the US Chiefs of Staff regarded support for operations in China as of greater strategic value than advances in SE Asia, they concurred and, on 23 February, Mountbatten gave priority to plans for a rapid drive southwards in Burma, positioning his intended major amphibious and airborne assault on Rangoon, Operation 'Dracula'. Plans for a reduced landing, named 'Modified Dracula', continued.

Not only had all the battle areas been photographed by the normal P.R. Squadrons, but 57 per cent of the total area of Burma had been mapped, an area equivalent to three times the size of England. It was found, however, that these maps had only limited value unless fixed ground or air positions could be obtained when the photographic survey was in process. The only solution to this was the use of radar, but there were no existing radar aids suitable for air survey work. New types of radar sets were evolved by radar experts in Britain, and by January 1945 a technique had been developed to enable small-scale tactical maps (1/50,000 and 1/100,000) to be prepared with a radius of 250 miles from a ground Radar Station. Although experimental work still continued, it was considered that the experiments were sufficiently far advanced for four P.R. aircraft to be specially fitted with radar and sent to India in April, 1945. Unhappily, further delays took place in testing and fitting the apparatus and it was necessary to inform Air Command South-East Asia that no more of these aircraft would be arriving until after the monsoon period.

By this time the Chinese mapping projects of the 24th Sqn were virtually completed; use of advanced bases at Liuchow and Chanyi had made possible the mapping of some 360,000 square miles—accomplished in 357 hours flying time—with materials and fuel flown by more than 80 round trips over the 'Hump'. These flights cost six B-24 and one B-25 aircraft, although none were lost during actual photographic missions.

Some aerial mapping of northern areas of Burma and of the coast at high and low tides was begun by the squadron. Of a mission on 21 January, the 24th Sqn recorded, "Five of our B-25s took to the air early in the morning for mapping over North Central Burma. No enemy action was encountered and all the sorties were successful. The aircraft flew approximately 2,300 miles of flight lines. Considering the fact that the planes had to travel between 550 and 600 miles to and from the target area, this is regarded as an excellent day's performance".

After these assignments the squadron began mapping other areas of south-east Asia, flying from forward bases at Tulihal, one of the Imphal airfields, and from Cox's Bazar.

Two crossings of the Irrawaddy near Myinmu were made by 20 Div on the night of 12 February and the Japanese promptly began moving their reserves against what appeared to be a pincer-movement against Mandalay.

Lt-Gen Slim's plan for 'Extended Capital' now developed, the intention being to cut the enemy's communications with the north of Burma by employing fast-moving forces south of the Irrawaddy Bend, thereby breaking Japanese resistance in central Burma.

The advance by IV Corps from Gangaw had also reached the west bank of the Irrawaddy. Although 7 Indian Div captured Pakokku on 10 February, the Japanese HQ moved reinforcements to oppose 20 Div's move which seemed to be the western arm of the XXXIII Corps pincer-movement against Mandalay. At Pakokku IV Corps made a feint attack before launching the main assault across the river at Nyaungu 10 miles to the south, at the boundary between the Japanese 15th and 28th Armies. The crossing was made across a three-quarter mile wide stretch of water, onto a small beach leading to a ravine between high cliffs and the Japanese thought this still to be a diversion from the effort against Mandalay. With the beach-heads secured, 17 Div and 255 Indian Tank Brigade began a drive towards Meiktila on the 26th and, within a week, had taken the airfield at Thabutkon, 60 miles away. Reinforcements and materiel were soon flown in for an attack on Meiktila, only 10 miles on.

The Fleet Air Arm's contribution to the preliminary reconnaissance for Operation 'Zipper' (an assault on Malaya) began with Operation 'Stacey', a series of twenty-two sorties frown from HMS *Empress* by the Hellcats of 888 Sqn over a three-day period. Beginning on 26 February from a flying-off position in the Andaman Sea, mid-way between the Nicobar Islands and Phuket Island, 888 Sqn's CO, Lt B.A. MacCaw, in Hellcat Mk.II(P) JV230 was 'squirted-off' by *Empress*'s catapult in clear, still weather for a photographic sortie to Penang and Langkawi Islands while the other four pilots flew to cover the coast and special targets from Victoria Point to near

164: *The escort carrier HMS* Ameer *at full speed with Hellcats parked forward. This shows how limited was the space available for flying-off and recovery of a Flight of four aircraft. The slightest misjudgment could result in damage to several aircraft*

165: *Its tailhook and rear fuselage broken away after hitting the rounddown, JW738, '6N', of 804 Sqn goes over the port side of HMS* Ameer *on 26 February 1945. The pilot, Lt RJH Cross, was rescued unharmed, another testimonial to the strength of the products of the Grumman 'Ironworks'*

166: *Indian troops of 4/15 Punjab Regt crossed the Irrawaddy into the main beachhead on 14 February. P-47 Thunderbolts on 'cabrank' patrol then bombed Nyaungu village which was declared 'cleared' two days later*

167 Left: An 804 Sqn Hellcat leaving Ameer's 'accelerator' on 12 February 1945, still wearing the early squadron symbol '2', with freshly-applied white bands

168 Below: A by-pass rail bridge built on trestles beside the piers of a 'blown' rail bridge, photographed on 14 February 1945 by a Mosquito of 684 Sqn, NS622, flown by Lowcock and Stevens. The print is reproduced here slightly larger than life-size

the Siam-Malaya border. The ability to process film on board enabled results to be plotted and the next day's flying planned. Camera failures made much of the first day's effort abortive but on the 27th, from a position 100 miles further north, successful cover was obtained of the same areas. The following day Lt Sakhanovsky returned early with camera trouble in JX682 but he resumed his sortie in the spare Hellcat, JV225. In addition to extensive survey cover of the Kra Isthmus, the Hellcats photographed the airfields at Bangsak, Hunlok and Bandon, Phuket, Langkawi and other islands and anchorages. Lt Gooden in JX673 flew across the isthmus to the airfield and harbour at Singora on the Gulf of Siam and Sub-Lt J.W. Tomlinson in JX676 covered Nancowry Harbour in the Nicobars. 804 Sqn flew Combat Air Patrol over the Task Force but, apart from investigating radar plots of 58 Bomber Wing's Super-fortresses, the fighters on CAP saw no other aircraft until 1 March when the carriers were located and attacked by enemy aircraft.

Flying from *Ameer* and *Empress*, 804 Sqn's Hellcats, shot down two Oscars, one of which fell to the guns of Sub-Lt G.F. Ferguson in Hellcat JW723, '6G', and a shadowing Dinah whose destruction was shared by another F6F-5P, JW730, '6K', flown by Sub-Lt C.D. Barnett. The Task Force withdrew to a position west of Sumatra where, on 4 March, 888 Sqn flew five more PR sorties, Lt Godden in JV225 to Simaloer and Nias Islands, Sub-Lt Tomlinson in JX676 to Penang and Butterworth airfield in northern Malaya, Lt MacCaw and the other pilots to obtain 1,600 sq miles of survey cover of the north coast of Sumara from Lho'nga to Pangkalan Brandan and all the airfields in the north, thirteen in number including a new site at Idi. The carriers then returned to Trincomalee.

Up to twelve B-29s were flying each day from Kharagpur over Siam and Malaya during Operation 'Stacey'; Lt MacCaw reported, "Much time has been taken in pursuing our own, rather than enemy aircraft, found to be B-29s which frequently did not show IFF (Identification, Friend or Foe) and were a considerable nuisance".

On the coast, by the 18th, XV Corps had occupied Kangaw and landed at Dalet Chaung and Ru Ywa, the Hurricanes of No.2 Sqn IAF providing continuing tactical reconnaissance and close-support for the ground forces. Meanwhile, the forward detachment of No.1 Sqn IAF moved south to Sinthe, twenty-five miles west of IV Corps' Nyaungu bridgehead. Enemy ground fire caused damage to several of the Hurricanes as 'Extended Capital' developed; on 26 February KZ581, flown by Flg Off Gupta, was badly damaged—the same day Flg Off Norris, flying LE169, was hit in the chest and crash-landed in friendly territory. Although recovered by a tank crew, he died in hospital the following day.

The need for additional supplies to maintain 14th Army's momentum meant that XV Corps had to be reduced in size and the Arakan operations almost came to an end. The limited activity which continued, however, contained a large enemy force in Arakan and the Bassein area until April, by which time the Japanese Burma Area Army had begun to disintegrate. Preparations for a later offensive to the south were continued during the month by F-13As of C Flight, US 1st PR Sqn which carried out sixty sorties, thirty-five of these at the request of SEAC Headquarters. Many of these flights were of fifteen hours duration, mostly for map-updating, others to obtain briefing photographs and target-damage cover. On 29 February B-29s attacked the rail workshops north of Kuala Lumpur in Malaya, then, despite Mountbatten's reservations, made a further attack on Singapore Naval Base to deny the Japanese any possibility of major repairs to their warships, on the night of 2/3 March.

Kimura reacted as Slim had foreseen, diverting troops intended for the battle around Mandalay to attempt the recapture of Meiktila. An efficient British radio-intercept service and tactical air reconnaissance provided constant Intelligence for air strikes on the several Japanese headquarters causing a total breakdown of tactical control.

The enemy fought doggedly throughout March to hold off XXXIII Corps while striving to regain control over the airfields upon which IV Corps now depended for its materiel. The fighting for Meiktila Main airfield continued, with attempts by Japanese patrols to infiltrate at night. They were less successful than a business set up by a group of local girls who carried on their profession for the benefit of British troops in the fuselage of a Dakota lying wrecked on the airfield.

As Katamura's 15th Army faced destruction, so elements of Honda's 33rd Army were committed to hold an area south of the Irrawaddy bend, stretching from the Meiktila-Mandalay railway westwards to the river at Myingyan but they were unable to withstand continued assaults by IV Corps' mobile columns. Myingyan was taken on 22 March and made ready to receive supplies rafted 50 miles downstream from depots on the Chindwin River. Honda, now given overall command in Central Burma, was unable to relieve the pressure on his forces around Meiktila and when the last of his troops were driven from the town and the survivors retreated into the Shan Hills, his situation was clearly irretrievable.

Late in February, the drive towards Meiktila under way, Chiang Kai-Shek demanded the return of the Chinese forces in NCAC for an offensive in China, insisting that they must not advance further south than Kyaukme, eighty miles north-east of Mandalay. This would leave the Japanese free to deploy most of their troops from the Northern Front to face 14th Army which would also become responsible for the defence of the Burma Road. Additionally, the left flank of 36 Div, part of NCAC advancing southwards down the Irrawaddy towards Mandalay, would be exposed to attack while the USAAF transport squadrons supplying 14th Army would be withdrawn. Not only would 14th Army's supplies be jeopardized but the opportunity of inflicting a substantial defeat on the Japanese could well be lost and the enemy given time to reorganise and force 14th Army into a situation of stalemate. Recapture of Rangoon before the monsoon became essential.

For the US Government, committed to support China's resistance to the Japanese, only the battles in Burma which led to the securing of Myitkyina and the supply route to China had any sound strategic value. 'Extended Capital' and the battles that followed "were not part of a grand strategy—they were fought to recapture the useless terrain of Burma", concluded a US Army report. "Whether this was done because of British post-war political interests or a lack of conception on the part of senior Allied commanders is a matter of controversy. Regardless of the reason it was a strategic error in that a tremendous air potential, which might have been shifted to China, was dissipated in the battles for Rangoon". In the event, the capture of Rangoon removed the need for intensive air supply. On Mountbatten's representations supported by the British Chiefs of Staff (still favouring an early recapture of the Singapore base), it was agreed that US transport aircraft would remain in Burma until 1 June 1945 or the recapture of Rangoon, whichever was earlier. Mountbatten and his Joint Planning Staff, however, were looking ahead; they saw Singapore as their main objective, the only possible base for further extended operations east of Malaya. A plan was proposed for the capture of Phuket Island (operation 'Roger'), for use as a forward air base and anchorage in June, to be followed by a landing in western Malaya (Operation 'Zipper'), in October.

The influence of politics on military decisions was of little importance to operational units; the 40th PR Sqn continued its support, flying 176 successful missions during February. Much of the squadron's effort was aerial survey, with 6in vertical or 'trimetrogon', and 12in vertical installations. It was calculated that some 184,000 square miles of territory in Burma and Western Thailand were covered.

Meanwhile Japanese Southern Army HQ, the superior authority, had decided to transfer, in conjunction with a general withdrawal of their garrisons in outlying islands, their 5th *Hikoshidan* (Air Division) from Burma into Indo-China, which Southern Area Army intended to hold against all Allied assaults. The removal of aircraft, however, upset Burma Area Army's plans for defence of the Irrawaddy line and Meiktila. The move began in February but was spread over three months and the Division continued rather ineffectual operations over Burma, including the use of Dinahs by 81st *Sentai* (Air Regiment), the only Japanese photographic reconnaissance unit of any strength in the SE Asia Command area of operations. The enemy's 70th and 74th *Dokoritsu Chutai* (Independent Air Companies) in Java

and Sumatra also flew Dinahs but had, together, fewer than a dozen aircraft at any time. No new aircraft were delivered to the Japanese 5th *Hikoshidan* in Burma or to the 9th *Hikoshidan* in Sumatra but losses were made up from a substantial reserve of fighter, bomber and reconnaissance aircraft held by the 1st *Yasen Koku Hokyusho* (Field Replacement Depot) in Malaya.

After Meiktila was taken and the last defences before Mandalay fell on 16 March, Slim regrouped his forces; IV Corps was given the task of driving southwards through Toungoo and Pegu towards Rangoon while XXXIII Corps headed for an alternative route down the Irrawaddy, through Magwe and Prome. The British 36 Div, always in the forefront of NCAC's southward advance, headed for the Mandalay-Lashio railway but the Japanese wrecked the Gokteik Viaduct on 17 March.

No 681 Sqn was detailed to discover the extent of the damage and two Spitfires were sent out on the 21st. Flt Lt D. Gadd, flying MB911, 'Y', took low-level obliques and, although his Spitfire suffered hydraulic and engine-trouble on the return flight, resulting in a crash-landing at Monywa, Gadd was able to fly another aircraft back to base at Alipore. A week later the British made contact with Japanese forces at Kyaukme, securing the Burma Road. Its task completed, 36 Div began moving west to the Mandalay area to come under 14th Army command.

Finding their lines of supply from the south cut between the river and Meiktila, the Japanese put in a massive attempt to destroy the forces of IV Corps but raids by mobile columns and air strikes destroyed their tactical headquarters. By the end of March Meiktila Main airfield, although still under fire and occasionally partly occupied by enemy troops, was in British hands and a reinforcing brigade was flown in from Akyab. Further north, a brigade of 19 Div, moving only by night, took Maymyo and isolated Mandalay from the Japanese forces facing NCAC before Lashio.

On 8 March Lts J.B. Ringo and F.L. Butler of the 20th PR Sqn, flying a mission to photograph bridges along the road from Hsipaw to Loilem came under fire from an anti-aircraft battery. Both pilots made several strafing attacks at low level and took obliques that later showed their target to consist of four 40mm guns, all of which appeared to have been put out of action.

The enemy units cut off to the east of Mandalay headed for the Shan Hills, intending to re-form further south before a mechanised column reached Mandalay and the ruined city was cleared by 11 March.

During March and April Wg Cdr Stevens flew a series of sorties in the modified Mosquito PR Mk.XVI, NS622, returning to obtain low-level obliques of bridges and other potential targets for attack along the infamous Burma-Siam railway and the line north from Bangkok. The sorties

169 Above: This oblique from 28 Sqn shows ferries unloading onto the Nyaungu beachhead during the build-up for IV Corps' advance on Meiktila. The narrow defile above the beach appeared to the Japanese an improbable route for a major river crossing

170 Right: The wreckage of the Gokteik viaduct, destroyed by the Japanese, photographed by Flt Lt D Gadd of 681 Sqn on 21 March 1945

extended through central Siam to Chiengmai.

Following these sorties and observation by the B-24s of Strategic Air Force, the bridges came under attack again on 22 March when the steel bridge and the trestle bridge (Q.654A) were hit by Liberators of. 159 Sqn and 356 Sqns RAF.

The by-pass bridge was back in use until 3 April when B-24s of the 7th BG, bombing from 4,000 to 6,000ft, knocked down a 60ft length and devastated the approaches. Yet again the wooden bridge was quickly rebuilt, so on the 22nd another attack was made, damaging both structures. Two days later 40 B-24s of Strategic Air Force bombed the bridges along 200 miles of the railway, destroying 30 and damaging six more. The Burma-Siam railway was now of no use for the reinforcement of the Rangoon area or of Moulmein.

On 5 April Mosquito NS657, 'A', of 684 Sqn, flown by Flt Lt R. Stoneham, was at the beginning of its run down the Burma-Siam railway when the starboard engine speed began to increase from 2,000 to 3,000rpm. The pilot throttled back but this had no effect—propeller pitch was altered without result—and the aircraft began vibrating as the engine speed reached 5,000 revs. The navigator, R.

Burns, who was in the nose position, saw that the engine was on fire and the extinguisher was operated. The aircraft lost height rapidly and, by the time it cleared the coast near Moulmein, was down to 1,000ft. A height of 600ft was maintained over the Gulf of Martaban and, when land was again sighted near Bassein, Stoneham jettisoned the wing-tanks, enabling the aircraft to climb to 1,500ft. By this time the R/T became so faint that it was impossible to call Cox's Bazar, but after hard work had been put in on the business of getting the undercarriage down, the pilot made a landing on the port engine. This was a superb effort, displaying great coolness in a distress position some 500 miles from the ALG. For this feat the pilot was subsequently awarded a Certificate of Gallantry.

Operations in Arakan by Nos.2 and 4 Sqns RIAF ended under the increasing severity of the pre-monsoon storms in April and, following up XXXIII Corps' drive southwards, 28 Sqn lost two aircraft within a few days. On the 18th, during a photographic recce of Yowhla, Flg Off J. M. Williams' Hurricane suffered a coolant leak and he force-landed near Pyinmana. Sqn Ldr Parnell's aircraft was hit by anti-aircraft fire near Toungoo on the 22nd and he crash-landed west of Oktwin; although he was seen to run from the aircraft into nearby cover, he could not be located when a search was made.

171: '74', a 10th AF B-24J Liberator of the 436th Bomb Squadron, low over the wreckage of the Bilin railway bridges

172: The railway yard at Kuala Lumpur, devastated by the last preparatory raid by XX Bomber Command B-29s on 10 March 1945; the aiming point, the 'round-house'. The B-29s of the 58th Wing were not renowned for precision bombing—this accurate attack was made from an altitude of 700ft. This vertical was taken from Mosquito RG187 of 684 Sqn's Cocos Islands Detachment on 19 July

173: *The rebuilt bridge over the Mu River going up in smoke again during an attack by 10th AF bombers. These raids were all part of the campaign aimed at destroying Japanese lines of communication and transport, thereby strangling the Japanese forces by denying them supplies and reinforcements*

174: *During a ten-day siege of Fort Dufferin, on the outskirts of Mandalay, in mid-March 1945, the attacking forces were resupplied by a series of airdrops. Here a Dakota drops materiel onto Mandalay racecourse, a half-mile to the north of the Fort. The strategic Pagoda Hill can be seen in the distance*

175: *A raid photograph taken on 20 March by a B-25H of the 3rd Bomb Sqn, US 10th Air Force, showing the results of RAF Thunderbolts attacking the ramparts of the Fort which was abandoned that day by its Japanese garrison*

Last operations in Arakan

In Arakan, XV Corps' operations were reduced as a result of the supply demands made by IV and XXXIII Corps on the Central Front and a landing by No.3 Commando Brigade at Kangaw on 22 January met furious resistance. The action was supported by the most intensive air effort yet undertaken by the Allied Air Forces of Eastern Air Command. During this, the fiercest battle in Arakan, fighter bombers used Napalm for the first time. Although "devastating" against troops in the open and against buildings of frame and thatch, it was observed that the intense flame soon died away, so from early February the close-support squadrons gave up the weapon for the less spectacular but more effective 500lb General Purpose high-explosive bombs. At Myebon the commandos fought through swamps intersected by tidal waterways or 'chaungs' in an amphibious battle ending in a landing at Ruywa. The 'Battle of the Chaungs' was typified by a cartoon in *SEAC*, the forces' newspaper, in which the question was asked, "Whose creek did you say we were up?". A further landing at Letpan took place on 13 March and the main purpose of the Arakan Campaigns, to establish bases for air-supply within the 250-mile economical range of Douglas C-47 aircraft serving the Central Front, had been achieved. XV Corps continued pressure around Toungup, however, compelling Kimura to retain a substantial force in Arakan to protect the western flank of his forces in Central Burma.

No.2 Sqn IAF sent a detachment to Akyab, on to Dabaing on 6 February, when Plt Off D'Souza crashed while on a photographic sortie. The detachment returned to Akyab on the 17th. There on 3 March Flg Off S.V. Hyder's aircraft was badly damaged in mist when, it seems, he taxied into the path of a Spitfire PR.XI of 681 Sqn on take-off. The Spitfire, PA860, 'G', appears to have been a write-off.

The capture of Mandalay and Meiktila precipitated the full-scale battle in open 'tank country' that Slim had intended, giving 14th Army an opportunity so to shatter the Japanese forces that a "race against time" to reach Rangoon would be practicable before the beginning of the monsoon rains.

The Japanese, unaware of the supply problems that had caused a reduction in the strength of XV Corps, saw the coastal operations in Arakan as a threat to their supply route along the Lower Irrawaddy Valley and mounted several air attacks. On 3 March ten Tojos made a surprise attack on Akyab airfield, damaging five Hurricanes of No.2 Sqn RIAF (the IAF became the Royal Indian Air Force on 1 March). On the 5th Flg Off R.L. Farquarson of 28 Sqn was forced to bale-out on a sortie over Maymyo but a party of troops sent to search for him failed to make contact.

160 Sqn's night photography experiments were continuing in a Liberator Mk.III BZ900, 'C', which was modified to carry thirty-six 4.5inch photo-flashes contained in a carrier manufactured at R&DU at Cawnpore and installed in the bomb-bay. These flashes were automatically launched at set intervals by electrical impulses and fused to burst at a pre-determined height. The shutter of a K.19A 'night camera' was operated by a photo-electric cell actuated by the light from the flashes. On 12 March Flt Lt Leeper flew BZ900 to Cox's Bazar for a special operation over Arakan at the request of HQ XV Corps, hoping to detect enemy transport which was, by this time, only moving by night. From the night of 13 March the first sorties took place each night until the 20th, covering much of the road from Toungup to Prome and from An to Minbu. The operation was not entirely satisfactory, due to the difficulty of pinpointing targets and to haze which reduced the effectiveness of the photo-flashes.

During the second week of March 1945, Liberators FL935 and FL936 were again flying over northern Sumatra but dense cloud prevented photography. No 684 Sqn's China Bay Detachment continued flying to Sumatra, Car Nicobar and Nancowry and, on 10 March, NS675, 'Z', (Flt Lt J. Irvine and Flt Sgt W.G. Bannister) flew through frontal cloud to Phuket to obtain beach cover. There was broken cloud over the target but, by diverting to each separate area as it became clear, almost complete cover was obtained although this entailed three full circuits of the island. The total flying time for 2,848 miles was 8hr 48min, a new distance and endurance record.

On 25 March, Sqn Ldr Berry, OC No.4 Sqn RIAF, carried out a tactical recce in Hurricane HC740, 'M', along the road from Taungup to Prome which winds over the 3,427ft Taungup Pass. The next day six Hurricanes bombed the road, causing a series of landslides. A photo-recce by Flg Off Surendra in 125, 'R' and Flg Off M.D. Khanna in 415, 'O' on the 28th showed the road, the enemy's main supply line and escape route between the Irrawaddy Valley and the Arakan coast, had been completely blocked. 681 Sqn, whose Spitfires had flown over 1,000 operational hours during February (up to ten sorties per day) as the Army moved south, was daily seeking targets in southern Burma. On 23 March Flg Off C.V. Papps in PL969, 'P', made a forced landing south of Cox's Bazar while returning to Alipore; he was spotted by the pilot of a USAAF Stinson L-5 who landed nearby and carried Papps and his cameras to Cox's Bazar. The squadron's Forward Detachment moved from Imphal to Monywa early in the month, then forward again to Meiktila Main airfield to join 28 Sqn's B Flight which moved south on 6 April.

The aerial survey of the Malay Peninsula was almost complete and, after a final raid on oil-installations off Singapore and a series of mine-laying operations, 58th Bomber Wing was transferred to the control of XXI

Bomber Command in the Pacific on 29 March. Only a further half-dozen daily PR sorties by Superfortresses remained to be completed in April. Continuing cover of Phuket Island and Northern Sumatra was obtained by Flg Off L R. Jones of 160 Sqn in FL936 on 1st and 8 April, and Flg Off J. Jackson flew the Liberator to Simaloer on the 12th. During March No.7 Sqn RIAF, earlier a light-bomber squadron, moved to Imphal and on the 26th flew their Hurricane IICs to Sinthe, replacing No.1 Sqn whose operations ended on the 31st with tactical recces over Thazi, Seikpyu aud Singu and a final photographic sortie by the CO, Sqn Ldr Rajaram, in LD630 escorted by Flg Off Cariappa in LD838. During its record 14-month operational tour, No.1 Sqn IAF flew 4,813 sorties, with a rate of aircraft serviceability "second to none in the world!"

During the month the 40th Sqn flew 278 operational missions and 1,963 hours. Its photo lab produced 113,488 prints, a record for the American squadron which had difficulty in getting supplies and material from Cox's Bazar to Manyubin. On one occasion supplies were so reduced that the photo lab was unable to operate until an F-5E brought hypo from Alipore.

No.7 Sqn began tactical reconnaissance operations on 28 March and, on the 29th, Flg Offs Kochar and Prasad flew as 'weavers' for the more experienced pilots of No.1 Sqn on PR sorties to Mahlaing and Thabutkon. Next day Flt Lt Dewan, with Engineer as No 2, and Sqn Ldr Lal with Flg Off Ghisad as 'weaver', flew No.7 Sqn's first PR sorties.

Operations continued into April following up 5 and 17 Division's advance to the Yamethin area, then in support of 20 Division's parallel drive southwards down the Irrawaddy. On 28 April Flg Offs Rikhye and Rao were met by intense small-arms anti-aircraft fire near Allanmyo where the Japanese fought desperately to hold off XXXIII Corps' mobile columns while their remaining forces in Arakan attempted to withdraw across the river. They were intended to protect the Pegu area until the monsoon, due in three weeks' time, halted 14th Army's double drive towards Rangoon . Rao's Hurricane was hit and burst into flames; the pilot barely had time to transmit "I am shot ..." before the aircraft fell into the Irrawaddy. Four other Hurricanes of No.7 Sqn were damaged by small-arms fire the same day at Allanmyo and two days later Flg Off Prasad was shot down into the river a few miles further south at Sadangaung.

Flt Lt Mathews had an unnerving experience of a different sort when, the Squadron's Record Book notes, he "learned that a Snake was his co-pilot"; over a yard in length, it crawled down his neck and arm and settled by his left foot. He flew back with his revolver in his left hand, covering the snake. "Flg Off Mathews", the record concludes, "is now an authority on airborne snakes in this squadron."

As earlier noted, in November 1944 the British Chiefs of Staff had directed that a base should be developed in the Cocos Islands, situated in the Indian Ocean 650 miles south-west of Java and the farthest east of any territory still in British hands. Although the Japanese had occupied the Christmas Islands, 200 miles south of Java, they had made only reconnaissance flights to the Cocos group and occasional air raids against the small British garrison there, protecting a cable station on Direction Island. The British intention was to construct a defended airfield on West Island, code-named 'Brown', for a regular air-link between Ceylon and Australia and as a staging-post for heavy bomber operations similar to 'Boomerang'. When the plan was formulated, Operation 'Capital' was still intended to be the only major British offensive and it was then anticipated that 14th Army could only establish a front from Mandalay to Akyab before the 1945 monsoon. 'Extended Capital' and the proposed 'Modified Dracula' now radically changed the situation, their likely success offering the use of heavy bomber airfields in Southern Burma.

The remaining units of the Japanese 15th Army were left to hold a line from Yenangyaung on the river to Thazi, east of Meiktila, until such time as the south-west monsoon might cause grave logistical problems for 14th Army's mobile forces. Slim was deeply worried by the impending loss of the American C-47 squadrons, leaving his Army with greatly reduced air supply. These squadrons were committed to the China-Burma-India Theatre of Operations only until land routes to China were secure and it had been made clear by the US Chiefs of Staff that the reconquest of Burma was simply a British colonial concern and that no matter what the military situation, the aircraft would be withdrawn in June. Another reason for haste was the need for airfields near Prome on the Lower Irrawaddy and Toungoo in the Sittang Valley, so that cover could be provided for Operation 'Dracula'.

It was decided that the landings be brought forward as 'Modified Dracula' and Rangoon recaptured so that forces could drive north to meet Slim's double drive. 14th Army's principal effort was to be a thrust down the 'railway corridor' to Toungoo and Pegu by IV Corps, while XXIII Corps made a parallel drive down the Irrawaddy through Prome, cutting off Sakurai's 28th Army in Arakan.

On 10 April the advances began, led by 5 Div, aiming to reach Rangoon in the thirty days before the monsoon was expected. IV Corps moved fast, using *Blitzkrieg* tactics; armoured spearheads would seize an airstrip, then RE airfield-construction units travelling with the armour would make good a runway for a battalion to be flown in to secure the area—and the pattern would be repeated every 20 or 30 miles along the 'corridor'.

176: *Aircraft losses were not always due to enemy action; this Indian Air Force Tac/R Hurricane IIc collided with a Spitfire of 681 Sqn on take-off. No details of the incident are recorded but this was almost certainly the occasion when Flg Off Hyder, of No.2 Sqn RIAF, "crashed in bad visibility" at Akyab on 3 March 1945*

177: *The Spitfire involved was PA860, 'G'. Both pilots walked away across a spreading pool of aviation spirit*

178: *Hurricane FR.IIc LD903, 'N', of No.10 Sqn RIAF, being armed at Kyaukpyu in April 1945. Although the squadron's aircraft were fitted with camera mountings, operations were mainly strikes against the enemy withdrawing from Arakan*

Preparing for 'Zipper'

The preparatory reconnaissance for 'Zipper' continued with Operation 'Sunfish' when Force 63, the battleships HMS *Queen Elizabeth* and the Free French *Richelieu* with a supporting force and the escort carriers *Emperor* and *Khedive*, sailed on 8 April for a series of bombardments, air-strikes and photographic reconnaissance of Malaya. Seven Hellcats from 888 Sqn were assigned to *Emperor* but one of the PR aircraft crashed into the barrier when landing. The reconnaissance was intended for 12 April but had to be postponed because *Emperor*'s catapult was faulty, so the battleships shelled Sabang while destroyers shelled Oleelhoe. On 11 April attacks were made on Koetaradja and Lho'nga airfields by *Khedive*'s 808 Sqn Hellcats—an Oscar was shot down by Sub-Lt J.R. Foxley in Hellcat Mk.II(P) JV311 and a Dinah was destroyed by Sub-Lt S.C. Richardson in another fighter-reconnaissance Hellcat, JW705. Five of 888 Sqn's PR Hellcats were flown off on the morning of 14 April, from a position west of Padang, to obtain cover of the proposed landing-beaches near Port Swettenham and Port Dickson on the west coast of Malaya, and the towns of Kuala Lumpur and Seremban. The weather over the Strait of Malacca was bad—not only were the photographs poor in quality but Sub-Lt J.W. Tomlinson, whose JX683 developed engine-trouble, was forced to bale-out ten miles off the coast. He was picked up by fishermen and given up to the enemy. Like a number of Naval airmen captured in Sumatra, he was later killed at the end of the war. Of seventy-five miles required beach cover, the other Hellcats photographed only half, and only a fifth of an intended 1,290 square miles of inland areas.

The following morning, from a position closer to land, three aircraft made four-hour sorties and obtained forty-five miles of the fifty required of the beaches, and half the cover of specific targets. Again the Task Force came under air attack and an Oscar was destroyed. On 16 April while a strike was made on Emmahaven, four more sorties were flown by 888 Sqn, this time achieving almost all the required cover of beaches and inland targets. During the three days of operations, some 2,000 sq miles of survey cover of Malaya and 3,500 sq miles of Sumatra were obtained.

The commanding officers of all the RAF photographic squadrons changed during the month: Sqn Ldr A.E. Guymer took over 28 Sqn; Wg Cdr D.B. Pearson DFC, who had been a Buffalo pilot of No.4 PRU before the fall of Singapore, replaced Wg Cdr Procter in 681 Sqn. During April 1945, operations over Burma were becoming hazardous with the approach of the monsoon season and No.2 Sqn RIAF ended their sorties on 15 April, apart from a few minor recces which proved costly: Flg Off Salahuddin crash-landed in Japanese-held territory on 5 May, escaping with minor injuries and the next day Plt Off Serapati crashed in enemy territory but made his way back to safety. No 684 Sqn also encountered difficulties;

on 18 April RG125, 'V' (Flt Lt Newman and Flt Sgt Preston) left Alipore for a sortie from Cox's Bazar but crashed *en route*, killing the crew. On the 22nd Flt Lt T. Bell and Flg Off J. Plater in NS675, 'Z', were sent to cover Nancowry Island but there was exceptionally bad weather along their route and, when they failed to return by dusk, it was assumed that they had crashed into the sea. The same day Flt Lt Stoneham and Flg Off Burns in NS646, 'I', flew to Victoria Point; they were caught in severe storms and returned to Cox's Bazar with only sufficient fuel for a further ten minutes' flight. The leading edges of the wings and the tail-plane were damaged and required repairs before the Mosquito could continue to Alipore.

When Mountbatten gave priority to the Rangoon assault, Operation 'Roger' was abandoned and the date for 'Zipper' was advanced to August. The lack of a forward airfield was made up by the provision of additional escort carriers and aircraft for the East Indies Fleet. In addition, the Cocos Islands plan, 'Pharos', which had begun in March, was sufficiently advanced for 'Brown' to receive aircraft late in April. The long-awaited base for long-range photographic reconnaissance was at last available.

No.7 Sqn IAF, equipped with Hurricane Mk.IVs, moved from Imphal to Sinthe to begin Tac/R operations on 28 April, losing Flg Offs Rao and Rikhye to anti-aircraft fire that same day. Two days later Flg Off Prasad also was shot down by AA fire.

With operations by Northern Combat Area Command virtually completed and the safety of the supply route to China assured, US 9th PR Sqn returned from Myitkyina to Dinjan and became non-operational late in April. Tactical reconnaissance cover on the coast was under some strain so, on 12 April, the 40th TR Sqn sent F-6 aircraft of Flight 'A' to Mawnubyin 1 airfield (Akyab) to obtain low-level photographs of the approaches to Rangoon and the first mission, led by Lt Ringo, was flown the next day. A second four-plane mission on the 14th came under concentrated fire from Elephant Point on the west bank of the Rangoon River. During another photo run at 150ft on 16 April the F-6 of the flight leader, Lt E.H. Dougherty was hit, crashed and caught fire. The following day Lts Ringo and Huelsnitz, returning to Mawnubyin, became separated in a rain storm near Kaiktaw and Lt Ringo failed to return. The last mission by four aircraft was led by Lt J.J. Kendrick on 20 April, to obtain low obliques of the east bank of the river, under constant fire from five anti-aircraft gun positions.

Besides attack photographs, Mosquitos and Beaufighters on offensive reconnaissance operations frequently used their cameras, fitted in the nose, to record potential targets and from March onwards, the Beaufighters of 27 Sqn, soon to be engaged in Jungle Rescue and Special Duties, were fitted with vertical F.24 cameras. Detachments from 27 Sqn were stationed at Meiktila and Akyab to locate crashed aircraft, using their cameras to record the condition of the aircraft and the surroundings, for the briefing of rescue or recovery teams. A typical 27 Sqn report was that made by the crew (R.E. Jones and G.A. Exley) of Beaufighter TF.X RD280, flying from Monywa on 20 April; "Search for Hurricane reported in position LQ6188. 5/10 cu with scattered thunderstorms.

Hurricane located at LQ585815 at north end of landing strip about 400 yards long. An American L-5 was also landed there. Message dropped to person standing by aircraft to forward details to 221 Grp". This was Flg Off Williams' Hurricane, force-landed two days earlier.

179: *Flg Off Williams' Hurricane FR.IIc located on a landing strip near Pyinmana by a 27 Sqn Beaufighter on 20 April 1945. The 28 Sqn aircraft carried no White markings above the wings and tailplane*

180: *A North American F-6K of the 20th PR Sqn in April. The 'trimetrogen' camera ports can be seen just forward of the tail-wheel covers and the oblique camera window in the fuselage side. F-6Ks carried six 0.50in wing guns*

181: *Hurricane IV, KZ393(?), 'G', of 28 Sqn, wears the White Identification Bands introduced in late January 1945 over its Temperate Land camouflage scheme*

182: *The Hurricane FR.IIcs of No.2 Sqn RIAF, as seen here at Akyab, were fitted with oblique and vertical camera mountings and retained their four 20mm cannon. Unfortunately for modellers, the original picture is not clear enough to allow the interesting nose art to be deciphered, but it appears to be an eagle with upstretched wings in front of a sun with the name 'Koel'*

183: *Beaufighter TF.X KN393, 'W', of 27 Sqn fitted with a camera in a square housing on the tip of the nose. The code letter appears to be in Red with a White outline*

184: *This Hurricane of 28 Sqn gives scale to the Ava bridge over the Irrawaddy. It was one of many which bore no White identification bands above the wings and tailplane*

"A race again time"

Rangoon retaken

During the last days of April 1945 the 'Modified Dracula' convoys bound for Rangoon encountered violent storms before the landings were made—then the monsoon rains began, two weeks earlier than expected.

For the next two weeks the weather was bad—an intertropical front of unusual severity stretched from Mergui southwards to Kra and the weather over the Gulf of Martaban made it almost impossible for 684 Sqn's Mosquitos to provide the consistent cover demanded on seven consecutive days.

Besides a covering Naval force which sailed from Trincomalee to screen the southern approaches to Rangoon and intercept any Japanese ships which might sail from Singapore to attack the troop convoys, the ships of Force 63 carried out diversionary attacks (Operation 'Bishop') on the Nicobar and Andaman Islands. On 30 April an early bombardment was followed by an air-strike on the two Car Nicobar airfields and, late in the day, Port Blair and its airfield were shelled. The Hellcats of 804 Sqn, flying from HMS *Empress* with one section in *Shah*, spotted for the guns and, next day, used their cameras for the first time to record the damage.

The Hellcats and Seafires of the Escort Carrier Squadron undertook combat air patrol (CAP), reconnaissance and strikes from the end of February to the beginning of May. Re-named 21st Aircraft Carrier Squadron, the escort carriers provided close support for the Rangoon landings, 'Dracula', on 2-6 May before

continuing a programme of operations over the Andaman Sea and Strait of Malacca until the end of the war.

By this time 14th Army was thrusting down the Irrawaddy Valley and preparing for a drive down the road/rail 'corridor' towards Toungoo but it seemed unlikely that Rangoon could be reached before the outbreak of the monsoon 'officially' forecast to begin about 15 May. On 3 April Mountbatten gave orders for the start of 'Modified Dracula', to ensure supply to the Army when air transport was reduced by the intended withdrawal of USAAF squadrons and restricted also by the weather. Forces assembled at Akyab and Ramree began sailing on 27 April and the assault was planned for 2 May.

The advances brought 14th Army forward units out of the 'dry belt' which had so well suited the armoured columns. Now they moved southwards in conditions of increasing temperature and humidity. On 18 April a column of 20 Div reached the Irrawaddy south of Magwe, by-passing Sakurai's main defences facing 7 Div further north. On 20 April the first rain of the season fell in the Sittang Valley but the drive continued and 5 Div's armour occupied Toungoo two days later.

By late April XV Corps had control of the whole Arakan coast and Sakurai's situation was critical, his only hope of salvation being to hold XXXIII Corps long enough to cover withdrawal of his Army eastwards from

185 Above: *808 Squadron's Hellcat II JV292, 'C7T', from HMS* Khedive *took part in the preliminary support for operation 'Dracula' and attacks on Mergui and Victoria Point airfields. 2-6 May 1945. Camouflage is Temperate Sea Scheme with an interesting interpretation of the instructions regarding White identification bands*

Arakan. Although unaware of the imminence of Operation 'Dracula', Kimura realised that Pegu must be held, even though Rangoon be abandoned, until the monsoon had begun; he could then withdraw his scattered units under cover of the rain storms and free from air-observation, across the Sittang to re-group 80 miles to the east along the Salween River.

For the last stages of Slim's advance, possession of the airfield group at Toungoo was essential. These airfields were in use on 30 April when 17 Div with close air support cleared Payagyi near Pegu, where stood the last defences before Rangoon.

The favourable weather conditions of the previous month over Arakan were not repeated in April when some reconnaissance sorties by the 40th PR Sqn had to be abandoned but in spite of the weather 167 missions were flown and the photo lab turned out 56,000 prints.

On 1 May 'Dracula' was mounted, troops of 50 Indian Parachute Brigade landing at Elephant Point by the mouth of the Rangoon River. The story of the re-occupation of Rangoon has often been told. Even as the Rangoon landings began, it became clear that, apart from isolated pockets of resistance, the Japanese had abandoned the city. On the afternoon of 1 May 1945 (D-1) the crew of one of 176 Sqn's Beaufighters, returning from an attacks on gun-positions and shipping, reported seeing the words "JAPS GONE" in white on the red roof of Rangoon Central Gaol, used as a POW camp. On D-Day, 2 May, an F-5E of the 40th PR Sqn, on one of the last USAAF sorties over Burma, brought back photographs of messages painted on the roof by prisoners—the messages read, "BRITISH HERE" and "EXTRACT DIGIT". Crews of 267 Sqn Dakotas, dropping suplies to Indian troops in Rangoon, reported another message painted on a nearby road: "JAPS EVACUATED—DO NOT PRANG RANGOON".

The sea-borne assault on Rangoon began on 2 May, tactical reconnaissance being flown for the first time by Seafire FR. Mk.IIIs of 807 Naval Air Sqn from the escort carrier HMS *Hunter*, while 808 Sqn's Hellcats from *Khedive* joined RAF fighter-bombers in attacks on gun positions along the Rangoon River.

A brigade of 26 Division landed and advanced on the port area of Rangoon. Late on the 2nd torrential rain began falling and, as the docks were re-occupied the following day, the monsoon rains having begun two weeks earlier than forecast, the temperature was recorded as 104°F.

On 6 May IV Corps' armoured spearhead, reduced to a crawl by rain and mud, linked up with a column from Rangoon at Hlegu, only 28 miles away. XXXIII Corps was still struggling down the Irrawaddy Valley against stubborn resistance from the largely intact Japanese 28th

Army withdrawing from Arakan into the Pegu Yoma. There the enemy would pose a severe threat of some 15,000 men in organised formations spread along the hills from Prome to Pegu.

The scattered Japanese remnants retiring from Meiktila meanwhile came under control of the Japanese 56th Div from China, marching south to join Kimura's main defence line on the Sittang and Salween Rivers. The difficulties now experienced by aircraft operating from the few all-weather airfields, and the impossibility in storm conditions of using *kachcha* strips, showed clearly that if Rangoon had not been occupied on the eve of the monsoon, close-support and air-supply for IV and XXXIII Corps could not have been maintained.

On 30 April No.7 Sqn RIAF moved south to 'Maida Vale' at Magwe for continuing tactical support of 7 and 20 Divs. In the Irrawaddy Valley there were still substantial enemy forces opposing XXXIII Corps but by 15 May the troops of the Japanese rearguard withdrawing from Arakan were dispersed by 7 Div. northwest of Allanmyo. At Kama, thirty miles downstream, the Japanese 54th Div, intact from Arakan , was trapped and defeated, the survivors escaping into the jungle-covered hills east of Prome. Here they were formed into columns and prepared to break-out from the Pegu Yoma to rejoin the main enemy force which still held ground west of the Sittang River, east of Pegu.

XXXIII Corps, meanwhile pressed on towards the Irrawaddy Delta and the port of Bassein. No.7 Sqn was daily involved with tactical recces and occasional PR sorties; by Sqn Ldr Lal with Flg Off Dewan on 5 May and with Flg Off Chandra on 11 May. On the 15th Flg Off Engineer failed to retuirn from a sortie to Henzada and his CO led a four-hour search the following day without success. Ground forces later reported the Hurricane burnt out and the pilot dead. It had been intended for the squadron to be withdrawn on 16 May but HQ XXXIII Corps requested a further ten days' operations when the weather improved. On the 20th Flg Off Mathews, in LD680, making a forced-landing, crashed and was injured but rescued from the bank of the Irrawaddy by a passing Royal Navy gunboat. The following day Flg Off Vazir was lost in HV796, before operations ended on 22 May with tactical recces around Tonbo.

By this time, the RAF Liberators of 234 Gp Strategic Air Force were fitted with mission-recording cameras and frequently carried hand-held cameras for miscellaneous photography *en route* and over their targets. In many cases, these relieved the PR squadrons of the need for 'post-raid' damage assessment sorties.

During the first three weeks of May, 681 Sqn flew a number of sorties from Alipore as far as Moulmein and Amhurst. The Detachment with 221 Gp moved from Imphal to Meiktila to cover the enemy escape routes in

186: *Operation 'Dracula'; under leaden grey skies, landing craft move up the Rangoon River on 2 May 1945. Smoke rises in the distance from defence positions bombed by RAF Thunderbolts*

187 Left: *Rangoon Central Jail photographed on 2 May 1945 by an F-5E of the 40th TR Sqn. 'JAPS GONE' can be seen painted on the roof a cell block*

188 Below: *Another view of Rangoon Central Jail; this time the picture was taken by P/O Lee on 3 May. Apart from the cell blocks, one with the legend 'BRITISH HERE' on the roof, most of the administrative buildings can be seen to have been completely gutted*

189: A later message from the inmates of Rangoon Jail showing their increasing desperation with the slow progress towards their relief:'EXTRACT DIGIT'

190: The camera window and its protective oil channel can be seen beneath this Hellcat II.PR (Type 2 mountings), JV282 of 808 Sqn, seen being winched over after an accident aboard HMS Khedive on 9 March 1945 while being flown by Sub-Lt J E Jackson

191: Hellcat II, JW723, '6G', of 804 Sqn, bounced over the wires aboard the escort carrier HMS Ameer on 28 May 1945, "demonstrating the destructive power of the Hellcat" on three aircraft parked forward. This aircraft and the Sea Blue Hellcat II (JX827 or JX889) show the typical position of the White wing band in relation to the outer edge of the roundel. The pilot of the offender, Lt TH Pemberton, escaped with a severe fright

the Shan Hills and the airfields at Kengtung in eastern Burma and Chiengmai in Siam. Following the occupation of Rangoon, an advance party of 681 Sqn was stationed at Mingaladon and the squadron, forced by the monsoon to abandon many sorties, was able to receive direct advance warning of adverse weather conditions over Southern Burma. On the 25th the Forward Detachment moved to Mingaladon from Meiktila.

To test the Spitfire's range and performance when fitted with a drop tank, Wg Cdr Pearson flew four hundred miles northward on 26 May, climbing to 29,000 ft over the cloud layer covering West Bengal and Bihar. Taking Mt. Everest as his point of reference, before turning back he took photographs of the mountain and the Rongbuk glacier.

The USAAF photographic squadrons and supporting units had, by this time, completed their required task as part of an integrated Force in SE Asia Command and, after a few sorties early in the month, were virtually non-operational, waiting to move from India and Burma into China.

Towards the end of May 1945 the weather improved for a brief period and up to three sorties were flown each day by 684 Sqn's Mosquitos as far south as Phuket Island. Increased attention was given to the port of Bangkok and the Burma-Siam railway as a search was made for evidence of enemy reinforcements moving up to their defences on the Salween River. A feature of these operations was the increasing use of low-level photography to obtain details of Japanese-held ports on the islands off the coast and of bridges on the Mergui-Moulmein coastal road.

The prospect of new reconnaissance variants of the Spitfire and Mosquito arriving in Air Command SE Asia led to the formation of a new unit at Ratmalana in Ceylon on 11 May. A PR Development Flight was set up with two Mosquito and two Oxford aircraft for experimental work and air-testing of cameras and installations, under the direct control of HQ 222 Gp. A new RAF headquarters, 347 (PR) Wing, was formed late in April and became effective on 9 June. The new HQ absorbed the RAF Element of PR Force which was closed down when the US forces ended offensive operations in Burma and Eastern Air Command was disbanded on 1 June. Gp Capt Wise returned to the UK and command of the new wing was assumed by Gp Capt C.E. Stuart Beamish DFC, who had previously commanded RAF Benson.

Although the weather severely hampered air operations by the Tac/R aircraft, on 26 May HQ RAF Burma signalled 221 Grp with a chilling message: *"Air C-in-C is concerned at large numbers of Japanese apparently escaping eastwards into Siam and south towards Malaya. From every point of view better to kill them now when in reduced circumstances rather than allow them time* *to re-equip and re-form. Air C-in-C is of opinion that every effort should be made to destroy Japs by air attack with good results in spite of difficulties in operating during monsoon. He suggests a new technique in hunting Japanese from the air whereby the whole area occupied by the enemy could be divided into sections for regular air reconnaissance with small striking forces standing by at call. Important to encourage new interest and enthusiasm in aircrews and squadrons in killing the Japs on every possible occasion especially at present time when large numbers are trying to escape. Should be possible develop a keen squadron competitive spirit on these lines".*

On 28 May 'A' Flight of 28 Sqn moved south to Mingaladon joining the Forward Detachment of 681 Sqn, which had moved on the 22nd. No 28 Sqn immediately returned to ops along the Mawchi Road and the following day to Pa-An and Kamamaung, with Tac/R sorties to Sittang, Mokpalin, Bilin and as far as Moulmein during the next few days. Sqn Ldr J. Rhind, arriving on 5 June to take Command of 28 Sqn, found the squadron's 'Initial Equipment' sadly depleted although several Hurricane Mk.IVs had been delivered to replace the older Mk.IICs. Sorties continued over the Sittang River, to Penwegon and Shwegyin until early July, by which time only two Hurricanes of 'A' Flt remained serviceable at Mingaladon —and one of these was destroyed when a Beaufighter of 27 Sqn ran into it. At Meiktila, after tactical reconnaissance over the Sittang Valley bv 'B' Flight's three remaining Hurricane IICs on 6 July, 28 Sqn became virtually non-operational.

During 14th Army's advances, the remaining Hurricane IIs and Spitfire VIIIs of the RAF's fighter squadrons had been almost exclusively operated in the ground-attack role. When they were withdrawn in May to prepare for the assault on Malaya, it was intended that they should continue to operate in support of the Army. At the beginning of June, No.10 Sqn IAF left Burma for Chettinad in India and began conversion to the Spitfire FR.XIVE. No.6 Sqn RIAF and 28 Sqn were programmed to re-equip with the new Spitfire but, for reasons that remain obscure, 28 Sqn (the only operational fighter-reconnaissance squadron in Burma by June 1945) continued flying a diminishing number of Hurricanes for the remainder of the campaign.

The Mosquitos of 684 Sqn's China Bay Detachment, under the command of Flt Lt H.C. Lowcock, continued reconnaissance over Port Blair and Car Nicobar almost every day, alert for signs of a Japanese withdrawal by sea which, when attempted, was stopped by the Navy.

At the end of March 1945, Sqn Ldr K.J. Newman DFC and Wt Off R.K. Smith DFM were ordered to fly Mosquito 'A' back to the UK for complete overhaul at De Havillands. This aircraft had done some extremely valuable work during its life with the Squadron and had been brought out from the UK by this crew in December

192: *Mount Everest photographed by Wg Cdr Pearson of 681 Sqn, the frame marked with the negative reference, date, lens focal-length, altitude and the squadron number*

CT/189   26MAY45   F.14/1 29000 681

193: *A Mosquito PR.XVI of 684 Sqn approaches the summit of Everest on 1 July 1945*

194 Left: *Hurricane FR.IIc LF208 of 28 Sqn RAF (ex-No.1 Sqn RIAF) with vertical camera installed and newly-applied Identification Bands. Flying in the pre-monsoon weather of April 1945 was made even more hazardous by the smoke haze that persisted when the weather cleared*

195 Below: *The first Mosquito PR.34, finished in Aluminium and PRU Blue, arrived at Karachi on 1 June 1945 after a record-breaking flight of 12hr 45min from Benson*

197: Mosquito FB.VIs of 110 Sqn showing the alternative Identification Bands—White against the Dark Green and Medium Sea Grey of the camouflage and Dull Blue on Aluminium. The various maintenance markings on HR631 are of interest, as is the cover over the pressure head on the fin leading edge and the sturdy picketing stake restraining the tail-wheel

198: Not of the best quality, but included on account of its rarity value, this picture shows Mosquito FB.VI RF780, 'P', of 47 Sqn in Dull Aluminium finish. Aircraft of 47 and 110 Sqns were fitted with cameras and were employed on Tac/R duties

196 Left: Mosquito PR.34 RG203, 'E', of 684 Sqn's Cocos Island Detachment in July 1944 shows the Dull Aluminium uppersurfaces and PRU Blue undersides usual on these aircraft. Note the ubiquitous jeep

199 Right: The nose cameras fitted in many Mosquitos were not only used during individual strikes. Here is recorded an attack by FB.VIs against river-port storage areas at Yenangyaung on the Irrawaddy, 12 April 1945

200: *The bomber squadrons' Mosquito FB.VIs were fitted with nose cameras to record their strikes. Here an aircraft of 110 Sqn is photographed from a following aircraft as it releases bombs on an enemy encampment on 3 June 1945*

201: *A shot taken by the nose camera of Beaufighter NV951 (Flg Offs AH Reick and NT Allen) of 177 Sqn, during an attack on a Mitsubishi Ki-21 'Sally' at Kaikpi, south of Bassein on April 1945. During the Chinese campaign and the early part of the war against the Western powers, the Ki-21 was a potent bomber, but by 1945 it was a sitting duck, whether in the air or on the ground*

1943. Up to this time she had flown a total of 495 hours, covering a distance of some 123,750 miles and had completed 56 operational sorties.

The aircraft behaved perfectly during the journey back to the UK and when she finally landed at Hatfield the only snag reported was a slight mag. drop on the port engine.

While the crew were in the UK they carried out trials on the new Mosquito Mk.34 to discover whether or not this type of aircraft was suited for work in the Far East. The tests were successful and on 29 May four aircraft set out for Karachi from Benson to make a bid for the England to India record. Three of the aircraft were flown by crews from 544 Sqn and one by the crew from 684 Sqn. The three aircraft from 544 Sqn reached Karachi safely. The winners (Flt Lt E.A. Weatherill and Flg Off L.G. Grover) completed the route in 12hr 27min. The aircraft flown by Sqn Ldr Newman, however, experienced a serious mag drop after take-off and the pilot decided to return to Benson. On the following day the defect was rectified and late that evening the aircraft once again took off for Karachi which was reached 12hr 25 min after take-off from Benson (with one stop at Cairo West for fuel) thus breaking the record set the previous day by two minutes.

On 1 June 1945, three of the four Mosquitos arrived at Alipore and the first Mosquito Mk.34s were placed on the Squadron's strength. A fuel consumption test was carried out in India by Flt Lt D.D. Warwick and Flg Off G. Jones in one of these aircraft. They were airborne for 9hr 25min and had half an hour's fuel left on landing.

By the middle of the month, action in Burma had been brought almost to a halt by the weather but port facilities at Rangoon were soon in operation. During May, a major change was made in the command structure in preparation for Operation 'Zipper', by a new formation, XXXIV Corps. Much of 14th Army was withdrawn to India, leaving some elements to continue limited operations under a new Headquarters 12th Army.

The 40th TR Sqn had ceased operations and now moved from the rapidly flooding airfield at Mawnubyin to Alipore. Dogged by a lack of transport the squadron made use of the 8th Recce Group's Courier Flight of B-25s for personnel, C-47s of Eastern Air Command for freight and F-5s with containers beneath the wings for baggage.

The fighter-reconnaissance squadrons of the Royal Indian Air Force were remarkable for their consistent records of availability. No.7 Sqn continued operations until 23 May when its tour of operations ended; aircraft serviceability during May was "an incredible 99.43%".

Following Mountbatten's instruction that there should be no further attacks on installations at Singapore by XX Bomber Command, the Imperial Navy was able to continue using the Naval Base without hindrance and, with air cover restricted by the monsoon storms, British supply convoys to Rangoon remained vulnerable to naval attack. Reconnaissance showed the presence still at Singapore of a substantial Japanese naval presence but, despite surveillance whenever the weather permitted, the 13,000 ton heavy cruiser *Haguro* and the destroyer *Kamikaze* were able to depart unseen. Sailing northwards they were spotted by a British submarine in the Strait of Malacca and, when intercepted by the 26th Destroyer Flotilla of the East Indies Fleet, the *Haguro* was sunk during the last true naval engagement of the war off Penang early on 16 May.

On the 24th, from Alipore and using Kyaukpyu as an advanced landing ground, Wg Cdr Lowry and Flg Off Stevens flew to Tenasserim and Kra in NS622, 'X', to take high-level verticals before coming down to a height of only fifty feet for oblique photographs of St Luke, St Matthew and Domel Islands. On 28 May RGl25, 'V' (Flg Off C.G. Andrews and Wt Off H.S. Painter) covered targets in the Siam Valley. Cover was obtained of Don Muang airfield (Bangkok), the water-front at Sattahib and bridges on the Bangkok-Phnom Penh railway line. A 'first-sighting' message was radioed back about shipping observed at Sattahib; on the strength of this report Liberators attacked two merchant ships and port installations on 30 May and 1 June.

Operations by 681 Sqn became increasingly difficult as the weather deteriorated during the following few weeks, although intensive work by RE airfield construction units ensured that the all-weather airfields remained serviceable. A number of sorties were flown by the Spitfires over the routes used by the Japanese forces still in retreat from Central Burma, east of the Sittang River, and over the airfields in Siam where the enemy still had a substantial fighter reserve. From one of these sorties on 7 June, PL841, 'E', flown by Flg Off Woodhouse, failed to return.

A small detachment from l60 Sqn was established at Akyab with Liberator Mklll BZ950, 'H'. On 22 May Flt Lt L.R. Davidson flew the aircraft to Kyaukpyu for a mission as far as Singapore, covering the west coast of Malaya from a height of 25,000ft. The crew of the Liberator saw two enemy aircraft taking off from Port Swettenham airfield and one attempted to overtake but was lost as the daily build-up of cloud began. A week later the same aircraft obtained additional excellent cover of the landing-beaches proposed for 'Zipper' in the Port Dickson area, then flew back to Alipore to await processing of the prints for delivery to HQ 222 Gp and HQ SEAC in Ceylon on the 31st.

From China Bay other aircraft of 160 Sqn, operating further south than the worst of the monsoon weather patterns, were able to continue with PR sorties. On 4 June BZ900, 'C' made a night recce of Eastern Sumatra and two nights later, repeating the operation, FL936 flown by Wt Off J.J. Baker encountered strong head-winds on the return journey but managed to reach China Bay on two engines. On the 9th BZ950 (Plt Off J. Hines) crashed immediately after take-off for the Cocos Islands, killing all the occupants. For the rest of the month l60 Sqn's Liberators were occupied with Special Duties over Malaya but cameras were carried and photographs were taken of specific targets as far north as Kota Bharu, at the extreme limit of the aircraft's range. No 681 Sqn's operations from Mingaladon continued through the month of June, mainly sorties over the Burmese airfields still in enemy hands at Kengtung and Martaban in Eastern Burma, and those in Siam where the Japanese still had substantial numbers of operational aircraft: at Chiengmai, Tak and Mesarieng, and as far south as Prachuab Khirikhand.

In addition to processing and interpreting the results of the PR squadrons' sorties, 347 Wing HQ received film from tactical reconnaissance flights by the Mosquito FB.VIs of 908 Wing, twenty-five sorties by 110 Sqn and fifty-six by 47 Sqn. Although 681 Sqn put up fifty-five sorties in all during the month, 684 Sqn was able to fly only six from Alipore although the China Bay Detachment continued their routine cover of the Islands throughout June.

With their operations restricted by monsoon storms, 684 Sqn's Mosquitos at Alipore, besides training flights, undertook other un-warlike activities. Not to be outdone by 681 Sqn, on 16 June Flt Lt G. Edwards and Flt Lt J. Irvine flew north to the peak of Makalu in Nepal, then to Everest, ten miles further west. Edwards circled the mountain for twenty minutes, taking photographs with cameras mounted in wing-tanks. Nepal was a neutral state and the Everest flights caused a minor diplomatic upset when details were released to the Press. It was explained that the aircraft was lost due to the extensive cloud cover and the crew were only able to fix their position by recognizing the mountain.

The same week, Naval Force 63, including the carriers *Stalker*, *Khedive* and *Ameer*, the last carrying 804 Sqn and six aircraft of 888 Sqn, sailed for operation 'Balsam', the purpose of which was to obtain final cover of the intended landing-beaches for 'Zipper', north and south of Port Dickson on the west coast of Malaya. Each of 888 Sqn's Hellcats carried out a prolonged sortie on the l8th and again on 19 June. Another three reconnaissance sorties were flown the following day. Beach cover was completely successful and most of the required cover was obtained of roads, bridges and airfields while the Naval force remained undiscovered in the Malacca Strait. With the operation completed and the need for secrecy ended, the Hellcats of 804 Sqn and 808 Sqn (from *Khedive*) and Seafires of 809 Sqn (from *Stalker*) attacked the airfields at Medan, Bindjai and Lhokseumawe in Northen Sumatra. The Hellcats of 804 and 888 Sqns were flown off to RN Air Station Tambaram in Madras when the carriers returned to Ceylon.

On 23 June, 171 Wing was informed that the Mosquito PR Mk.34 had been "released for Service in temperate and tropical conditions". By the end of June seven had been delivered to India. These aircraft had a range much greater than that of the Mk.XVI and were developed from the Mosquito B.XVI for use in the Far East to cover the 2,000 mile gap over Sumatra, Malaya and Java, between the operational radii of aircraft based in India or Ceylon and those based in Australia, New Guinea and the Pacific Islands. Two 100 gal wing-tanks were usually carried by the earlier PR Mosquitos, supplemented by 90 gal belly tanks on some of the Mk.XVIs, but the PR.34 was fitted with two 200 gal wing-tanks and had additional internal tankage—1,267 gal in all to give an operational radius of some 1,800 miles.

Merlin 76/77 Series engines gave the aircraft a speed of 425mph at 30,500ft. Five cameras could be mounted in the bomb-bay; two 'split' F24 cameras forward and another pair aft of the fuel-tanks, with one oblique F24 camera.

Four PR.34s left Alipore during the last week of the month for China Bay, then continued to the new Cocos Islands base as No.2 Detachment, all having arrived by the 29th, briefed to undertake urgent and extensive reconnaissance of Malaya and Sumatra.

Photographic reconnaissance showed renewed attempts to repair both the Tamarkand bridges, so Liberators of the RAF's 159 and 356 Sqns returned on 24 June. 356 Sqn's ORB recorded, "All eight aircraft detailed to attack the target at low-level (200/500ft). At the end of the attack the bridge which was originally intact was broken at three places and damaged at others, together with its northern approach. Gun positions in the vicinity of the target were also strafed but flak (Heavy, light and MG.A.A.) was meagre, spasmodic and inaccurate. Photographs were obtained, all aircraft carrying 5in mirror cameras and five aircraft carrying hand-helds".

By this time the Japanese Army Air Force had removed many of its units from South-East Asia to bases along the eastern Pacific coast northward from Indo-China for defence of Japan. Pre-war agreements between the Siamese (Thai) and Japanese Governments had brought no good to Siam but some destruction, and left the small Thai air force with a variety of obsolete Japanese warplanes. Their pilots offered no opposition to the RAF Liberators bombing the railway and recording the results of their attacks. This was 356 Sqn's last operation before moving from the base at Salbani to 'Brown' on the Cocos Islands to prepare for 'Zipper'.

From Alipore on 1 July another flight was made to Everest by two Mosquitos, one fitted with cine-cameras, but heavy cloud and snowstorms prevented a clear view of the mountain. The first sortie by 684 Sqn's No 2 Detachment from Cocos was flown by the squadron's CO, Wg Cdr Lowry, with Flt Sgt Pateman in RG185, 'Z', over the Port Swettenham area on 3 July. The following day Sqn Ldr Newman and Wt Off Smith in RG186, 'G', covered the airfields at Kuala Lumpur and Port Swettenham and, on the return flight, Fort de Kock airfield, north of Padang in Sumatra; thereafter an average of one sortie per day was maintained over the west coast of Malaya. Flt Lt D. Warwick and Flg Off G. Jowles in RG184, 'X', covered Port Dickson, Morib airfield and another new airfield at Pakanbaroe in central Sumatra. During the next few days, other airstrips at Kerling and Kampong Choh were photographed while No 1 (China Bay) Detachment continued their sorties over Car Nicobar, the Andamans and Northern Sumatra. 160 Sqn's Liberators also continued their reconnaissance sorties over Malaya; Flg Off Durant flew Liberator MkVC BZ862, 'J', to Kuala Lumpur on 3 July but found no aircraft on the airfield.

A fifth Mosquito PR.34, RG191, 'M', joined 684 Sqn's Cocos Islands Detachment on 10 July but on the 14th flying out on a sortie, the port engine began vibrating when 450 miles from base. The pilot, Flt Lt Edwards, feathered the propeller and jettisoned his wing-tanks but the aircraft lost height and crashed into the sea on final approach. For several days the Mosquitos' objectives were cloud-covered but Newman and Smith in RG185 obtained satisfactory cover of Johore Bharu and Singapore Island on the 16th, while BZ825, 'O', of 160 Sqn flown by Flt Lt I.A. Muir, checked Ipoh airfield . Warwick and Jowles of 684 Sqn covered more airfield sites in RG186 on 22 July, at Batu Pahat, Yong Peng and Kluang, all in Johore State of Malaya. Then Sqn Ldr Newman and Flt Sgt Pateman in RG184 obtained further airfield cover on the 26th, of Airmolek in Sumatra; of Changi on Singapore Island; Tebran, ten miles north; Batu Pahat and Lumut (Sitiawan) on the west coast.

No 681 Sqn also received new aircraft—the first four Spitfire PR Mk.XIXs, the beginning of a re-equipment programme. The PR.XIX was the final reconnaissance version of the Spitfire, a combination of the F Mk.XIV fuselage and modified Mk.V 'bowser' wings as fitted to the PR.XI. Larger internal wing tanks, each holding 86 gal, increased the total tankage to 256 gal, giving the aircraft a range of 1,550 miles. The engine was a Griffon 66 fitted, like that of the Spitfire XIV, with a Rotol five-bladed airscrew. A Marshall blower pressurised the cockpit to provide reasonable comfort for the pilot at the operational ceiling of 40,000 ft. A 'universal installation' in the fuselage provided mountings for either two F52 or F8 vertical cameras or one oblique and two vertical F24 cameras.

The first PR.XIX to arrive ran into a heavy storm while approaching Alipore and landed with the Christofin covering the airscrew blades badly damaged. The same fault, surface stripping from the blades, occurred on the propellers of the other new aircraft and prevented their use for medium or long-range sorties. 'Between-flight'

inspections and improvised field repairs (the application of Bostik, dope and black enamel) enabled the Spitfires to be kept flying but it was reported that one aircraft, which took off with a perfect airscrew, landed three hours later with 3 sq ft of covering stripped off.

On the last day of the month Flt Lt R.B. Rowley, flying BZ830, 'I', on 160 Sqn's last reconnaissnace to Port Swettenham, returned after a flight time of 21hr 15min with the gauge indicating only 10 gal of fuel remaining. By the end of July 1945, 684 Sqn's final reconnaissance task in preparation for Operation 'Zipper' was two-thirds complete. No processing or interception facilities were provided at 'Brown', so a number of Beaufighters of 171 Wing Command Flight were attached permanently to 684 Sqn as a high-speed Courier Flight, replacing all but one of the B-25Cs, to ferry personnel and to rush camera magazines from the detachments to Alipore which remained the squadron's base. A detachment was established at Chittagong but only one operational sortie was flown from Bengal during the month; huge masses of cumulo-nimbus cloud along the Bengal and Arakan coast made flights virtually impossible. From Mingaladon, however, 681 Sqn was able to mount forty-one sorties, most of these to provide information about enemy positions and movements along the railway and roads between Pegu and Moulmein.

In Southern Burma the fighting continued despite appalling weather. On 3 July the Japanese, who still had a large and organised force in the Sittang Bend area, west of the river, attacked Waw, east of Pegu. Their intention was to cut 12th Army's frail line of supply along the road and rail 'corridor' from Rangoon to Toungoo and central Burma, compelling the British to reinforce the area, thereby weakening 'stronghold' positions along the corridor. This would offer the opportunity for the Japanese troops cut off in the Pegu Yoma to break out eastwards and join their forces east of the Sittang. Neither of the enemy's intentions was realised; the counter-offensive at Waw petered out after a week of storms which brought almost all movement to a halt and 12th Army's forces were deployed in depth to intercept the escaping enemy columns as they crossed the corridor. By mid-July the attack at Waw had come to nothing.

On the 19th, elements of the Japanese 28th Army moving eastwards were engaged south of Toungoo. Day after day, Japanese columns came up against 12th Army's string of strong-points along a 50-mile stretch of the corridor or, having slipped through the line, were hunted through the flooded fields in the Sittang valley where many were caught by fighter-bombers or simply drowned as they attempted to cross the river. This 'Battle of the Break-out', the greatest slaughter of the war in the Far East, continued until 4 August. Of 18,500 Japanese troops who came out of the Pegu Yoma, only 7,500 reached safety east of the Sittang while 12th Army's casualties during the period were 96 killed and 322 wounded.

202: The low-level attack on the Mekong bridges by Liberators on 24 June 1945, as seen from an aircraft of 159 Sqn flown by Sqn Ldr Watson

203: RAF Liberators carried cameras, either hand-held or with mirror-mountings, for strike-record photography such as this showing bombing of the steel bridge by 159 Sqn in March. Beyond stands the broken trestle bridge

204: The air defence of the area was in the hands of the Thai Air Force, who were equipped with obsolete Japanese fighters such as this Nakajina Ki-27 ('Nate') at Bangkok/Tan Son Nhut. Their resistance was little more than a token gesture, for the Air Force was one of the centres of clandestine resistance to the Japanese. Just visible under the wing is the national marking adopted during the time of Japanese occupation; a white rampaging elephant (the symbol of the Thai Royal house) on a red square

205: *The escort carrier HMS* Attacker, *an oiler alongside, in Trincomalee Harbour in June or July 1945. Seafires of 879 Sqn are ranged on deck*

206: *F6F-5P Hellcats of 896 Sqn aboard HMS* Empress, *two wearing Temperate Sea Scheme and the other Sea Blue finishes. The newer aircraft have curtailed identification bands and White-outlined 'Small' roundels*

207: *The placing of the wing bands on Hellcats was occasionally adjusted to avoid overlap of the national markings, as can be seen on some of these, including F6F-5P aircraft, of 896 Sqn aboard* Empress *in July 1945*

208: *Hellcat FR.II JW370, 'K6K', of 804 Sqn off Bela-wan Deli on the last day of Operation 'Balsam', 20 June 1945*

209: *During Operation 'Livery' in July, this coastal steamer was one of many targets strafed by 804 Sqn's Hellcats*

210: *Another rail target, this time at Dhung Song, attack-ed by Hellcat PR.IIs of 804 Sqn on 25 July*

211: A flight of Hellcat PR.IIs of 888 Sqn in locally-mixed blue finish, early in 1945. In the centre is JV222, at the back is either JV225 or JV228, both of which were with the squadron. Nearest is the newest aircraft, JX???, minus 'Royal Navy' legend. Note the variations in the fuselage roundels

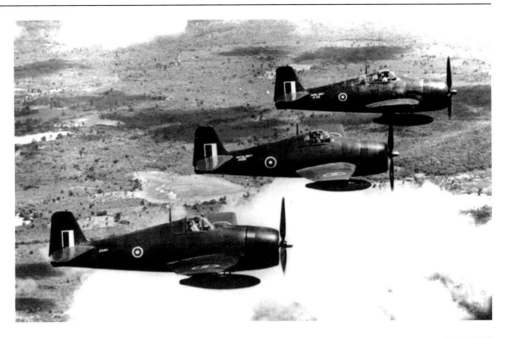

212: The Tamarkand steel bridge Q.654 was under repair when this photograph taken in April 1945. Q.654A, the by-pass bridge 100m downstream, was in use at that time. Extensive sand-banks can be seen on both sides of the river

Naval Operations

The East Indies Fleet

In July Mountbatten was told of the Allied intention to demand 'unconditional surrender' of the Japanese Government and of the possibility that the atomic bomb would be used against the Japanese homeland. Although this made his preparations for 'Zipper' appear "rather unrealistic" plans for the landing went ahead. On 19 July a mine-sweeping force sailed for the Andaman Sea to clear the approaches to Phuket Island (Operation 'Livery') with the escort carriers *Empress* and *Ameer*, whose 804 Sqn was again accompanied by a section from 888 Sqn. 804 Sqn took part in attacks on the airfields at Hinluk (Phuket) and Bandon in Siam, and at Sungei Patani in northern Malaya on the 24th while 888 Sqn flew two sorties over Hastings Island and the following day flew final Naval PR sorties to Davis Island. 804 Sqn's Hellcats attacked Phuket Harbour and the railway yard at Dhung Song, camera-fitted Hellcats JW710, JW743 and JX802 ('K6C' flown by Lt J Myerscough) having made runs over the targets before attacking. The Hellcats flew to Sungei Patani airfield again on 26 July, JW710 recording damage.

In three days of attacks, some 150 Hellcat sorties destroyed more than 30 enemy aircraft on the ground. It was later estimated that the aircraft of the 21st Aircraft Carrier Squadron destroyed more than a third of the Japanese aircraft remaining in the SEAC area in the first half of 1945. That day the carrier force was attacked by a formation of suicide aircraft. Three Aichi D3A2 'Val' dive-bombers were destroyed by anti-aircraft fire (although the Hellcats were flying CAP they were not directed onto the attackers) but two found targets. One crashed and sank the minesweeper *Vestal*, the other hit *Ameer* causing fire to break out. The fire was soon extinguished and the carrier put in to Akyab for repair.

During the three days of 'Livery', 804 Sqn flew eighty offensive recce and strike sorties, destroying thirteen enemy aircraft on the ground and fourteen locomotives.

Photo-reconnaissance by the Mosquitos of 684 Sqn's Cocos Islands Detachment showed two cruisers of the Imperial Navy, *Myoko* and *Takao* remaining at Singapore Naval Base. On 30 July the Royal Navy's midget sumarines XE-1 and XE-3 entered the Johore Strait to attack them. The time available was so limited that only the 33-knot, 10,000ton heavy cruiser *Takao* could be approached and charges attached to her hull. Later reconnaissance by 684 Sqn showed that when the charges exploded the cruiser settled on the bottom. The commander of XE-3, Lt I. Frazer, and his diver, Ldg Seaman J. Magennis, were each awarded the Victoria Cross for their action.

213: *Hirara airfield on the west coast of Miyakojima, Okinawa, receiving a severe pounding from aircraft from HMS* Victorious *during Operation 'Iceberg 5' on 16 April*

Delayed action in the Pacific

The British Pacific Fleet

Fleet Admiral Ernest King, the anglophobic US Chief of Naval Operations, considered the war against Japan to be entirely an American affair, intending to conduct his campaign in the Pacific Ocean "without reference to the British". He proposed that the activities of the British Pacific Fleet be confined to the area of South-East Asia Command, although there could be no use for such a major naval force in the Bay of Bengal or in East Indies waters. Gen Douglas MacArthur, Supremo of the South-West Pacific Operational Area, whose restrictions on operations by his Dutch allies were causing complaint, intended that Australian forces should continue further SWPOA actions in New Guinea, Borneo and the Philippines, hoping the BPF would be assigned to support these operations. He also initiated moves to enlarge Mountbatten's SEAC to include the Netherlands Indies and the hinterland of the South China Sea as far north as Hong Kong, thereby avoiding the awkward political problems that would certainly affect these areas when they were liberated from Japanese rule.

In December Adm Sir Bruce Frazer, commanding the

British Pacific Fleet, met Adm Chester Nimitz, Commander-in-Chief, Pacific (CINCPAC) at Pearl Harbor and agreed to place the Fleet under Nimitz's control in the Central Pacific, with the same operational status as a Task Force of the US Navy. After further dissension the US Chiefs of Staff gave way to British interests and the BPF assembled at Sydney, the warships as Task Force 112 and the Fleet Train as TF-111, awaiting orders to begin operations.

Although the British Pacific Fleet was to operate no longer under control of South-East Asia Command, the ships, squadrons, aircraft and crews remained the same. Their further operations are included here.

During January 1945 the Japanese High Command was compelled to consider a reduction in their long defensive perimeter, not only on the now relatively unimportant Burma Front but throughout the Pacific Ocean where, as a consequence of US naval air power and lack of fuel, the Imperial Fleet had been reduced to near impotence. They prepared plans for alternative strategies to counter possible American military operations—and for a hitherto inconceivable possibility—an invasion of the Japanese Home Islands of Kyushu and Honshu. They began concentrating their fighter aircraft there, no matter what the needs in other regions, and authorised the conversion of some Army air units into suicide formations; these took as their symbol the Chrysanthemum badge of a 14th-Century Samurai warrior and the name *Kikusui Tokkotai* (Floating Chrysanthemum Special Attack Units).

214 Above: The Corsairs of No.47 Naval Fighter Wing ready for take-off from HMS Victorious *during Operation 'Iceberg', Lt Col Hay in his unmarked JT456 to the fore. As can be seen, the flight deck of a fleet carrier during preparations for launching dozens of propeller-driven aircraft was an extremely dangerous place. All the aircraft wear the 'roundel and bar' marking introduced in March-April 1945*

157

The Imperial Navy had already begun employing suicide tactics with great success against the American Fleet. In November 1944, during an action off Samar in the Philippines, the first organised suicide attacks were made on an escort carrier Task Unit of Task Group 77. With such actions in mind, Adm Onishi had established in the Philippines a *Shimpu Tokobetsu Togeki-Tai*, known to the Americans as the *Kamikaze Tokkotai*; both expressions have essentially the same meaning—Divine Wind Special Attack Unit. A6M Zekes were used by the *Shikishima Tokkotai* against the escort carriers (CVE), one crashing onto *St. Lo* which sank within an hour. Within a few weeks eight American fast carriers (CV) suffered various degrees of damage from *Kamikaze* attacks, usually by teams of five suicide aircraft escorted by fighters.

At the beginning of the year the Japanese Staffs prepared plans to combat the American threat under the name '*Ten-Gô*' (Providence or Heavenly Power). These plans were '*Ten-ichigô*' (Providence No.1), for defence of the Ryukyu Islands; '*Ten-nigô*' (No.2), defence of Formosa (Taiwan); '*Ten-sangô*' (No.3), of the China Coast and '*Ten-yengô*' (No.4) of Indo-China and Hainan.

By this time the US Navy deployed 17 fleet carriers (CV) and light fleet carriers (CVL), some 50 CVEs and 20 major warships in the Pacific. The full weight of *Kamikaze* attack fell upon the US Navy's Luzon Attack Force when it headed for landings on the northernmost of the Philippine Islands, sinking the CVE USS *Ommaney Bay* and damaging CVEs *Kadashan Bay*, *Kitkun Bay* and *Salamaua* within ten days.

Meanwhile, the B-29s of XX Bomber Command, which had operated with impunity in their bombing of Japanese industry, late in 1944 had begun taking losses from *Tai-atari* (battering-ram or body-crashing) attacks by Ki-44 Tojo fighters of the 47th *Sentai's Shinten Seiku-tai* (Heaven-Shaking Interceptor Flight). The US Army Air Forces began pressing for bases nearer Japan so that the bomber offensive could be stepped up, these bases to be occupied as part of the American 'island-hopping' strategy, the first objective being Iwo Jima in the Volcano Islands by the end of February 1945. There the *Kamikaze* struck the carrier *Saratoga* and put her out of action, then the CVEs *Lunga Point* and *Bismarck Sea*, this last blowing up with the loss of 200 lives, but the island was overrun by mid-March. Its No.1 airfield was soon in use by B-29s of a new XXI Bomber Command for its programme of fire raids on Japanese cities.

When the British Pacific Fleet (designated Task Force 113) moved to a forward base on Manus in the Admiralty Islands, the Navy was surprised to find that, although Manus was a Crown colony, the Fleet was not permitted to make use of shore facilities without approval from the US Chief of Naval Operations. As the Fleet Train (now TF-112) arrived on 7 March there were still no instructions from Washington but Adms Nimitz and Halsey, commanding the US Third Fleet, were eager for the BPF to take a part in operations and an American-built camp on Ponam Island was made available. Faced with a *fait accompli*, Adm King now warned that the BPF remained subject to seven days' notice to move to Borneo if Washington so decided.

The ships of the Fleet and the Fleet Train then moved on 19 March to the US Navy's Pacific base at Ulithi Atoll in the Caroline Islands to prepare for action. Although only of Task Group size, the Royal Navy's 1st Aircraft Carrier Squadron of fleet carriers; *Illustrious*, *Indefatigable*, *Indomitable* and *Victorious*, was assigned to the Fifth Fleet as Task Force 57 with a minimal photo-reconnaissance capability aboard just two of these carriers.

On 20 March the carriers of the US Navy's TF-38 came under attack while their aircraft were operating over Japan's Inland Sea. A *Kamikaze* of the 721st *Kokutai* (IJN Air Wing) pierced the flight-deck of USS *Franklin* and exploded in the hangar beneath; the ship was saved but saw no further action. Two minutes later *Wasp* was hit but was able to continue operations for three more days.

Okinawa, the largest island of the Ryukyu Group, only 350 miles from Kyushu, was now intended to be the forward base for a later invasion of Japan, Operation 'Olympic' in November 1945. Increasingly heavy attacks on the Ryukyus made it clear to Japanese Imperial Headquarters that the islands would be the next object of assault. On 20 March orders were issued to put into motion the counter-attack plan *Ten-Ichigô*, with massive *Kikusui* attacks on the American Fifth Fleet. Sixty-nine Army *Sentai* were made available as *Tokkotai* to begin immediate training of new pilots for suicide operations.

Seventeen US Navy CVs, four Royal Navy carriers and 18 American escort carriers (CVE) with about 1,900 aircraft were committed to support an invasion of Okinawa, Operation 'Iceberg', beginning 1 April. To oppose them the Japanese Navy and Army air forces had some 6,000 aircraft. While Task Force 58 began relay attacks in preparation for a landing, the BPF's Task Force 57 was despatched to the western flank of the operational area, to the Sakishima Gunto, half-way between Formosa and the Japanese Homeland.

There were six airfields on the islands of Ishagaki, Mihara and Miyako, staging-posts between the major Japanese bases on Formosa and Okinawa. It was feared that these Sakishima airfields could be used as bases for attacks on the American forces landing in Okinawa so TF-57 was ordered to 'neutralise' them by cratering the runways. The attacks were planned as a series of two-day strikes separated by two- or three-day periods of RAS (Replenishment at Sea) by ships of the Fleet Train, during which the operational duty would be taken over by an escort carrier division of the US Navy.

215 Right : *The IJN light aircraft carrier* Kaiyo *under attack and on fire, photographed by one of HMS* Formidable's *Hellcat PR.IIs on 24 July 1945. This is the only time that RN aircraft have attacked an aircraft carrier*

216 Below: *Seen from HMS* Victorious, *the BPF under attack by Kamikazes off Okinawa. An RN fleet aircraft carrier can be seen in the distance. Burning on the water are two Japanese bombers after being shot down by Seafires and AA fire. Marked is a third bomber on its run in. Just visible on the original print is a Hellcat at 11 o'clock and a Seafire at 1 o'clock pulling clear of the Air Defence Zone*

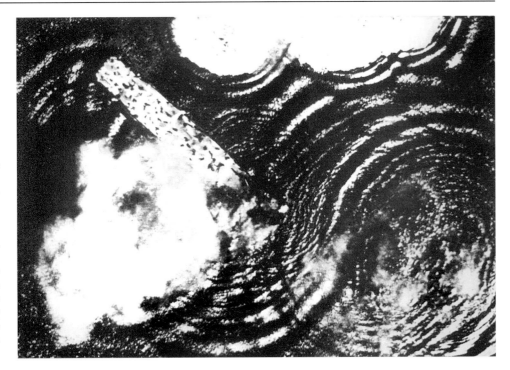

217: *In a desperate measure to turn back the Allied forces, the Japanese refined their Kamikaze tactics by developing a rocket-powered human-guided missile, to be carried within the bomb-bay of specially modified Mitsubishi G4M bombers. These formed the the 721st Kokutai, seen here*

218: *On their only mission with the rocket-powered MXY7 Ohka (Cherry Blossom) suicide bombs, the G4M bombers carrying the rocket craft were intercepted by the CAP well before they came within range of the US Fleet. Consequently the Ohkas were all jettisoned, along with their pilots, a measure which did not prevent all the bombers from being shot down. Not a single aircraft came anywhere near the US vessels. This example, carrying a cherry blossom symbol, was captured intact on Okinawa*

219: *While the Kamikazes were attacking the British and US Fleets, the naval attack aircraft were striking at the Kamikazes' home bases. This is Matsushima airfield on mainland Honshu, Japan, seen on 9 August 1945 in a picture taken by Sub-Lt MJ Brown, flying a camera-equipped Seafire ('135/S') of 887 Squadron from HMS* Indefatigable. *Little remains of the installations and aircraft except smouldering wreckage*

220: *Wally Knight flying Corsair II JT633, '120/P', of 1834 Sqn from HMS* Victorious *in late July 1945 makings. The remains of the 'T' of the former No.47 Fighter Wing can be just made our beneath the '1' of the fuselage number. Flying this aircraft on 4 May 1945, Sub Lt Pocock shared in the destruction of a Nakajima C6N Kamikaze bomber off the Sakishima Gunto. Noteworthy is the pinup; several Corsairs of the BPF carried such noseart*

221: *Modified 32in roundels are marked on the Temperate Sea Scheme camouflaged Hellcats of HMS* Indomitable's *1839 and 1844 Sqns, seen during April or May 1945*

222: *Seafire FR.III, NN621, '115/N' of 880/801 Sqn, normally aboard HMS* Implacable, *ashore in Tasmania in 1945. This was Lt Cdr 'Mike' Crosley's machine and was finished in Temperate Sea Scheme with the BPF roundels. As the Commanding Officer of the squadrons and presumably for identification purposes, his aircraft appears to wear a Dull Blue rudder with a vertical White stripe. An illustration of the aircraft is included in the colour section of this book*

Four squadrons of Avengers and one of Fireflies from the carriers of TF-57 were to make up to four strikes on each day of operations, some 40 aircraft at a time, with support from the Corsairs and Seafires of the Fleet. All were under the tactical control of Maj (now Lt-Col) Hay of *Victorious* and Cdr N.S.Luard DSC, Air Co-ordinator aboard *Indomitable*. Lt-Col Hay and his 'Sheepdog' Flight of Corsairs reconnoitred and photographed the airfields and other enemy installations before each strike 'serial', so that the runways could again be bombed where they had been repaired. After rapid consideration of their findings further targets could be allocated, then damage-assessment photographs were taken during and after the strikes.

For 'Iceberg 1', the first series of attacks, 26-27 March, five sorties were flown by the PR Flight of Hellcats from *Indomitable*, finding aircraft on the ground at Hirara and Ishagaki, although the other airfields appeared deserted. The strikes found many aircraft in the air and about 40 were destroyed for the loss of 19 British aircraft. The Japanese reacted to 'Iceberg 2', attacks on Sakuma and Ishagaki airfields (31 March-2 April) with *Kamikaze* attacks on the carriers; one crashed into *Indefatigable* but the carrier's armoured deck prevented serious damage and the ship was operational within an hour. Five PR sorties were flown for 'Iceberg 3', 6-7 April, before strikes on Hirara, Nobara, Ishagaki and Sukuma. A number of *Kamikaze* attacked the Fleet on the first day, one striking *Illustrious*' island bridge but causing little damage.

The US Navy carrier *Hancock* was put out of action on the 8th by Kamikaze aircraft seemingly from Formosa. It was believed that the Imperial Navy's experienced pilots were based there, while the pilots of the *Tokkotai* operating from Kanoya on Kyushu were student pilots trained only for a suicide attack and, therefore, less able to make a successful approach to a target.

'Ten-Ichigo' was launched on 6 April, when wave after wave of *Kikusui* aircraft attacking the radar-picket destroyers off Okinawa when no American carriers were found there; the enemy losses were heavy—335 *Kikisui* and some 130 other bombers destroyed. As there appeared to be no way of preventing the suicide attacks, Adm Rawlings was requested to take TF-57 to strike at the airfields on Formosa instead of returning to the Sakishima Gunto. Whereas the US Navy carriers had suffered grievously from the suicide attacks, the armoured decks of the British carriers had prevented serious damage. For the Formosa operation, 'Iceberg 4', 12-13 April, Lt-Col Hay and his Corsairs obtained photographic cover of Yonkuni-Shima and the airfields at Iamsero, Okasaki and Matsuyama. During the strikes that followed, 16 enemy aircraft were shot down but it became clear that the bases in Formosa were not being used for major attacks on the American Fleet. On 16 April, as the British Task Force began 'Iceberg 5' with three more PR Hellcat sorties over Miyako and a strike led by Lt-Col Hay on Hirara airfield in the Sakishima Group, the US carriers

Enterprise, *Franklin* and *Yorktown* were attacked and *Intrepid* was put out of action by A6M Zekes and Ki- 61 Tonys but a formation of 16 G4M Betty bombers from the 721st *Kokutai* carrying rocket-powered MXY7 *Ohka* (Cherry Blossom) 'Special Attackers' of the *Jinrai Butai* (Thunderclap Unit), each with a 1,200kg explosive warhead, were intercepted by Hellcats from *Hornet*. The *Ohkas* were jettisoned in the sea far from their targets and all the Bettys were shot down.

During the RAS that followed 'Iceberg 5', *Illustrious* left the British Pacific Fleet for a long-overdue refit and was replaced by HMS *Formidable* which joined TF-57 for 'Iceberg 6' (20-22 April), attacks on the Sakishima airfields at Hegina and Nobara with photographic cover. Then, after spending 32 days at sea, the British Pacific Fleet retired to re-equip and replenish at Leyte in the Philippines. Washington again proposed that the Fleet should be sent south-west to Borneo but, because of the continuing threat to the US Navy's carriers, Adm Nimitz, who regarded Task Force 57 as his "most flexible reserve", insisted on retaining the Royal Navy's carrier force for further attacks on the Sakishima Gunto.

TF-57 returned to action on 3 May for 'Iceberg 7', again beginning with sorties by *Indomitable*'s PR Hellcats and strikes on Ishagaki airfield. This time Miyako was bombarded by the 14in guns of the battleships HMS *Howe* and HMS *King George V,* the results being recorded by Lt-Col Hay. The *Kamikaze* offensive was resumed the following day when about 20 aircraft attacked the Task Force. Only two A6M Zekes avoided the Combat Air Patrol and penetrated the Fleet's anti-aircraft barrage, one sliding off *Indomitable*'s flight-deck, the other hitting *Formidable* by the 'island', where the damage was soon repaired. New pilots of the PR Hellcats, Lt T.D.Handley and Sub-Lt R.E.Goadsby, were praised for the quality of their coverage of the airfields and other possible targets; "Although trained for FR on Seafires, with no experience on Hellcats, their results were good enough to permit assessment of runway serviceability and aircraft strength".

Operations on 8 May, the first day of 'Iceberg 8', were hampered by bad weather but PR Hellcat sorties were possible the following day when Miyako and Ishagaki were again attacked. At 1700 a suicide aircraft crashed into *Formidable* and destroyed 18 aircraft on deck but there was little damage to the carrier and she was operational again within the hour. A second aircraft hit *Victorious*, set fire to the ship and damaged the forward lift motor then, before the fire could be brought under control, another *Kamikaze* hit the flight-deck and destroyed four aircraft.

Subsequent Operations 'Iceberg 9' (12-13 May) and 'Iceberg 10' (16 May) again required PR sorties from *Indomitable*, finding runways at Hirara and Nobara airfields repaired and serviceable but these sorties and the usual pre-strike reconnaissance by Lt-Col Hay brought no reaction from the enemy. The results of reconnaissance during 'Iceberg 9' were sourly criticised; "coverage of targets thought to be not as good as before, as pilots trained in Tac/R rather than strategic reconnaissance". For the PR pilots flying for 'Iceberg 10', however, there was considerable praise—after three sorties on the 16th, a thousand 'verticals' of "excellent quality" awaited interpretation, supplemented by many 'obliques' from the strike aircraft of *Victorious* and *Formidable*. For 'Iceberg 11' on 20 May, two more Hellcat sorties were flown from *Indomitable* over Miyako and Ishagaki while Lt-Col Hay carried out weather reconnaissance. *Formidable*, having few aircraft remaining serviceable, left for Manus and Sydney on 22 May.

When Task Force 57 joined the US Fifth Fleet, it had been intended that the attachment should be until the last week of May, by which time it had become apparent that the Japanese were no longer using the Sakishima airfields as staging-posts to Okinawa, the greater part of which was in American hands. For 'Iceberg 12' (24-25 May) Miyako and Ishagaki were again subjected to strikes from *Indefatigable*, *Indomitable* and *Victorious* before the rest of the Fleet returned to Manus and thence to Sydney at the beginning of June.

Meanwhile, on 27 May, Adm Halsey had replaced Adm Spruance and the US Fifth Fleet had become the Third Fleet.

The newest fleet carrier of the Royal Navy, HMS *Implacable*, had arrived at Manus to begin operations with the British Pacific Fleet. On 10 June she left with HMS *Ruler*, an escort carrier of the Fleet Train, and support vessels as Task Force 111/2 for a series of strikes against the islands of Truk Atoll in the Caroline Islands, a Japanese forward naval base from which the Imperial Navy had long-since withdrawn its warships to the Philippines and Singapore. Truk had been by-passed by the American 'island-hopping' strategy but still posed some threat to the supply routes across the Pacific. For this Operation 'Inmate' on 14-15 June, pre-strike photographic reconnaissance by Seafire FR.IIIs of 890 Sqn from *Implacable* showed few worthwhile targets remaining for *Implacable*'s Avengers and Fireflies and *Ruler*'s Hellcats, after repeated strikes by US Navy aircraft. Although 'Inmate' achieved no substantial results, the operation provided experience for the crew of *Implacable*, to be tested in earnest when the carrier began operations with the Fleet, its number of major warships reduced by damage and refits to *King George V* and the three carriers of the 1st Aircraft Carrier Squadron, *Formidable*, *Indefatigable* and *Victorious*. Six Hellcats of *Indomitable*'s PR Flight were transferred to *Formidable*, their operations to come under the control of Maj PP Nelson-Gracie RM on 4 July when he became Air Group Leader, 1st Div, 1st AC Sqn as Lt-Col Hay left the Fleet and soon afterwards returned to Britain.

On joining the US Third Fleet, the British Pacific Fleet

was re-designated Task Force 37 to begin operations with Vice-Adm McCain's TF-38 off the Japanese Home Islands. On 17 July the aircraft of TF-37 struck targets north of Tokyo, preceded by four PR sorties by the Hellcats from *Formidable*. Appalling weather delayed the next strikes until 24 July, by which time *Indefatigable* had joined TF-37, the four PR Hellcats covering airfield targets on Shikoku. While US Navy aircraft sank a Japanese carrier and three battleships at anchor off Kure on the Inland Sea, four Royal Navy aircraft hit and set on fire the light aircraft carrier *Kaiyô*. Reconnaissance and attacks from TF-37 continued the following day, then *Formidable*'s Hellcats intercepted a formation of B7A Grace torpedo bombers approaching the Task Force; three bombers were shot down and the others driven off.

The next series of operations began on 28 July with three PR sorties followed by strikes on the dockyard at Harima and the naval base at Maizaru on the shores of the Inland Sea, where the Hellcats found further targets for attack on the 30th. The intended two-day RAS period was lengthened by the ships encountering a series of typhoons and by a delay when the first atomic bomb was dropped on Hiroshima on 6 August. On 9 and 10 August further attacks were made against airfields and shipping off Honshu, then *Formidable*, *Implacable* and *Victorious* returned to Sydney, leaving a small force with *Indefatigable* and *King George V* as Task Group 38.5 of McCain's TF-38. On 13 August the Tokyo area was attacked and, although surrender negotiations were under way, further strikes were launched at dawn on 15 August and the Avengers from *Indefatigable* were attacked by a dozen A6M Zekes. In the last fighter combat of the war, eight of these were shot down by the carrier's Seafires, one of which was lost. Further planned strikes were cancelled and the Task Group remained on 'stand-by' until the Japanese surrender.

By August the 11th Aircraft Carrier Squadron, HMS *Colossus*, *Glory*, *Venerable* and *Vengeance*, was formed at Sydney, ready to join the British Pacific Fleet. The carriers were assigned to the re-occupation of the British Far East colonies and *Venerable* joined *Indomitable* at Hong Kong where, on 31 August and 1 September, their aircraft made the last attacks of the war, destroying groups of suicide boats of the Imperial Navy.

Soon afterwards, many of the Lend-lease aircraft were dumped overboard, the US Navy having no need of them, the terms of their provision being that aircraft retained after the end of hostilities were to be purchased. Lend-Lease ended on 8 May and no more aircraft were supplied to the British Government. Henceforth, it was intended that the squadrons of the RAF and the Royal Navy be entirely re-equipped with British aircraft.

The destruction left the Fleet with a greatly reduced complement of aircraft. The empty spaces of the carriers' hangar decks were then used for the urgent 'Repatriation of Allied Prisoners of War and Internees' programme, RAPWI, known to those whose return was inevitably delayed as 'Retain All Prisoners of War Indefinitely'. The Lend-lease escort carriers of the East Indies Fleet and of the Fleet Train in the Pacific were soon decommissioned and were returned to the United States between December 1945 and late 1946.

223: A Spitfire FR.XIVE of No.11 Sqn RAF takes off from HMS Trumpeter *during Operation 'Zipper' on 9 September*

224: RAPWI. A poor quality, but rare, picture taken from a wartime newspaper showing HMS Searcher *docking at Madras, loaded with released POWs. The pendant number '40' shows clearly against the hull camouflage.* Searcher *was returned to the US Navy in November 1945*

225: The Lend-Lease Agreements required serviceable aircraft diverted to the British Government to be paid for, or returned to the United States at the end of the war. Some of the RN aircraft were made 'unserviceable'; they and others which suffered accident damage, like this Corsair IV, KD172, aboard HMS Speaker, *were simply dumped over the side. The BPF markings show well against the Sea Blue finish*

No end to hostilities

No sorties were flown by 684 Sqn during the first week of August 1945; the weather over Malaya was bad and some of the required additional beach-cover was particularly exacting, as photographs were of use only if taken at low-tide. Operations by 681 Sqn from Mingaladon were hampered by the monsoon but successful flights were made to Koh Si Chang, along the enemy's railway system and the roads and tracks east of the Salween where Japanese troops were still moving south from the Shan hills. At Alipore 684 received instructions to prepare for a move to Mingaladon; all equipment was packed and the ops room was closed down but the move was soon delayed.

684 Sqn's Courier Flight, which had operated the B-25Cs without accident (apart from the loss of MA957 on a rescue flight in November) suffered its first loss on 2 August when Beaufighter Mk.X NV371 caught fire soon after take-off from Mingaladon and crashed some thirty miles south of Rangoon, killing the crew (Wt Offs Munday and Earl) and its passengers.

During a continuing series of low-level attacks on the Burma-Siam railway, the main Japanese supply route to their base at Moulmein, the Liberator B.VIs of 231 Group RAF supplemented the cover obtained by the reconnaissance squadrons. All the heavy bombers were fitted with mission-recording cameras and several aircraft on each raid carried hand-held cameras. Throughout 1944 and into early 1945, reconnaissance had built up almost complete information about the locations of prisoner-of-war and internment camps in enemy-occupied territory; this had proved invaluable as the Japanese had frequently sited PoW camps adjacent to potential targets for bombing.

Three Spitfire PR.XIs from 681 Sqn were allocated to 28 Sqn at the end of July, for familiarisation by the Hurricane pilots who were delighted at the prospect of re-equipment with new aircraft, only some half-dozen Hurricanes being still serviceable. The pilots were checked during the first three days of August by Wg Cdr R.H. Courtney of 906 Wing at Mingaladon, then were amazed and horrified to hear that the squadron was to be re-equipped with twelve Hurricane Mk.IVs as soon as the aircraft had been fitted with camera mountings. Few of these aircraft were delivered and the Spitfire PR.XIs were used for Tac/R sorties over the Sittang Valley, while a few Mk.VIIIs were made available until such time as 28 Sqn could be fully equipped with Spitfire FR.XIVs. The remaining Hurricanes were used for short-range photographic sorties for the Army until 29 August, when the squadron ended ops and began to prepare for Operation 'Zipper'. The PR.XIs were returned to 681 Sqn, marked with white 'tactical markings'.

On 4 August a force including six escort carriers, with 804 and 808 Sqns aboard sailed for a series of strikes against the principal airfields in Malaya and northern Sumatra. The operation was cancelled when the atomic bombs were dropped over Japan.

On 16 July a successful test of a plutonium bomb had been made in New Mexico. By the end of the month another plutonium bomb and a 'uranium bomb' were ready for B-29s to drop on Japan. Ten days later, from the Potsdam Conference, the Allies demanded Japan's unconditional surrender but a delay in acknowledging this demand was interpreted by the Americans to be rejection. In consequence a uranium bomb was dropped over Hiroshima on 6 August and, when no Japanese reply to the Potsdam Declaration was forthcoming, a plutonium bomb was dropped on Nagasaki three days later.

The decision to use the atomic weapon remains controversial. It was later claimed that by these actions thousands of Allied casualties were prevented at the cost of more than 130,000 Japanese civilian lives. In retrospect it seems evident that the destruction of the two Japanese cities might have been avoided by the exercise of patience, awaiting the outcome of negotiations between the Japanese and the USSR which declared war on 9 August. A distant 'demonstration' of the atomic bomb might have been sufficient finally to persuade the Japanese government and Emperor of the futility of further hostilities.

During the month two Mosquitos crashed; a Mk.XVI, NS528, broke its back as a result of a heavy landing at Alipore on 11 August and a newly-arrived Mk.34, RG213, 'O', crash-landed in the sea at China Bay on the 19th while attempting to land on one engine. The crews were unhurt but both aircraft were written-off.

Although further reconnaissance was cancelled, cover was still required of selected targets three times each in a fortnight, from Penang to Soerabaja, and more intense anti-aircraft fire was encountered during these sorties than at any previous time, particularly over Palembang in Sumatra, where the main fighter force of the Japanese 9th *Hikoshidan* (Air Division) was still concentrated to defend the oil installations.

A further programme of reconnaissance over Indo-China and Siam was intended but, due to weather conditions and problems caused by uncertainty about squadron moves, only 24½ operational hours of reconnaissance sorties were flown from Alipore during the month, and no satisfactory photographs obtained. A small servicing detachment was stationed at Mingaladon in anticipation of 'Zipper' which was intended to be mounted late in the month but was now postponed and modified to an occupation rather than as an assault-landing. From the Cocos Island base, the four crews of 684 Sqn, now with seven Mosquito PR.34s available, flew 208 operational hours in August, including a record flight by Flt Lt J.R. Manners and Wt Off F.A. Burley, in RG210, 'J', of 2,600 miles in 9hr 5min, to Penang Island and Taiping in northern Malaya on the 20th.

In Burma limited fighting continued until the Japanese Government announced 'unconditional surrender' on 14 August 1945; then orders were issued to cease air operations so far as "consistent with the safety of Allied forces".

The following day, in an unprecedented and extraordinary radio address in which he made no mention of defeat or surrender, Emperor Hirohito told the Japanese nation, "We declared war on America and Britain because of our earnest wish to protect the future of Japan and the stability of East Asia, it being far from our intentions to violate the dominion of other nations or to initiate territorial expansion... We are determined to facilitate an honourable peace for future generations by yielding to the unbearable... having been able to protect and preserve the fabric of the Imperial State".

With the capitulation of Japan, the need for further Intelligence of the theatre ceased to be an urgent one, and the survey and photographic cover then required could be obtained from forward bases, as the British took over the enemy-occupied zones. No use was therefore made of the radar air survey Mosquitos which were becoming available.

On 16 August 1945 the Combined Chiefs of Staff, under intense American political pressure, confirmed the appointment of General Douglas MacArthur as Supreme Commander of the Allied Powers in Japan. At the same time the area of operations controlled by South-East Asia Command, previously bounded by the eastern border and coastline of Siam, Malaya and Sumatra, was extended to include the entire Netherlands East Indies, French Indo-China, Hong Kong and the area of the South China Sea—all the territories controlled by the Japanese Southern Area Army.

Without consideration of the imminence of 'Zipper', which was already under way, or the problem of rescuing some 12,500 prisoners-of-war and civilian internees in more than 250 camps spread across SE Asia, MacArthur ordered that no Allied landings be made on enemy-held territory until he had received a formal Japanese surrender. Accordance with such an order would have entailed a delay of up to two weeks before prisoners could be released from the dire conditions of their captivity.

In South-East Asia Command his edict was acknowledged but ignored; PoW camp reconnaissance continued and medical teams and supplies were dropped to the camps by parachute.

It was already too late for some; between 18 and 20 August nine Naval airmen, including 888 Sqn's Sub-Lt J.W. Tomlinson, were taken from Changi Gaol to the beach near Tanjong Changi and there beheaded by an over-zealous officer of the Japanese Navy who then committed suicide.

226: Seafires of 807 Sqn bore No.4 Fighter Wing's symbol '5' and the squadron symbol 'D' aboard Hunter *for the re-occupation of Singapore, 11 September 1945. Lt Cdr George Baldwin had his aircraft NN300, 'D50', stripped back to bare metal, with Black or Dull Blue bands and anti-glare panel*

227 Above: *Two 'erks' demonstrate the empty weight of a wing tank of the type fitted to Mosquito PR.34, RG203, 'E', of 684 Sqn on the Cocos Islands. Finish is Dull Aluminium above, PRU Blue below with 32in 'SEAC' roundels. Dull Blue bands on the tail. RG185, 'Z', lurks in the background*

228: *A few FR aircraft had their serials repeated on the tail fin. This is Hurricane IV KZ248 of 28 Sqn, which carries its serial in small white figures above the fin flash. Wing and tail bands are not applied. Kuala Lumpur 1946*

229: *After the return to Malaya, 28 Sqn's last remaining Hurricane FR.IV, KZ248, stands alongside a 'clipped-wing' Spitfire FR.XIVE finished in Dark Green and Dark Earth camouflage*

230: An 804 Sqn aircraft took this oblique of disabled enemy fighters, Ki-43 Oscars and a Ki-44 Tojo, during a pass over Port Swettenham airfield as the landings for Operation 'Zipper' began on 9 September

231: Mitsubishi Ki-57 'Topsy' transport aircraft carrying a Japanese delegation to the surrender ceremony in Burma, approaching Mingaladon under escort on 28 August 1945. Spitfire PR.XIs and a PR.XIX stand in blast pens in the foreground

The post-war period

Before the formal surrender ceremony was staged by MacArthur aboard USS *Missouri*, one unauthorised landing was made by Flt Lt Anderson and Wt Off Painter of 684 Sqn on the last day of August. On a sortie over Singapore from the Cocos Is base 'Brown' in RG210, 'J', they landed with engine-trouble at Kallang airfield and, to their relief were politely accommodated and fed by the Japanese who radioed news of their safety.

At HQ 247 (PR) Wing, future reconnaissance and survey programmes were under review. Large areas of foreign territory in SE Asia remained unsurveyed and it was clear that after political control had been recovered from the Japanese, further extensive survey flights by the RAF would not be tolerated by the returning Dutch and French colonial governments. Continuing aerial survey of the East Indies, Siam and Indo-China was proposed to be completed before political objections could be raised but Air Command SE Asia deferred approval because of the practical difficulties caused by repatriation of personnel and problems of transport.

The occupation forces for Siam and Indo-China were to be flown in. 684 Sqn was required to fly from Mingaladon to obtain cover of Saigon and the airfield at Tan Son Nhut, Hanoi town and the nearby airfields at Bac Mai and Gia Lam on 1 September, and to the Cambodian city of Phnom Penh and its airfield the following day.

For several days Gen Itagaki, commanding the 7th Area Army comprising the troops in Malaya, Singapore and the Netherlands East Indies, declared his intention of continuing the fight but he was over-ruled and, when his superior, Gen Terauchi, C-in-C Southern Area Army, suffered a heart attack, Itagaki was appointed in his place, commanding all Japanese forces within the original boundaries of South-East Asia Command.

On 3 September a token occupation force was landed at Georgetown, Penang Island, and a British naval force sailed south for Singapore. On the 6th, 681 Sqn made one further sortie before all outstanding PR tasks were cancelled, only one aircraft being maintained on stand-by.

The modified Operation 'Zipper', without preliminary bombardment, went in over the beaches near Port Swettenham and Port Dickson on 9 September, with tactical air support on a reduced scale by the Hellcats of 800 Sqn in HMS *Khedive* and 804 Sqn in *Emperor* which made final recces of the airfields at Morib (Kelanang) and Port Swettenham. Forty-two Japanese aircraft were counted, all immobilised by removal of their propellers in accordance with the terms of surrender, and photographs were taken along the routes inland from the landing beaches. No 804 Sqn recorded, "the Army was very impressed with the way in which it was possible to order photographs of bridges in the morning and have them delivered after lunch".

Extensive reconnaissance by 681 Sqn began over the prison camps at the Siamese end of the Burma railway and beyond as far as Nakawn Nayok, seventy miles east of Bangkok, and over enemy airfields to assess their suitability for the landing of emergency medical teams and the air-lifting of prisoners by RAF transport squadrons. During one of these sorties on 18 August, Flt Lt Papps came under fire when he flew PL920, 'J', over Moulmein. Another sortie which aroused considerable interest and emotion was that on 25 August when Flt Lt Death in PL920, 'D', obtained low-level oblique cover of three camps on the Burma railway near Kanchanaburi. After some difficulty in locating the camps, he made four runs at 200ft over the camp at Tansamrong and reported, "Prisoners in this camp were crowded at the front of the camp, swarming over the watch-towers, showing great excitement, waving and shouting at the aircraft. A Union Jack was spread on the ground near the road 20ftx30ft". Death followed up with two runs over the other camps where the PoWs, free of Japanese control, showed equal excitement.

A 'local agreement' to cease fire was signed by Japanese representatives in Rangoon on 27 August and, in spite of MacArthur's edict, the first prisoners were flown out from Siam the following day.

At the end of the month, Operation 'Birdcage' began — aircraft dropped 'Nickel' bombs of surrender leaflets to the Japanese guards and Allied prisoners of war and internees in more than 30 camps along the Siamese border, from Chiengmai to Tavoy and Ross Island, and along the Burma-Siam railway to Kanchanaburi and Bangkok, followed by Operation 'Mastiff', the landing of medical relief teams and stores.

As an essential part of 'Zipper', Thunderbolt fighter-bomber squadrons were to fly from Burma into the Malayan airfields at Port Swettenham and Morib (Kelanang) to support Operation 'Tiderace', a rapid drive down the Malay Peninsula. When a reduced-scale 'Zipper' was mounted by XXXIV Corps on 9 September, it was feared that the Japanese might oppose the landings but, in the event, no resistance was offered. Spitfire F.XIVs and the FR.XIVs of 28 Sqn were immediately flown from the escort carrier HMS *Trumpeter* to Port Swettenham airfield.

The enlargement of area caused great difficulties for South-East Asia Command and for the United Kingdom Government which was committed to the protection of Allied colonial interests and had already promised immediate repatriation of long-serving members of the British forces from the East.

With the withdrawal of No.2 Sqn RIAF from Dabaing and of No.7 Sqn from Sinthe, all the fighter/ground attack and fighter-reconnaissance squadrons of the RIAF were returned to India. Their Hurricanes were replaced by Spitfire Mk.VIIIs, most of these transferred from the RAF fighter squadrons which were to receive Spitfire Mk.XIV aircraft. By August, only No.8 Sqn RIAF had returned to Burma, equipped with Spitfire LF.VIIIs for fighter-bomber operations against the Japanese. No.6 Sqn, based at Kohat, was prepared for 'Air Control' duties on the North-West Frontier and No.7 Sqn awaited re-equipment at Lahore, eventually receiving Spitfire FR.XIVs in November 1945. Early in 1946, No.6 Sqn was fully equipped with the FR.XIVE and was allocated two Spitfire PR.XIs in April to undertake photographic sorties. Two months later, No.7 Sqn RIAF also received two PR.XIs. The other RIAF squadrons were re-equipped with Spitfire Mks.VIII and XIV for the fighter role, No.4 Sqn forming the Indian component of the Allied Occupation Force in Japan until late in 1946.

If imitation is, indeed, the sincerest form of flattery, the Admiralty had expressed appreciation of the operations of 888 Sqn in the East Indies Fleet most sincerely by establishing another photo-reconnaissance squadron on 1 June. This was 809 Sqn, equipped with six PR Hellcats, which was intended to serve with the British Pacific Fleet but the squadron was disbanded before sailing, on 11 September.

On 12 September Gen Itagaki surrendered his forces to Adm Mountbatten at Singapore; the war in South-East Asia was at an end.

No 684 Sqn's Mitchell Mk.II MA956, 'E', had remained unserviceable at Alipore until struck off charge at the end of April but the remaining B-25C, N5-14, 'Z', was still operational after more than five years in service and eighty-six operational sorties. On 19 September the B-25C was removed from the squadron strength and allotted to 163 RSU at Alipore for disposal.

681 Sqn's operations ceased until 25 September when Wg Cdr Pearson led six Spitfires southwards along the isthmus and down the west coast of Malaya towards Kuala Lumpur, flying at low-level because one aircraft carried the squadron's dog, Dicer, as a passenger and he could not be persuaded to wear an oxygen mask. The hinterland of the peninsula was covered in storm cloud which had closed down K.L airfield, so Wg Cdr Pearson advised his pilots to avoid heroics and, if necessary, to land on one of the sandy beaches. Fortunately visibility on the coast was sufficiently good for the Spitfires to land at Port Swettenham, a field manned by Japanese and a small detachment of Indian troops. There, Dicer chased about the airfield, the first Allied dog to return to Malaya. The Spitfires were later flown in to Kuala Lumpur but, as the airfield lacked any 'back-up' and processing facilities, all six soon returned to Mingaladon from where the few

Hurricanes and Spitfires of 28 Sqn flew occasional photo-recces over Eastern Burma to keep track of groups of Japanese still moving southwards. The long-awaited Spitfire FR.XVIs were delivered in October and 28 Sqn flew south on 3 and 4 November to the airfield at Bayan Lepas (Penang), escorted by the Air-Jungle Rescue Beaufighters of 27 Sqn and later moved south to Kuala Lumpur.

The British Military Government administrations set up in the re-occupied territories required further surveys. A detachment from 681 Sqn intended for Hong Kong suffered disaster at Mingaladon; one of the pilots, Flg Off W.K. Williams, wrote, "Probably the most spectacular 'write-off' of 681 Sqn's Spitfires was in (if my memory serves me correctly) November 1945 at Rangoon, when on the morning we were all due to take off for Hong Kong, a Dakota swung on take-off and destroyed a number of the Spits which were lined up adjacent to the runway". The destructive aircraft was of 31 Sqn, making a single-engined landing.

Despite the moral stance of pre-war Japanese Governments and the dream of a 'Greater East Asia Co-prosperity Sphere', Japanese military expansion brought no material benefits to the peoples of South-east Asia. Effective and just colonial administrations were replaced by exploitive and harsh military rule, and war damage was repaired only where it suited the Japanese victors.

The Philippine Islands, their economies ruined, bred a strong guerilla movement, as did Malaya where the principal industries of rubber and mining were allowed to degenerate into near-ruin; the greater part of the population supported a British-armed but Chinese communist-inspired Malayan Peoples' Anti-Japanese Army awaiting the return of British forces. In the Netherlands East Indies, where the Dutch were reputed to be hard masters (although there was less prejudice against families of mixed race than in British colonies or in India) the Japanese had a degree of self-interested co-operation from those who hoped for an independent Indonesia.

Fighting broke out in Java where the British and Indian troops of 23 Div landed to cover the evacuation of Dutch civilians from internment camps early in October. A 681 Sqn detachment of Spitfires, bound for Kai Tak (Kowloon) suffered a series of mechanical failures and only one aircraft, PL982, 'Y', completed the journey. The others, having reached Kuala Lumpur, remained there until December, when two aircraft were detached to Kemajoran (Batavia, now Jakarta) in Java to operate as 904 Wing PR Flight.

In Annam (Eastern Indo-China) a revolt began against the French authorities and 684 Sqn moved base from Alipore to Tan Son Nhut (Saigon) on 16 October to provide reconnaissance support for troops arriving from France.

232: *After re-equipping primarily with Spitfire XIVs, two fighter-reconnaissance squadrons of the Royal Indian Air Force were allocated PR.XIs for high-level photography. Here, lined up for inspection with the squadron's other aircraft, was PL987 of No.6 Sqn RIAF*

233: *681 Sqn's Spitfire PR.XI, PL897, 'B', detached to 904 Wing PR Flight at Kemajoran in 1946, was finished Medium Sea Grey on sides and uppersurfaces with White bands, PRU Blue underneath*

234: *N5-172, a North American B-25D (42-87256) which served with No.18 (NEI) Sqn of the* Militaire Luchtvaart *from 1944 until late in 1946. In July that year the Netherlands took over the task of keeping order in the East Indies and the* ML *consequently formed a PR Unit, the* Photo Verkennings Afdeling, *of B-25s. N5-172 was transferred to the new unit late in 1946. All camouflage paint has been stripped off, leaving just the Dutch national flag and red propeller warning stripe*

235: *A Dakota of 31 Sqn makes a supply drop to an internment camp relief team after preliminary reconnaissance by 681 Sqn. Note the unusual position of the aircraft identity letter on the rudder*

236: *Seen from the despatcher's position in the Dakota, the dropping zone identifying mark laid out adjacent to the camp*

237: *One of the courier Beaufighters of 684 Sqn at Kuala Lumpur alongside a Dakota IV bearing the pre-war 'Type A' roundels and larger finflash proposed by HQ ACSEA. The Dakota is finished in US Basic Camouflage with Medium Green blotches, the ideal finish for the type in South-East Asia*

Three days later three of the Mosquitos flew with Spitfires of 273 Sqn in a display of air-power over Dalat, 130 miles to the north-east, where Annamite rebels were in control. Reconnaissance sorties were flown over the area for several weeks to establish the location of the rebel forces, while new survey cover was obtained of the Saigon area. The seven Mosquito PR.34s of 684 Sqn's No 2 (Cocos) Detachment were flown to Seletar (Singapore) but RG184, 'X', failed to arrive and was presumed to have crashed in the sea.

HQ 347 Wing was disbanded on 30 November but the two photographic reconnaissance squadrons and 28 Sqn remained active. The two Spitfire squadrons remained at Kuala Lumpur, 681 Sqn sending two more aircraft to Tan Son Nhut on 21 December, until both 28 and 681 moved south to Seletar on 8 January 1946. The only operational flights made during December were to obtain up-dated cover of the Burmese oil-fields at the request of Air HQ Burma. On 29 January 684 Sqn was moved to Don Muang (Bangkok), followed at the beginning of March by the No 2 Detachment. No 681 Sqn was fully re-equipped with Spitfire PR.XIX aircraft.

By the end of 1945, all the escort carriers had left the East Indies Fleet. Of the Hellcat squadrons, only No.888 remained, stationed at Sembawang on Singapore Island from where the Hellcats undertook 'infill' survey until disbanded in August 1946.

By February 1946 the RAF in the Far Fast had begun a return to a peace-time establishment, apart from detachments at Tan Son Nhut to maintain a staging-post on the route from Singapore to Hong Kong and the Occupation Forces in Japan, and the squadrons supporting the forces in the Netherland-Indies.

Tactical reconnaissance for the Army in Java and Sumatra was undertaken by the fighter squadrons stationed there, Nos 60, 81 and 155, but camera-fitted Mosquito FB.VIs of 47 and 84 Sqns carried out a number of armed reconnaissance tasks until more faulty wing-structures were discovered and, on 20 January 1946, many of the Mosquitos in the Command were again grounded for inspection. Throughout February the Spitfires of 904 Wing PR Flt were occupied over the Indonesian-held areas of Western Java, with repeated sorties to Buitenzorg, Tijandoer and Bekasi, or over the strongholds of the Republican forces, the *Tentara Republik Indonesia*, at Djokjakarta, Cheribon and Semarang in Central Java.

Late in May a detachment of Mosquito PR.34s from 684 Sqn was stationed at Kemajoran to prepare for a four-month topographical survey of Java before Dutch forces took over completely from the British Army. The Spitfire PR Flt was, meanwhile, engaged in a 'Special Rice Survey' for an assessment of the coming rice crop and during the next few weeks, as the Dutch Army took over control from the British, tactical reconnaissance was generally

undertaken by B-25s of the Royal Netherlands-Indies Army *Militaire Luchtvaart*. These aircraft were bombers of No 18 (NEI) Sqn, overhauled and fitted with Fairchild K.17 cameras for vertical photography and, in some cases, with oblique, hand-operated cameras in the side gun-positions. Unlike the RAF B-25Cs, which carried a crew of four, the ML B-25s had two pilots, radio-operator, observer, flight engineer and a camera-operator. Nor did they have the large bomb-bay fuel tanks that made the RAF aircraft so remarkably effective. Late in the year, several B-25Cs and B-25Ds were transferred to a new *Photo Verkennings Afdeling*, (PR Section) under the command of Lt Fridjof Olsen, who had been a member of the '*patrouille Bangalore*' in 1942 and later served with No.18 NEI Sqn of the *Militaire Luchtvaart*.

In May 1946, 681 Sqn moved to Palam (Delhi) and was there re-numbered No.34 Sqn on 1 August. A detachment of the squadron's Spitfire PR.XIXs stationed at Kallang on Singapore Island was principally engaged in survey but also flew some tactical recces to supplement operations by the Spitfire FR.XIVs of 28 Sqn during October and November, over the Bidor and Tapah areas of Western Malaya, seventy miles north of Kuala Lumpur, where terrorists attempted to take local control.

No 684 Sqn at Don Muang was re-numbered No.81 Sqn on 1 September 1946; the Mosquito detachment was withdrawn from Java in November but the aircraft were temporarily grounded with defects in their flap-operating systems. Whilst they were modified, several sorties were made with the squadron 'hack' Harvard, FT374, fitted with a camera.

Following the withdrawal of British troops from the Indies and a general repatriation of Japanese prisoners, SE Asia Command ceased to exist on 31 November 1946.

By the beginning of 1947 it seemed that order had been largely restored in Malaya (although this was merely the calm before a storm) and 28 Sqn's IE was reduced to eight Spitfires when the squadron moved to Tengah in February. All RAF commitments in the Indies were over and there was a general run-down in the Far East Air Force.

From April 1947 the Spitfire FR.XIVs of 28 Sqn were gradually replaced by Spitfire FR.XVIIIs; these aircraft had mountings for one F.52 vertical camera or one oblique and two vertical F.24 cameras in the fuselage, instead of the single oblique F.24 camera of the FR Mk.XIV. Early FR.XVIIIs were powered, like the FR.XIV, by the 2,050 hp Rolls Royce Griffon 65 engine; later aircraft had the 2,340 hp Griffon 67 engine. Armament was similar —two Hispano 20mm cannon and four 0.50-inch Browning machine-guns—but with additional provision for mounting eight rocket-projectiles. No.81 Sqn also received a Mk.XVIII (later to be followed by more), an ex-28 Sqn aircraft, TP407, as a replacement but this aircraft was used for PR sorties, fitted with twin vertical cameras.

On 31 July, 34 Sqn was disbanded and seven of its Spitfires went to 81 Sqn at Seletar, the equipment was now Mosquito PR.34, Spitfire PR.XIX and FR.XVIII aircraft, the last providing the PR squadron with a strike capability for the first time. The Mosquitos extended their survey operations to other territories—a detachment to Labuan for a survey of British North Borneo and Sarawak in September and another to Hong Kong, while the squadron's base was moved to Changi (Singapore) in November. In January 1948, 28 Sqn moved to nearby Sembawang.

By mid-1948 terrorist activity in Malaya had become so widespread that a State of Emergency was declared in July. No.81 Sqn's Hong Kong Detachment was ordered back to Singapore, to operate from Tengah while the other Spitfires were detached to Kuala Lumpur. From there, P.H. Watson flew Spitfire PM574 on the first tactical PR sortie in support of the Army on 9 July.

Thereafter 28 Sqn, also operating mainly from Kuala Lumpur, became increasingly involved in tactical reconnaissance in support of Operation 'Firedog', the twelve-year struggle against Communist terrorists, successors to the wartime MPAJA, while 81 Sqn continued PR, usually at heights above 16,000ft so that the terrorists would not be aware that they were kept under observation.

235 Below: Wg Cdr DB Pearson DFC with ground-crew of 681 Sqn at Kuala Lumpur in 1945. The Spitfire PR.IX, PL781, 'F', was finished in Medium Sea Grey on the uppersurfaces, PRU Blue below

The use of Roman numerals for the aircraft Mark numbers was discontinued in June 1948 and the Marks were thereafter denoted by Arabic numerals, thus the Spitfire FR.XVIII became FR.18.

The following year another threat developed when it was feared that Communist armies in China, on the brink of victory over Chiang's forces, would invade Hong Kong. As part of a build-up of British forces in the colony, in May 1949, 28 Sqn flew its Spitfire FR.18s (brought up to full squadron strength of sixteen aircraft) to Kai Tak where the squadron effectively reverted to the fighter role. Fortunately the threat did not materialise.

Spitfire PR.19s remained with the Mosquitos of 81 Sqn when, in 1950, the squadron's Spitfire FR.18s were attached to 60(F) Sqn at Tengah as 'C' Flight to take part in strikes against terrorists on the mainland of Malaya.

The story of Operation 'Firedog' has been thoroughly covered by other writers. Wartime aircraft types were replaced by new aircraft and, by January 1952, only five Spitfires and eight Mosquitos were still operational with 81 Sqn. It is worth recording here that Sqn Ldr W.P. Swaby, commanding 81 Sqn, flew the last Spitfire 'war flight' in PR PS888 on the day the last Spitfires were struck off charge, 1 April 1954. The Mosquitos remained in service through the following year, the last operational sortie being flown on 15 December 1955 by Mosquito PR.34A, RG314.

COLOUR STANDARDS & COLOUR REFERENCES

A sheet showing the Colour Standards of the Air Ministry and wartime Ministry of Aircraft Production was included, in facsimile, in *British Aviation Colours of World War Two**. Some of these MAP colours have since been incorporated into British Standard 381C *Colours for identification, coding and special purposes* which includes small 'chips' of the Standard colours and a schedule of their light reflectivity or brightness. The current BS 381C provides exact matches only for those aircraft camouflage colours (originally listed as 'Aircraft Series') that are still in use. US Federal Specification No.595 and its revisions are often used as a reference source for both American and British aircraft colours but, like BS 381C, the FS.595 reference numbers are of no help in matching colours which have no equivalent among the Standard's wide range of colour samples.

We often have difficulty in describing or accurately identifying colours because of our generally loose naming of them. For example, we may be familiar with the range of camouflage greys used on British Service aircraft, yet only Sky Grey was a true grey that can be accurately matched by mixing black and white. Dark Green, the most widely used camouflage colour was (and still is) a dark olive-green which appears more greenish to the eye because of a physiological phenomenon termed 'green shift'. This colour cannot be matched by mixing blue and yellow, with or without black and/or white, as can a true green.

236 Above: 'Spit and polish' is the most fitting description of this overall PRU Blue Spitfire Mk.XI of 681 Sqn, cleaned for inspection by the King of Nepal at Alipore early in 1945. This aircraft retained 32in dia roundels, repainted Dull Blue/Light Blue

The Munsell Reference System

The Munsell System describes each colour in terms of three variable qualities or 'dimensions' which Munsell named Hue, Value and Chroma. Hue is the attribute of a colour that indicates its position in the visible spectrum, Value denotes the tone of a colour on a scale from dark to light, and Chroma indicates 'saturation' or strength of a colour.

The British Standards Institution, in its colour specifications, refers to the reference system devised by A.H. Munsell and explained in *A Grammar of Colour*. The Munsell System is based on a presumption that all colours can be matched by mixing pure pigments of five 'primary' colours: pale cadmium yellow, cadmium red, cobalt violet (purple), cobalt blue and cadmium green with varying quantities of black and white.

The Munsell References express Hue as a number followed by the initial letters in English, of the primary colours—Y, R, P etc—and their 'secondaries'—YR, RP etc. Each of these ten hues is divided into ten 'steps' but, as the differences between them are supposedly not perceptible to the eye, only four are normally used, numbered 2.5, 5, 7.5 and 10. Thus, 5GY represents a bright green-yellow. A second number indicating Value (tone) from dark (0) to light (10) is followed by an oblique stroke and a final number indicating Chroma, usually from /0 to /18. So the colour 'Sky' is given the Reference 5GY 7/2; a green-yellow, in strength seven-tenths between black and white, with low intensity of colour. 'Neutral' greys, mixed from only black and white and having neither Hue nor Chroma, are denoted by the initial N and a Value number only; Sky Grey is N 7.

The System enables tonal values to be compared, as light reflectivities can be found by substituting the Value number in the equation: Reflectivity = V(V-1)%. Because of the limited number of Value steps shown in BS 381C,the Munsell references and their reflectivities, as given in the Standard, are approximate.

The Methuen Reference System

An alternative colour reference system is that in the *Munsell Handbook of Colour* by Kornerup and Wanscher (Methuen & Co Ltd, 1963). This compact book, intended for designers and colour technicians, provides 1,266 colour samples and enables the user to match colours closely enough for all practical purposes.   Colours are classified in a manner similar to that of the Munsell System, with symbols for Hue, Tone and Intensity but, unlike Munsell, recognising that these last two attributes are interdependent.

Hue is indicated by a (page) number from 1 (greenish-yellow), through yellow (2), red (10), purple (15), blue (21) and green (27) to 30 (yellow-green). Tone is indicated by letters; A (light) to F (dark) and the range *can* be extended further. Colour strength or Intensity is shown by a final number, 1 to greatest strength 8.

A disadvantage of the Methuen System is that the tones in the book are limited to six (A to F), but these are of equal lightness or darkness for all colours.

It should be noted that, in black and white photographs, the relative tones of camouflage are no sure guide to colours. There are a number of factors that can affect the tones of the camouflage in black and white photos, which might be differently interpreted by the eye:

- weathering of the painted surface
- . intensity of light on the painted surface
- light reflected from the surface
- ambient light temperature (degrees Kelvin)
- colour balance of the film (dependent on the make)

- accuracy of film exposure
- contrast characteristics (hard or soft) of the print paper
- accuracy of exposure of the print.

Although photographs show considerable variations in the contrast between uppersurface camouflage colours, the true colours and tones were less varied than they often appear in photographic prints.

Most pictures of aircraft by 'official' photographers were undoubtedly taken using a light or medium yellow filter over the camera lens. Such filters were commonly used with 'pan' film to darken the tone of blue sky and to increase cloud contrast. They also darkened the Green of camouflage and tone of PRU Blue which remained generally consistent in tone through long periods of exposure to sunlight. 'Unofficial' photographers —squadron personnel—probably did not have the benefit of using filters for their photographic efforts and their pictures may show considerable variations in the tonal value of aircraft finishes. However, the tone of the 'PRU Blue' finish applied to the first Mosquitos and reinforcing B-25s of 684 Squadron late in 1943 was probably a different instance. The paint appears surprisingly pale in photos and it may be assumed that the colour was certainly lighter than MAP PRU Blue of new aircraft delivered from Britain from that time onwards.

The matching of colours is, of course, a subjective matter; the references given here have been tried and checked in diffuse daylight but readers will probably prefer to make their own comparisons if colour cards or chips are available to them. In a few cases no Methuen colours exactly match the camouflage finishes.

The tables included here list the camouflage colours mentioned in the text, the equivalent BS 381C and FS.595 references, and reflectivities. Some of the reflectivity figures are taken from *Camouflage and Surface Finish of Aircraft*, an unpublished MAP Scientific War Record (1947) by G. Palmer of the Royal Aircraft Establishment, Farnborough.

237: The tones of photographs can be deceptive, as shown here; the Temperate Land camouflage pattern on this Beech Expediter is barely perceptible in the strong sunlight. Such aircraft were used by most Command Communications Flights but none were provided to meet the transport needs of PR Force

RAF Museum Series, Arms and Armour Press, 1976

TABLE 1

BRITISH CAMOUFLAGE COLOUR EQUIVALENTS

Selected Colours from MAP DTD Technical Circular No.360		BS381C Colours		FS595a Colors	Methuen References	Approx Munsell References	Approx Diffuse Reflectivity
SPEC.DTD 83A & 308							
REF. (5gal): 1944							
Sky Grey	33B.295			36463	24C2	N7	43%
Ocean Grey	33B.486	Dk Admiralty Grey	632*	26187	24DE3	7B 4.5/1	16%
Medium Sea Grey	33B.492	Medium Sea Grey	637	36270	22DE3	10B 5.5/1	26%
Dark Sea Grey	33B.221	Dark Sea Grey	638	36173*	22F3	4PB 4/1	13%
Extra Dark Sea Grey	33B.227	Extra Dark Sea Grey	640	36118	23F2	10B 3.5/1	10%
Light Slate Grey	33B.236	Light Slate Grey	639	34159	28E3	10GY 4/1.5	14%
Dark Slate Grey	33B.224	Dark Slate Grey	634	34096	29E3	5GY 4/1	12%
Midstone	33B.356	Midstone	362	30266	4D7	2.5YR 5.5/6	25%
Light Earth	33B.230			30257	5CD4	8.5YR 6/4	30%
Dark Earth	33B.182	Dark Earth	450	30118	5E4	10YR 4/2	13%
Light Green	33B.233				30EF4	10GY 4/1	11%
Dark Green	33B.185	Dark Green	641	34079	2F4	10Y 3/1.5	7%
Extra Dark Sea Green	33B.388			34092	27F4	2.5G 3.5/2	8%
Sky	33B.335	Sky	210	34424	29B3	5GY 7.3/1.5	43%
Sky Blue	33B.298			35414*	24AB3	7PB 7.4/2	52%
Deep Sky	33B.493	Azure Blue	104	15050*	20E7	5PB 3/8	8%
Azure Blue	33B.468			35231*	20-21B5	5PB 6.5/6	30%
Dark Mediterranean Blue	33B.318				20EF6	7.5PB 3/6	8%
Light Mediterranean Blue	33B.319				21D4-5	7.5PB 5/5	16%
PRU Blue	33B.494	PRU Blue	636		23DE4	10B 4/3	14%
PRU Mauve	33B.594†				18D4	2.5P 5/4.5	22%
Dull Blue	33B.327			35053	21F7	5PB 2.5/8	4%
Dull Red	33B. 230	Venetian Red	445*	20152	8DE7	10R 4/8	10%
Yellow	33B.156	Golden Yellow	356	33538	4-5A8	10YR 5.5/6	57%
White	33B331			37875	1A1	N 9.1	74%
Night	33B.188				21H2	N 0.5	4%
Bright Blue	33B.68(1gal)	Roundel Blue	110	35031*	20E7	7.5PB 2.5/7	8%
Bright Red	33B.72(1gal)	Post Office Red	538	21105	11-12B8	5R 4/12	12%

Additional Colours mentioned in the text

NIVO‡	33B.123			34096*	28F4	7GY 3.5/1	10%
PRU Special Pink	33B.NIV**	Shell Pink	453*	31668*	12B1-2	5.5RP 8/2.5	57%
RAAF Light Green				34151	1F6	2GY 3.6/3.0	9%
RAAF Light Earth		Light Brown	410*	39219	5E6	9YR 4.5/3	15%
BS.381C No.1 Sky Blue		Sky Blue	101		25B4-5	2.5BG 6.5/3	33%
MAP Sky Blue '40					24B2-3	8B 7.5/1.5	49%
'Duck-egg Blue'/RAAF Sky		(cf Humbrol No.23/MB)		35622	25-26B3	3GY 8/2	53%
RAAF Sky Blue '41				35550	24B3-4	7B 7/2.5	40%
Dark blue ('royal blue')		Oxford Blue	105*	25051*	21E8	7.5PB 2.5/8	6%
Light blue (Blue:White, 4:1)				35450*	22-23A4-5	5.5PB 7/6.5	41%

* = near match

† = equivalent to a mixture of one part Identification (Bright) Red 33B.72, two parts PRU Blue 33B.494 and five parts PRU Pink 33B.NIV

‡ = possibly 'Night Varnish, Orfordness' or 'Not in vocabulary, Orfordness'

** = 'not in vocabulary of stores'

British Aircraft Camouflage

No schemes of aircraft camouflage and markings have been so frequently misrepresented as those applied to operational aircraft of the wartime Commands in India and South-East Asia during the Second World War. In a great number of books and magazine articles by specialist writers, the colours used on aircraft of these Overseas Commands have often been incorrectly described and illustrated, principally because of a failure to refer to documentary evidence from the period, readily available for many years in the Public Record Office at Kew.

In some cases, the wording of Air Ministry Orders was ambiguous or incorrect, requiring the issue of Amending Orders. Although each Standard finish was denoted by an 'official' name and had a distinct Stores Reference within the series 33B (matt cellulose lacquer) the Ministry frequently used loose descriptive terms such as 'light blue' and 'duck-egg blue', such names sometimes causing misunderstanding.

Oft-repeated errors, resulting from misunderstanding of the Air Ministry Orders (reprinted in *British Aviation Colours of World War Two*) have become accepted as truth. Simply by their repetition, such errors have given the impression that aircraft markings in the Far East were sometimes applied in a haphazard manner, thus explaining the different markings occasionally to be seen in photographs. In fact, variations in markings were made in strict accordance with the operational requirements of the Overseas Commands, these sometimes at variance with the camouflage schemes and markings required by the Air Ministry and those applied in the factories under the supervision of the Resident Technical Officers of the Ministry of Aircraft Production.

In February 1933 the Royal Aircraft Establishment at Farnborough was instructed to devise a scheme of camouflage suitable for aircraft on the ground and when in flight over terrain similar to that of Southern England, where greens and browns predominate. After a series of trials, disruptive patterns were recommended of a drab olive-green, Dark Green, and a yellowish brown, Dark Earth, each colour to occupy 50% of the plan area of an aircraft, as described in a *Note on colour schemes to decrease the visibility of aircraft from above* sent to the Air Ministry in August.

When the Italians invaded Abyssinia in October 1935, it was decided to camouflage the aircraft forming the Emergency Air Garrison of Malta, and a 'War Emergency Marking' replaced the National marking on the camouflaged surfaces. This was the roundel of Dull Red (V.NR.5, 'Night-flying Red') and Dull Blue (V.NB.6, 'Night-flying Blue') used on night-bombers, now generally termed the Type A roundel.

At the time of the Munich Crisis in September 1938,

the Temperate Land Scheme C.3A of Dark Green and Dark Earth was applied to first-line aircraft of the RAF, and the Temperate Sea Scheme S.1E to many aircraft of the Air Branch, Royal Navy. By the outbreak of war, eleven months later, virtually all operational aircraft of the Home Commands were camouflaged, the new monoplane fighters and bombers so finished at the factory in accordance with a series of Air Diagrams which illustrated the patterns and colours required on each make of aircraft.

The surfaces of the lower wings of biplanes, their fuselage sides and tailplanes were to be finished in lighter tones, so that those areas receiving less intense light would appear similar in tone to the areas in direct light from above. This principle was called 'shadow shading', a term misunderstood at the time and generally assumed in the Press to be the official name for disruptive camouflage.

The later US Army Air Corps 'Basic camouflage' of Dark Olive Drab with Neutral Gray under surfaces used the same principle, named 'counter-shading'.

From the beginning, a characteristic of the aircraft of the Heston Flight had been the adoption of special camouflage for its high-flying aircraft. A later Air Ministry Order A.513 of July 1941, *Camouflage Colouring and Markings of Aircraft*, stated, *"Aircraft of photographic reconnaissance units are to be coloured and marked in accordance with operational requirements, and the colour schemes used need not conform to the standard system"*. In May 1939 Cotton's Lockheed 12A, G-AFTL, was painted with 'Camotint', a glossy pale green-grey akin to the colour of a mallard's egg, a shade which Cotton had observed to cause an aeroplane "apparently to disappear against a clear sky". The Camotint was claimed to render an aircraft invisible at 10,000 ft and it was reported that Wg Cdr Cotton had flown over Heston for half an hour without having been seen.

Some sources have given the manufacturer of 'Camotint' as Titanine Ltd but the Royal Aircraft Establishment at Farnborough recorded the receipt of a sample of 'Camotint gloss lacquer' from Cellon Ltd on 21 November 1939. The RAE was asked to produce 'smooth-finish, none-gloss' paints in Dark Green, Dark Earth and 'duck egg green' to finish three Blenheims and enough 'duck egg green' for one Spitfire of the Photographic Development Unit.

The pale olive-grey was added to the Colour Standards of the new Ministry of Aircraft Production and called 'Sky', an unsuitable name as the colour had no resemblance, apart from light tone, to either Sea Grey (the "Dirty White", used beneath Fleet Air Arm aircraft) or to Sky Blue, favoured for fighter undersurfaces by the Royal Aircraft Establishment, Farnborough. The RAE reported that its "light grey-green" had slightly greater reflectivity than Camotint.

Throughout the late 'thirties the aircraft of the Home Base Fighter Command were finished with Aluminium dope on under surfaces, even when camouflage was introduced, but from April 1939 the undersides of the port wings were painted Matt White (33B15) and the starboard wing Matt Night (33B/25). With so distinctive a means of identification, the underwing National markings were considered unnecessary and were deleted by the fighter squadrons from 10 June.

When operational trials of the Camotint finish as an alternative under surface colour were undertaken early in 1940, the Royal Aircraft Establishment reported that the colour was too bright for concealment of an aircraft at altitude greater than 10,000ft. At lower level, the RAE preferred the current Sky Blue but it says much for Wg Cdr Cotton's influence and, perhaps for simple observation, that the HQ Staffs of Bomber Command and, later, of Fighter Command believed Sky to be the most suitable colour for the undersides of their day-flying aircraft under most weather conditions. There is no doubt that camouflage trials by the Photographic Development Unit exerted an influence on the choice of Colour Standards, out of all proportion to the size and importance of the Unit.

After a Hudson of the PDU was shot down by a British fighter, further mistakes were feared and a folder was distributed on 31 March 1940, showing the colour schemes in use on photographic reconnaissance Spitfires and Blenheims (overall 'Duck-egg Blue' or 'Duck-egg Green') and the Hudsons (dappled camouflage of Dark Green and Medium Sea Grey with diagonal bands of Sky on upper surfaces, and Sky under surfaces).

Since the outbreak of war, in accordance with the Air Ministry's earliest camouflage requirements, upper surface camouflage colours were all Type 'M' matt finish but Sky, intended as camouflage for under-surfaces where there was no specular reflection, was produced with finely ground pigments as Type 'S' smooth finish. When the aircraft of Wg Cdr Cotton's Unit were refinished in Type 'S' paint, an increase in the speed of the Blenheims of 20 mph was recorded.

By mid-1940, HQ Fighter Command had decided to change the markings of its aircraft. An Air Ministry Leaflet, *Introduction of New Type Roundels and changes in the colouring of Squadron and aircraft code letters*, issued on 30 April, listed revised proportions for National Marking II on fuselage sides and National Marking III beneath the wing-tips; these markings are generally known as Type C1 and Type C roundels. Code letters were to be changed from Medium Sea Grey to Sky. Instructions were issued on 6 and 12 June for undersides of fighter aircraft to be Sky Type 'S' when sufficient dope became available, the starboard wing remaining in black on many aircraft.

In an Appendix to a document dated 11 August, the Air Ministry set out: *"Fighter aircraft to be Temperate Land Scheme with undersides duck egg blue. Fleet Air Arm aircraft to be Temperate Sea Scheme of Dark Slate Grey and Extra Dark Sea Grey with undersides duck egg blue"*, for it was supposed that 'Sky Blue' might be mistaken for the RLM 65 Hellblau of German fighters, and Fighter Command confirmed the use of Night beneath the port wings of day fighters from 5 January 1941.

Since the beginning of the application of camouflage, each scheme had been applied as pattern A and 'handed' as pattern B to aircraft of alternate serial numbers. From 14 January this system was given up on production lines and only pattern A camouflage was applied to aircraft built in the UK, as confirmed by MAP Directorate of Technical Development Circular No.144 in March 1941. From 22 April, fighter aircraft were again to be all 'Duck-Egg Blue' beneath.

In March, HQ Fighter Command expressed the view that the Temperate Land Scheme colouring, intended for aircraft flying below 10,000 ft, was too dark at altitudes above 20,000 ft and as fighter aircraft were increasingly active across the Channel, colours were requested that would be more effective over the sea. Following flight trials of several schemes at the Air Fighting Development Unit, Duxford, it was decided to replace Dark Earth by a new colour, Ocean Grey, and to replace the under-surface Sky by the darker Medium Sea Grey on Fighter Command aircraft.

On 15 August 1941, the new colouring came into operation; in place of Dark Earth, a colour mixed from seven parts of Medium Sea Grey and one part of Night. New identification markings were to be added; Yellow strips along the leading edges of the wings; the spinner and an 18in band around the rear of the fuselage to be Sky. It was noted that *"the requirements for overseas fighters remain unchanged"*. The colour scheme set out in the Signal (S.7013) was an interim measure; the new Standard colour, Ocean Grey, was to replace the Dark Earth but was not yet available in sufficient quantity for refinishing and factory production.

On Spitfires used for low-level reconnaissance, the finish remained Sky for a while. To Spitfire PR.IBs a darker colour was applied, a medium grey-blue produced by Titanine Ltd under the trade-name 'Cosmic Blue'. This was 'PRU Special Blue' later included in Ministry of Aircraft Production Colour Standards and added to BS 381C as PRU Blue. For Type G Spitfires fitted with various oblique cameras for low-level reconnaissance just below cloud-base, after some experimentation the colour adopted was a light greyish-pink, 'PRU Special Pink', which was soon found to be less visible in hazy conditions than Sky. This finish was again used on fighter-reconnaissance Spitfires late in the war. Another finish for intended application to under-surfaces of low-level reconnaissance aircraft was PRU Mauve; this was not used on aircraft in the Far East.

It is hardly surprising that misunderstandings arose from the use of 'Sky' in Ministry of Aircraft Production Colour Standards in May 1940 or 'Duck-egg blue (Sky Type 'S')' in Air Ministry Order A.946 of 12 December and other documents, for the light olive-grey colour.

Under the direction of the MAP Resident Technical Officers, all new aircraft were finished at the factories in the required camouflage of Temperate Land Scheme and Type 'S', (Smooth) Sky late in 1940 but, perhaps because Ministry of Aircraft Production Technical Circulars and Colour Standards were not usually issued to Engineer Officers at operational level, under whose authority changes were made to aircraft in service, confusion arose.

Whether decisions about the required under-surface colour were made at Group, Wing or Squadron level is immaterial; in some cases it seems the assumption was made that MAP Sky Blue was intended but many aircraft were refinished in a stronger, greenish blue close in hue and tone to Colour No.1 Sky Blue of BS 381C:1930 (later Colour No.101, since deleted). Harald Penrose, test-pilot at Westland Aircraft, confirmed to the Author that early Whirlwind fighters had blue under-surfaces of such a colour.

Although the new MAP assured the Air Ministry that 'Duck-egg blue' and Sky were identical (Stores vocabulary reference 33B.335), there is no doubt that an alternative 'unofficial' colour, distinct from the grey-green Sky, was used on many aircraft in 1940-1941 and widely known as 'Duck-egg blue'.

In *Aviation History Colouring Book No.30*, aviation historian Ian K. Baker included a colour chip matching a sample of a finish, identified as Sky Blue of 1942 from an RAAF wartime store. A possible match for the under-surfaces of the Buffalos of No.4 PRU and of 67 Sqn in 1941, the chip almost exactly matches the colour of Humbrol Enamel No.23 Duck-egg Blue (Methuen 25-26B3) alternatively the Buffalos may have been finished beneath with a less reflective Sky Blue (Methuen 24B34) of which a sample has been discovered in Australia.

Meanwhile, research and trials of high-altitude camouflage continued. In the Middle East pilots of No.2 PRU were concerned at the visibility of their aircraft but trials with Hurricanes finished in dark tones of Light Mediterranean Blue showed even this colour to be still too light in tone.

Boeing Fortress Is (B-17C) were made available to Britain in the spring of 1941 for use by 90 Sqn. To a Signal on 30 April from Burtonwood, where incoming aircraft were modified to RAF requirements; *"I understand that the aircraft will operate by day, in which case the camouflage should be dark earth and dark green for upper and keel surfaces and Duck-egg blue camotint for undersurfaces"*, HQ Bomber Command replied on 2 May that the "high PRU Spitfire (blue) scheme" would be more suitable for high-altitude bombers. On 14 May the Air Ministry notified Commands that B-17Cs would be 'special blue' beneath, the 'Cosmic Blue' initial dope obtained from the Unit at Benson.

Trials at Farnborough and Boscombe Down had already shown that for camouflage at 35,000 ft both Sky and PRU Special Blue were inferior to more intense blues. Trials by the High Altitude Development Flight at the Aircraft and Armament Experimental Establishment, continued in July 1941 of variations on MAP Colour Standards Azure Blue and Titanine Ultra Blue (ultramarine) with three Spitfires, two having under-surfaces and sides in 'dark' and 'extra dark' Ultra Blue, the third in PRU Special Blue. Trials Report No.17 confirmed that the 'extra dark' shade was "almost invisible" although "the white of the roundels renders even a perfect camouflage completely useless as they remain conspicuous at practically all angles of sight", and recommended adoption of the 'extra dark' shade, made "more dull and matt"—the RAE recommended adoption of this colour and the name 'Deep Sky'.

The Air Ministry sent the Report to Bomber Command on 5 September with an added comment, "You will note that the colouring at present in use on PRU aircraft and Fortresses is not so good as the ultra blue extra dark shade produced by the RAE Farnborough". It was suggested that Fortresses be finished beneath "a navy blue colour having 10% reflection", so HQ Bomber Command instructed the PRU to carry out tests with Deep Sky. There seems to have been no interest at the PRU in changing the camouflage colour of the high-flying Spitfires although the RAE reported that PRU Blue was "considerably lighter and plainly visible at 30 deg to the Zenith into the sun".

This was not the end of the story. On 6 October the British purchasing Commission to the US required Boeing Fortress IIAs (B-17E) intended for the RAF to have under-surfaces and sides of "deep sky colour" but most were instead finished Sky beneath. The Japanese entry into the war caused a re-appraisal of USAAC aircraft requirements and delivery of B-17s was delayed until the spring of 1942. The colour used on these aircraft (Fullers colours) and on the first Consolidated Liberator IIs (B-24D) for Britain (Dupont 'Duco' colours) was that recommended by the RAE, termed 'Deep Sky Blue' in the United States. The aircraft intended for delivery under Lend-Lease legislation were diverted to the US Army Air Corps after the attacks on Pearl Harbour. They mostly retained the factory-applied colours and were merely re-marked with US insignia before the B-17Es began operations with the US Eighth Air Force in England and the B-24Ds ('Blue-bellies') with the Halverson Project

No.63 (HALPRO) force in Egypt. Other aircraft ordered from the United States were specified to have Sky undersides; and again American manufacturers changed the name—to 'Sky Gray'—another possible cause of confusion. Hudsons diverted to the Royal Australian Air Force early in 1942 from British Purchasing Commission contracts are reported to have been sprayed MAP Sky Blue beneath instead of the Aluminium lacquer of earlier deliveries, the RAAF having chosen the colour in preference to Sky as more suited to operations based in Australia.

Dark Mediterranean Blue had been used occasionally as an experimental upper surface camouflage on flying boats before the war; now a somewhat more dull shade of blue was chosen as a satisfactory all-over finish for high-flying PR Hurricanes and later for the first Spitfire PR.IVs by the PR Unit in Egypt, and given the indeterminate name 'royal blue', perhaps with reference to BS 381C Colour No.6 Royal Blue, which was much darker in tone than is usually associated with the name. The two Hurricanes flown out to Burma in January 1942 and the Hurricanes and B-25Cs of No.5/No.3 PRU (India) were finished in this dull blue, as were later Hurricanes and the first Spitfires transferred from Egypt to India. The refinishing of aircraft in 'royal blue' for No.2 PRU ended when replacements for the first Spitfire PR.IVs were delivered in factory-finish of PRU Blue.

Junkers Ju 86P high-altitude reconnaissance bombers had been flying over Britain since 1940; even after their operations over South-west England became a threat in August 1942, there was a delay of some months before pressurised Spitfires entered service, capable of making successful interceptions. They were the Spitfire HF.VI and HF.VII and a new high-altitude camouflage scheme was introduced on 7 June 1943 for these 'very high-flying day fighters'—Medium Sea Grey upper and side surfaces, PRU Blue beneath. Type B roundels were applied, 42in diameter above the wings and 32in on the fuselage, with a 24in square Red and Blue fin flash. Surprisingly, no changes were suggested for photographic reconnaissance Spitfires which carried similar roundels and a fin flash l2in square; 5in Red, 2in White and 5in Blue.

On the outbreak of war with Japan in December 1941, aircraft of the Royal Air Force and the Indian Air Force in India Command and Far East Command were, with rare exceptions, finished in accordance with Air Ministry Order A.513 of 10 July 1941. The few aircraft of the Air Branch, Royal Navy (the Fleet Air Arm) complied. The standard camouflage was Temperate Land Scheme C.3A of Dark Earth and Dark Green (commonly "sand and spinach"), that of floatplanes and flying-boats was Temperate Sea Scheme S.1E and of the few Royal Navy aircraft Temperate Sea Scheme S3; both schemes of Extra Dark Sea Grey and Dark Slate Grey (perhaps "slime and sewage"). The lower wings of Naval biplanes were finished Dark Sea Grey and Light Slate Grey. Undersurfaces were required to be either Night (a mix of black and ultramarine) for bombers or Sky for other types but some aircraft retained pre-war Aluminium undersurfaces or, in the case of Naval aircraft, Sky Grey. Notable exceptions were the Buffalos in Temperate Land Scheme with light blue beneath.

National Markings were those used world-wide; Marking I of 'Ministry of Aircraft Production, Directorate of Technical Development, Air Diagram No. 2001' of May 1941 (now known as roundel Type B) above and Marking II (Type A) beneath the wings and Marking III (Type A1) on fuselage sides, with variously-sized tail-fin flashes. The serial number (Identification Marking B) was marked on the rear of the fuselage in Night.

So, until the later months of 1943, the camouflage of all day-flying operational aircraft in India and Bengal was the Temperate Land Scheme with Sky undersurfaces, excepting only the dull, dark blue finish of the photo-reconnaissance machines. New aircraft in camouflage of Medium Sea Grey or PRU Blue had not yet been seen in the Command and these two closely related colours may have caused some misunderstanding when PRU Blue was required to be applied to Mosquitos and B-25C aircraft. The signal from Air HQ asserting that Mosquitos of 27 Sqn (i.e. the Mk.II aircraft) were camouflaged for PR work would not have been based on direct observation; all such information was passed on 'secondhand' by telegraph from geographically distant units; New Delhi was 750 miles from Agartala and Dum Dum, 300 from Allahabad and 600 miles from Karachi. The first Mosquito F.IIs delivered to India from April 1943 onward were finished in a Dark Green disruptive pattern over Medium Sea Grey.

Sky was soon replaced as an under-surface colour for Hurricane Mk.IIs (and other operational aircraft) by Medium Sea Grey, and in October 1943 the first Spitfires and Mosquitos in factory-applied PRU Blue were delivered to the photographic squadrons.

British National Markings

The British National marking was periodically changed to meet operational needs. Air Ministry and Ministry of Aircraft Production documents usually referred to the roundels as National markings I, II, III and IV, retaining these names even when the roundels, illustrated in revisions to Air Diagram No.2001, appeared markedly different. To clarify the matter, initially for aircraft modellers, in 1956 the writer on aviation matters Bruce Robertson, then Editor of the Inter-Services Aircraft Recognition Journal, devised a system which classified the roundels as Types A, B, C and D. These classifications have become so widely used as to encourage the belief that they formed an official system but this is not so.

Whilst most black-doped night-fighters and some bombers carried a marking consisting simply of a White ring during the final year of the First World War, other night-flying aircraft retained the Red, White and Blue (Type A) roundels required by RFC Routine Order No.76 of 12 November 1914. In mid-1918 it was decided that from 29 August (Order No.939) rudder stripes would be omitted from night-flying machines and White would be omitted from their roundels. The Red circle and the Blue ring would be expanded outwards and inwards respectively to meet half-way across the space occupied by the White ring, the proportion of Red to Blue diameter thus becoming 2 to 5 (ie the Type B roundel).

This 'Night-flying' roundel of the First World War, still applied to the NIVO-finished heavy bombers of the RAF during the inter-war years, was adopted as National Marking I to be painted on the upper wing surfaces of all British Service aircraft. During the period 1938-1940 several sizes and types of fuselage markings were in use but they were standardised by the issue of Air Diagram No.2001 in December 1940, revised in May 1941. The diameter of the Dull Blue ring was to be 2in less than the chord width from leading edge of the wing to the aileron cut-out, measured on plan. In practice the proportion varied slightly between aircraft types, exact sizes being shown on Air Ministry-approved camouflage pattern drawings. The Red, White and Blue under-wing Marking II (Type A roundel), where required, also varied from type to type but the fuselage Marking III (type A1) for all smaller aircraft was of 35in diameter, of Red, White, Blue and Yellow, each colour band 5in wide.

The Type A1 fuselage roundels were considered too clearly visible against camouflage and night finish so, in late 1941, a modified roundel was proposed with areas of colour so proportioned that each would reflect equal amounts of light; the areas were thus in inverse ratios to the reflectivity of the colours. The resulting unequal and very narrow white and yellow rings of the roundel were considered impractical and this 'Equal Reflectivity Roundel' was abandoned. A compromise was reached with a new range of markings proposed at the end of the year. These standardised markings, it was explained, were based on the principle that the resolving power of the eye is limited, and therefore an area of light tone or white will blend into surrounding darker areas at a certain distance. The requirement was that markings should become visible only at a distance where the type of aircraft could be recognised under average weather conditions and visibility.

The new Markings II and III (roundels Type C and C1) were illustrated in a further revision to AD No.2001 dated June 1942.

The few aircraft of India and Far East Commands that were prepared for photographic reconnaissance late in 1941 wore standard camouflage and markings. With the arrival of the first two PR Hurricanes from Heliopolis, where it was usual to paint National Marking I on upper and lower wing surfaces, it was clear that the Dull Blue of the Type B roundel was difficult to distinguish from the dark blue finish, the marking appearing as a Dull Red disk which could be mistaken for the Japanese *Hinomaru* (sun-disc). Before arrival at Mingaladon, the outer edges of the roundels were over-painted with Yellow rings to define them against the background colour but even this precaution did not prevent the destruction of Z4949 by a pilot of 17 Sqn.

238: By late 1941, the Temperate Land Scheme camouflage was required for fighters overseas, with 'Type A1' roundels. This Hurricane IIB, BE163, was wrecked after running into a monsoon storm drain during the battle for Singapore. No squadron codes were applied to the Hurricane reinforcements which went into action as soon as they had been assembled and air-tested

239: *The 'Type C1' roundels were applied to the initial batch of Hurricane IIBs of 28 Sqn, among them BG802 seen here, in Temperate Land Scheme camouflage with Sky undersurfaces*

240: *Hurricane IIB BH125 carried no National markings on the fuselage sides and had 4in wide Yellow outlines to its wing markings. This aircraft of No.3 PRU and 631 Sqn crashed when the undercarriage failed at Chittagong in August 1943. Of note is what appears to be a cartoon figure just below the radio antenna—or is it simply weathered paintwork?*

241: *Operational trials of new markings for India Command began with the Hurricanes of 28 Sqn in June 1943. In this instance the Dull Red of the markings was merely painted over with White*

242: *Simple overpainting with White was soon found to be too conspicuous and the proportion of White to Blue in the roundels was changed, as shown by the provisional markings set out on 24 July 1943 and displayed here on Hurricane Trop IIB BE198*

243: *Late in 1943, markings were still not standardised. here, BE198 in July markings flies alongside BM982, 'C', wearing September-pattern 16in 'small' roundels*

244: *Some Hurricanes arrived in India in Home Fighter Command markings with Yellow wing leading edge stripes. None were issued so finished to squadrons in Assam or Bengal, although a few were assigned to training units and this Mk.IIC, KZ371, 'R', went to No.1 Sqn IAF at Miranshah in North-West Frontier Province*

US camouflage schemes

Colours for aircraft of the US Army Air Corps from 1919 until June 1941, then of the US Army Air Forces, at first conformed to a series of colour samples included with US Army Quartermaster Corps Specification 3-1. A Joint Aircraft Committee was set up by the US Army and Navy after the outbreak of war in Europe to consider co-ordinating factory-applied camouflage colours of aircraft built for the Army and Navy and for the British Services and by mid-1940 the Air Corps had approved a revised and limited range of colours. This was issued on 16 September 1940, as Air Corps Bulletin No 41 but some colours from Spec 3-1 remained in use until stocks were run down. The surface of these paints, as generally applied to combat aircraft of the US Army and Navy, had a smooth 'non-specular' (matt) finish similar to the MAP Type 'S' finish.

By the summer of 1940, American aircraft were being supplied to the British Government in the current Air Ministry disruptive camouflage patterns and colours, as typified by camouflage of the Curtiss Hawks flown by the American Volunteer Group in 1942. The US Army Air Corps Board considered such camouflage patterns valueless, as they were not visible at any great distance.

A USAAF Basic Camouflage Scheme, applied to most aircraft of the Army Air Forces, was set out in USAAF Technical Order No 07-1-1 which specified upper surfaces of the aircraft to be Dark Olive Drab 41 edged with 'splotches' of Medium Green 42 (these but rarely applied to fighters) and 'shadow-shading' (ie, lighter-toned under-surfaces) of Neutral Gray 43. This camouflage was used until the autumn of 1943 when colours for the US Army, the US Navy and for application to aircraft supplied to Allied countries under Lend-Lease legislation were modified as described below.

Complications arose when aircraft for the American and British Services were allocated from the same production series. A Technical Sub-Committee on Camouflage, including a representative of the British Air Purchasing Commission, of the Joint Aircraft Committee met to consider 'Standardization of Camouflage, Case No.58'. The camouflage schemes required by the British Ministry of Aircraft production were reviewed and it was noted that, whereas the US Army and Navy had universal systems considered suitable for all theatres of operation, the British had different systems depending on the role of the aircraft and the locality to which assigned. A series of discussions followed and on 13 July 1942 having considered the colours used by the USAAF, the US Navy Bureau of Aeronautics and the British, the Committee prepared a list of 'non-specular' colours to be applied to aircraft for all their Services. The Committee's recommendations, including adoption of an inclusive 'Army-Navy Standard Color Card', were submitted at the end of July in Report No.3 but they were not to come into operation for many months.

A degree of confusion was caused by a decision to change Dark Olive Drab, Color No.41, to match the US Army's 'Lustreless Olive Drab Standard', when it was discovered that the special 'infra-red formula' of Dark Olive Drab No.41 had been abandoned but this did not materially affect the appearance of the camouflage still to be applied to aircraft allocated to the British Government under Lend-Lease. It was made clear that the Air Ministry was not prepared to accept the United States Basic Camouflage schemes on operational aircraft but the Air Commission representative reported that the upper surface camouflage of 75% of British operational aircraft required the use of variations on a 'Dark Green'. He confirmed that the Air Commission was empowered to accept Army Olive Drab in place of the British 'Dark Greens' throughout the camouflage programme and that aircraft produced with only Olive Drab on upper surfaces would be acceptable, the other colours to he added after completion by the manufacturers or at modification centers.

The current policy of pooling of aircraft was given as a very strong reason why a basic camouflage should be agreed upon for use by the Services of both Nations.

Simple colour schemes of a few greys and blues for US Navy aircraft were decided by the Navy's Bureau of Aeronautics. A shading scheme of Semi-gloss Sea Blue "graded" into Insignia White beneath was authorised by the issue of BuAer Spec. SR-2e on 5 January 1943. No American aircraft were at that time supplied to Britain finished in US Navy Bureau of Aeronautics colours.

The colours of US Navy carrier-borne aircraft were selected to match the camouflage paintwork of the aircraft carriers; Bureau of Aeronautics Light Gray was equivalent to the US Navy Haze Gray, BuAer Blue Gray was similar to Dark Gray, BuAer Dark Gull Gray to Ocean Gray and BuAer Sea Blue to Navy Blue.

Research by the Author has shown that the ANA 'equivalent' colours were not used on aircraft for the Royal Navy by Chance-Vought and Grumman, these being finished for some further time in the MAP Temperate Sea Scheme. The *Handbook of Erection and Maintenance Instructions for the Grumman F6F-5 and Hellcat Mk.II* (15 April 1944) still included the same camouflage colours for the British aircraft as for the Hellcat Mk.I, namely Extra Dark Sea Grey and Dark Slate Grey with Sky undersurfaces.

Approved Army-Navy Aeronautical colour cards were distributed to paint manufacturers in May 1943 and an ANA Bulletin No.157, 'List of Standard Aircraft Camouflage Colors', was issued on 28 September. ANA Bulletin No.157a dated 24 March 1944, set out the 'ANA equivalent' colours intended to replace the earlier

USAAC Bulletin No. 41, BuAer and Ministry of Aircraft Production colours. Meanwhile, in October 1943 camouflage had ceased to be a requirement for most Army aircraft but was still to be applied to aircraft built for the US Navy and for the British Services. On Army aircraft produced with Basic Camouflage finishes, ANA Olive Drab 613, Medium Green 612 and Sea Gray 603 were intended to be used but stocks of the Bulletin 41 colours took some time to be exhausted—indeed, some manufacturers continued to order and apply the 'old' colours. Uncamouflaged aircraft bore Dark Green 30 anti-glare panels.

An alternative finish for high-flying aircraft was proposed to the US Army Air Corps by Samuel Cabot who offered a paint with surprising properties. From the inception of Service camouflage during the Great War, the idea of concealing positions and weapons by the use of 'invisible paint' had become a too-familiar joke—but now it seemed a possibility. Cabot proposed a paint made from a dispersion of colloidal zinc oxide in a linseed-oil base. He claimed that, when thinly sprayed over a black undercoat, a blue colour resulted from the scattering of daylight by the extremely fine particles of the pigment, smaller than the wavelength of blue light. By varying the thickness of the translucent paint film, a range of tones could be obtained, from black through shades of blue to near-white and, when carefully applied in a number of coats, the finish reflected daylight so as to replicate the light from the sky beyond, thereby making invisible an aircraft to which it was applied.

The principle behind Cabot's proposal was investigated and recommended for trials. The paint had a unique property; the intensity of reflected light increased with the thickness of the paint film so that, at oblique angles to an observer, such as in shadow beneath the wings, engine nacelles and booms the finish appeared brighter instead of darker, and 'natural' shadow-shading occurred on these curved surfaces. The colour changed from an intense blue in bright sunlight to a neutral grey under overcast. It was accepted that an aircraft could not be concealed under all conditions of daylight and weather but the finish was considered to be most useful for airplanes intended to operate at "extreme altitudes" (40,000ft). During subsequent flight trials it was noted that the blue effect was a perfect match under a cloudless sky with a degree of haze in the atmosphere. Possibly because of this observation, the finish was named 'Haze Paint'. By mid-1944 nearly all the fleet carriers of the US Navy in the Pacific Theatre were finished in Camouflage Measure 21, overall Navy Blue with their flight decks Deck Blue No.3. By the end of the year most of their aircraft were (to BuAer Specification SR2-d, effective 22

245: Early 1945; F6F-5 Hellcats awaiting collection by USN pilots at Grumman's Bethpage field, each aircraft having the last three numerals of its BuAer number painted on the engine cowling. As can be seen from their numbers, 900 and 920 for the Royal Navy were Glossy Sea Blue; undersides appear paler due to reflected light off the snow

246: An F-4A, 41-2364 of the 3rd Photo Group (Recon), 12th AF in North Africa early in 1943. The worn appearance of the National Insignia on the boom is typical of markings applied over Haze Paint

March) finished in matching ANA 607 Glossy Sea Blue overall, with a subsequent Spec SR-2e of 25 June, effective 7 October, for all carrier-based aircraft to be so finished.

Although the camouflage diagram was included in a later issue of the 'E and M Handbook' dated 1 July 1945, Grumman and the builders of the Corsair had begun finishing aircraft intended for the Royal Navy in Glossy Sea Blue at the beginning of 1945. Aircraft so finished were supplied from the Blackburn Aircraft Company's 'US East Coast Maintenance Centre', Roosevelt Field, Long Island, to the East Indies and British Pacific Fleets during the first quarter of the year.

TABLE 2

US CAMOUFLAGE COLOUR EQUIVALENTS

Selected Colours from USAAC Bulletin No.41		BS381C Colours	FS595a Colors	Methuen References	Approx Munsell References	Approx Diffuse Reflectivity
Color Card for Camouflage Finishes 16 September 1940						
Dark Olive Drab	41	Olive Drab 298	34086	3F4	8.5Y 3.5/1	8%
Neutral Gray	43		36173	22DE2	6PB 4.1/2.5	12%
Insignia Red	45	Venetian Red 445*	30109	8DE7	10R 4/8	11%
Insignia White	46		37875	2A1	N9.2	75%
Insignia Blue	47		35044	20F7	7PB 2.5/6	4%
Identification Yellow	48	Golden Yellow 356	33538	4-5A8	-10YR 5.5/6	56%
Selected Colours from USAAF Bulletin No.48						
Color Card for Temporary Camouflage Finishes 26 May 1942						
Dark Green (anti-glare panels)	30	Deep Brunswick Green 227	34092*	26F5	9.5G 3/4	6%
Selected Colours from Army/Navy Bulletin No.157						
List of Standard Aircraft Camouflage Colors 28 September 1943						
Non-spec Light Gray	602		36440	30C2	5Y 7.5/1	43%
Sea Gray	603	Extra Dark Sea Grey 640	36118	22F2	10B 3.5/1	12%
Semi-gloss Sea Blue	606		25042	22G4	4.5PB 3/2	7%
Non-spec Sea Blue	607		35042	22G4	4.5PB 3/2	7%
Non-spec Intermediate Blue	608		35164	21D3	6.5PB 5/3	23%
Sky	610	Sky 210	34424	29BC3	5GY 7.3/1.5	43%
Non-spec Olive Drab	613	Very Dark Drab 437	34087	4F4	6.5Y 3/1.5	7%
Glossy Sea Blue	623		15042	22G4	4.5PB 3/2	7%
Non-spec Insignia White	601		37875	2A1	N 9.2	75%
Non-spec Black	604		37038	1H1	N 1.2	1%
Non-spec Insignia Blue	605		35044	20F7	7PB 2.5/6	4%
Non-spec Orange-Yellow	614	Golden Yellow 356	33538	4-5A8	10YR 5.5/6	56%
Non-spec Dull Red	618	Venetian Red 445*	30109	8DE7	10R 4/8	11%

Non-spec = Non-specular
* = near match

US National Markings

Apart from a red star to identify its aircraft during the Mexican Civil War in 1916, the United States of America made no use of a national insignia before joining the Allies in the First World War against the Central Powers on 6 April 1917. On 19 May a marking was approved consisting of a red disc within a five-pointed white star on a blue circular ground but this was changed on 11 January 1918 to a cocarde, a white disc with a red surround and a blue outer ring, so that all Allied aircraft carried markings of roundel form. On 30 April 1919 the earlier insignia was reinstated and remained the national marking until, after the Japanese attacks of 1941 and 1942, red markings were removed from US aircraft.

From 15 May 1942 the standard marking on aircraft of the US Army Air Force was the 'cocarde' described in USAAC Technical Order No.07-1-l, a "*five-point white star within a blue circle*" (ie USAAF Bulletin No.41 colours Insignia White 46 and Insignia Blue 47 or Navy Bureau of Aeronautics equivalent colours), placed on the top surface of the left wing and lower surface of the right wing.

On Army aircraft the size was set at 80% to 90% of the wing chord between the leading-edge and the aileron cut-out. On the fuselage the insignia was to be of maximum diameter 75% of the fuselage height, midway between the wing trailing-edge and the tailplane leading-edge. Each aircraft was identified by a radio 'call-number' (the USAAF serial less its first digit) in 12in x 9in figures of Yellow 48 on dark camouflage, Black 44 on light surfaces.

Carrier-borne aircraft of the US Navy bore similar cocardes of Insignia White and Insignia Blue on their Basic camouflage of counter-shaded Blue Gray and Light Gray, the wing markings of various sizes to a maximum of 65in and fuselage markings of 24in diameter.

In accordance with an Amendment to Operation Order No.9 of 26 September 1942, Army and Navy aircraft intended for Operation 'Torch', the invasion of French North Africa (8 November) were marked with an Identification Yellow 48 ring, nominally 6in wide, around their under-wing and fuselage insignia.

The Navy Bureau of Aeronautics Spec SR-2c which changed the camouflage colours of carrier aircraft to Sea Blue and White with effect from 1 February 1943 confirmed sizes of wing markings to be of standard sizes, from 20in to 60in in 5in increments, of a size nearest to 90% of the fixed wing-chord. Fuselage markings of 20in to 50in, 75% of the fuselage height, were required by Army-Navy Specification AN-1-9 of 1 March. Navy aircraft were simply marked on the tail-fin with their 'BuAer' numbers in Black

A major alteration was made on 29 June 1943 when it was feared that the US insignia might be mistaken for the Luftwaffe black and white marking. Insignia White rectangles were added to each side of the Blue disc, the entire marking having a Red surround. The use of Red brought such strong objections from the Pacific Commands that the colour of the surround was changed to Blue from 14 August (ANA Spec. AN-I-9b). The Insignia remained unchanged until the end of the war.

247: This is a very plain natural metal Consolidated F-7B, 44-2452, of the 24th Combat Mapping Squadron, from Gushkara in India. The unit was tasked during 1944-45 with mapping over half a million square miles of the Chinese coast from the mouth of the Yangtze River down to Indo-China.

India Command and SEAC Markings

As early as July 1943, Air HQ India was receiving complaints from the squadrons that continual sunshine caused severe fading of the camouflage and markings on the upper wing surfaces of their aircraft, to an extent which might cause confusion between British and Japanese markings. In April HQ Bengal reported that the Blue of the RAF Type B roundels often merged with the general camouflage, so that the marking apeared to be only a red disc. It was proposed that India Command should authorise use of the 'complete' British (presumablyType C1) roundel but alterations should be permitted and suggested that Yellow bands be applied 'as on UK Mustangs', ie 12in wide chord-wise bands above and beneath the wings.

The use by the enemy of their Kawasaki Ki.56 'Thalia' army transport also caused concern. This aircraft appeared almost identical to the Lockheed Hudson, both designs being derived from the Lockheed 14 civil airliner.

At the end of the month a further request was made on behalf of USAAF Gen Caleb Haynes, Combat Cargo Task Force commander, after a Hudson in which he was travelling was disturbingly intercepted and 'buzzed' by US fighters, and the Air Ministry was asked to permit the addition of a Yellow band encircling the upper wing roundel, as earlier applied to PR Hurricanes and Spitfires. In reply Air Ministry proposed the adoption of markings similar to those used by the RAAF in the Pacific Theatre of Operations, eliminating the Red. Air HQ Bengal immediately agreed to the proposal which would bring RAF markings into line with USAAF markings (one a white disc within a blue surround, the other a white star within a blue surround). On 24 June, having obtained Admiralty agreement, Air HQ India proposed the introduction of the proposed new markings for all operational aircraft east of Meridian 60°E, ie east of the Gulf of Oman:

Roundel (circles to be concentric)			
Position	Aircraft	White	Blue
Fuselage sides	Small	6-inch dia	16-inch dia
& under wings	Medium	9-inch dia	32-inch dia
	Large	9-inch dia	48-inch dia
Above wings	All	9-inch dia	Existing dia

Flash (blue towards leading edge)			
Aircraft	Size	White	Blue
Small	24x18 inches wide	6-inches	12-inches
Medium	24x24 inches wide	9-inches	15-inches
Large	24x36 inches wide	9-inches	27-inches

It was stressed that practical trials must be undertaken before the new India Command markings were adopted, to confirm that the area of white in the markings was acceptable. An amendment dated 24 July required the

colours of the fin flash to be reversed, White to be towards the leading edge. Among other aircraft, B-25Cs of No.3 PRU and some Hurricanes of 28 Sqn were already painted with the provisional markings, but more recommendations followed when it was found that the White areas defeated the 'low-visibility' principle upon which the Type C1 roundel had been based; "*Even 9in diameter White centre circle is too obvious. Real solution is 9inch circle mixture, four parts White one part Blue. This imparts good marking just off-white and visible at 1,700ft range. Consider markings fighter aircraft should be same size as for small aircraft ie White circles 6ins repeat 6ins*". While RAF and IAF markings were simplified, American markings had, meanwhile, been altered; the new 'star-and-bar' marking with Red surround was adopted on 29 June but the Red outline was changed to Blue in September. On 29 September revised India Command markings were set out:

Roundel (Concentric circles)			
Position	Aircraft	White*	Blue
Fuselage sides and	Small	6-inch dia	16-inch dia
above wings	Medium	12-inch dia	32-inch dia
	Large	18-inch dia	48-inch dia

Flash (white towards leading edge)			
Aircraft	Size	White*	Blue
Small	24x16 in wide	8in	8in
Medium	24x22 in wide	11in	11in
Large	24x34 in wide	17in	17in

*White being too conspicuous, a mixture of four parts of white and one part of blue to be used instead.
The markings for small aircraft to be used on fighters.

During the following weeks, the revised markings, later commonly termed 'SEAC markings' because their introduction coincided with the formation of that Command, were applied to all aircraft in India and Burma. The fuselage roundels of the Liberators were repainted, but with 24in centre disks, ie the Red and White of the type C1 roundels were over-painted light blue.

681 Squadron was reinforced in mid-1943 with Mosquitos from 27 Sqn and B-25Cs from the US Tenth Air Force. Unlike the aircraft of the squadron's Initial Equipment, these acquisitions were to be re-finished in PRU Blue. From (perhaps unreliable) photographic evidence, it seems that the locally-produced finish was appreciably lighter in tone than MAP PRU Blue. At this time, August 1943, no new aircraft in factory-fresh PRU Blue (reflectivity 14%) had yet reached India. It is suggested that the finish applied to the Mosquitos and B-25Cs had a reflectivity of about 25%, the colour a medium blue-grey.

The requirement for Temperate Land Scheme camouflage on fighters, fighter-bombers and bombers was reaffirmed by Air Force Order (India) No.70 of 4 April 1944. An Appendix listed all the aircraft types in the Command and classified them (somewhat inconsistently) as 'Large', 'Medium' and 'Small' for the application of the approved markings. This simply confirmed that 'Small' markings were applicable to Hurricanes and Spitfires, and 'Medium' markings to Mosquitos. Mitchells (B-25C) were listed among the aircraft to have 'Large' markings but this requirement was ignored and 'Medium' markings were applied to the new aircraft.

Anomalies in the finishes of aircraft delivered to overseas Maintenance Units were a minor source of irritation. In September 1944 Air Ministry Order A.864/44 was issued, requiring all aircraft to be coloured and marked in accordance with Ministry of Aircraft Production DTD Technical Circular No. 360 but Air Ministry informed ACSEA, *"concern exists in the Service as this circular is not held by units. As the circular cancels all previous Air Diagrams units have no accurate information on identification markings. It is pointed out that new publication AP.2656A External Aircraft Finishes is under preparation and will include the data provided by DTD.360".*

Air Publication 2656A was issued in October, incorporating the current requirements for aircraft camouflage and markings previously set out in a series of Air Ministry Orders, revised Air Diagram 2001 and the latest edition of MAP DTD Circular No.360. Table 1 appended to AP.2656A listed the markings for high-flying photographic reconnaissance aircraft as National Marking I (Type B roundel) on the upper surfaces of the wing-tips and on fuselage sides, code letters to be Dull Red and the serial number in Night. From that time, the aircraft factories, and operational and maintenance units applied finishes and markings to the same standard requirements, *excepting* aircraft of the tactical and strategic formations of Eastern Air Command (South-East Asia).

In Europe, other changes were made. By the end of November 1944 there was increasing concern in the Air Ministry at the number of RAF aircraft fired upon by Allied fighters and ground troops during the slow approach to the Rhine. On 6 December the Ministry notified all Commands; "considered that the number of friendly aircraft shot down by our forces could be substantially reduced if National markings on all RAF and Fleet Air Arm aircraft were to revert to the system of red, white and blue roundels". HQ 2nd Tactical Air Force, the Command most directly involved, thought it inadvisable to so compromise the camouflage and recommended the addition of a 2in Yellow surround to the upper wing National marking I (Type B roundel) and, with certain reservations the Admiralty and other Commands (excepting Bomber Command and SEAC) on 24 December approved replacement of the upper wing marking with National marking II (roundel Type C), with effect from 7 January 1945.

HQ Air Command S.E. Asia was prepared to accept aircraft delivered bearing the tri-colour roundels but proposed replacing them with India Command markings at Maintenance Units. Aircraft delivered to the Pacific Area for the Royal Navy would be similarly re-marked. Aircraft bearing the new markings did not begin arriving in the Far East until the second quarter of the year.

On 3 January, however, HQ 2.TAF ordered the removal of the Sky colour from the spinner and fuselage of fighter aircraft and required the roundels on upper and side surfaces to be Red, White, Blue and Yellow, as National Marking III (Type C.1 roundel). Accepting the *fait accompli*, the Air Ministry issued a directive on 7 January, informing all Commands that the upper wing roundel should be changed to National marking III.

From late 1943 until early 1945, RAF and IAF camouflage in SEAC remained the same; fighter-reconnaissance Hurricanes were finished in Dark Green and Dark Earth with Medium Sea Grey under-surfaces, while photo-reconnaissance Spitfires and Mosquitos were all-over PRU Blue, only the early B-25s remaining in dark blue.

In mid-1944 US-built aircraft began arriving in India in clear-varnished or natural metal finish, unpainted except for National Markings and Olive Drab 613 anti-glare panels. In view of forthcoming operations from airfields within reach of the enemy's main air bases, at HQ ACSEA there was some resistance to the use of 'bare-metal' aircraft although many USAAF formations (including the 9th PR Sqn) had already accepted uncamouflaged aircraft.

At the beginning of March Prime Minister Winston Churchill had noted that American aircraft were being manufactured unpainted. He asked whether it was intended to "adopt a similar policy with regard to British aircraft". The Air Council replied that the lighter-gauge metal used in British aircraft and the consequent need to fill imperfections made it essential to retain painted finishes as protection against corrosion but, by the end of November, HQ ACSEA had decided to allow aircraft to remain uncamouflaged, excepting only night fighters and general reconnaissance aircraft.

For tactical reasons, camouflage was retained on Hurricanes and PRU Blue on 681 Sqn's Spitfires, but a change was soon authorised for Mosquitos. The cause of structural failure in these aircraft was not fully established —de Havillands maintained that prolonged exposure to high temperature and humidity caused distortion of the airframe and deterioration of the adhesive. As a means of reducing the heat absorption of the aircraft's upper surfaces, a new paint scheme was recommended by J.G. Fisher of ICI, reporting to the Air Ministry, and supported by Maj H. de Havilland—a proposal that all Mosquitos for SE Asia should be finished overall Dull Aluminium.

Several changes in the structure of command took place at that time, HQ Third Tactical Air Force became HQ RAF Burma in December 1944 and was re-named Air HQ Burma on 27 February 1945, controlling all RAF and IAF units in Eastern Air Command. It may be assumed that this Headquarters authorised the application of serial numbers 4in high on the vertical tail surfaces of RAF aircraft delivered soon afterwards to training and operational units.

From the end of April the marking appeared on many aircraft of Nos. 221 and 224 Groups; the serial number usually repeated on the lower part of the tail-fin, forward of the flash, usually of 4in digits. Some of the late Hurricane Mk.IVs of 28 Sqn carried the fin serial as did a few of the Spitfires that replaced them later in the year.

Another change, to take effect from 26 July, was the application to aircraft of all RAF Units not engaged in active operations of serial numbers in Night, of a height equal to half the wing chord, measured one third of the distance from fuselage centreline to wing tip. The photographic squadrons in SE Asia were still operational; underwing serials appeared on their aircraft much later.

A change in the style of aircraft identification lettering was soon introduced in the Command. Instead of the rectangular letters and figures that had, with occasional variations in shape, been in use since before the outbreak of war, the new style included rounded forms of letters such as B,C, J and so on, to standard sizes as set out in 'Identification Letters and Serial Numbers' appended to Bomber Command Engineering Staff Instruction Leaflet AC/Con/59. Such markings were applied at Maintenance Units to all aircraft entering service and to other aircraft at regular periods of maintenance.

248: This overall PRU Blue Spitfire PR.XI, PA935, 'R', probably of 681 Sqn, was refinished and carried the 'Small' markings on wing uppersurfaces and fuselage sides, with 24in x 18in flash, in accordance with AFO(I) No.70/1944. On the original print it can be seen that the serial has been repainted with the aid of a stencil

249: Spitfire FR.XIV, NH 869, 'H', of 28 Sqn also wore a tail-fin serial. There was so little surface area free from the other markings that the serial was superimposed on the identification band. Just visible under the windscreen is a small and unfortunately illegible personal emblem

Identification Bands

Meanwhile, on 27 January 1945, HQ ACSEA issued an instruction for all aircraft of Eastern Air Command, except four-engined aircraft and night fighters, to carry the identification markings already applied to Thunderbolt fighter-bombers of the Command, with effect from 1 February.

The markings consisted of 28in-wide bands across the wings, mid-way between wing-root and wing-tip, and 18in-wide across the tail surfaces. A 17in-wide band applied to the cowlings of Thunderbolts was interpreted for other aircraft as painting the spinners. An accompanying diagram bore a note, "*Stripes and numbers (A) for uncamouflaged aircraft will be identification blue, (B) for camouflaged aircraft will be white*". On 3 February the Air Ministry urgently telegraphed ACSEA to insist, "*White stripes should not, repeat not, extend on to the control surfaces*"; this was to prevent the balance of the controls being upset. The expression 'stripes and numbers' was taken to mean all identification markings, codes and serials—consequently most camouflaged aircraft, including the fighter-reconnaissance Hurricanes, were thus re-painted at overhaul periods with White serial numbers and letters.

The Hurricanes were also marked with White identification bands but, as with the Hurricanes of ground attack squadrons, the markings were soon removed from upper surfaces of many of the aircraft to maintain the camouflage intact when operating from forward airstrips.

A number of PR Mosquitos, still under inspection and repair at No.1 CMU, Kanchrapara, were repainted Dull Aluminium like the FB.VIs and marked with Blue spinners and bands. As a result, by March 1945, the aircraft of 684 Sqn were flying in three different paint schemes; PRU Blue, Aluminium or Aluminium with Blue bands, all with 32in diameter Blue and light blue roundels and 24inx22in wide fin flashes.

250: *Yet another variation on markings; Spitfire FR.XIVE MV363, 'H', 'Mary', intended for the fighter role with 11 Sqn, had 12in White bands on the tail surfaces*

251: *By 1947, replacement aircraft for the fighter-reconnaissance squadrons were delivered in standard late-war 'Day Fighter' camouflage with Fighter Command markings. This is TP377, 'Y', a Spitfire FR.XVIII of 28 Sqn at Sembawang*

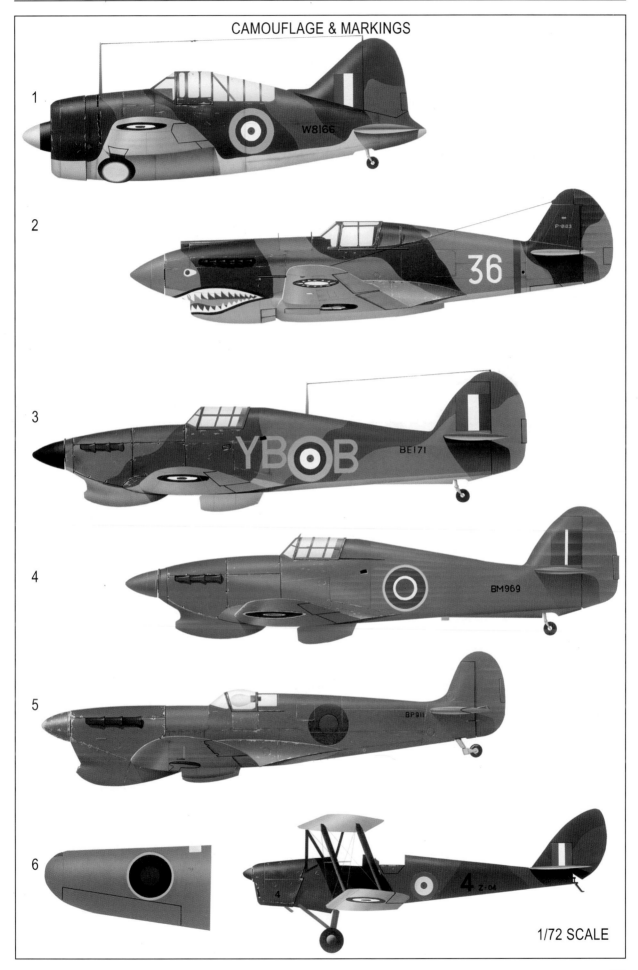

1

2

3

4

5

6

W8166

P-8123

36

YB◎B   BE171

BM969

BP911

4   Z-04

4

1/72 SCALE

7

8

9

1/72 SCALE

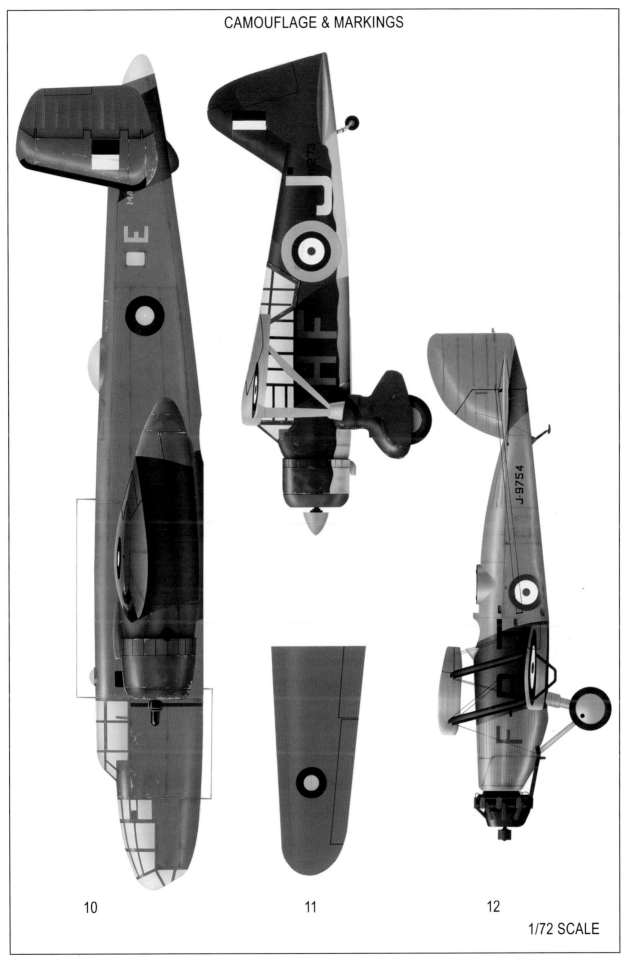

10

11

12

1/72 SCALE

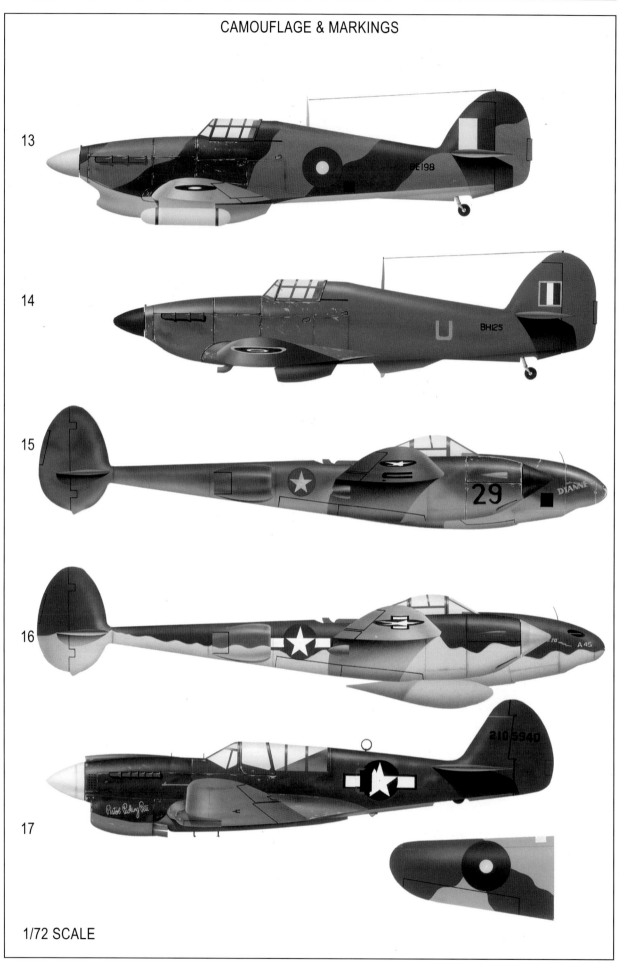

13

14

15

16

17

1/72 SCALE

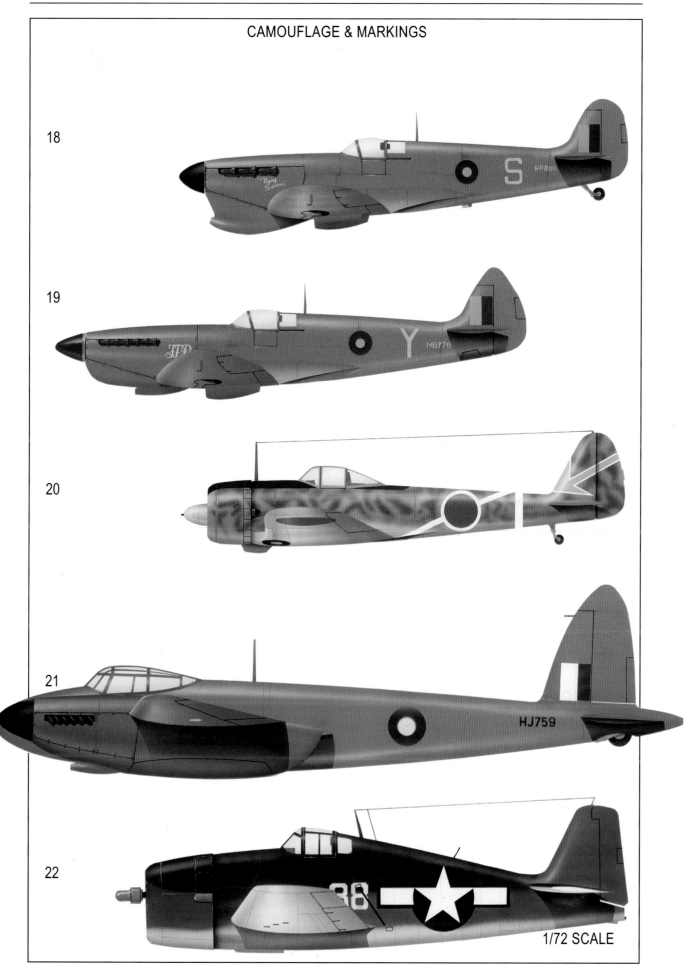

18

19

20

21

22

1/72 SCALE

23

24

1/72 SCALE

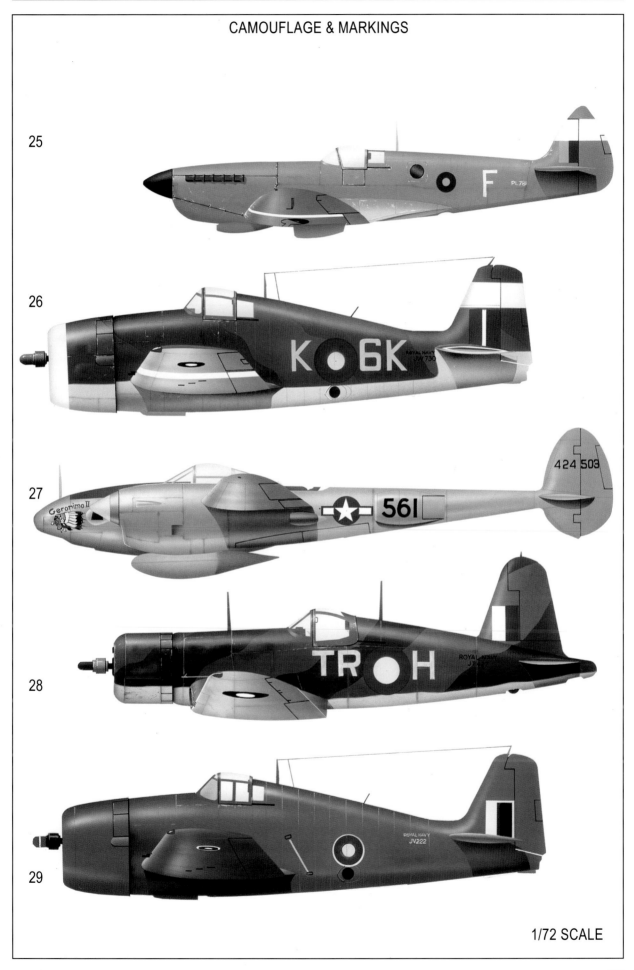

25

26

27

28

29

1/72 SCALE

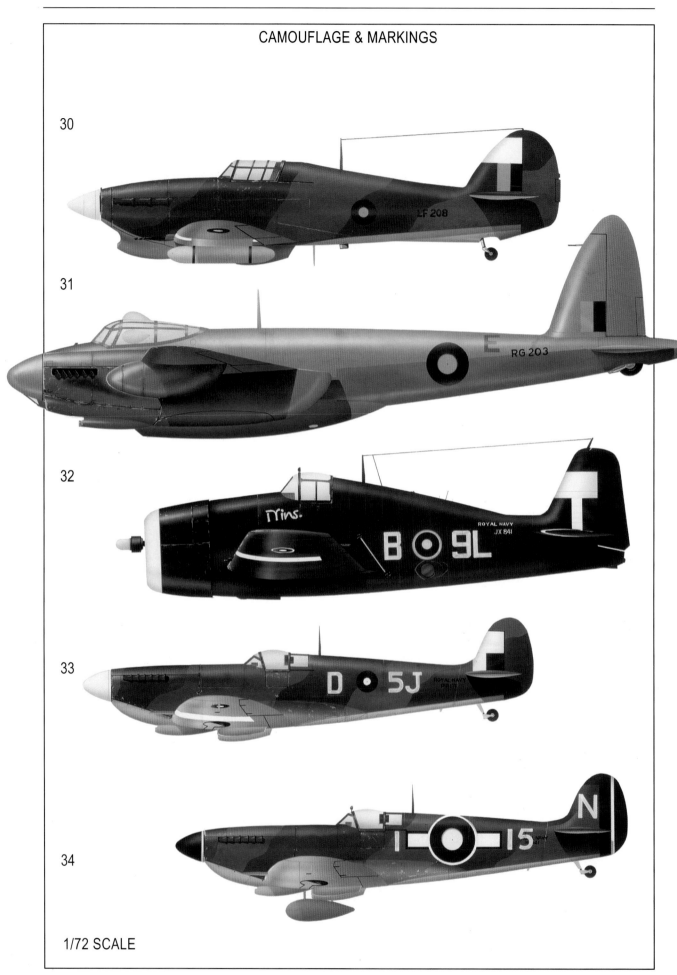

30

31

32

33

34

1/72 SCALE

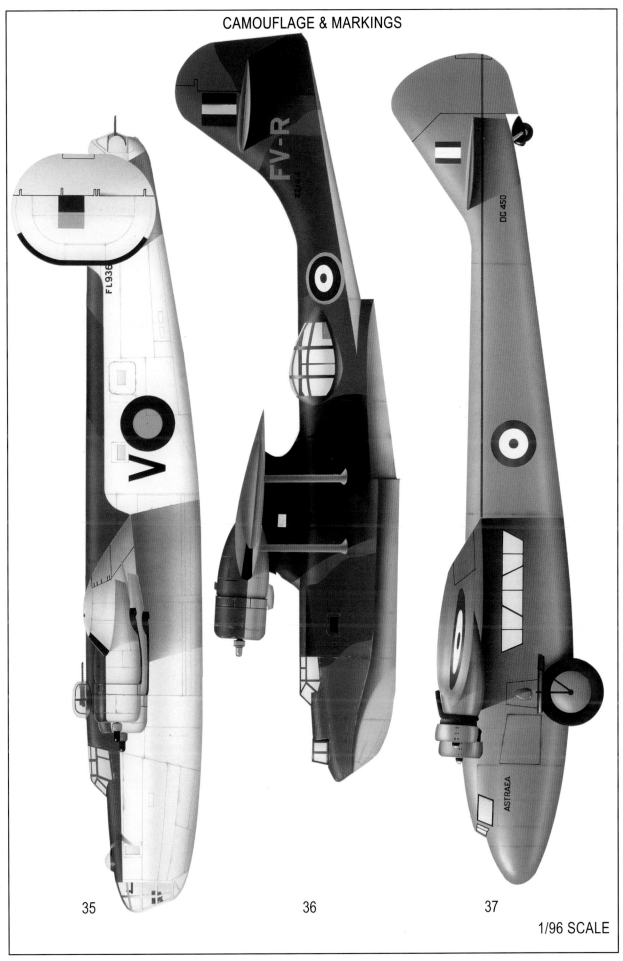

35

36

37

1/96 SCALE

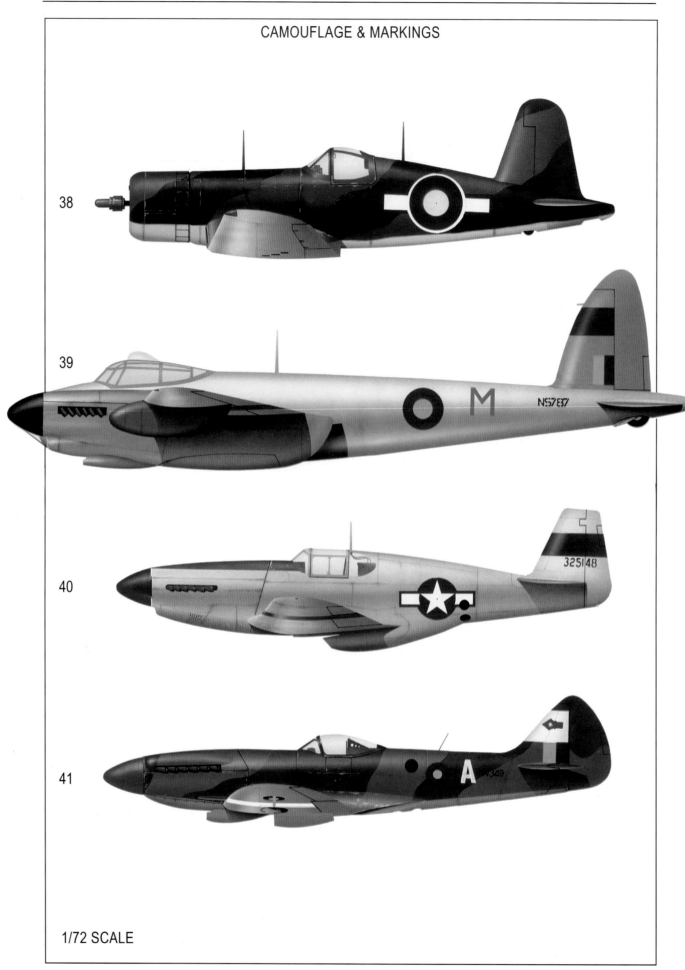

38

39

N57837

O M

40

325148

41

A

1/72 SCALE

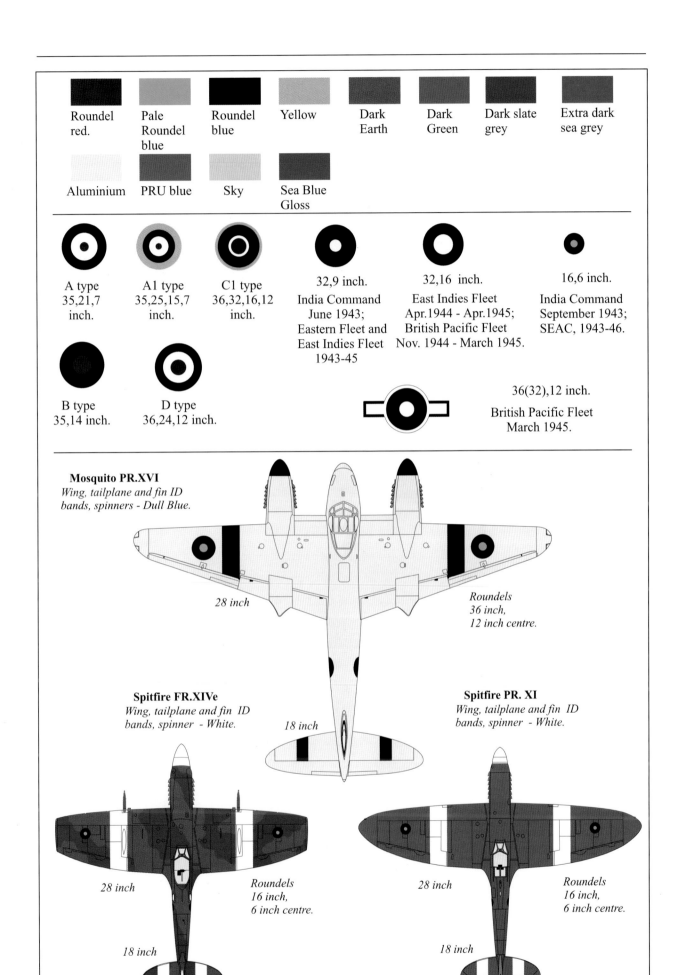

Roundel red. Pale Roundel blue Roundel blue Yellow Dark Earth Dark Green Dark slate grey Extra dark sea grey

Aluminium PRU blue Sky Sea Blue Gloss

A type
35,21,7
inch.

A1 type
35,25,15,7
inch.

C1 type
36,32,16,12
inch.

32,9 inch.
India Command
June 1943;
Eastern Fleet and
East Indies Fleet
1943-45

32,16 inch.
East Indies Fleet
Apr.1944 - Apr.1945;
British Pacific Fleet
Nov. 1944 - March 1945.

16,6 inch.
India Command
September 1943;
SEAC, 1943-46.

B type
35,14 inch.

D type
36,24,12 inch.

36(32),12 inch.
British Pacific Fleet
March 1945.

Mosquito PR.XVI
*Wing, tailplane and fin ID
bands, spinners - Dull Blue.*

28 inch

Roundels
36 inch,
12 inch centre.

18 inch

Spitfire FR.XIVe
*Wing, tailplane and fin ID
bands, spinner - White.*

28 inch

Roundels
16 inch,
6 inch centre.

18 inch

Spitfire PR. XI
*Wing, tailplane and fin ID
bands, spinner - White.*

28 inch

Roundels
16 inch,
6 inch centre.

18 inch

© M.D.Howley 1998

203

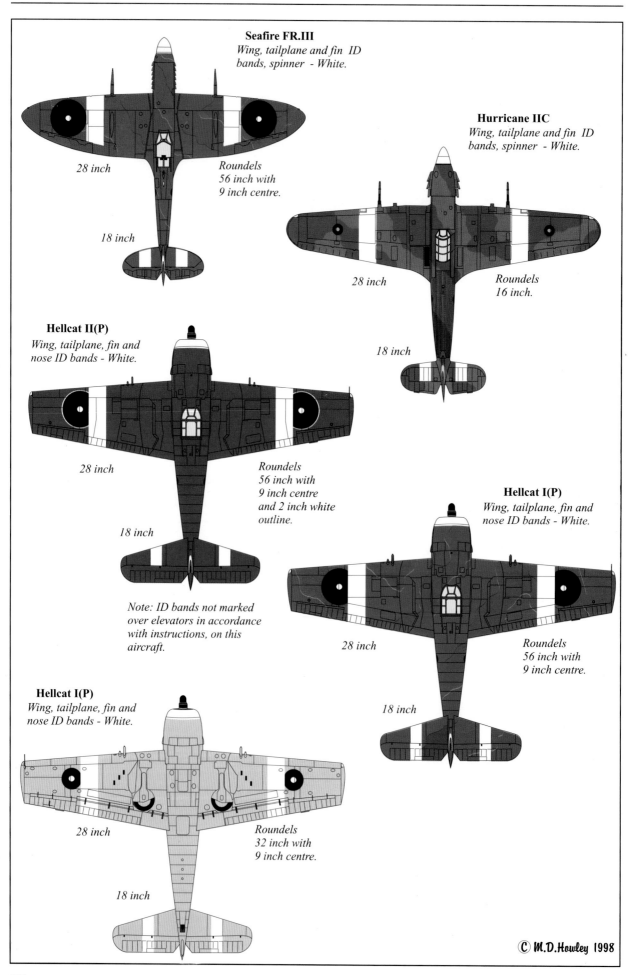

Seafire FR.III
Wing, tailplane and fin ID bands, spinner - White.

28 inch

Roundels 56 inch with 9 inch centre.

18 inch

Hurricane IIC
Wing, tailplane and fin ID bands, spinner - White.

28 inch

Roundels 16 inch.

18 inch

Hellcat II(P)
Wing, tailplane, fin and nose ID bands - White.

28 inch

Roundels 56 inch with 9 inch centre and 2 inch white outline.

18 inch

Note: ID bands not marked over elevators in accordance with instructions, on this aircraft.

Hellcat I(P)
Wing, tailplane, fin and nose ID bands - White.

28 inch

Roundels 56 inch with 9 inch centre.

18 inch

Hellcat I(P)
Wing, tailplane, fin and nose ID bands - White.

28 inch

Roundels 32 inch with 9 inch centre.

18 inch

© M.D.Howley 1998

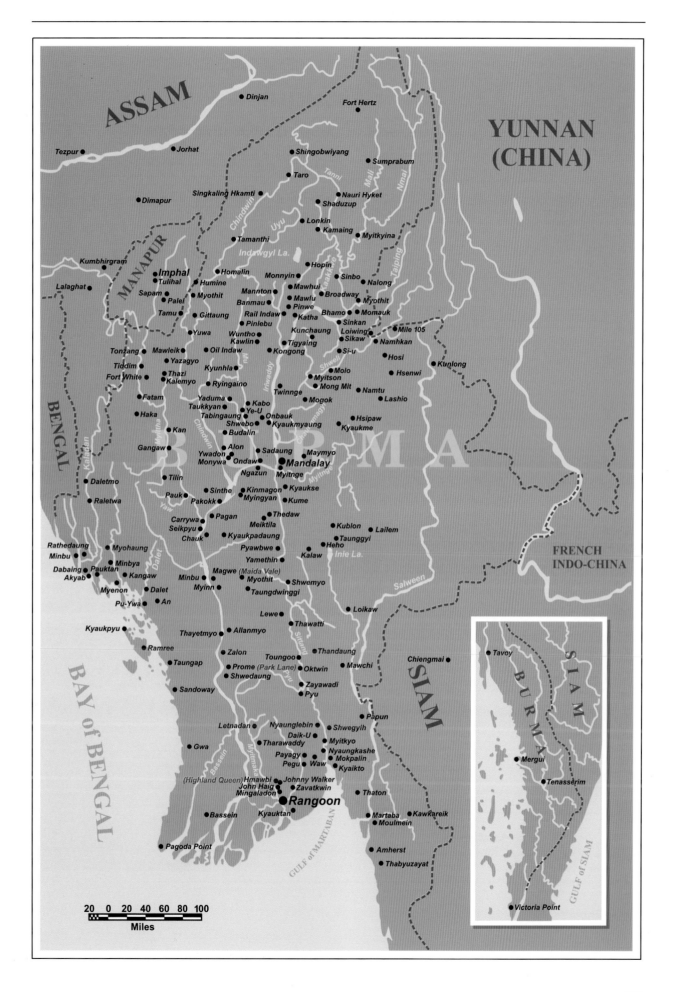

ASSAM

YUNNAN
(CHINA)

Tezpur
Jorhat
Dinjan
Fort Hertz
Shingobwiyang
Sumprabum
Taro
Singkaling Hkamti
Nauri Hyket
Shaduzup
Dimapur
MANAPUR
Lonkin
Kamaing
Myitkyina
Kumbhirgram
Homalin
Hopin
Lalaghat
Imphal
Tulihal
Humine
Monnyin
Sinbo
Nalong
Sapam
Myothit
Mawhui
Broadway
Myothit
Palel
Banmau
Mawlu
Bhamo
Momauk
Tamu
Gittaung
Rail Indaw
Pinwe
Sinkan
Yuwa
Pinlebu
Katha
Loiwing
Mile 105
Tonzang
Mawleik
Wuntho
Kunchaung
Namhkan
Mawleik
Kawlin
Tigyaing
Si-u
Hosi
Tiddim
Yazagyo
Oil Indaw
Kongong
Molo
Hsenwi
Kunlong
Fort White
Thazi
Kyunhla
Myitson
Namtu
Kalemyo
Ryingaino
Twinnge
Mong Mit
Lashio
Fatam
Yaduma
Kabo
Mogok
Haka
Taukkyan
Ye-U
Onbauk
Hsipaw
Kan
Tabingaung
Shwebo
Kyaukmyaung
Kyaukme
Budalin
Gangaw
Alon
Sadaung
Maymyo
Ywadon
Monywa
Ondaw
Mandalay
Daletmo
Tilin
Myitnge
Raletwa
Sinthe
Kinmagon
Kyaukse
Pauk
Pakokk
Myingyan
Kume
Carrywa
Pagan
Thedaw
Kublon
Lailem
Seikpyu
Meiktila
Taunggyi
Chauk
Kyaukpadaung
Heho
Rathedaung
Pyawbwe
Kalaw
Inie La.
Minbu
Myohaung
Yamethin
Dabaing
Minbya
Magwe (Maida Vale)
Akyab
Pauktan
Kangaw
Minbu
Myothit
Shwemyo
Myenon
Dalet
Myinn
Taungdwinggi
Pu-Ywa
An
Loikaw
Kyaukpyu
Lewe
Thawatti
Thayetmyo
Allanmyo
Ramree
Zalon
Thandaung
Taungap
Toungoo
Prome (Park Lane)
Oktwin
Mawchi
Chiengmai
Shwedaung
Zayawadi
Sandoway
Pyu
Papun
Letnadan
Nyaunglebin
Shwegyih
Gwa
Daik-U
Myitkyo
Tharawaddy
Nyaungkashe
Payagy
Mokpalin
Pegu
Waw
Kyaikto
(Highland Queen) Hmawbi
Johnny Walker
John Haig
Zavatkwin
Mingaladon
Rangoon
Thaton
Bassein
Kyauktan
Martaba
Kawkareik
Moulmein
Pagoda Point
Amherst
Thabyuzayat

B U R M A

BENGAL

BAY OF BENGAL

GULF of MARTABAN

SIAM

FRENCH
INDO-CHINA

Tavoy
SIAM
BURMA
Mergui
Tenasserim
GULF of SIAM
Victoria Point

20 0 20 40 60 80 100
Miles

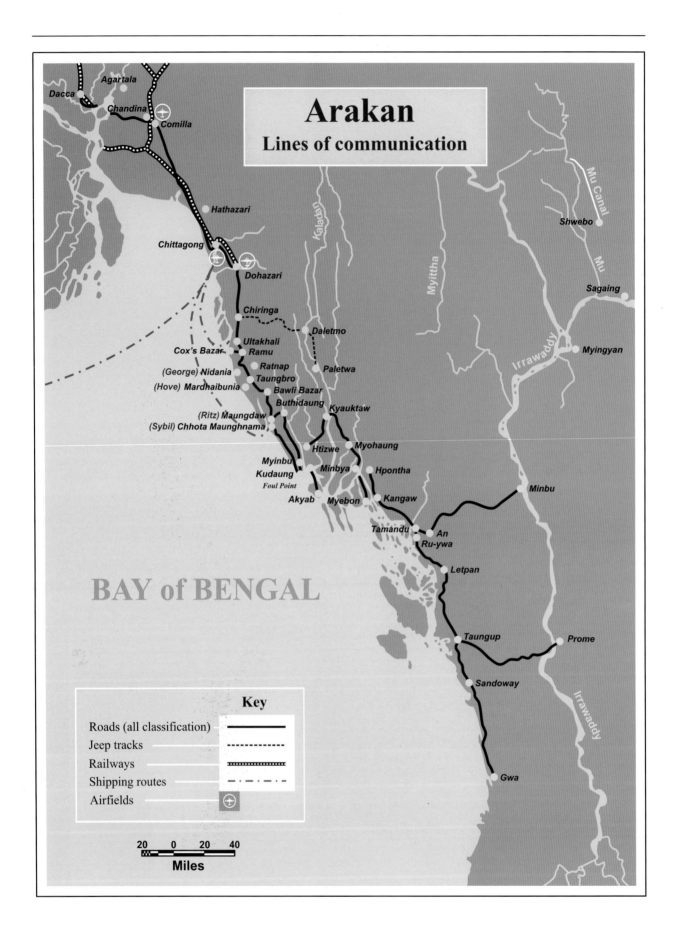

Arakan
Lines of communication

Key

Roads (all classification)	——
Jeep tracks	- - - -
Railways	▦▦▦
Shipping routes	—·—·—
Airfields	⊕

20 0 20 40
Miles

BAY of BENGAL

Dacca
Agartala
Chandina
Comilla
Hathazari
Chittagong
Dohazari
Chiringa
Daletmo
Ultakhali
Cox's Bazar Ramu
(George) Nidania Ratnap
Taungbro Paletwa
(Hove) Mardhaibunia
Bawli Bazar
Buthidaung
(Ritz) Maungdaw Kyauktaw
(Sybil) Chhota Maunghnama
Htizwe Myohaung
Myinbu
Kudaung Minbya Hpontha
Foul Point
Akyab Myebon Kangaw
Tamandu An
Ru-ywa
Letpan
Minbu
Taungup Prome
Sandoway
Gwa
Shwebo
Sagaing
Myingyan
Mu Canal
Mu
Myittha
Kaladan
Irrawaddy

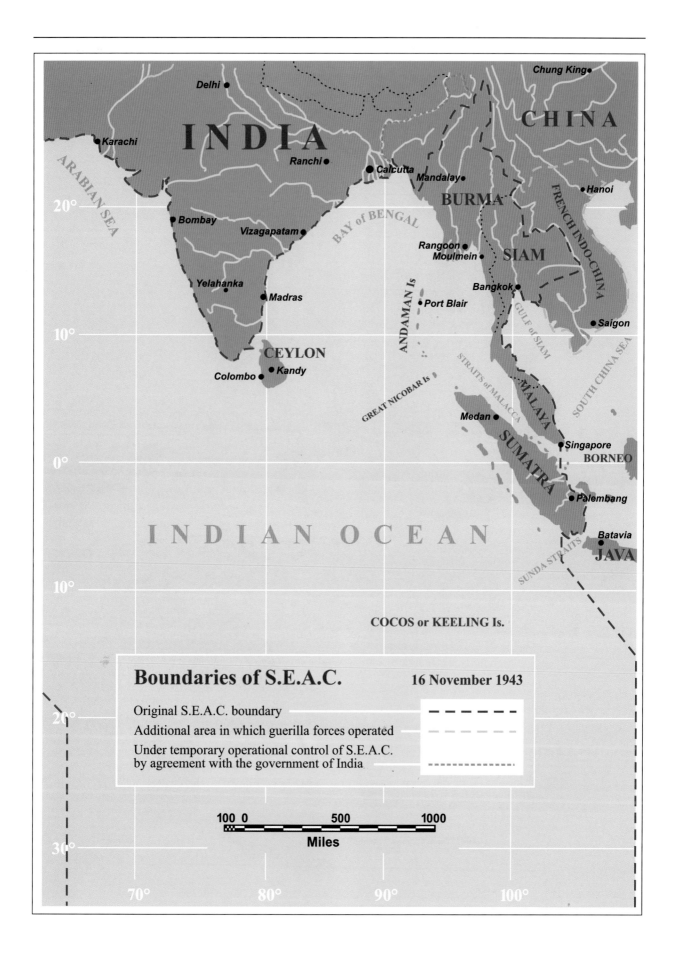

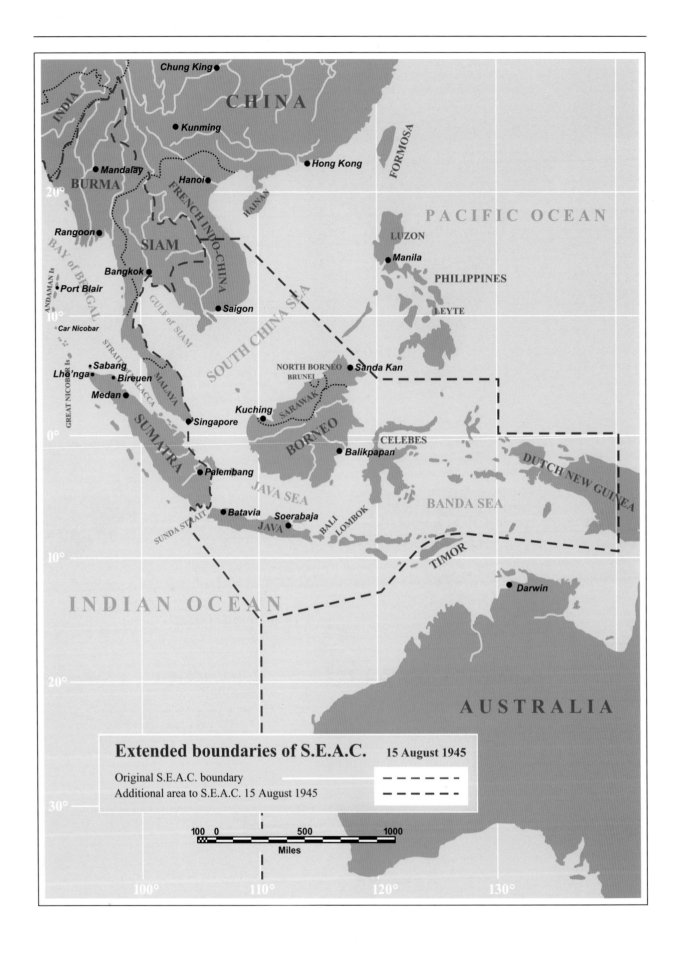

Chung King●
CHINA
● Kunming

● Mandalay
● Hanoi
BURMA
FRENCH INDO-CHINA
● Hong Kong
FORMOSA
HAINAN
PACIFIC OCEAN

20°
INDIA

Rangoon●
SIAM
LUZON
● Manila
PHILIPPINES

BAY OF BENGAL
Bangkok●
ANDAMAN Is
Port Blair●
10°
● Saigon
GULF of SIAM
LEYTE

Car Nicobar●
SOUTH CHINA SEA

GREAT NICOBAR Is
Lho'nga● ● Sabang
STRAITS of MALACCA
MALAYA
● Bireuen
Medan ●
NORTH BORNEO
BRUNEI
●Sanda Kan
SARAWAK
Kuching●

● Singapore
0°
BORNEO
● Balikpapan
CELEBES

SUMATRA
● Palembang
JAVA SEA
BANDA SEA
DUTCH NEW GUINEA

SUNDA STRAIT
● Batavia
● Soerabaja
BALI LOMBOK
JAVA
10°
TIMOR
● Darwin

INDIAN OCEAN

20°

AUSTRALIA

Extended boundaries of S.E.A.C. **15 August 1945**

Original S.E.A.C. boundary ---- ---- ----
Additional area to S.E.A.C. 15 August 1945 ---- ---- ----

30°

100 0   500   1000
Miles

100°   110°   120°   130°

252: *684 Sqn's Mosquito PR.XVI, NS787, 'M', shows the Dull Blue identification bands cut short at the control surfaces as per instructions. Although the aircraft itself is overall Dull Aluminium, the underwing tanks are still finished in PRU Blue. This is another example of a serial being applied by means of a stencil*

253: *Spitfire PR.XI PL781, 'F', of 681 Sqn carried thinly-applied White identification bands on Medium Sea Grey uppersurfaces*

254: *Royal Navy aircraft also carried White identification bands as required by Eastern Air Command from 1 February 1945. This Hellcat II, JX885, 'K6T', of 804 Sqn was unusual in having Sky codes, and a nose band which did not reach to the front edge of the engine cowling. As seen here, the aircraft is returning to HMS* Attacker *following raids on Medan in June 1945*

Royal Navy Distinguishing Symbols

Eastern Fleet Markings

In contrast to the two-letter squadron codes applied to aircraft of the RAF, the 'symbols' (Royal Navy parlance for 'markings') used on Naval aircraft may appear confusing but, in fact, they were in accordance with a simple system in use from mid-1940.

Late in 1943 the squadrons aboard the fleet carriers of the Eastern Fleet were organised into new Tactical Units: Torpedo-bomber-reconnaissance Wings and Naval Fighter Wings, each squadron identified by a single figure. By mid-1944 their squadron figure symbols were prefixed by Tactical Unit letter symbols. These Wing-letter and Squadron-number symbols and individual aircraft letters 24in (occasionally 18in) high were painted on the fuselage sides in Sky against the Temperate Sea Scheme camouflage.

In 1944, when operating in Home, Atlantic or Mediterranean waters, the Royal Navy's escort carriers bore the initial letter of the ship's name painted on the flight deck, and aircraft of the squadrons based on these vessels carried on their fuselage sides their 'parent' carrier's 'deck letter' as the first of a two-letter identification symbol. The aircraft flying from HMS *Emperor*, *Hunter*, *Khedive* and *Stalker*, for instance, bore these markings until they were sent to serve in the Indian Ocean. On joining the Eastern Fleet, where this identification system was not employed, the carrier's deck letter was painted out and replaced by the pendant code, (as painted on the sides of the hull). The deck marking was similar to the 'hull number' on the decks of US Navy CVEs (carriers, heavier-than-air aircraft, escort) in light grey.

Several of the Naval fighter squadrons equipped with camera-fitted aircraft were embarked at various times in different escort carriers so that, in photographs, their aircraft markings are no reliable indication of the ships from which they flew, these often being identifiable only by their hull camouflage patterns, deck letters or pendant numbers.

The British Eastern Fleet was divided on 22 November 1944 into two parts. An East Indies Fleet now included an Escort Carrier Squadron with several squadrons of Hellcats and later one of Seafires to provide reconnaissance, air cover and spotting for the other warships of the Fleet along the coasts of Burma, Sumatra and Malaya, for South East Asia Command. A British Pacific Fleet included capital ships and four armoured fleet carriers with supporting vessels, intended to join the US Navy operating in the Central Pacific Ocean.

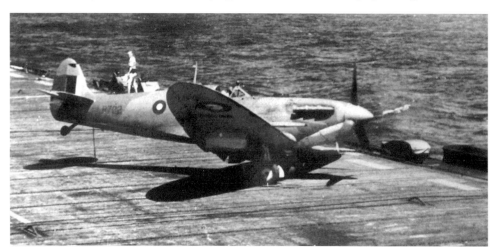

255: LR702, 'Z', a Seafire LIIC of 834 Sqn on the escort carrier HMS Battler *falls foul of the Seafire's weak undercarriage enroute from Durban to Mauritius, 23 February 1944. The machine is wearing only the National markings, the squadron symbols have apparently not yet been applied*

256: Even during the last weeks of war, the markings on Naval aircraft were still not standardised. This Hellcat II, JX675, 'B9H', of 898 Sqn, wore 32in/16in roundels at Ratmalana in Ceylon during training for Operation 'Zipper'; the squadron was assigned to HMS Pursuer *but took no part in offensive operations*

East Indies Fleet and British Pacific Fleet Markings

Until the end of January 1945 the National markings on the aircraft of both the Fleets remained unchanged, namely those approved in June 1943. On 1 February the White cowling, wing and tail bands required on tactical aircraft of Eastern Air Command were applied to the aircraft of the East Indies Fleet with some exceptions, for instance the PR Hellcats of 888 Sqn. On the fighter and fighter-reconnaissance Hellcats the White wing bands were positioned halfway along the wings, so that they overlapped the inboard edges of the upper wing roundels. There followed a re-allocation of squadron symbols, as later confirmed by Confidential Fleet Admiralty Order No.1099 (Aircraft Distinguishing Symbols), the numbers 5 to 9 being applied to single-seat fighter squadrons. In consequence the Hellcats of 804 and 808 Sqns, previously coded 2 and 1 respectively, were remarked K6 and K7, the K being previously the Tactical Unit symbol of No.3 Naval Fighter Wing. The letter-number-letter symbols were retained in the Eastern Fleet to which were allocated the symbols A to J, and in the British Pacific Fleet with symbols N to Z; in practice it was convenient for 'K' to remain on the operational aircraft of No.3 NFW.

As earlier noted, a change in the requirement for upper wing markings was notified in Air Ministry Orders on 7 January, the National Marking I (Type B roundel) to be replaced by Marking II (Type C) of the same diameter on aircraft of the RAF. Admiralty approval had already been obtained and was confirmed in CAFO No.618 dated 5 April. Some American-built fighters for newly-formed or re-formed Naval squadrons were shipped directly from New York to South Africa for squadrons working up in preparation for operations in South-East Asia. Most of these aircraft were re-marked at the Modification Center before delivery but the markings were again changed before issue to the squadrons, the Yellow fuselage roundel surround deleted and the Red of all the markings over-painted with White to the sizes prescribed in the CAFO. On aircraft already in service, the wing markings remained as set out in AFO (India) No.257/43, but the fuselage roundels of a few aircraft were modified to meet the new requirements. It has sometimes been supposed that variation in proportion was due to errors in application, but this was not the case—a different rule was applied. The new 32in marking was similar in appearance to the 'Medium' fuselage roundel already to be seen on some Fleet aircraft, the different markings distinguishable by the proportion of White to Blue; 18in to 36in and 12in to 32in.

No record has been found of any Order rescinding the February 1945 instruction for the application of identification bands. Aircraft of the RAF continued to bear these markings for two years after the surrender of Japan, as might be expected where operations in conjunction with the Army were still necessary, as in the Netherlands Indies.

For the Royal Navy the situation was different. After the recapture of the area west of the Sittang in Burma, the need for Naval support of amphibious landings was greatly reduced. Although the Hellcat fighter and fighter-bomber squadrons, Nos.808, 896 and 898, were equipping with new aircraft aboard the escort carriers of the East Indies Fleet at that time, some of the aircraft had their roundels modified as described in CAFO No.618, some were without the White identification bands, of which there was no mention in the Fleet Order. Those aircraft were employed briefly on operations during July 1945.

The simple Blue and White roundels were soon to be superseded on the aircraft of the British Pacific Fleet. No record survives in Royal Navy or US Navy archives but an Instruction or Order for a further change in the National Marking for aircraft of the BPF was authorised while the Fleet prepared for action at its forward base, Manus Island. The new marking has sometimes been wrongly called the SWPOA marking but it was applied only to BPF aircraft, which saw no service in that area of Command; the RAAF, RNZAF and the Royal Netherlands-Indies Army operating over the territories of the SW Pacific Ocean each had their own form of marking.

The new BPF marking was confirmed in CAFO No.618; *"in the British Pacific Fleet the national marking consists of a blue ring with a narrow white border and a white circular centre. On either side of the roundel are white rectangular panels similar to those used in the United States insignia"*. The marking was identical in outline and proportions to that of US Navy aircraft, a 'roundel-and-bar' instead of the 'star-and-bar' insignia, applied to the fuselage sides, above the port wing and beneath the starboard wing. The marking appeared in two sizes, based on Dull Blue and White roundels of 32in and 48in diameter with a White bar at each side, of length equal to the half the diameter and width equal to the radius. A surround was added, one-eighth of the radius (ie 2in and 3in) in width, White around the Blue of the roundel, Blue around the White bars. The 48in size marking was soon applied to all BPF aircraft, excepting various small aircraft and Seafires which had insufficient area on the fuselage sides. Fin flashes were deleted from all BPF aircraft after the first weeks of operations.

At the end of June 1945 new identification symbols were introduced, based on the pre-war marking system of the Fleet Air Arm. Each aircraft bore its parent carrier's deck letter in White on the tail-fin and a number, 18 or 24in high, on the fuselage sides.

In accordance with US Navy practice, in June 1945 the Wings aboard the BPF carriers became Carrier Air Groups, the deck letters being in effect tail-fin CAG identification symbols. The Corsairs of the PR Flight of No.47 NFW aboard *Victorious* were marked with the tail symbol 'P' of No.1 CAG and the Hellcats of *Indomitable*'s

PR Flight with the symbol 'N' of No.11 CAG.

The aircraft number was of three figures, usually placed ahead of the fuselage roundel but sometimes (as on Seafires) split either side of the National Marking or on the fin beneath the deck letter. The number codes began with the numeral 1 for single-seat fighters and fighter-reconnaissance aircraft, code range from 111 to 199, with the numeral 2 for two-seat fighters and fighter-reconnaissance aircraft, and 3 for three-seat aircraft. The

markings were in use on aircraft aboard the fleet carriers of the BPF operating as Carrier Unit 17.1.1 during, strikes against Formosa and Japan in July and August 1945.

A similar system of markings was adopted on 27 July for the US Navy's Fast Carriers of Vice-Adm McCain's Task Force 38, having deck letters painted on the tail and wing-tips, and numbers on the fuselage sides. Both the Royal Navy and the US Navy continued using variations on this marking system for several years after the war.

257 Above: This Sea Blue Hellcat Mk. II, JZ777, of 896 Sqn on the 'accelerator' aboard HMS Empress carried the usual markings, with White surrounds to all roundels with no identification bands

258 Left: Taking a wave-off, this Hellcat II, JW738, of 804 Sqn displays the White 'tactical' bands painted the full chord of the wings and tailplane. It appears that RN aircraft were not so susceptible to control imbalance as their RAF counterparts

259: *In contrast to JZ777, this Hellcat II(P), JX841, bore the White identification bands and the 898 Sqn symbol, 'B9', as well as the name of the pilot's choice. 'Mins' was non-operational aboard HMS Pursuer in July 1945*

260: *This Seafire of 894 Sqn displays Eastern Fleet markings, the aircraft and Squadron symbol 'H6Y' in 24in high figures and 16in roundels in six places. This picture shows well how labour intensive and time-consuming the manual wing-folding of the early Seafires was*

261: *A Seafire of 801 Sqn in* Implacable's *barrier. Those aircraft of 880 Sqn which carried out photographic reconnaissance during Operation 'Inmate' were similarly marked but with numbers within the series 135-159*

Post-War Colours and Markings

After the end of the war, the reduction in the number of units overseas; the introduction of new aircraft and the likelihood of frequent transfers between Commands caused the Air Ministry to consult with representatives of the Admiralty and RAF Commands before establishing standards of finish and markings suitable for a peace-time establishment.

On 19 October 1945, approval was given to a simplified schedule of colour schemes. This required that *"all wooden and fabric aircraft (for example, Mosquitos) should be silver doped with the exception of night fighters and night bombers. All photographic reconnaissance aircraft to be silver doped"*.

So far, the Air Ministry had "permitted licence" in the camouflage PR aircraft; 681 Sqn's Spitfires carried both 'small' and 'medium' roundels and 684 Sqn's Mosquitos were finished as we have seen, since early 1945, either all PRU Blue, all Aluminium or Aluminium above and PRU Blue underneath.

By then 28 Sqn was re-equipped with Spitfire FR.XIVs of standard 'clipped wing' type, already refinished in India with Temperate Land scheme camouflage to AFO (India) No.70 of 1944, and with White identification bands. Serial numbers and aircraft letters were also White. Later deliveries of FR.XIVs, some of which equipped Far East fighter squadrons, had 'full span' wings. These aircraft were sometimes left in factory finish of Dark Green and Ocean Grey but with their Fighter Command markings and National Markings over-painted Dark Green before India Command (SEAC) markings were applied. Serial numbers were in Night.

From late 1946, 28 Sqn's aircraft had their spinners painted in Flight colours, Red or Blue.

A revised system of colouring and markings was provisionally issued in April 1946. HQ Air Command SE Asia *"considered that RAF aircraft should display Red White and Blue roundels and fin markings, especially when operating through foreign countries"*. As a result, many units and detachments repainted the national markings, some with the pre-war Type A roundel and fin flashes of equally wide stripes. Others painted over the 'SEAC' markings with Marking II (Type C roundel) and the fin flashes set out in DTD Circular No.360 and Air Publication No.2565A in Dull Red, White and Dull Blue, usually when the aircraft were re-finished after major maintenance.

In 1947, the Spitfire FR.XIVs of 28 Sqn were supplemented by FR.XVIIIs in 1945-style Fighter Command camouflage with Sky band and spinner, and Type C roundels above the wings, as originally authorised on 7 January 1945. Although the Air Ministry additionally approved the use of Yellow surrounds to the roundels, it appears that they were not applied during production of the aircraft.

A new colour schedule, intended to be included in a revised edition of AP 2656A, was issued as Air Ministry Order A.413 on I5 May 1947. Fighter and PR aircraft were to be painted with a *"silver finish with the smoothest surface possible, to produce the best performance"*. In fact, as A.413 was applicable only to aircraft that required re-doping in the normal course of maintenance, very few (Spitfires) were re-finished.

A new style of roundel also was introduced; although the Order stated that it had been decided to revert to the pre-war roundel on all aircraft, the diameters of the colours were to be in the proportions 1:2:3 instead of the pre-war 1:3:5. The new marking is usually classified as 'Type D':

Roundel Position	Aircraft	Red	White	Blue
Above wings	Sizes as before, between 2ft 6in and 7ft dia			
Fuselage sides	Small	6in	12in	18in
& below wings	Medium	12in	24in	36in
	Large	18in	36in	54in
Fin Flash	24-inches in height			
	Aircraft	Red	White	Blue
	Small	6in	6in	6in
	Medium	8in	8in	8in
	Large	12in	12in	12in

All fighter and fighter-reconnaissance aircraft were to be marked as Medium aircraft.

The pre-war identification colours Bright Red and Bright Blue (later BS 381C colours Post Office Red No 538 and Roundel Blue No 110) were in short supply and were to be used "only when repainting becomes necessary", consequently because of the lack of the new colours, the revised markings were usually applied in MAP Dull Red and Blue. A further Instruction was issued on 28 October, confirmed by AMO. A.977 now requiring 'strategical PR aircraft' to be painted (as so often, indeterminately) with "a blue finish".

Air Publication 2656A had required PR aircraft to be finished in PRU Blue but noted, "The Service is permitted licence in the camouflage of P.R. aircraft", thereby perhaps allowing authority for the use of Aluminium or Medium Sea Grey on the upper surfaces. During the years after the war a confusing series of Orders and Amendments were issued. Silver "with the smoothest surface possible" for upper and lower surfaces of PR aircraft was a requirement of Air Ministry Order A.413 of June 1947, then again smooth blue (A.977) later in the year. It was not until the issue in April 1951 of AMO A.217, an Order that changed the colour schemes of most types of aircraft, that Medium Sea Grey upper surfaces with PRU beneath was established as the scheme for photographic reconnaissance aircraft.

New high-gloss finishes were required; Medium Sea Grey on upper surfaces and PRU Blue beneath, to Boundary Pattern No 2 of AP.2656A, ie, the vertical tail surfaces and lower three-quarters of the fuselage sides were PRU Blue. These colours were generally applied to the Spitfires and Mosquitos of 81 Sqn, although a few Mosquitos remained in smooth Aluminium finish until the end of their service with the squadron.

262: 681 Sqn's Spitfire PR.19 PM574 in Aluminium finish with 16in 'Type C' roundels (National Marking II) on fuselage and wings, as required in January 1945, and 12in square PRU fin flash

263: A Dakota C.4, KG492, wearing the revised markings set out by ACSEA in April 1946, reverting to the pre-war 'Type A' roundels. Although stripped of camouflage, the machine retains an interesting anti-glare panel forward of the windscreen

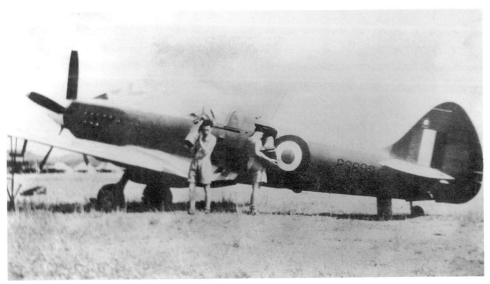

264: Unloading the cameras from a Medium Sea Grey and PRU Blue Spitfire PR.19, PS890 of 81 Sqn during the Malayan Emergency. A small version of the unit badge can just be made out on the fin above the flash

265: *There were still variations in markings even after AMO A.217/51 finishes had been applied, as shown by these Spitfire PR.19s of 81 Sqn. The far aircraft carried markings of the diameters set out in AMO A.413/47, the nearer aircraft was incorrectly marked with 36in roundels above the wings*

266: *This Mosquito PR.34 of 81 Sqn in Medium Sea Grey and PRU Blue finish shows the wing leading edges to have been repaired, defacing the 'Type D' roundels*

267: *No.81 Sqn's Mosquito PR.34, RG314, in standard Aluminium finish of the time, taking-off from Seletar for the last Mosquito sortie on 15 December 1955. There appears to be the hulk of another aircraft just visible below the tail of RG314*

268: A really low-level beat-up by Mosquito PR.34 RG177 which wears the Medium Sea Grey and PRU Blue scheme. Spinners could be black or a Flight colour. Seletar, May 1953

269: Both world-beaters in their day, the careers of the superlative Mosquito and the hapless Blenheim in the reconnaissance role could hardly have differed more. This Blenheim Mk.I, L4827, of 60 Sqn wears the 'night bomber' camouflage of Dark Green and Dark Earth upper-surfaces with Night below. Later variants wore Sky undersides

270: The Blenheim Mk.IVs in the Far East were mostly used as bombers, many being destroyed on their airfields like this one, believed to be from No.60 Sqn. That unit had a mixed complement of both Mk.I and Mk.IV versions and both types were used for makeshift reconnaissance as an adjunct to their bombing sorties

271: The Blenheim Mk.V (or Bisley) was long past its sell-by date when it was issued to units in the Far East. Virtually helpless against enemy fighter opposition, all had been mercifully replaced by Hurricanes by October 1943. This example wears the standard 1942-43 Temperate Land Scheme for day bombers of Dark Green, Dark Earth and Sky

RAF/IAF RECONNAISSANCE AIRCRAFT
Colour Schemes & Markings

1941-1942

Blenheim Mk.I and Mk.II

The Blenheim Mk.I bomber entered service in 1937. From early 1939 it was superseded by the 'long-nosed' Blenheim Mk.IV and the Mk.V (originally called Bisley) but although phased out of service in the United Kingdom by the autumn of 1942, the Blenheim remained in service as the standard bomber in India.

The camera-fitted Blenheim Mk.Is of 34 Sqn and later of 60 Sqn were finished in standard Bomber Command camouflage of Temperate Land Scheme with Night undersides. Upper wing markings were of 59in diameter, fuselage roundels 42in and fin flashes 24 x 28in. Squadron identification markings in Medium Sea Grey were: 34 Sqn: EG; 60 Sqn: MU. The Blenheim IVs and Vs were also finished in the Temperate Land Scheme but with Sky under surfaces. Only aircraft identification letters were carried on later aircraft.

Lockheed Hudson

The Hudson was a military version of the admirable Lockheed 14 airliner. Initially ordered by the RAF in 1938 for use as a navigational trainer, the aircraft proved highly effective as a maritime reconnaissance bomber.

The Hudson GR.Mk.IIs of No.8 Sqn RAAF, in handed A and B pattern Temperate Land Scheme camouflage, have been usually described as finished Dark Green and Dark Earth but the historian Ian K. Baker writes of RAAF camouflage in his Aviation Colouring Book No.301, "Official painting instructions consistently indicated Foliage Green and RAF Dark Earth (later shortened to Dark Earth) as the colours for upper surface camouflage through 1940 and '41. Undersides were Aluminium at that time. Then, during 1942, Sky Blue became the colour for undersides. The same year, Earth Brown became the brown officially named for use with Foliage Green in upper surface camouflage". Bearing in mind that No.8 Sqn's aircraft were specifically ordered by the Australian Government, there seems little doubt that they were finished in either Foliage Green (or the closely matching USAAC Medium Green 42) and Dark Earth, with Aluminium-lacquered undersurfaces marked with roundels and black 'A16-' serials. A16-76, the crew of which aircraft observed the destruction of 'Force Z', bore the code 'NN-F'. The Hudson GR.IIIs of the Akwing General Reconnaissance Flight were finished Dark Green and Dark Earth with Sky under-surfaces, standard National Markings on upper and side surfaces but none beneath the wings.

Westland Lysander

Lysanders had a major role in supporting the British Expeditionary Force in France, 1939-1940, but proved highly vulnerable in their army-co-operation role. In India Lysanders replaced obsolete Audax aircraft which had served in India for many years, and the obsolescent Lysanders were adequate for the tasks to which they were assigned, some remaining in service for 'special operations' in Japanese-occupied territory until 1945. The aircraft were camouflaged and marked in standard fashion, those of 28 Sqn bearing the squadron marking BF and of 20 Sqn the letters HN.

Brewster Buffalo Mk.I

The Buffalo, as supplied to the RAF, was a land-based version of the US Navy's first carrier-borne monoplane fighter, the F2A. When first tested in 1940 for the British Air Purchasing Commission to the US, it was considered so inferior in performance to contemporary British and German fighters that the Air Ministry diverted the RAF's deliveries to Far Fast Command where it was assumed that the aircraft of the only possible adversary, Japan, would be no match for the little fighter.

All the Buffalos delivered to Singapore in February and to Rangoon in May 1941 were camouflaged in the Temperate Land Scheme, those aircraft with 'even' serial numbers to Pattern A and those with 'odd' serials to the 'mirror' Pattern B to comply with Air Ministry Orders. Presumably the Air Purchasing Commission contract required under-surfaces to be 'Duck-egg blue' (Sky Type S) but it is well-established that the colour was not that intended. Upper wing roundels Type B were of 40in diameter, under-wing Type A of 30in and on fuselage sides 35in diameter.

The Buffalos used for photographic reconnaissance from Seletar and Mingaladon were drawn from reserve stocks and were the only PR aircraft finished 'Duck-egg blue' beneath. It is understood that no markings were applied to the aircraft of No.4 PRU or to 67 Sqn's camera-fitted Buffalo; its regular pilot, Flg Off Bingham-Wallis, wrote, "W8 241—I am sorry to say that I cannot give you the code letter. It became fashionable in the Squadrons to only show Code letters in our log books, but for some unknown reason 8241 was shown under its number. Our aircraft in Rangoon were painted pale blue under-colour. Of the original 30 aircraft there, approximately 20 were painted half black and half blue beneath, ie on the mainplane. Shortly after they were assembled and painted (we painted the black) the Air Ministry orders were changed and the remaining aircraft were left as delivered from the manufacturers, pale blue underneath. The band of blue forward of the tailplane would be a shade lighter than the sky blue". No record exists of the exact colour of the under-surfaces but it is certain that Brewster's interpretation of Duck-egg blue was markedly different from Sky, probably close to Methuen ref. 24B3-4, slightly darker than MAP Sky Blue, as applied to aircraft of the RAAF delivered in 1942.

Bristol Beaufort Mk.V

The design of the Beaufort torpedo-bomber was largely derived from that of the Blenheim, the Beaufort Mk.I with Bristol Taurus engines entering service with Coastal Command in 1940. Agreement had earlier been reached with the Government of Australia for large-scale production there of the aircraft and orders were placed in July 1939 for Beauforts to be built by the Department of Aircraft Production. Beaufort Mk.I L4448 was shipped to Australia to act as a pattern aircraft and prototype (later numbered A9-1001). Production of Beauforts with Pratt & Whitney Twin Wasp engines was begun in 1941, in England as the Mk.II and in Australia as the Beaufort Mk.V. The first DAP Mk.V, T9540, was completed in August, one of a batch intended for RAF re-equipment in the Far East but when Japan entered the war it was agreed that later aircraft should be retained for the defence of Australia.

The Mk.I aircraft of Coastal Command were camouflaged in the Temperate Land Scheme, as was L4448 with 'Duck-egg blue' under-surfaces. Only from 3 August 1941 did HQ Coastal Command require all its aircraft to be finished in the Temperate Sea Scheme and Sky beneath.

Doubts have been expressed about the camouflage colours of the six Mk.Vs flown from Australia to reinforce 100 Sqn at Seletar. It has been suggested that they were finished in RAAF Foliage Green and RAAF Light Earth, darker in tone than the MAP Colour Standards equivalent, a reasonable match to the Temperate Land colours of L4448. Although T9540 was used for a series of demonstration flights in Australia late in 1941, no records remain of the camouflage but it is clear that the colours were not very different from those of L4448 or of the Vildebeests that the first six Beaufort Mk.Vs were to reinforce and replace in 100 Sqn. There is a possibility that T9540 was first flown with under-surfaces simply varnished aluminium, but before leaving for Singapore the six aircraft were finished beneath in 'Duck-egg blue', almost certainly the RAAF version of Sky Blue.

National Marking I of 59in diameter was carried above the wings, Marking II of 42in on the fuselage sides and the standard 28in x 24in flash on the tail-fins. At Seletar the Beauforts were marked with the 100 Squadron identification letters 'NK' in Medium Sea Grey, and the identification letter 'A' applied to T9540 before it was used for its historic reconnaissance flight.

De Havilland Tiger Moth Mk.II

Perhaps the most unlikely aircraft of the PR Units was a Tiger Moth. From nine 'Tigers' employed by the Burma Volunteer Air Force for coastal reconnaissance was one attached to No.3 PRU and flown by Plt Off D. Harris of 28 Sqn on tactical reconnaissance over Central Burma.

The BVAF Tiger Moths were camouflaged in the standard Temperate Land Scheme with Aluminium undersurfaces to the pattern of Air Diagram No.1169 and given serials/codes beginning 'Z-' in Black, 12 in high aft of the fuselage roundels. Of the nine machines, two are known certainly to have survived the first Burma campaign; both Z-04 and Z-09 were flown in India later in 1942.

Z-04 was one of the light aircraft of the BVAF Communications Flight at Akyab before evacuation in March 1942 so it is almost certain that the Tiger Moth flown by Harris from Magwe at that time was Z-04, handed over to No.3 PRU at Lashio in April 1942.

Hawker Hurricane

The Hurricane has been described in detail in a host of specialised publications. The first monoplane fighter to serve with the RAF, when it entered service early in 1938 it was soon realised that the aircraft had great potential for development. With increased power, alternative wing designs and the ability to carry several types of armament, the Hurricane remained the principal ground-attack and Tac/R aircraft in the Far East.

Photo-Reconnaissance Hurricane Mk.IIA & IIB

The Hawker Hurricane Mk. IIA and IIB (Tropicalized) fighters varied principally in their armament. They carried, respectively, eight and twelve Browning machine-guns within the wings. When converted in the Middle East for photographic reconnaissance they were virtually identical; all armament was removed and camera mountings were installed in the lower part of the fuselage and enclosed by a removable protective fairing.

The once fighter Hurricanes converted for use by No.2 PRU, Heliopolis, were finished in shades of blue, some in colours similar to Light and Dark Mediterranean Blue or Azure Blue over-all, but others of these PR Hurricanes were painted at Almaza in a matt finish made up of 5gal of ICI 'Bosun Blue' (ultramarine) with 3lb of black pigment added, mixed with 16lb of zinc powder and turpentine. The resulting colour of this peculiar mixture was described as 'royal blue' (an indeterminate name applied in this case to a colour slightly more dull than the Deep Sky proposed by the RAE), claimed to render the aircraft "invisible to the eye at 14,000ft". Such was the finish applied to the two Hurricane Mk.IIs intended for No.4 PRU at Seletar and retained at Rangoon in January 1942. Both aircraft carried 49in diameter (Type B) roundels above and beneath the wings, as was usual for

272: *Lockheed Hudson Mk.I (the RAAF designation, akin to the Mk.IV for the RAF) of No.8 Sqn RAAF at Mingaladon, sometime before February 1942 when it was written off. A-16-15, 'NN-G', was from the first production batch of 50. These early aircraft had their black serials wrongly applied, as shown, with an extra hyphen. It wears Foliage Green and Dark Earth uppersurface camouflage, with lacquered Aluminium undersides. Note that the Medium Grey identification letters have been painted over the cabin windows*

273: *Lysander Mk.II N1273 of No.28 Sqn over the mountainous terrain of the North-West Frontier near the Khyber Pass. Although wearing the typical camouflage and markings with which aircraft from 28 Sqn went to war in Burma on army co-operation duties in February 1942, 'BF-J', was not one of them as it crashed on take-off from Kohat on 19 December 1941*

274: *Lysander Mk.II P9182, 'BF-D', of 28 Sqn at Kohat in mid-1942, with the squadron identification letters painted over before being repainted in Dull Red. Note the highly unusual angled fin flash*

275: *Buffalo Mk.I W8215 being assembled at Mingaladon. On delivery the Buffalos were finished light blue on their under-surfaces and carried no Sky 'fighter markings'*

276: *In squadron service the Buffalos were painted, like Home Base Fighter Command aircraft, with Sky fuselage bands and spinners. The port undersides were refinished Night. Here is W8245, 'RD-D', of 67 Sqn at Mingaladon in 1941. This was one of the very few Buffalos to survive the Burma campaign, returning to Dum Dum in March 1942 before eventually finding its way to 151 OTU at Risalpur in early 1943. Apart from a full set of 'fighter markings' W8245 also wears a very neat, but non-standard, white outline to its serial number*

277: *A poor photograph but included as it features an extremely rare aircraft. This is Tiger Moth 'Z-09' once of the Burma Volunteer Air Force. It is seen here in India, probably late in 1943, back in use as a communications taxi. Two Tiger Moths from the BVAF (Z-04 and Z-09) are known to have survived the disaster in Burma; of the pair it is believed that Z-04 was the example used by Flg Off Harris on Tactical Reconnaissance missions throughout the retreat to India*

No.2 PRU at that time, and 35in (also Type B) roundels on the fuselage sides. Serial numbers were in Night, 4in high.

To define the markings a Yellow surround 4in wide was painted over the outer edges of the Type B wing and fuselage roundels, the Dull Blue rings being reduced to about 40in diameter on the wings and to 28in on the fuselage, the Dull Red centres untouched.

The later PR Hurricanes delivered to form 'S' Flt of No.3 PRU (India) in 1942 were similarly finished in No.2 PRU's royal blue but the roundels differed from one aircraft to another. The wing markings remained 49in diameter, the standard size for the aircraft with Yellow outer rings of 2in or 3in, the Blue ring in some cases repainted to maintain the Red centre at two-fifths the diameter of the Blue. Some of the Hurricanes carried Marking III (roundel Type C1) on the fuselage sides but these appear soon to have been deleted so that all the aircraft of N.3 PRU carried no National Markings other than on the wings, and only a serial number and identification letter on the dark blue finish of their fuselages.

Tactical Reconnaissance Hurricane Mk.IIB & IIC

Air Ministry Order A.413 dated 10 July 1941 had clearly set out the camouflage required on aircraft intended for service overseas as the Temperate Land Scheme (Dark Green and Dark Earth) or the 'Tropical Land Scheme' (Dark Earth and Midstone) "applied according to the nature of the country in which they were to operate". The first of these schemes was used on aircraft in India and South-East Asia Command until early 1945. In a number of otherwise reliable publications, the 'Day Fighter Scheme' of Home Base Fighter Command has been described and illustrated as applied to fighter aircraft in the Far East Commands, probably a result of mis-reading Appendix I to the Order, summarising colouring. This showed only the Tropical Land Scheme to be applied to the upper surfaces of aircraft for service abroad. The matter was again confused by AMO A.664, Appendix I listing the colouring for 'Day Fighters, abroad' as 'Day-Fighter scheme or Desert scheme'. This was corrected in AMO.1096 of 8 October 1942 by the insertion of "temperate land scheme" and, for under surfaces, "Sky, azure or light Mediterranean blue".

A few of the first Hurricane IIBs flown from the Canal Zone to Burma for 17 Sqn remained in the Tropical Land or 'Desert' Scheme camouflage. BE171 had Type A (Red, White and Blue) roundels above the wings, the White ring perhaps added en route to identify more clearly an aircraft finished in camouflage colours not hitherto seen in Burma.

The usual National Markings of the period were applied to the other aircraft; 49in diameter Blue and Red roundels above the wings, 40in Type A roundels beneath,

35in Type A1 fuselage roundels and 24x27in high fin flashes. No Fighter Command markings, namely yellow leading edge stripes, Sky spinner and fuselage band were applied. Squadron letters 'YB' were 30 inches in height, in Medium Sea Grey. Other Hurricanes of 17 Sqn including those used for tactical reconnaissance by 28 Sqn pilots at Mingaladon, were camouflaged in the Temperate Land Scheme with Sky undersurfaces.

Converted at No.301 Maintenance Unit, Karachi, for the tactical role, fighter-reconnaissance Hurricane Mk.IIBs were subjected to few alterations. The two outboard guns were removed from each wing and additional tankage was built in. Mountings for cameras were installed behind the cockpit, allowing vertical photography through a port in the floor of the fuselage and obliques to be taken through a port in the lower side of the fuselage. It was usual to use under-wing fuel tanks as a permanent attachment to increase range, although the drag of the tanks reduced speed and manoeuvrability.

From May 1942 all newly-built Hurricanes were marked with 36 inch fuselage roundels (termed Type C1), 32 inch Red, White and Blue under-wing roundels of similar pattern (Type C), 49 inch Red and Blue roundels were retained on the upper surfaces. Most aircraft in service were also re-marked, although the old Type A underwing roundels often remained.

At the end of 1943 the Hurricane Mk.IIBs were largely replaced in 28 Sqn and the fighter-reconnaissance squadrons of the Indian Air Force by Hurricane Mk.IICs, similarly fitted with camera mountings and external fuel-tanks or with bomb racks. Nearly all these aircraft also had their armament reduced by the removal of the two outboard cannon. Later, Hurricane Mk.IV aircraft were similarly converted. The Mk.IV had a 'universal wing' with eight machine-guns and the facility to attach various 'stores'; fuel-tanks, bombs or rocket projectile rails.

The 'required' camouflage was again a repeat o[the Fighter Command scheme—Dark Green/Ocean Grey— and National Markings were those authorised on 29 September 1943. A number of Hurricanes reached squadrons in this hybrid colour-scheme but virtually all those delivered to operational areas were finished in the standard Temperate Land Scheme as specified in DTD Circular No 360 for 'fighter aircraft overseas'.

On 27 October 1943, Air HQ India instructed subsidiary Units; *"Some Hurricane aircraft are being received into India camouflaged with the desert scheme, and carrying the UK identification markings with yellow borders. These are to be re-camouflaged before despatch"*.

None of the photographic reconnaissance aircraft carried squadron markings. Aircraft letters, when used, had been painted Medium Sea Grey until this time but a change was made from 30 April to letters of 'Duck egg blue'. The Air Ministry continually referred to the colour Sky as 'duck egg blue' and, as with the underside colour of the Buffalos in 1941, some confusion arose as to the Ministry's intention. As a result, aircraft code letters were variously painted in Sky and light blues, usually 24 inches in height.

North American B-25C

RAF B-25Cs

The B-25C aircraft for the *Militaire Luchtvaart* were delivered to Karachi in factory-finish of USAAC Basic camouflage of Color No.41 Olive Drab with under-surfaces of Color No.43 Neutral Gray, wearing the Netherlands national marking of the period. In September 1939 a Dutch Fokker T.8W floatplane was shot down by a German fighter, its markings of red, white, blue and orange apparently mistaken for British roundels. The following month the Dutch marking was changed to be an orange equilateral triangle outlined with black and this marking was applied to the B-25Cs.

When assigned to No.5 PRU for reconnaissance the aircraft were re-finished in a blue similar to the 'royal blue' colour of the Hurricanes received from No.2 PRU, with National Marking I (Type B roundel) on the upper surface of the wings. Their ML 'N5-' registration numbers were retained and appear to have been applied in Night, 8in high, and 24in aircraft identification letters in Sky or a light blue to the rear fuselage sides. No changes were made to the finish or to the markings until July 1943 when new markings were approved for use in India Command.

Grp Capt J.D. Thirlwell, who flew both types of aircraft with No.5 PRU in India, wrote, "As far as I can remember the Hurricanes and Mitchells were the same hue of blue". Criticism of the colour by *kapt* Wittert van Hoogland, commanding the ML detachment, was unjustified, for the dark blue applied under Sqn Ldr Pearson's direction had proved satisfactory on high-flying aircraft in the Middle East where Pearson had earlier been stationed.

The two B-25C aircraft allocated to 684 Sqn on 5 July 1943 were, of course, in USAAC Basic Camouflage but British serials from a block reserved for aircraft taken over in India were applied in RAF service. Both aircraft, MA956 and MA957, had originally been intended for Lend-Lease delivery to the British Government in April 1942 but were later diverted to India and retained by the US Tenth Air Force. Their US insignia were replaced by the Blue and White markings authorised on 4 July but both aircraft were soon re-finished overall and the (September 1943-style) Dull Blue and light blue India Command 32in markings were applied in service with 684 Sqn. The Red propeller warning bands painted on the fuselages of US B-25Cs were omitted.

Having advised against attempting to identify colours from the tonal values of black and white prints, it may seem provocative even to consider an exception, but from such photographic evidence as exists it appears that the two ex-Tenth Air Force B-25Cs transferred to 684 Sqn on formation were similarly finished in a colour somewhat lighter in tone than the MAP PRU Blue finish (reflectivity 14%) of the Mosquitos which were to be delivered before the end of 1943 from Britain.

The colour may have quickly faded—at that time blue was considered a 'fugitive' colour—but it is more likely that the paint, produced in India, was simply of a lighter tone. It is suggested that the reflectivity of finish was similar to that of Medium Sea Grey (about 25%) but that this locally-mixed version of PRU Blue contained less black and more blue pigment resulting in a colour equivalent to Methuen 22C4.

Dutch B-25s

The B-25s flown by No 18 Sqn and the PR section of the *Militaire Luchtvaart* under RAAF N.W. Area Command were originally finished in the USAAF Basic Camouflage Scheme of Dark Olive Drab 41 with Neutral Gray 43 under-surfaces or the later scheme of Olive Drab 613 and Sea Gray 603. Some were stripped of paint when overhauled and modified for PR use, matt black anti-glare panels were painted forward of the cockpit on these 'natural metal' aircraft. All the B-25s had Insignia Red warning bands level with the airscrews on each side of the fuselage.

'N5-' serial numbers were painted on the sides of the nose section and on vertical tail surfaces in 9in digits, Insignia Yellow on camouflage, black on bare metal. The national marking, carried above the port wing, beneath both wings and on each side of the fuselage, was a Dutch 'flag' of Red White and Blue, 1.5m x 1m. The fuselage and under-wing markings were outlined in White on camouflaged aircraft.

Although MacArthur's HQ, SWPOA, refused to permit the ML-KNIL bombers to operate freely over the East Indies, the Australian Command was sympathetic to the Dutch aspirations. A couple of B-25s were re-marked with double-sized flags and allowed to overfly camps in Java where Dutch civilians were interned, literally to 'show the flag', late in 1944.

A dozen B-25C and B-25D aircraft of the Netherlands Army, most already refurbished and used as transport aircraft, were fitted with cameras after the end of the war against Japan. All were stripped of their camouflage and carried the tricolour '*vlaag*' on wings and fuselage and their 'N5-' registration numbers on the fuselage and the vertical tail surfaces.

When, early in 1947 a new Army Air Force, the *Nederland Legerluchtmacht*, was formed, these aircraft were all renumbered, the serial ('M-') carried on the rear

278: *It seems that Mainten-ance Units, as well as the Army, sometimes failed to understand the special requirements of the fighter-reconnaissance squadrons. This Hurricane Trop IIB, BG872, with no long-range tanks or camera-mountings, was delivered to 28 Sqn but soon transferred to 146(F) Sqn. Camouflage was the Temperate Land Scheme with Sky undersurfaces*

279: *The 'royal blue' Hurricane Mk.IIAs used by No.5 PRU had National Marking I (the Type B roundel) above the wings and on the fuselage sides, 5in Yellow surrounds. The fairing for the projecting lens of the vertical camera can be seen lying on the ground near the tailwheel*

280: *This Hurricane Tac/R Mk.IIB of 28 Sqn crash-landed at Cox's Bazar on return from operations. Only eight guns were moun-ted on these aircraft; here the fabric covering over the muzzles has been shot away, showing that the aircraft has been in action*

281: *One of 681 Sqn's dull dark blue B-25Cs undergoing maintenance. For several months after the retreat to India, these were the only reconnaissance aircraft capable of reaching Rangoon*

282: *Taken in late 1944, this photograph shows a B-25C at Comilla wearing the lighter tone of PRU Blue, applied late in 1943, perhaps faded during the following twelve months*

283: *B-25C N5-128 (once 41-12935) was delivered to the Dutch in August 1942. The aircraft survived in service until February 1945. The Donald Duck device is presumably an early version of the No.18 Sqn (ML-KNIL) emblem*

fuselage sides. The flags on wings and fuselage were replaced by the pre-war national marking, a tricolour segmented roundel with an orange centre disk. Small flags were painted on the tail fins.

Supermarine Spitfire

The British aircraft considered during the war to be ideally suited to medium-range photo-reconnaissance was the Spitfire. Beginning with the Mk.I conversions of 1939, Spitfires performed outstandingly in the PR role and their success ensured a continuing high priority for later Marks to be adapted for reconnaissance; all following Cotton's principles; unarmed and relying on speed and altitude for safety.

After a series of Spitfire I conversions had been used operationally, the Heston Aircraft Co Ltd undertook further developments. The Spitfire C was the first to carry a vertical camera within the fuselage, two cameras in a blister beneath the port wing and an additional fuel-tank beneath the starboard wing. The next variant, used in considerable numbers, was the Spitfire D with internal wing tanks and either two F.8-20in, F.24-20in or F.24-14in 'split' cameras in tandem within the fuselage. The Spitfire F allowed installation of two F.8-20in vertical cameras or two F.24-20in vertical cameras and an F.24-14in oblique camera. Externally, the aircraft differed in appearance by the addition of 'teardrop' bulges on each side of the cockpit hood to allow better downward and rear vision and an increase in depth of the engine cowling to enclose a larger oil-tank.

Until the end of the war there was a steady improvement in Spitfire performance and an increase in production of the PR versions. To accord with the usual Air Ministry notation of aircraft types, the Spitfire D became the PR Mk.IV in quantity production, with an oblique camera mounting behind the pilot. Despite the small dimensions of the aircraft, the fuselage was wide and high enough to accommodate varying camera combinations; the standard British F.24 cameras weighed between 35 and 78 lb, depending on lens and the film magazine, so, the performance was not adversely affected by the fitting of multiple camera installations. 229 PR.IVs were built with Merlin 45 to 65 series engines and provision for 'tropicalization' to be used in the Middle East and the Far East.

The Spitfire PR.XI was developed from the Mk.IX fighter, combining the experience gained from the PR.IV with the performance of the Merlin 61 to 70 series engines. The Mk.XI had increased fuel tankage, an enlarged rudder and a 'Universal Installation' allowing two F.52 or F.8 vertical cameras, or two F.24 verticals and one F.24 oblique camera to be fitted.

Late in July 1945 a few Spitfire PR.XIs of 681 Sqn at Mingaladon were put at the disposal of 28 Sqn, also at Mingaladon, which had only five or six Hurricanes remaining serviceable. There is no documentary evidence to show what colour was used but the Spitfires were repainted on their sides and upper services in a light, glossy finish. Unlike the markings and lettering of "un-camouflaged aircraft" used on Aluminium-finished Mosquitos, the Spitfires carried White lettering and serials as for "camouflaged aircraft", required by HQ ACSEA on 27 January 1945, implying the use of a camouflage colour, almost certainly Medium Sea Grey. In 1942 a camouflage scheme for Day-Fighters (High-Flying), of Medium Sea Grey over PRU Blue, had been included in MAP DTD Circular No.360 for use on Spitfires; this scheme was still included in Air Publication No.2656A which set out camouflage requirements until after the end of the war but the Author has been unable to trace anyone serving in either 28 or 681 Sqns who has any recollection of the colour scheme of these PR.XIs.

Several PR Spitfires also were given the White tactical markings; it seems that all the aircraft so marked were intended to operate in the Tac/R role on detachment to Kai Tak, Hong Kong, and to Batavia in Java where they flew under control of Air HQ, Netherlands East Indies.

The Spitfire FR.XIV was the first production variant to have the Griffon 65 engine and the 'E' wing armament of two 0.50in machine-guns and two 20mm Hispano cannon. The FR.XIVE, usually with 'clipped' wings for increased low-level manoeuvrability, and rear-view cockpit hood had provision for an F.24 oblique camera behind the pilot. Deliveries of the FR.XIVE to India began early in 1945 as replacements for the out-dated fighter-reconnaissance Hurricanes but none were used operationally before the end of the war. The final FR variant was the Spitfire FR.XVIII with a re-designed wing assembly and mountings for an oblique and two vertical cameras.

The final Spitfire photo-reconnaissance variant was the PR.XIX, Griffon 66 engine, developed from the Mk.XIV fighter. The PR.XIX had provision for two F.52, F.8 or F.24 vertical cameras and alternative port and starboard oblique camera mountings. The Griffon engine allowed provision for pressurization of the cockpit, excellent for long-distance flights at 40,000ft. The PR.XIX was used for only a brief period by 681 Sqn before the end of the war.

In similar fashion to the PR Hurricanes, the early Spitfire PR.IVs operating in the Middle East were painted dark blue. Those ferried to India late in 1942 wore National Marking I of 42in diameter above and beneath the wings and 32in diameter on the fuselage sides. No fin flashes were marked. Serial numbers were usually Night. The roundels were retained in service with No.3 PRU(India), 1in or 2in Yellow surrounds having been added to define the Type B markings. 24in high identification letters were applied in Sky on the rear fuselage sides. When, in October, the first Spitfire PR.XIs were delivered to India, they also were in production finish of PRU Blue with Type B roundels, as described above, but they and the earlier Spitfires were re-marked to India Command require-ments; roundels and flashes in Dull Blue and the 4:1, White/Blue mix. A number of the Mk.IVs and most of the new Mk.XIs were re-marked with 16 inch fuselage roundels. 18in Sky letters were applied, aft of the roundels. The size and colour of serial numbers on the Spitfires varied; either in Night or Sky, 6 or 8 inches in height.

Spitfire FR.XIVs delivered to 28 Sqn, like the Mk.XIVs of the fighter squadrons taking part in the landings in Malaya, were refinished in Temperate Land Scheme camouflage with l6in India Command roundels and White spinners, identification bands, serials and lettering. They were supplemented late in 1945 by aircraft from Maintenance Units in India in 'Day Fighter' camouflage; most remained in Dark Green/Ocean Grey but were re-marked and their Sky fuselage bands painted over with camouflage colours. The aircraft in Temperate Land Scheme colours can invariably be identified in photographs by their having White serial numbers.

The Spitfire FR.XVIII reinforcements remained in their factory finish of Dark Green and Ocean Grey with Medium Sea Grey undersurfaces. Some were delivered to 28 Sqn with the Sky 'fighter band' around the fuselage rear; this marking was painted out in service.

Consolidated-Vultee Liberator

The Liberator bomber was built in greater numbers than any other American aircraft. Liberator VLR (Very Long Range) ocean patrol bombers began service with Coastal Command late in 1941. The Liberator GR.III and GR.V flown by 160 Sqn from Ceylon, had greater fuel-tankage and range than the earlier Marks. These B-24Ds supplied under Lend-Lease and offset from USAAF contracts were painted as required in the instructions issued by the Ministry of Aircraft Production in August 1941, applicable to land-planes of Coastal Command; Temperate Sea Scheme camouflage on upper surfaces, Glossy White on under-surfaces, merged into Matt White on the sides, including the tail-fins and rudders. On some aircraft, de-icing strips were over-painted White. Serial numbers were Light Slate Grey and aircraft letters Red. 56in Type B roundels were marked above the wings, 54in Type C1 roundels on the fuselage sides and 36x24in high flashes on the tail fins on both sides.

On 23 April 1943 a camouflage test was carried out with an aircraft of 160 sqn, which was clearly visible from the ground at a height of 15,000ft. On Liberator GR.IIIA FL 945:H the White was painted over during the next few days with a coat of Sky dope and, on the 29th, a further test was made with FL929:W for comparison, both aircraft flying over Sigiriya at heights of 1,000, 2,000, 5,000, 10,000

and 15,000 ft. The Sky finish appeared to ground observers slightly more satisfactory but the difference in visibility, depending to some extent on cloud conditions, was not sufficient to warrant repainting all the Liberators—in any case, no more Sky dope was available. In November 1943 a revision to DTD Circular No 360 changed the camouflage scheme to Extra Dark Sea Grey on the upper surfaces and glossy White on the under-surfaces and sides but aircraft in this scheme did not reach the Command for some months.

The Liberator B.VIs of 159 Sqn had no squadron codes or special markings, unlike the other four Liberator squadrons that made up No.231 Grp whose aircraft carried White and Night markings on their vertical tail surfaces. Most of the B.VIs were delivered in US Army Basic Camouflage of Dark Olive Drab with Neutral Gray undersurfaces, a few partly re-finished with Night beneath. At the beginning of 1945 aircraft were delivered to the squadrons without camouflage, the Alcald unpainted except for markings and a Dark Green anti-glare panel in front of the pilots cabin. Some of the Liberators were fitted with vertical cameras to record the results of their attacks, in particular 159 Sqn which specialised in low-level operations. After the war ended 159 and 355 Sqns, the latter using a rudder marking of two horizontal White bars across a background of Night, were employed until May 1946 on aerial survey over Bengal.

De Havilland Mosquito

The other principal British photo-reconnaissance aircraft beside the Spitfire was the Mosquito. Even the first Mosquito could match the speed and had twice the range of the Spitfire. Notwithstanding the success of the Spitfire in all theatres of war, and despite setbacks caused by structural failures, the Mosquito has been considered the best reconnaissance aircraft of the war. Eight PR variants were produced, beginning with the very first Mosquitos delivered to the RAF. Subsequent versions used for PR in the Far East were the Mk.II fighter, the Mk.VI fighter-bomber, the PR.IX, PR.XVI and PR. 34. The Mosquito fuselage was large enough for several alternative camera mountings, the usual combination a single short focal-length camera and a pair of 'split vertical' long-lensed cameras, whilst forward obliques could be taken with a camera in the nose. The cabin accommodated the pilot and navigator; it was not easy for a Spitfire pilot to photograph winding linear targets such as railway lines but the Mosquito navigator could give warning of changes of course at short notice.

Designed to meet a specification for a fast medium-bomber, the Mosquito was immediately seen to be ideal for photo-reconnaissance. The first 50 'bomber-reconnaissance' aircraft were designated PR Mk.Is, followed by a day-and-night 'intruder' version, F Mk.II which was short-lived in service and was soon replaced by the ubiquitous fighter-bomber, FB Mk.VI. The first

284: *The elegant silhouette of the Spitfire is displayed to perfection in this shot of a home-based PR.XI rolling over against the sun to reveal the staggered vertical camera ports beneath the fuselage*

285: *A pair of F.8 cameras ready for mounting in a Spitfire PR.XI of 681 Sqn at Alipore. The pilot is Plt Off 'Bluey' George. Note the open fuel filler point*

286: *This Spitfire PR.IV on arrival in India from Egypt clearly shows the contrast between the shine of the lacquered roundels and the 'dull' finish of the dark blue camouflage*

287: *As Wing Commander, Freddie Procter DFC was permitted to apply his initials to his 'personal' aircraft as code letters. As 681 Sqn was not allocated a two-letter code, he had his Spitfire PR.XI, MB776, marked elegantly with his monogram, 'FDP' on the engine cowling*

288: *Spitfire FR.XIV NH866, 'L', of 28 Sqn (?) in Temperate Land Scheme camouflage, with White bands, spinner, codes and serials. The serial had been applied in 4in digits on the fin in accordance with the instructions of March-April 1945. This particular aircraft served as the prototype for the strengthened fuselage common to the FR and LR variants of the Griffon-engined Spitfire. It arrived in India in July 1945*

fully satisfactory version to equip 681 Sqn was the PR Mk.IX, converted from the standard bomber Mk.IX. A distinct advance on this model was the high-altitude PR variant of the B Mk.XVI with a pressure-cabin, which became the main equipment of 684 Sqn early in 1944. A further development which 'filled the gap' between the operational radius of the PR.XVI and the extreme limits of SEAC was the 'extra long-range' Mosquito PR.34, its tankage increased from 547gal to 1,267gal, giving the aircraft a range of 3,500 miles. Five cameras could be housed in an enlarged bomb-bay, two 'split' F.52 cameras in the forward fuselage, two more and an oblique F.24 in the fuselage rear. The cabin was pressurised by a blower which maintained 21b/sq in above external air pressure, in effect equivalent to a reduction of 10,000 ft of altitude.

Although HQ India Command informed 681 Sqn that the "Mosquitos allotted to 27 Sqn are PRU type fitted with cameras and camouflaged for PRU work", this was incorrect. These Mk.II aircraft were indeed camouflaged, each with provision for only one camera to be fitted. When the versatility of the Mosquito was first realised in March 1942 it was decided that all Mosquito FB.VIs should be factory-finished with Medium Sea Grey on all exterior surfaces, so that the various camouflage schemes of different Commands could be applied to them after delivery, according to the operational of the aircraft. It is not clear, however, to what extent this requirement remained in force as Air Ministry Order A.1096 of 8 October 1942 stated, *"Mosquito aircraft with a day role are to bear standard day fighter camouflage and colouring. National and tactical markings are to conform to the scheme for day bomber aircraft. The spinner is Ocean Grey. The code letters are Sky"*. A further instruction stated, *"Full (sic) markings are to be applied to this aircraft with the exception of the yellow leading edge stripe"*; the 'full' Home Base Fighter Command Markings consisted of Sky spinners and fuselage band and Yellow leading-edge stripe.

The four Mk.II aircraft of 27 Sqn were finished with

the standard Dark Green disruptive pattern over Medium Sea Grey, without the Sky fuselage band, i.e. in the colour scheme approved for night fighters. There is no record of the finish applied to the first Mk.VIs intended for weathering trials. It is just possible that they were finished in overall Medium Sea Grey but there is no doubt that later aircraft from the same production batch were in Green/Grey camouflage with Sky spinners and fuselage bands. All were re-finished in PRU Blue in service with 681 and 684 Squadrons.

The first Mosquito PR.IX arrived in October, the finish MAP PRU Blue which was the standard finish for all Marks of PR Mosquitos until early 1945.

On 20 January, HQ Base Air Forces, South-East Asia signalled the Air Ministry, *"Decided to supersede camouflage finish on Mk.VI and Mk.IX and XVI Mosquitos with Aluminium on all surfaces. Request flow similar"*; (ie for aircraft to be delivered already so finished). The scheme received immediate approval and the Air Ministry issued an Instruction, dated 15 February, that "consequent upon the exacting climatic conditions", Mosquito FB.VIs in ACSEA should be given two coats of Aluminium finish above and beneath, whilst Mosquito PR.XVIs should be similarly finished on upper surfaces only, remaining PRU Blue beneath. In fact, the few Mk.XIVs painted Dull Aluminium were so finished on upper and lower surfaces, like the Mk.VIs.

The PR Mk.34, a pressurized reconnaissance version of the Mk.XVI bomber was the final operational PR Mosquito. It was intended specifically as a 'very long-range' aircraft for use in the Far East, and the first four were delivered to India at the end of May 1945. All were finished PRU Blue on undersurfaces with Dull Aluminium on their tailfin and uppersurfaces. The 'SEAC' 32in roundels were added and aircraft identification letters in Dull Blue.

289: Spitfire FR.XIV MV349, 'A', in Dark Green and Ocean Grey upper-surfaces and Medium Sea Grey below. Serials are Night and identification letters are White. The factory-applied roundels and Sky fuselage band have been overpainted with Dark Green. Spinner is Red and 28 Sqn's demi-Pegasus badge appears in a pre-war style arrowhead on the fin

290: *At the end of 1946, Spitfire FR.XIV MV304 of 28 sqn remained in late wartime camouflage and markings, only the identification letter was reduced in size, while MV373 in Aluminium finish had its roundels changed to National marking II*

291: *PM514, a Spitfire PR.XIX of 681 Sqn, newly delivered to Seletar, wearing the factory-applied Home Base PR markings*

292: *A poor picture, included only for its rarity value. This is Spitfire PR.XI PL951, 'K', of 681 Sqn carrying the White identification markings intended for aircraft on tactical reconnaissance duties. Seen at Alipore, the aircraft was re-marked with 16in 'Type C' roundels but retained the India Command fin flash*

293: *A murky shot of a Liberator Mk.VI, EV833, 'X', of 354 Sqn on patrol on an armed reconnaissance 'Maxim' anti-shipping mission somewhere off the Arakan coast during late 1944-early 1945. The protuding ventral radome houses the AN/APS15 search radar. Camouflage is the standard Temperate Sea Scheme with SEAC roundels and fin flashes*

294 Far left: *Installing a Fairchild K.19 'night camera' in the bomb-bay of a 160 Sqn Liberator*

295 Left: *Seen against a background of towering monsoon clouds is another Liberator VI, this time from 355 Sqn, whose Night and White rudder stripes can just be made out. This aircraft is finished in US Basic Camouflage with appropriate wing and fuselage SEAC roundels*

296: *After bombing the rail-yards at Amarapura on 25 January 1945, the aft oblique camera of Sqn Ldr Brighouse's 356 Sqn Liberator recorded the southern part of Fort Dufferin, Mandalay. At that time the only sign of enemy activity was the construction of some gunpits within the middle compound*

297: *Photographic reconnaissance aircraft were not intended to have identification bands applied, but, by April 1945, some Mosquito PR.XVIs of 681 Sqn were so marked with Dull Blue when Alumininum finish was applied. MM367, 'U', wore the new finish while NS645, 'P', remained in PRU Blue*

298: *This 684 Sqn Mosquito PR.XVI starting up at Alipore in April 1945 shows the Dull Blue spinners and identification bands applied to the aircraft finished in Aluminium*

299: *After first forming, 681 Sqn received several aircraft form No.681 Sqn. among them was this Mosquito II, DZ697, 'J', seen in India at about the time the squadron formed. It had the misfortune to be the first aircraft lost by its new owners, being shot down over Rangoon on 2 November 1943. The interesting personal emblem on the crew access door is unfortunately indecipherable*

ROYAL NAVY RECONNAISSANCE AIRCRAFT
Colour Schemes & Markings

Grumman Hellcat I and Hellcat II

252 F6F-3 Hellcat Mk.Is were provided to the Royal Navy under the Lend-Lease agreements. All were required to be modified in a number of ways, this work being done by Blackburn Aircraft Ltd. Some of the original equipment was unsuitable; radio equipment, gun-sights and oxygen equipment were changed. A special Blackburn modification was the installation of different types of mountings for cameras within the lower rear fuselage, one vertical and two for alternative oblique F.24 cameras.

The first deliveries were named Gannet but the names of Grumman aircraft for the Fleet Air Arm were changed late in 1943 to accord with the US Navy names; thus Tarpon became Avenger, Martlet became Wildcat and the new fighter became Hellcat.

The Hellcats of HMS *Indomitable*'s PR Flight, like all other F6F-3s of the Royal Navy, were camouflaged in Ministry of Aircraft Production colours to the Temperate Sea Scheme and bore the National Markings approved for the Eastern Fleet; small areas of the original markings were overpainted where necessary with Dark Slate Grey.

The Insignia Blue of the roundels was extended inwards with White centre disks added and the White of the fin flash widened to form a 16 x 24in marking. These Hellcats, first employed during September 1944, were drawn from Nos.1839 and 1844 Sqns, and coded '5' and '6' respectively, the squadron numbers to the left of the fuselage roundel, aircraft letters to the right. The Wing symbol 'R' was added in October 1944.

No.888 Sqn's Hellcats were similarly camouflaged when they arrived in Ceylon, where it was proposed that they be painted PRU Blue but no paint of that colour

300 Above: *This Temperate Sea Scheme-finished Hellcat FB.II JX725, 'B8D', of 896 Sqn gives a very clear view of the freshly applied identification bands and East Indies Fleet roundels.. The picture has, however, anomalies. The tail bands do not cover the elevators, in similar fashion to RAF and IAF aircraft. Additionally, although the squadron identification symbol, 'B8 is that of 896 Sqn, allocated to HMS* Empress *in June 1945, and* Ameer *for strikes on the Nicobar Islands (Operation 'Collie') during July, the plainly visible deck letter, 'A', is that of HMS* Attacker. *It could be that despite the fuselage markings the aircraft is in use by another squadron or there was a degree of cross-decking following the cancellation (11 August) of the only operation involving all three carriers* was available, consequently they were refinished early in 1945 with a blue mixed from Dull Blue and a small proportion of White, probably a near-match to the 'royal blue' still applied to the B-25Cs of 684 Sqn's Survey Detachment, a familiar sight at China Bay during the late months of 1944. Markings varied slightly between the PR Hellcats but complied in principle with India Command markings—55in wing roundels, 16in fuselage roundels and 18 x 24in fin flashes (6in White, 12in Blue). No squadron markings were applied but the propeller hubs were painted with White bands, one for No.1 Flight, two for No.2 Flight, none on the CO's aircraft.

A series of improvements in capability culminated in a new model, the F6F-5, the prototype flying for the first time on 4 April 1944.

The Blackburn Aircraft Company had been allowed to set up a Modification Center at the US Naval Air Facility, Roosevelt Field, Long Island (some eight miles from Grumman's Bethpage plant), in 1940. There Blackburn was to carry out alterations to Naval aircraft supplied against British Government contracts. Among the great number of modifications made to the Hellcat Mk.I and Mk.II was a redesign of the fuel-venting system. Although no mention appears in US Navy or Army records of such problems, there were several fatal accidents to Republic Thunderbolts of the RAF which were attributed to venting faults—both Hellcat and Thunderbolt were fitted with similar Pratt and Whitney Double Wasp R.2800 engines and ancilliaries. Another major modification was the installation of at least three different camera mountings within the rear fuselage. One permitted the use of oblique cameras, another of vertical cameras, a third of both at the same time. In later documents (including Grumman post-war archives) these different aircraft have been designated FR.I and II, and PR.I and II but it appears that all were classed as Hellcat Mk.I(P) or Mk.II(P) at the time. The aircraft with mountings for oblique cameras only were issued principally to 804 Sqn to serve in the fighter-reconnaissance role.

It had been intended that each Naval fighter squadron should have four fighter-reconnaissance aircraft and it appears that the requirement was implemented for squadrons in the Far East by February 1945. The fighter-bomber Hellcats of Nos.808 and 898 Sqns were supplemented by a few aircraft (sometimes termed Hellcat FR.II) for Tac/R and strike-recording; in addition, each squadron was provided with one Hellcat II(P) (also termed PR.II). 898's JX682 carried the 'Type 1' camera mounting as fitted to 888 Sqn's aircraft but JV282 of 808 Sqn was fitted with a simple timber frame for a single F.52 camera. This 'Type 2' mounting was used in a number of replacement aircraft, JW and JX-serial Hellcat II(P), later delivered to 888 Sqn although neither a K-17 or K-18 camera could be fitted without fouling the control lines or causing 'cut-off' on the film. 888 Sqn, however, devised

a steel frame which could accommodate all types of camera except the K-18—but still only one could be installed at a time.

By the end of hostilities, seventeen Hellcat II aircraft modified strictly for the PR role were in squadron service or in store at the Royal Naval Air Stations at Cochin and Katukurunda.

No.804 Sqn was unusual in eventually being equipped entirely with F6F-3 and F6F-5 model Hellcats for use in the Tac/R role. During 'working-up' for operations the squadron's aircraft carried the symbol '2' but this was changed to '6' early in 1945, in accordance with CAFO No.1099. By April 804 Sqn's Hellcats were marked with the prefixed symbol 'K' of No.3 Naval Fighter Wing.

All the Hellcats were marked with the White wing, tail and cowling identification bands of fighter aircraft as earlier described. An Instruction was issued on 9 March, effective the following day, requiring the bands to be omitted from control surfaces but the aircraft were already painted with full-chord wing and tail markings before the escort carriers of the East Indies Fleet sailed for Operation 'Stacey' at the end of February. Unlike the 16in diameter 'small' roundels on the wings of RAF and IAF fighter aircraft, most of the Hellcats retained their 55in roundels on upper wing surfaces, the White bands impinging upon these, and 32in roundels beneath.

The East Indies Fleet and British Pacific Fleet received a number of Hellcats from Roosevelt Field finished Glossy Sea Blue during the second quarter of 1945, the 'ROYAL NAVY' marking and serial numbers Insignia White. The factory-applied National Markings were replaced with the 1943-pattern Admiralty-approved India Command markings or with BPF markings, the former outlined with two inch White borders to define them against the Blue ground.

Chance Vought F4U-1D Corsair II

Designed to meet a US Navy requirement for a completely new fighter fitted with the most powerful radial engine then available and having a revolutionary 'cranked' wing to provide clearance for the necessary large-diameter propeller, the Corsair proved to be one of the great American fighter aircraft. After carrier trials in 1942 and 1943, the US Navy considered the limited forward view and the under-carriage design unsafe for deck-landings, so most of the early production aircraft went to the US Marine Corps for use as land-based fighters.

Early F4U-ls, however, were accepted by the Royal Navy as suitable for carrier operation in 1943 and first equipped squadrons of the Fleet Air Arm in June and July. F4U-1B aircraft had a revised 'bubble' canopy and wingspan reduced by 17in, allowing their folded wings to be accommodated within the limited-height hangar decks

301: *Hellcat IIs of 896 Sqn, presumably aboard the escort carrier HMS* Empress *in late July 1945. The nearest aircraft JX878, 'B8B', hit the barrier on landing on 21st of that month. All the aircraft are finished in Temperate Sea Scheme camouflage with East Indies Fleet markings*

302: *Hellcat II JZ935, '145/ W', of 1839 Sqn has hit* Indomitable's *barrier on landing, 5 August 1945. The pilot, Sub-Lt TB Speak appears to be uninjured— unlike the aircraft which has had its engine cowling neatly sliced open by the barrier wire. The all-Sea Blue aircraft wears correctly applied BPF roundels, although the size of the bars has required the serial to be moved high on the fuselage*

303: *This Corsair II, JT441, '7X', of 1830 Sqn hit* Illustrious' *barrier in a fiery crash on 28 November 1944, the fate of the pilot (Sub-Lt JL Roberts) not being recorded. This overhead view gives a very good idea of the appearance of the Corsairs just after the formation of the Britsh Pacific Fleet. The requirement for White identification bands was still three months away, and the roundels are still those ordered for the Eastern Fleet in June 1943. Of interest are the Red squadron symbols with White outlines*

304: *Corsairs aboard HMS* Illustrious *being re-armed in March-April 1945 show off their newly-applied BPF roundels*

305: *En route from the UK to India, the roundels of the Corsairs were modified by painting White over the Dull Red, (with odd results) as here on Mk.IV KD747, 'X', of 1843 Sqn. At Coimbatore the aircraft were marked with India Command markings, some later with British Pacific Fleet markings. The aircraft has apparently just floated into the barrier on HMS* Arbiter, *25 March 1945. The pilot, Sub-Lt Ferguson of the RCN, was uninjured*

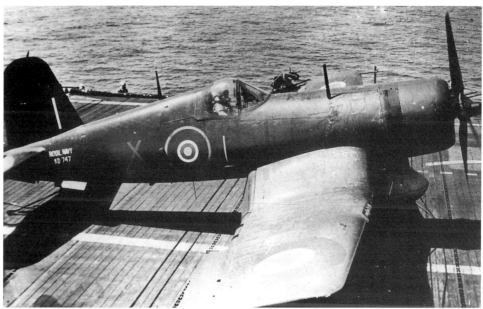

306: *'Type C' roundels, authorised from 7 January 1945, were applied above the wings of the Sea Blue Corsair IVs seen here on their way to the Far East aboard* Arbiter *in February 1945. While attempting to land KD571 has perched itself on the earlier arrivals. Note the pilot has yet to extricate himself*

of Royal Navy carriers. Corsair Mk.IIs built by Chance-Vought were, like Hellcats, modified at the British Modification Center, Roosevelt Field, a major alteration being replacement of the original machine-gun mountings which were found to fail after a few hundred rounds had been fired. A few Corsairs were fitted with vertical and/or oblique camera mountings similar to those installed in Hellcats.

All the early Corsairs were finished in the Temperate Sea Scheme camouflage, Extra Dark Sea Grey and Dark Slate Grey on upper surfaces, Sky beneath. Although the scheme is sometimes described and illustrated as 'two-tone grey', the colours were dissimilar in hue.

As on other Naval aircraft, the 4in Marking 'ROYAL NAVY', serial numbers, Wing symbols and Squadron codes were applied in Sky. The squadron symbol and aircraft letter were usually applied to the front undercarriage doors in Night. National markings were those approved by the Admiralty in August 1943, the 9in White disk superimposed on the 55in upper and 32in lower wing roundels. Fuselage roundels were either l6in Blue, 6in White (as applied to RAF and IAF fighters) or 32in Blue with l2in White centres.

The first Corsair IIs fitted with camera mountings were of 1833 Sqn, No.15 Naval Fighter Wing aboard HMS *Illustrious*. In mid-1944, at the beginning of Naval PR operations, the Corsairs carried only their squadron number '6' and individual aircraft letter. After August 1944, the Wing symbol 'A' was added. Corsairs of 1834 and 1836 Sqns of No.47 Wing on HMS *Victorious* were marked with codes '7' and '8' (later 'T7' and 'T8') respectively and Maj Hay, as Wing Leader flew Corsair II JT427 marked with the Wing symbol and his initials; 'TRH'.

Later, some Corsair IIs (F3A-1) and Corsair IVs (FG-1D) were issued as replacement aircraft to the British Pacific Fleet, some in over-all Glossy Sea Blue in mid-1945. All markings on these aircraft were in White.

When the Pacific Fleet marking was applied, the Corsairs of No.47 NFW were again marked with the letter-number-letter codes, split by the new marking on the fuselage but after Lt Col Hay's aircraft was accidentally damaged it was replaced by another Corsair II, JT456, which carried no individual markings.

Supermarine Seafire

Early models of the Seafire naval fighter were converted from several Marks of Spitfire, fitted with arrester-hooks. Based on the Spitfire Mk.V, the Seafire Mk.III, with folding wings and wing-tips to enable ease of handling aboard carriers, was produced in three versions, F.III (fighter), L.III (low-altitude fighter) and FR.III (fighter-reconnaissance), the last having mountings for oblique and vertical F.24 cameras. Range could be extended by fitting a 90gal drop-tank, flush-fitting beneath the centre-section.

Despite some success in the defensive Combat Air Patrol and the Tac/R roles, the Seafire was far from being an ideal aircraft for carrier operations. Its narrow-track undercarriage and light handling contributed to many deck-landing accidents, so that there was a continual interchange of aircraft between squadrons as aircraft were damaged and re-issued after repair.

The Admiralty's belief in the importance of tactical reconnaissance aircraft for spotting and amphibious-landing support was proved by the requirement that 129 of the Seafires built by Cunliffe-Owen Aircraft Ltd should be FR.IIIs.

No.807 Sqn was the first squadron to employ the Seafire FR.III in the Far East, in support of Operation 'Dracula', the Rangoon landings. Serving with the British Pacific Fleet aboard HMS *Implacable*, 801 and 880 Sqns were equipped with Seafire L.III and FR.III aircraft, operating during the attacks on Truk, Operation 'Inmate', and over the Japanese Home Islands until the end of the war.

All the Seafire FR.IIIs were finished in Temperate Sea Scheme camouflage with Sky undersides. The aircraft of 807 Sqn were marked with standard Eastern Fleet/East Indies Fleet National Markings (usually with l6in fuselage roundels) the No.4 Fighter Wing squadron symbol 'D5' to the left of the roundel on each side, and White identification bands and spinners. Those of 880 Sqn, half of whose equipment consisted of FR.IIIs, wore the British Pacific Fleet marking, at first coded with the No.30 Fighter Wing and squadron symbol 'P6'. These markings were later deleted and replaced by the markings of HMS *Implacable*'s No.8 CAG, 'N' on the tail-fin and the aircraft number on the fuselage sides.

In principle, the Seafires of 801 Sqn carried the numbers from 111 to 134 and those of 880 Sqn numbers from 135 onwards, but exchanges of aircraft soon caused the system to be ignored in some degree. In any case, the practice of operating as a Fighter Wing meant that operations were often carried out by pilots of both squadrons, on occasion flying aircraft of the other squadron.

307: *This view of a Seafire LIIC clearly shows the White identification bands and India Command style roundels adopted by the East Indies Fleet. 'D4M' was in use by 879 Sqn and was aboard the escort carrier HMS* Stalker *when this picture was taken, probably shortly after arrival in Malaya in summer 1945. Immediately after the Japanese surrender the squadron undertook photographic reconnaissance and Tac/R sorties over Singapore*

308: *Seafires of 801 Sqn in BPF markings aboard* Implacable; *several of these aircraft retained their starboard underwing 'Type C' roundels*

309: *Seafire L.III PP979, 'D5X', of 807 Sqn/4th Fighter Wing chews up the deck of HMS* Hunter *while being flown by Sub-Lt Logie of the RNZN on 26 June 1945. Finish is Temperate Sea Scheme with Sky undersides and the prescribed Eastern Fleet Markings with White identification bands and squadron symbols. Two days after this picture was taken the aircraft was struck off charge at Trincomalee*

US RECONNAISSANCE AIRCRAFT
Colour Schemes & Markings

The American Volunteer Group and the Curtiss H81-A-2 Hawk/Tomahawk

The H81-A1 Hawk, popularly known by its Army designation P-40, was the first Curtiss fighter to be powered by the untried Allison vee-12 engine. Supplied for use by the RAF, the aircraft showed poorly in comparison with British fighters then under development and saw limited service as the Tomahawk Mk.I. Improved export versions of the P-40C (Tomahawk Mk.IIA and Mk.IIB), were widely used in the low-level fighter-reconnaissance and ground-attack roles over Europe and in Africa.

Fifty-five 81-A3 Hawks, from some hundred diverted from Air Ministry contracts to equip the American Volunteer Group, were operationally serviceable to support the Chinese Army when the Japanese declared war on the Western nations but only one of these was used for photographic reconnaissance on behalf of Air HQ Burma.

The camouflage colouring of these aircraft has also been a subject for debate and disagreement among aviation historians for many years. Although the camouflage was specified to be Temperate Land Scheme with Sky beneath, research by Ian K. Baker and others has indicated that of the two uppersurface colours (in Dupont 1071-series nitrocellulose paints), Dark Green 1071-013 and Dark Earth 1071-065, the former was a poor match for the Air Ministry Standards Dark Green and was more like USAAC Bulletin No.41 colour Medium Green 42 (not to be confused with Dark Olive Drab 41).

Although Ian Baker has written, "The undersides of the Tomahawks were given a light grey about which we know very little... The colour may have been M-495 Non-specular Light Grey. Sky (0171-021) might have been the official requirement but it is not what was actually applied", it is clear from study of photographs of early Tomahawks, that a darker tone was used, perhaps again 'Duck-egg blue' or a variant of Sky Blue applied to other American aircraft built for the RAF.

On the AVG P-40s the British marking was replaced by that of the Chinese Air Force, a twelve-pointed star and ring above and beneath the wings, and most of the aircraft had around the radiator intake a shark-mouth marking copied from that on the Tomahawks of 112 Sqn RAF, itself adapted from the marking on the Messerschmitt Bf 110s of the Lufwaffe's *Zerstörer Geschwader 76*.

Chinese Air Force serial numbers beginning 'P-81-' were marked on the tail-fins in 2in white digits, and white identification numbers 18in high on the fuselage sides, some repeated 4in high on the engine side panels. It has been stated that these numbers were applied in order of delivery and assembly; this was certainly the case with replacement aircraft after March 1942.

A 4in wide coloured identification band; 1st Pursuit Sqn, white; 2nd Sqn, blue; 3rd Sqn, red, was painted around the rear fuselage of each aircraft. Those of the 2nd Sqn were marked with variations on a Panda Bear emblem aft of the cockpit, the H81-A3 fitted with a camera and flown by Ed Rector and Eric Shilling was most probably P-8123 with a blue band and the number 36 on the fuselage sides.

Curtiss P-40N

Although British experience had already shown that fighter aircraft performance was necessary to the survival of photo-reconnaissance aircraft, during 1941 the US Army Air Corps experimented with camera installations in several of its first-line aircraft. Various bomber and fighter aircraft were tried out and in spite of the fact that Spitfires carried smaller, lighter cameras than those available in the United States, the Curtiss P-40, one of the most promising American fighters at that time, appeared the most suitable although it could accommodate only one long-focal-length camera inside the fuselage. In due course, a number of the ultimate model of the Curtiss Hawk 'family' of fighters, the P-40N Warhawk, were fitted with camera mountings for use in tactical reconnaissance.

Deliveries of the Hawk P-40 series to the US Army were in Basic Camouflage of USAAC Bulletin No.41 colours, Dark Olive Drab 41 and Neutral Gray 43. All these aircraft had the additional Medium Green 42 splotches along the edges of wing and tail surfaces, up to and including the early P-40N series. The application of the splotches appears to have been abandoned on later Warhawks for the short period late in 1944 when ANA equivalent camouflage colours, Olive Drab 613 and Sea Gray 603 may have been applied.

USAAF North American B-25C, B-25D and F-10

Another aircraft that saw service in the photographic reconnaissance role was the B-25 series, some aircraft modified as the F-10. More than fifty of these aircraft had been converted by mid-1942, each carrying a wide-angle, three-camera 'fan' and a long focal length vertical camera. Few were used operationally; the performance of the F-10 was poor in comparison with the F-5 series of modified Lockheed fighters, so it was rarely used for reconnaissance over enemy-held territory. In May 1943 the Photograph Requirements Section of the US Air Staff decided that "tactically it was impossible to use these ships in the combat theaters". Thereafter the long-range missions were taken over by F-5s and F-7s, and the F-10s were used either for aerial survey or for courier tasks.

The camera-fitted B-25Cs of the US 9th PR Sqn were in standard USAAF camouflage of Dark Olive Drab 41 with 'irregular splotches' of Medium Green 42 along the edges of the wing and tail surfaces. Undersides were Neutral Gray 43. 'Call- numbers' were applied to the outer surfaces of tail-fins and rudders in 9 x 6in Identification Yellow figures. Because of the narrow clearance between the airscrew tips and the fuselage sides (less than a foot) an Insignia Red warning band was painted around. the fuselage in line with the propellers on all B-25Cs and B-25Ds.

The B-25Hs of the First Air Commando Group, occasionally used for reconnaissance early in 1944, were similarly finished in 'Basic camouflage' with the five diagonal White bands of the Group marking around the fuselage.

Consolidated-Vultee F-7

The US Air Forces desperately needed an extremely long-range PR aircraft to operate over the Pacific Ocean. Not only was long-range essential but the problems of getting to and from well-defended targets dictated a high-flying aircraft able to carry cameras sufficient to cover a great area in one mission. The most satisfactory aircraft available was the Consolidated B-24 bomber, in which up to eleven cameras could be mounted at one time when converted for PR use as the F-7. Unlike the Liberator GR.IIIs of 160 Sqn RAF, which were simply standard VLR aircraft fitted with camera mountings in the bomb-bay, the F-7 could carry three area-coverage 'fans' of 6in, 24in and 40in focal-length lenses, a single vertical camera and a 'tracking camera' for precise location recording. The F-7A, developed from the later B-24J, carried one 'fan' within the forward fuselage and another in the bomb-bay. As with other American PR bomber conversions, the F7 and F-7A retained the armament of the B-24. Fewer than a hundred B-24s were converted but, as the US Army's principal combat mapping aircraft they were used to collect photographs throughout the world to serve as the basis of a US Government world mapping programme.

The aircraft of the 24th Combat Mapping Squadron were finished in US Basic camouflage of Dark Olive Drab 41 and Neutral Gray 43 with serial numbers in Identification Yellow 484, and a few in Synthetic Haze Paint as described below. Some carried the squadron's unofficial emblem painted on the tail-fin outer surfaces but no other special identification markings.

Lockheed F-4 and F-5

In 1939 the Lockheed Aircraft Corporation produced a revolutionary twin-boom, twin-engined long-range fighter which, in service, became the P-38 Lightning. 119 of these fighters were converted for PR use by removing the guns from the nose cone of the nacelle and replacing them with camera mountings. Ports were beneath the nose for a three-camera area-coverage 'fan' and in the nacelle sides for obliques. These aircraft, F-4 and F-4A, were delivered from March 1942 onwards.

When the Air Corps Materiel Division issued a report *Haze Paint for Camouflage of Photographic Airplanes* in April 1942, the finish was specified for the Lockheed F-4. It was applied thinly over the black undercoat on upper surfaces, giving a dark slate-blue. More thickly applied to under-surfaces and in shadow areas it appeared a lighter blue-grey. Lockheed experienced considerable difficulty with the paint; being oil-based it was very slow to dry and picked up dust, whilst slight changes in film thickness caused "unacceptable" colour variations.

Only 110 of the F-4 and F-4A (re-engined P-38F) aircraft were so painted because it soon became clear that the Haze Paint deteriorated rapidly under severe weather conditions and that it was sometimes *too* effective—it glowed at height above 20,000 ft. A *final Report on Test of Haze Paint* of 23 October concluded that the paint, "while slightly superior to Standard camouflage under haze conditions, is not superior to other types of camouflage". Others of the F-4 series were finished in Basic camouflage but many of these, and some in Haze Paint, were refinished at Unit level in various tones of blue.

F-4s in Haze Paint were delivered for the 9th PR Sqn in September 1942, with standard Insignia White and Blue US national markings on the outer sides of the twin booms, above the port wing and beneath the starboard wing. The aircraft 'call number' was painted across the fin and rudder surfaces and the last three digits were repeated, in 8in Identification Yellow figures on each side of the nacelle.

At the beginning of 1943 an alternative finish was proposed, termed Synthetic Haze Paint, a deep ultramarine 'Sky Base Blue' coat overlaid with several coats of a pale synthetic enamel 'Flight Blue' graduated in similar manner to Haze Paint. The finish was approved, although it did not have the unique characteristics of Cabot's invention, and applied from March to some 30 of the F-5A and F-5B conversions of the P-38G fighter. Thereafter, Lockheed aircraft remained un-camouflaged, having only anti-glare panels in Dark Olive Drab 613. All these aircraft wore markings similar to those of the F-4 series.

Replacement F-5As of the 9th PRS arriving in India in Haze Paint or in Olive Drab 41 and Neutral Gray 43, later to be refinished beneath in a light blue. Some carried the squadron's approved circular emblem on the sides of the nacelle or had coloured bands around the propeller spinners. The squadron received a few un-camouflaged F-5Es (P-38J conversions) after June 1943; these were marked with three identification bands around the tail-booms aft of the radiator housings and with single letters 30in high on the outer faces of the tail-fins.

The F-5Es of the 40th PR Sqn, which joined PR Force in September 1944, had no special markings, merely the last digits of the serial number on the sides of the nose cone. Some were re-finished in service with either PRU Blue of Synthetic Haze paint.

North American F-6B TO F-6D

Although the Lockheed F-5 was sometimes used for low-level reconnaissance, it became obvious that a faster and more manoeuvrable aircraft was needed to replace the out-dated P-40 for tactical reconnaissance in support of ground forces in contact with the enemy.

The North American P-51 was considered for photo-reconnaissance during its development as a fighter. By July 1942 the RAF was using Mustangs for low-altitude oblique photography with a K-24 camera mounted behind the pilot's seat. At that time the USAAC Materiel Division at Wright Field was still showing interest in trials of camera installations in P-38 and P-40 aircraft but expressed the view that the mounting of cameras in the P-51 would so shift the centre of gravity as to seriously affect the handling of the aircraft. This view was undoubtedly motivated to retain this most promising of American aircraft for use only as a fighter but British success with the P-51, it seems, so influenced American opinion that authority was given for the conversion of 57 P-51s into F-6A tactical aircraft fitted with two 'split vertical' K-24 cameras. Subsequently, 35 P-51As became F-6Bs, 71 P-5lCs became F-6Cs, 71 P-51B and 20 P-51C aircraft became F-6Cs. The fuselage depth was greater than that of the Spitfire, providing alternative mountings for K-17, K-22 or K-44 cameras at various angles for specific tasks. It was intended that 200 P-51Ds would be converted to F-6Ds but the need for this superb fighter over-rode the Tac/R requirement and only 136 were completed. Later, P-51K aircraft were converted into F-6Ks with additional camera ports for high obliques.

The aircraft of the 20th Tac/R Sqn were used almost entirely in support of the Army. All were delivered in standard US Army markings, without camouflage but with Olive Drab 613 anti-dazzle panels and, from the end of February 1945, the Identification Blue wing and tail bands and spinners required on all un-camouflaged tactical aircraft in India and Burma.

US Navy Grumman F6F3 Hellcats

The Grumman Hellcat was one of the most immediately successful fighters of the war. The prototype flew in June 1942 and full-scale production began at the beginning of October, deliveries to the US Navy commencing in mid-January 1943. During that year more than 2500 F6F-3s were built, equipping most of the Navy and many of the Marine fighter squadrons in the Pacific Area. The principal variant was the F6F-3N night-fighter with APS-6 radar.

At the end of December 1943 the American Chief of Naval Operations instructed the Head of the Bureau of Aeronautics and the Director of US Marine Corps Aviation that the F6F-3 Hellcat should be employed in the photographic role and, in course of time, each Carrier Air Group included a number modified for that purpose. Initially a few Hellcats operated with camera pods beneath the fuselage but many F6F-3 and F6F-3N aircraft were fitted with an internal mounting for a 'high oblique', usually for a long-lensed K-18 camera, just aft of the wing-root.

Although new finishes for US Navy carrier-based aircraft were authorised in March 1944, the F6F-3 Hellcats aboard USS *Saratoga* for Operations 'Cockpit' and 'Transom' were still finished in the 1943 Basic (Non-specular) camouflage Scheme. The upper surface of the fuselage was Non-specular Sea Blue (ANA 607), blended on the fuselage sides into Non-specular Intermediate Blue 608; this again blended into Non-specular White 601 on all under-surfaces. The upper surfaces of wings and tail-plane were finished semi-gloss Sea Blue 606, with leading-edges in Non-specular Sea Blue. Tail-fin and rudder were Intermediate Blue. 50 in diameter Insignia Blue and White 'star-and-bar' insigne were applied to the fuselage sides. 55 in markings were painted above the port wing and beneath the starboard wing, the White of the upper marking being darkened by the addition of an equal part of Light Grey 602.

The model designation 'F6F-3' and 'NAVY' above the BuAer serial number, in Black 1in high, were applied to each side of the rudder and tail-fin respectively. By the beginning of 1944 most of the US Pacific Fleet aircraft carriers had adopted an 'unofficial' identification scheme, the Air Groups applying White symbols to the tail units of their aircraft. No record has come to hand showing which F6F-3s were used by Squadron VF-12 but aircraft identification numbers were marked on all aircraft in Insignia White, 16 x 12in figures just forward of the fuselage insignia and repeated in Black 9in figures on the forward undercarriage covers on Hellcats.

The aircraft of AG-12 carried Group identification markings consisting of a chord-wise 6in White bar on the upper surface of the tailplane, each side of the fin.

Boeing B-29 and F-13A

The B-29 was the 'super-bomber' of the USAAF, designed primarily to destroy Japanese industry. The first mission was an attack on Bangkok by aircraft of the 58th (Very Heavy) Bombardment Wing, based on a group of airfields close to the HQ of XX Bomber Command at Chakulia, 80 miles west of Calcutta.

A few early-production B-29s were finished in 'Basic camouflage' but most of the aircraft, including those modified for photo-reconnaissance, remained in 'natural metal' finish and retained their unit markings. For example, B-29B-30 42-24471 carried the call-number on the tail-fin in 12in high numerals, with the last three figures, 471, painted above in black, 24in high. The marking of the 468th (VH) Bomb Group, two diagonal stripes, was painted across the rudder surface, in Non-specular Bright Red (ANA 619) to denote the 794th Sqn. The name 'CHATANOOGA CHOO CHOO' was superimposed on the 'tail' of the 468th Group's 'comet' marking on each side of the fuselage forward of the wings. The F-13As of 'A' Flt, 1st PR Sqn, operating from the Calcutta area, carried no unit marking whilst attached to XX Bomber Command. Only the standard call-number was painted on the tail-fin but these aircraft, like most others of the 58th Bomb Wing, carried the usual nose art.

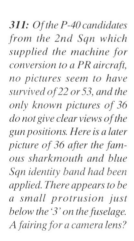

310: Although only one Curtiss P-40 of the 99 received by the AVG was converted into a makeshift reconnaissance aircraft, there is conflicting evidence as to which it was. According to different members of the Group it was variously No.36, 53 or P-8153 (fuselage number unknown). '53' had s/n P-8170; '36' was s/n P-8123. On balance it seems possible that the given serial is a misreading for that of No.36. Stripped of armament and fitted with a British camera in the luggage bay, it was flown by Ed Rector and Eric Shilling on missions. This is Ed Rector in the cockpit of 36

311: Of the P-40 candidates from the 2nd Sqn which supplied the machine for conversion to a PR aircraft, no pictures seem to have survived of 22 or 53, and the only known pictures of 36 do not give clear views of the gun positions. Here is a later picture of 36 after the famous sharkmouth and blue Sqn identity band had been applied. There appears to be a small protrusion just below the '3' on the fuselage. A fairing for a camera lens?

312: 41-29651, one of the first B-25Ds to be fitted with cameras. Unlike the RAF's B-25Cs, these aircraft retained their nose and upper-turret armament, which reduced their performance considerably and made them generally unsuccessful in the PR role

313: *To record raid results, enlisted men of the US 10th Combat Camera Unit operated cine-cameras such as this, mounted in the modified tail positions of late-model B-25s. The B-25J models had an aft-facing strike camera in the bomb bay. This proved to be a highly successful modification and recorded some of the most spectacular imagery of the entire war*

314: *A Consolidated F-7A in standard Dark Olive Drab and Neutral Gray finish shows the trimetrogon camera windows beneath the nose and ports for vertical cameras in the rear bomb-bay doors, which were sealed shut. 42-64245 was originally a Fort Worth-built B-24J*

315: *Pilots from the 9th PR Sqn seen at Dum Dum in front of a Lockheed F-5E-2, converted from a P-38J-15. The aircraft sports at least 103 miniature camera mission markers and an illegible name as well as a fine example of a pin-up. One of a hundred conversions from the fighter variant, all were delivered between June-August 1944. Unfortunately for modellers, although the fairing for the port oblique camera is clearly visible, the serial number of this all-metal finish aircraft is not. Note the shiny metal spinners*

316 Above: This early Lockheed F-4 of the 9th PR Sqn
shows the mottled appearance
of Haze paint. The early
underwing 'U.S. Army' marking was retained on many
aircraft throughout their
service in the CBI theatre of
operations

317 Right: An F-5B-1 of the
9th PR Sqn taxies out from its
dispersal at Rhumkhapalong
on the India-Burma border
for another mission. 'Miss Vir-
ginia E' appears to be finished
in weathered Haze Paint with
natural metal and white spinners

318: Inside the nose section
of a Lockheed F-5A. In
addition to the twin K.22 'split
vertical' cameras, this aircraft
carried a divided K.17 'trimetrogen' assembly with left-
oblique and vertical cameras
forward, right-oblique in the
aft mounting

319: *Although actually in service with VF-2 on 6 May 1944, this Grumman F6F-3 ready for launch from the catapult aboard USS* Hornet *wears the same Basic Camouflage as that which was carried by the Hellcats of VF-12 on* Saratoga. *For some reason very few pictures of the aircraft of the latter unit seem to have survived—possibly because the Indian Ocean was seen as a sideshow by the US Navy. Of note is the catapult strop and the prominent exhaust stains against the White undersides*

320: *A 3rd Photo Sqn F-13A, 42-24621, attached to XX Bomber Command in November 1944, carried thirty-one black and red mission markers below the cockpit windows—and a very fine piece of artwork*

321: *Tailpiece. This rear view of 'Yokohama Yo-Yo' shows the flat camera windows in the fuselage sides and belly aft of the national marking. In 1944 it cost about $400,000 to convert a B-29 into an F-13*

ACCENTUATING THE POSITIVE
Some recollections from the darkroom

Early in 1943, having just completed the RAF Photography Course at No.2 School of Photography, I was posted to the Far East via South Africa. I disembarked at Bombay and was soon posted to AHQ New Delhi, where I lived in the Irwin Stadium, and worked with other photographers, cartographers and model makers, in the Hyderabad Palace which was situated next door to Lord Louis Mountbatten's HQ.

The Hyderabad Palace was a beautiful building with alabaster pillars and marble floors, set in magnificent grounds, but the Nizam of Hyderabad had never lived in it, in fact the only time he set foot in it was when it was handed to him as a gift from the British Government. There we worked 24 hours round the clock on a 3 shift systems, 08.00 to 16.00 to 23.59 and midnight to 08.00 hrs. and were known as the Central Photographic Interpretation Section. It was here that I experienced my introduction to unorthodox photography. Someone 'up there' thought we should encourage Indians to join the RIAF, especially photography groups, and decided an advertising compaign was needed. This was to take the form of large oblique aerial photographs of notable Indian buildings, such as Bombay Gateway, the Vice-Regal Lodge, the Taj Mahal and so on, to be displayed at strategic places throughout India. An order for enlarged photographs approxmately 10ft square was requested, and sounded very attractive, but where would anyone find dishes large enough in which to process prints of this size? We had paper large enough, and the problem was solved by making the exposure, laying the exposed paper on the marble floor of the darkroom. Four 'bods', one at each corner of the print, complete with a household string mop and a bucket of developer, then swabbed the surface of the print. The print was then rinsed with water and fixed in the same manner and finally washed off with a hose pipe. I often wonder if the brown developer stains on those beautiful marble floors were ever removed or was it necessary to relay new floors?

In 1944, I was posted to 681 Sqn at Alipore near Calcutta. The squadron's photographers worked in Tagore Palace where many of the rooms had been converted into darkrooms. In the latter part of 1944, we were informed that volunteers were required to form a complete Photographic Reconnaissance Unit to operate with, and just behind, the 14th Army lines in Burma, and would be known as 681 Sqn PRU (Detachment), the first ever airborne photographic unit. In preparation we were issued with both British and American darkroom tents, film processors, printers and such like, and to familiarize us with all the equipment, we spent days erecting tents and testing the various bits and pieces. The British darkroom tents, developed I believe at RAE Farnborough, were cleverly designed consisting of a tubular frame painted khaki-green, which supported a canvas tent in the shape of a cottage, the whole kit packed into a crate approximately 8ft long x 3ft wide x 8in deep. When the tent had been erected using the tubular frame, the packing case doubled as a darkroom sink compete with drainage hole. Erecting the frame work was more like a Chinese puzzle, the sketchy instruction sheet being of very little use and one built the framework more or less by trial and error. When the darkroom was complete and ready for use, one soon realized it had been designed for use anywhere other than the tropics, ventilation being virtually non-existent, and would have served better as a Turkish bath rather than a tropical darkroom. The American equipment was just the opposite and very sophisticated in comparison. The tubular framework was colour coded so assembly was essentially self explanatory, yellow to yellow, red to red, blue to blue and so on until the framework was completed, when finally a canvas tent was fitted over the frame. Inside the tent were two small rooms built in the same way but made of a rubberized material with a blower unit situated between and connected to the two rooms, and when the darkrooms were in use cool air was blown into both rooms. On completion of work, each room had a wall which could be unzipped from floor to ceiling, and the wall rolled up to the roof to allow fresh air to circulate. Needless to say, the American darkrooms were the ones we used as darkrooms, whilst the British ones were used for offices, print sorting and finishing rooms.

Our first operational base was Imphal, shortly after being vacated by the 14th Army who had now started to push the Japanese southward from upper Burma. Having sited ourselves on the banks of a small river from where we could draw our water-supply for photographic use, the plan was basically for our Spitfires to fly sorties ahead of the 14th Army, over enemy occupied territory during the morning, and on return, all film would be processed during the afternoon, ready for printing through the night. Prints from the sorties would then be ready for first phase viewing by Photographic Interpretation Officers at 08.30 hrs. and useful information passed to the appropriate department in the 14th Army. On the first operation everything worked quite smoothly until the middle of the night when all prints had been produced, then we were faced with a big problem which had obviously been overlooked during the preparation days—how does one dry some 500 soggy fibre based prints, some 9in x 7in and others 5in x 5in? This was eventually overcome by passing the prints through a bath of meths, and taking one print at a time by a corner, a match or cigarette lighter was used to light the lowest corner. As the meths burnt off, the print was rotated to bring the dry portion to the lowest position. Some prints had to be reprinted having gone up in flames, and a few fingers suffered in the process, but we made it through the night, completing the job by about 03.00 hrs. Subsequently the job was made easier when some inventive character created several small 'stoves' from old developer tins, around which several of us could squat and light our methed prints and thus speed up the 'drying' process.

The developer tins or 'stoves' as they became known, were about 7in tall by 6in square with holes punched along each side about 3in up from the bottom. Sandy soil was placed in the bottom until the level was just below the holes, and meths poured into the soil and ignited. This would burn until the meths was exhausted when it could be replenished and the cycle started all over again. Later in the campaign, the drying system was improved by two factors; firstly, we were supplied with a new type of waterproof bromide paper which absorbed none of the solutions and hence dried quicker. Secondly, when this paper was used with another of our innovations, drying racks, the drying process was even faster. The waterproof paper, after leaving the final wash, was passed through a bath of meths, then squeegeed with a rubber rollered wringer to remove surplus fluids and finally laid out to dry. We were able to shorten the drying time by laying the prints on muslin 'shelves' stretched between four bamboo poles. This time was made even shorter by collecting the meths/water solution beneath the wringer and burning it in a trench beneath the muslin shelves. The wet prints were placed on the lowest shelf, and as they dried were moved up to the next shelf until collected finally off the top shelf completely dry.

Two catastrophes occurred in this drying tent; the first being when the lowest shelf and prints caught fire. A character who has remained nameless until this day naturally shouted "Fire!" and dashed out of the tent, grabbed the first can of water he saw and threw it over the muslin shelves, whereupon the complete rig disappeared in a ball of flame—the can of 'water' proved to be 100% meths, but the tent remained unscathed and proved it really was an American 'Green Canvas Fireproof Type'.

The second disaster occurred when Met. Section reported a dust-storm with gale force winds was moving down the Chindwin River and heading in our direction. In the distance we could see the sandy-coloured wall of 'fog' and so the order was issued for flaps on both ends of all office, workshops and personnel tents to be tied back to allow wind to pass through and thus leave tentage undamaged. Everyone obeyed the last order, including those working in the drying tent. Consequently, as the storm passed through, it took with it all the prints on the muslin shelves, spiraling into the air and depositing them among the jungle trees. After the storm had passed a crowd of us spent an hour retrieving the prints, and although we lost only a few, the whole lot had to be reprinted.

Life continued in much the same way throughout the rest of the compaign, our blood being spilt only once. This was due to an enemy air attack during the night. While we were all intent on our work, with lights blazing everywhere, no-one even heard the Japanese aircraft as the American direct drive generators which supplied our electric power created so much noise that they drowned the noise of the attacking aircraft. Not until we received a frantic message from our aircraft dispersal area to "get those *!!**! lights out" and heard the bombs exploding did we realise that we were being attacked. Orders were shouted to scatter and lay as flat as possible. No sooner said than done. The grass was cold and very wet and after the raiders had passed we found we were all streaming with blood—not from enemy action but from those horrible creatures called leeches we had picked up in the grass. We all spent the next half hour in a large circle facing the back of the man in front, removing the blood suckers with the aid of an unlit cigarette, as for some unknown reason they disliked either the tobacco or nicotine and withdrew themselves naturally, thus avoiding any poisoning if a head should be left in the skin.

As the war came to an end and we finally arrived in Mingaladon, close to Rangoon, we again lived in proper houses and, naturally, worked in another palace, once owned by a rich Chinese named Lim Tshin Song who had made a fortune from patent medicines. Until our arrival this had been occupied by the Japanese and used as their radio station from where they had broadcast their propaganda. A room off the main entrance had been converted into a sound-proof studio complete with recording units, and to achieve a fantastic soundproof effect, a false wall had been erected 3ft from the original wall and the cavity filled with teak sawdust. It took a gang of coolies two weeks to remove both the wall and the sawdust.

After a short stay in Rangoon we were to return to India to prepare for the invasion of Malaya, for although the war was over, the button for the invasion had been pushed. So off we went on the jaunt known as Operation 'Zipper'. It was rumoured that it got its name because "nothing was buttoned up"—or so it was believed—but that, as they say, is another story.

Mervyn Caswell ex-681 Squadron

322: *Typifying all the unsung members of the ground crews and service units who did not fly, but without whom the efforts of the PR aircrew would have been wasted, are these men of 347 Wing (681 and 684 Squadrons) PRU Detachments at Seletar, Singapore in 1945-46*

323: *This chart shows all the main types of cameras used by the RAF in World War II. The Williamson F.24 series on the top row were the principal information gatherers until about 1942, when the F.52 series (developed from the earlier types) was introduced. Shown to a different scale, the F.52s were capable of being fitted comfortably into a Spitfire and were probably some of the most reliable cameras of their day. An F.52, as carried by PRU Spitfires, was capable of taking 500 7in x 5.25in exposures from a single film.In general, the RAF cameras were very much lighter for a given performance than those used by their opponents, and thus allowed more effective fast single-seat aircraft to be used. On the bottom row are American Fairchild cameras. These were the basic US cameras for much of the war. Their high-definition capabilities made them much used for large-area coverage and mapping purposes*

F.24 CAMERAS
(250 EXPOSURE MAGAZINES)

14"   8"   5"   3¼"

F.52 CAMERAS
(500 EXPOSURE MAGAZINES)

MODIFIED AS MOVING FILM STRIP CAMERAS

36"   20"   14"   8"   5"

FAIRCHILD 'K' CAMERAS

K19B 12"   K8AB 12"   K17 6"

249

CAPTIONS TO COLOUR ARTWORK

PAGE 193

1: Brewster Buffalo, W8166, 4 PRU, Dec 1941: No codes, Night serial. Dark Green/Dark Earth/'Sky Blue' (Equivalent to RAAF Sky Blue, FS 35550/Methuen 24B3/4). Large Red/White/Blue 'Type A' roundels under extreme wingtips.

2: Curtiss 81-A3 Tomahawk, P-8123, '36', 2nd Squadron AVG, Dec 1941: USAAF Medium Green 42/Dupont Sandy Earth (FS 30219)/ Pale Grey (about USAAF ANA 512, FS16473 or a little paler) in standard P-40 pattern. White numbers on side of fuselage and serial on fin. Chinese markings on wings. Blue band around rear fuselage. Sharkmouth in Red/White/Blue. No wing guns fitted. Camera probably behind fuselage hatch with cutout in fuselage below. Colour scheme accurate, but aircraft not definitely confirmed as the PR ship.

3: Hurricane Trop IIB, BE171, 'YB-B', 17 Squadron, Jan 1942, as flown by Sqn Ldr 'Bunny' Stone. Tropical Scheme camouflage of Dark Earth/Midstone/Azure Blue. 30in codes in Medium Sea Grey. 'Type A' roundels above (49in dia) and below (40in dia) wings. Fuselage roundel 35in Type A1. Night spinner and serial.

4: Hurricane Trop Tac/R IIC, BM969, 3 PRU (India) 1942: Overall Royal Blue (Methuen 21E6/7—a fractionally darker blue than FS35109) with 2in yellow outlines to 49in dia Type B upper and lower wing roundels and 35in Type C1 fuselage roundels. Dull Red/ White/Dull Blue fin flash. Note camera fairings.

5: Spitfire PR IV Trop, BP911, 3 PRU, as it was received from the Middle East in November 1942. Overall Royal Blue (as Hurricane) with 42in type B roundels on wings, 32in on fuselage. No fin flash, Night serial.

6: Tiger Moth, 'Z-04', of Burma Volunteer Air Force. Nine aircraft of the type were in Burma, two at least of Australian origin. This is probably the aircraft used by Plt Off Harris for tactical reconnaissance sorties during the retreat to India. Dark Green/Dark Earth/ probably Aluminium undersides. 24in Night '4' on fuselage side (and possibly on side of engine cowling) and 12in 'Z-04' on lower edge of fuselage. R/W/B 'Type A' roundel on fuselage and below wings, Dull Red/White/Dull Blue fin flash.

PAGE 194

7: Bristol Blenheim I, L8609, 'MU-X', 60 Squadron, late 1941: Dark Green/Dark Earth/Night. Serials Night, codes Medium Sea Grey. MU aft of roundel on port side.

8: Bristol Beaufort V, T9540, 'NK-A', 100 Squadron RAF: RAAF Foliage Green, RAF Dark Earth and RAAF Sky Blue. Codes probably in Medium Sea Grey (NK aft of roundel on port side). Serial black. This aircraft carried out the first reconnaissance mission after the Japanese attack in Malaya.

9: Lockheed Hudson II (Australian), A-16-76, 'NN-F', 8 Squadron RAAF: US Dark Olive Drab 41/RAF Dark Earth, underside lacquered Aluminium. Serials black, codes Medium Sea Grey. The first 100 Hudsons for the RAAF all had their serials incorrectly applied at the factory with an extra hyphen between the 'A' and '16'. This aircraft was delivered in April 1940 and was lost during the retreats of March 1942.

PAGE 195

10: North American B-25C, MA956, 'E', 5 PRU, May 1942: India Command version of PRU Blue, Sky code and serial.

11: Westland Lysander II, N1273, 'HF-J', 28 Sqdn: Dark Green/Dark Earth/Sky. Roundels in six positions (note non-standard Dull Red centre on fuselage) and fin flash. Codes are in Medium Sea Grey, although 'J' could be white. Spinner may be yellow. This aircraft was lost after a take-off crash at Kohat on 19 December 1941. It had already seen service with 614 and 225 Squadrons.

12: Westland Wapiti V, J9754, 'PT-F', of No.1 CD Flight, IAF. Overall Aluminium dope and natural metal with glossy black struts. The squadron markings are still those of 27 Sqn RAF. 'PT' is Night, 'F', Red. National markings are in the pre-war Bright Red/White/Bright Blue colours.

PAGE 196

13: Hawker Hurricane Trop FR IIB, BE198, 28 Squadron, July 1943: Dark Green/very faded Dark Earth to about FS30219/Sky. Underside could also be Azure Blue as this aircraft was originally intended for desert service. 32in dia India Command blue/white roundels on fuselage, 49in above/below wings. Note long range underwing tanks in natural metal?. Spinner Sky. Night serial. Note square aperture for oblique camera aft of fuselage roundel. Inset: upper wing plan.

14: Hawker Hurricane FR IIB, BH125, 'U' of No.3 PRU/681 Squadron, India 1942. No tropical filter. Overall 'royal blue'. No fuselage roundels, above and below wings 'Type B' with 4in Yellow surrounds. Dull Red/White/Dull Blue fin flash also with 2in Yellow outline. Medium Sea Grey aircraft letter, Night serial. There may be a cartoon character on the side of the fuselage. See photo 240.

15: Lockheed F-4A, 41-2371, of 9th PR Sqn, 10th USAAF: Cabot Haze Paint finish, heavily weathered. The overall effect is a pale blue-grey with darker blue upper surfaces where paint is thicker. Very dark blue on wing leading edges. Spinners could be Olive Drab. Probably still carries 'US Army' under wings. Star in circle style national insignia lightly overpainted Haze. Black number '29' on outer face of engine nacelle. Name 'Dianne' in yellow on nose.

16: Lockheed F-4-1-LO of 9th PR Sqn, 8th PR Group, 10th USAAF, Pandaveswar, 1942-43: Medium Green uppersurfaces, Pale Blue (about FS 35550) below. Note drop tanks finished in similar fashion. Yellow spinners. Two guns were retained. Blue/White national insignia. Name 'FOTO-JO' superimposed over lightning flash and number A45 on nose, all in white.

17: Curtiss P-40N-10 Warhawk, 42-105940, 'Pistol Packing Pete' of the 20th TacR Sqn, 10th AF, USAAF: Well worn Dark Olive Drab 41/Neutral Gray 43 with Medium Green blotches on tail and wing leading edges. Serial appears to be in black. 'Star and bar' style national marking. White spinner and yellow name.

PAGE 197

18: Supermarine Spitfire PR.IV Trop, BP880, 'S', 'The Flying Scotsman', 681 Sqn, Chandina 1943: Overall PRU Blue. Letter and serial Sky. Name in White. September 1943-style 16in dia India Command Dull Blue/pale blue roundels on fuselage and wings. 24in x 16in fin flash.

19: Supermarine Spitfire PR.XI, MB776, 'Y' of 681 Sqn, as flown by Wg Cdr FD Procter, 1944: Overall PRU Blue, Sky aircraft letter, serial and small letter under nose. 16in September 1943 India Command roundels on fuselage. Upperwing roundels appear to be 48in. Ornate monogram on engine cowling in White. Spinner could be Dull Blue.

20: The opposition: Nakajima Ki43-II Koo Hayabusa (Peregrine Falcon) of the 64th Hiko Sentai of the Imperial Japanese Army Air Force. Flown by the 3rd Chutai leader, Chu-i (1st Lt) Hinoki Yohei, Mingaladon, Burma, autumn 1943: Finish is natural metal with an olive green mottle. Blue-black anti-glare panel. The arrow head unit insignia and propeller spinner are in yellow to indicate the 3rd Chutai, while the diagonal white band indicates a formation leader's aircraft. The white stripe around the fuselage and yellow wing roots were standard markings used by the Japanese to identify friendly aircraft.

21: De Havilland Mosquito FR.VI, HJ759, 681 Squadron, August 1943: Overall 'India Command PRU Blue', serial Night. June 1943

India Command Dull Blue/White 32in dia roundels on fuselage, 48in on wings. Fin flash is 24in x 22in Dull Blue/White. Later coded 'W'.

22: Grumman F6F-3, '88', of VF-12 aboard USS Saratoga for operations in the Indian Ocean. Believed to be the aircraft of the Air Group Commander, Cdr JC Clifton, during Operation 'Cockpit', April 1944: Weathered USN Basic Camouflage amouflage (Sea Blue/Intermediate Blue/Insignia White) with Insignia White tailplane tips and numbers behind cockpit. Black numbers on wheel doors. Propeller spinner could be polished metal or white.

PAGE 198

23: North American B-25C, MA957, 'K', 681 Sqn, India 1943: USAAF Basic Camouflage of Dark Olive Drab 41 and Neutral Gray with RAF modifications. The aircraft only flew very briefly in this scheme before being repainted PRU Blue, subsequently being re-lettered 'X'.

24: North American B-25C, N5-154, of the ML-Foto Afdeling, Netherlands East Indies July 1946: Stripped of all camouflage paint (including propellers) with Red/White/Blue flag markings, 1m x 1.5m. Serials in black. Red warning stripe in line with propellers. This aircraft had already seen considerable war service.

PAGE 199

25: Supermarine Spitfire PR.XI, PL781, 'F', of 681 Squadron, Kuala Lumpur 1945: Uppersurfaces Medium Sea Grey, PRU Blue below. 28in White bands on wings inboard of control surfaces and 18in across tail surfaces. 16in dia SEAC roundels. Night spinner. 24in high White aircraft letter and 8in serial.

26: Grumman Hellcat II(P), JW730, 'K6-K', of 804 NAS, Fleet Air Arm aboard HMS Ameer, 1945: Temperate Sea Scheme camouflage with Sky undersides. India Command June 1943-style roundels and White bands.

27: Lockheed F-5E, 44-24503, '561/Geronimo II' of the 21st PR Sqn USAAF, 14th AF, China 1944: Overall 'natural metal' with Dark Green 30 anti-glare panel. Black number on boom and weathered serial on fin. The name is probably red, face red/white/blue/black/brown. White spinners forward of propeller blades.

28: Chance Vought Corsair II, JT427, 'TR-H' of 47 NFW, flown by Lt Col R Hay, the Air Co-ordinator for the Wing, late 1944. Temperate Sea Scheme with India Command June 1943 Dull Blue/White roundels and squadron symbols.

29: Grumman Hellcat II(P), JV222 of 888 NAS, early 1945: Overall mixed blue (similar to the 'royal blue' on Hurricanes). 16in dia Dull Blue/White roundels with extra White outline.

PAGE 200

30: Hawker Hurricane FR Trop IIC, LF208, latterly of No.1 Sqn IAF, February 1945: Temperate Land Scheme uppersurface camouflage of Dark Green/Dark Earth with Medium Sea Grey undersurfaces. 28in White bands on wings inboard of control surfaces and 18in across fixed tail surfaces. 16in dia SEAC roundels. White spinner. Note outboard cannon each side removed.

31: De Havilland Mosquito PR34, RG203, 'E' of 684 Squadron, Cocos Island Detachment, July 1944. Dull Aluminium upper surfaces, PRU Blue below. 32in dia SEAC roundels on wings and fuselage, 24in x 22in fin flash. The aircraft letter apppears to be non-standard PRU Blue or a mixed blue similar to the centre of the roundels, serial Night.

32: Grumman Hellcat II(P), JX841, 'B9-L', 898 NAS, Fleet Air Arm, HMS Pursuer 1945: Overall glossy US Sea Blue with modified East Indies Fleet Dull Blue/White roundels, White letters and

name; 28in bands on wings, 18in on tail and 17in on nose.

33: Supermarine Seafire FR.III, PR171, 'D5J', of 807 NAS: Temperate Sea Scheme uppersurfaces with Sky below, 16in Eastern Fleet roundels, White squadron symbols, aircraft letter and spinner, Night serial and 'Royal Navy' titles. 28in White bands on wings, 18in on tail surfaces.

34: Supermarine Seafire FR.III, NN621, 'N/115', 880 NAS, HMS Implacable, July 1945. This aircraft was flown by the CO of No.30 Naval Fighter Wing (880/801 NAS), Lt Cdr 'Mike' Crosley. Temperate Sea Scheme uppersurfaces, Sky below. British Pacific Fleet roundels, with White squadron symbols and spinner, Night serial and 'Royal Navy' titles. The aircraft appears to have a Dull Blue rudder with a White vertical stripe, presumably as the Wing Leader's identity marking.

PAGE 201

35: Consolidated Liberator GR.IIIA, FL936, 'V', of 160 Squadron. Temperate Sea Scheme uppersurfaces, White undersurfaces, in accordance with AM instructions of August 1941. Delivered wearing Home Base national markings, these were later modified into SEAC-style fuselage roundels by overpainting the Red and White portions light blue and covering the Yellow by White. Fin flashes were also modified. Upperwing roundels should have been 48in dia. Aircraft letter and serial appear to be Night. A Churchillian-faced bulldog wearing a bowler hat and chewing a cigar appeared on the starboard nose, just above the DTD paint scheme marking (DTD C 308).

36: Consolidated Catalina I, Z2144, 'FV-R', of 205 Squadron, Malaya, December 1941. The aircraft in European Temperate Sea Scheme (Dark Slate Grey/Extra Dark Sea Grey uppersurface, Sky below). National markings are the standard Home Base types of the period. Squadron markings on the fin were a characteristic of the aircraft of this squadron and were all in Medium Sea Grey.

37: Armstrong-Whitworth XV Atalanta, DG450, 'Astraea', of 101 Coastal Defence Flight, IAF, St Thomas' Mount, Madras. Overall Aluminium dope and natural metal with a red stripe along the fuselage. National markings are all of the pre-war style, probably in the Bright Blue/White Bright Red. Serial black. See photo 13.

PAGE 202

38: Chance Vought Corsair II, JT456, aboard HMS Victorious in 1945, as used by Lt Col Hay as Air Co-ordinator of the 47th Fighter Wing, following the loss of an earlier aircraft. Temperate Sea Scheme with no squadron symbols, Night serial and 'Royal Navy' titles. 48in dia BPF roundels.

39: De Havilland Mosquito PR.XVI, NS787, 'M', of 684 Squadron in April/May 1945. Overall dull Aluminium. SEAC 32in roundels in four positions. Night or Dull Blue spinners, Night stencil-style serial and aircraft letter. 28in Dull Blue bands across wings, 18in across tail surfaces. Wing tanks appear to be PRU Blue.

40: North American F-6C, 43-25148, of the 20th TacRS, Myitkyina, Burma September 1944. Overall natural metal, Dark Green 30 anti-glare panel. Usual national insignia, black serial, 12in Insignia Blue bands across tail and wings.

41: Supermarine Spitfire FR.XIV, MV349, 'A' of 28 Squadron, late 1945-1946. Late-war period Fighter Command Temperate Land Scheme camouflage of Dark Green/Ocean Grey/Medium Sea Grey. The factory applied Sky fuselage band has been overpainted Dark Green. Sky aircraft letter, Night serial. 28in wide White bands on wings, 18in on tail. Spinner is Dull Red, 16in dia SEAC roundels. Note the Squadron demi-Pegasus badge on a disc on a pre-war style red 'arrowhead' on the fin.

APPENDICES

APPENDIX I: BRITISH AIRCRAFT CARRIER MARKINGS

FLEET AIRCRAFT CARRIERS OF THE BRITISH PACIFIC FLEET (March-August 1945) & THEIR AIR GROUPS

Carrier	Deck Letter	Carrier Air Group
HMS Formidable	X, R	No.2 CAG
HMS Illustrious (until April)	L, Q	No.3 CAG
HMS Implacable	M, N	No.8 CAG
HMS Indefatigable	D, S	No.7 CAG
HMS Indomitable	N, W	No.11 CAG
HMS Victorious	P	No.1 CAG

Four new Light Fleet Carriers joined the British Pacific Fleet for projected operatons against the Japanese Home Islands but were not operational before 15 August 1945:

Carrier	Deck Letter	Carrier Air Group
HMS Colossus	C, D	No.14 CAG
HMS Glory	L	No.16 CAG
HMS Venerable	B, T	No.15 CAG
HMS Vengeance	A, Y	No.12 CAG

ESCORT CARRIERS OF THE EASTERN FLEET, EAST INDIES FLEET & BRITISH PACIFIC FLEET*

Carrier	Pendant Number	Deck Letter (July-August 1945)
HMS Ameer	01	R
HMS Attacker	02	A
HMS Begum	38	B
HMS Emperor	98	E
HMS Empress	42	M
HMS Hunter	80	H
HMS Khedive	62	K
HMS Rajah	10	-
HMS Ruler	72	-
HMS Shah	21	S
HMS Smiter	55	-
HMS Speaker	90	G
HMS Stalker	91	T
HMS Trumpeter	09	O

* Excluding carriers on replenishment or transport duties

APPENDIX II: ROYAL NAVY FIGHTER WING & SQUADRON SYMBOLS

EASTERN FLEET, EAST INDIES FLEET & BRITISH PACIFIC FLEET 1944-1945

Squadron	Aircraft Type	Fighter Wing	Wing Symbol	Squadron Marking	Known PR/Tac/R Capability	Carrier
1833	Corsair II	No.15	A	6, A6	x	HMS Illustrious
1830	Corsair II			7, A7		
896	Hellcat IIFB	-	B	B8	x	HMS Empress, Ameer
898	Hellcat II			B9	x	HMS Emperor
800	Hellcat I, II	-	C	3, C3, K3	x	HMS Empress, Shah, Emperor
896	Hellcat IIFB			C8	x	HMS Emperor, Ameer
879	Seafire II, III	No.4	D	D4	x	HMS Attacker
807	Seafire III			D5	x	HMS Hunter
809	Seafire II			D6	x	HMS Stalker, Khedive
887	Seafire III	No.24	H	H5		HMS Indefatigable
894	Seafire II			H6		
808	Hellcat II	No.3	K	7, K7, C7	x	HMS Khedive, Emperor, Shah
804	Hellcat II			6, K6	x	HMS Ameer, Empress, Shah
801	Seafire III	No.30	P	P8		HMS Implacable
880	Seafire III			P7	x	
1839	Hellcat I	No.5	R	5, R5	x	HMS Indomitable
1844	Hellcat I			6, K6	x	
1834	Corsair II, IV	No.47	T*	7, T7	x	HMS Victorious
1836	Corsair II, IV			8, T8	x	
1841	Corsair II	No.6	-	-		HMS Formidable
1842	Corsair II			-		
888	Hellcat I(P), II(P)	-	-	-	x	HMS Indefatigable, Ameer, Empress, Emperor, Khedive, Shah

Corsairs only, Avengers used 'P'

SECRET. P O S T A G R A M. AIR MAIL.

From:- Air Headquarters, India.

To :- Air Headquarters, Bengal.

Ref :- 95/5/AIR.

Date:- 4th July, 1943.

AIRCRAFT IDENTIFICATION MARKINGS FOR INDIA COMMAND.

Reference your A.235 dated 1st July, 1943, the revised identification markings scheme applies to all aircraft. Markings on the under surface of mainplanes will be used only on those functional types as specified in A.M.O. A.664/42 (as amended by A.1096/43 and A.1677/43).

2. The proposed dimensions of the new markings are as set out in the table under para 3 below. Before these are finally adopted, however, it is requested that you confirm by practical trials with one of the operational squadrons under your Command, that the sizes of the white markings shown are large enough for identification purposes without seriously interfering with the camouflage scheme for dispersed aircraft. Should the trials indicate that larger or smaller white circles would be better, your recommendations should be forwarded. Later, when bright moonlight nights return, further trials should be carried out to confirm that the markings are not too conspicuous to enemy night fighters.

3. Roundel (Circles to be concentric)

Position	Type of Aircraft	White	Blue
Sides of fuselage, and under surface of main plane.	Small	6 inches dia.	16 inches. dia.
	Medium	9 inches.dia.	32 inches. dia.
	Large	9 inches.dia.	48 inches. dia.
Upper surface of main plane	All Types	9 inches.dia.	Diameter of existing blue.

Flash (Blue towards leading edge)

Type of Aircraft.	Width of flash	White	Blue	Height.
Small	18 inches	6 inches	12 inches	24 inches
Medium	24 inches	9 inches	15 inches	24 inches
Large	36 inches	9 inches	27 inches	24 inches

4. It is essential that this matter be treated with the greatest urgency to enable final instructions to be issued as soon as possible.

for Air Chief Marshal,
Air Officer Commanding-in-Chief,
AIR FORCES IN INDIA.

Copy to:- 6005/45/Eng.

For Official Use Only   A. F. Os. (L.) 69—70

AIR FORCE ORDERS (INDIA)

BY HIS EXCELLENCY GENERAL
SIR CLAUDE JOHN EYRE AUCHINLECK, G.C.I.E., C.B., C.S.I.,
D.S.O., O.B.E., A.D.C., COMMANDER-IN-CHIEF IN INDIA

Nos. 69—76

Air Headquarters, New Delhi, the 4th April 1944

70. Camouflage Colourings and Markings of Aircraft.—The following co-relates and augments instructions previously issued in Air Ministry and Air Force (India) Orders.

2. The camouflage schemes for the various aircraft types tabulated in A. M. O. No. A 664/42 (amended by A. M. O.'s. Nos. A. 1096/42 and A. 1377/42) hold good for aircraft in this Command with the following reservations :—

(i) *National Markings*, as specified in A. M. O. No. A664/42 are cancelled and are superseded by the new markings detailed in ABO (India/357/43).

(ii) *All Fighter Aircraft* will be camouflaged in accordance with the temperate land scheme as follows :—
Upper Surfaces.—Dark green and dark earth.
Under Surfaces.—Medium sea grey.

Tactical Markings.—Nil.
Code Letters.—Sky.
(iii) *Day Bomber Aircraft.*
Upper surfaces are to have the ' temperate land ' scheme.
(iv) *Night Bomber Aircraft.*
Upper surfaces are to have the ' temperate land ' scheme.
(v) *General Reconnaissance Aircraft in Coastal Areas.*
(Types :—Wellington, Hudson, Liberators) will have the scheme laid down for Coastal Command landplanes, viz.
Upper Surfaces.— Temperate sea scheme.
Under Surfaces.—White.
(Types :—Catalina, Sunderland) will have the scheme laid down in A. M. O. 664/42 for flying boats (target aircraft), viz.
Upper Surfaces.—Temperate sea scheme.
Under Surfaces.—White.
It is intended that aircraft used on G. R. role in Coastal areas at the present time having under surfaces painted azure blue will not be recamouflaged until such time as maintenance requirements dictate.
(vi) *Service Transport Aircraft.*
Upper Surfaces.—Temperate Sea scheme.
Under Surfaces.—Azure blue.
Spinner.—Either of the upper surface colours.
It is not intended that this camouflage scheme be introduced retrospectively.
(vii) *Training Aircraft.*
Upper Surfaces.—Temperate land scheme.
Under Surfaces.—Yellow.
(a) An exception is made in the case of Harvard Aircraft, which are received into the Command with both upper and under surfaces coloured yellow. The aircraft may remain in this state.
(b) Tiger Moth aircraft used for flying training are to conform to the requirements of A. F. O. (India) No. 400/43.

SIZE OF AIRCRAFT NATIONAL MARKINGS BY TYPES

Large	*Medium*	*Small*
Atalanta	Anson	Auster.
Catalina	Beaufighter	Argus.
Dakota	Beaufort	Audax.
D. C. 2	Blenheim	Battle.
D. C. 3	Dominie	Defiant.
Halifax	Dragonfly	Fox Moth.
Hudson	Lockheed 12 A	Gipsy Moth.
Lancaster	Lodestar	Harlow.
Liberator	Lodestar	Hart.
Mitchel	Mosquito	Harvard.
York	Valentia	Hurricane.
Warwick	Vengeance	Lysander.
Wellington	Waco	Leopard Moth.
		Miles Falcon.
		Mohawk.
		Moth Minor.
		Moth Major.
		Piper Cub.
		Percival Gull.
		Puss Moth.
		Proctor.
		Spitfire.
		Taylorcraft.
		Tiger Moth.
		Vega Gull.
		Yale.

[A. H. Q. (I)/06582/1/Eng.].

C.A.F.O. 618.—British Aircraft—Marking and Colour Schemes
(A. 01443/43.—5 Apr. 1945.)

I.—GENERAL

The standard recognition marking of British service aircraft and of Allied aircraft under British administration is as follows in all areas except South-East Asia and Pacific:—

(i) Upper surface of wings .. Red, white and blue roundels. The white may be omitted on aircraft whose primary role is night operations.

(ii) Sides of fuselage .. Red, white and blue roundels surrounded by a yellow ring.

(iii) Fin .. .. Red, white and blue vertical stripes, with the red colour leading.

(iv) Under surface of wings .. Red, white and blue roundels. Fighters and non-operational aircraft have red, white and blue roundels. Other aircraft have no marking.

2. *Far East Markings.*—(i) In *South-East Asia* the red is eliminated from the national marking. The roundel consists of a blue ring with a white circular centre. The fin is marked with one white and one blue stripe, the white leading.

(ii) In the *British Pacific Fleet* the national marking consists of a blue ring with a narrow white border and a white circular centre. On either side of the roundel there are white rectangular panels similar to those used in the United States insignia.

3. *Colour Schemes.*—Colour schemes are not in themselves a method of recognition. Owing to the wide range of colours used and the frequent changes made to meet operational requirements it is not practicable to summarize the operational colour schemes.

Non-operational training aircraft, prototype and experimental aircraft, and the majority of communication aircraft are distinguished by yellow under surfaces. Target-towing aircraft and training gliders have yellow and black diagonal stripes on the under surfaces.

4. *Civil Aircraft.*—National markings are as follows:—

(i) Upper surface of wings .. Registration letters undersigned with continuous red and blue stripes.

(ii) Sides of fuselage .. { Registration letters underlined with
Under surface of wings .. { continuous red, white and blue stripes.

Note.—Some civil aircraft bear roundels instead of the coloured stripes.

5. Holders of Air Ministry Document S.D. 158 (i) should consult Appendix "C" of that document for fuller details.

II.—PARTICULARS OF NAVAL AIRCRAFT

6. *Dimensions of National Marking.*—The radius of the outside circumference of each colour of the roundel is normally as follows:—

Red	6 in.
White	8 in.
Blue	16 in.

The flash on the fin is in the form of a square with 24-in. sides, or of an area conforming to this as nearly as the size and shape of the fin permits. The width of each vertical coloured stripe is:—

Red	11 in.
White	2 in.
Blue	11 in.

C.A.F.O. 618

Note.—The red colouring is replaced by white on aircraft employed in the East Indies. In the British Pacific Fleet the markings are modified as described in paragraph 2 (ii). The dimensions of national marks in these areas may also be modified to meet operational requirements.

7. *Colour Schemes.*

Type.	Upper Surface.	Under Surface.
Operational types, except where otherwise specified.	Temperate sea camouflage (dark slate and extra dark sea grey).	Sky.
Operational types manufactured in the U.S.A.	Glossy dark blue.	Glossy dark blue.
Aircraft employed mainly on A/S duties.	Temperate sea camouflage.	White (including sides of fuselage, fin, rudder, spinner, and interplane struts of biplanes).
Night fighters ..	Sky grey and grey green.	Sky grey and sky.
Non-operational types ..	Temperate sea.	Yellow.
Target towing aircraft ..	Temperate sea.	Black inclined stripes on yellow.

Notes

(i) On the instructions of the Flag Officer concerned, the temperate land scheme (dark green and dark earth) may be used on the upper surface of non-operational aircraft whose duties are mainly confined to flying over land.

(ii) The colours in which aircraft are supplied by the manufacturer may in certain circumstances differ from the standard scheme. These colours need not be altered unless desired.

(iii) Flag Officers concerned may authorize local modification to the colour, or the addition of tactical marking, provided that the Commanders of other British and Allied services in the area are notified. Any changes made should also be reported to the Admiralty.

8. *Other Markings.*—(i) Aircraft symbols: Symbols are to be carried on both sides of the fuselage and are to be as large as possible consistent with the type of aircraft. They are to be painted in the following colours:—

Operational aircraft (except A/S aircraft)	..	Sky.
A/S aircraft	..	Medium sea grey.
Training and ancillary aircraft	..	Yellow.

The symbols to be used are laid down in C.A.F.O. 1901/44.

(ii) Serial number: The words "Royal Navy" and the aircraft serial number are to be painted in black on the after part of the fuselage in the following dimensions:—

Height of each letter or figure	..	4 in.
Width of each letter or figure	..	2¾ in.
Width of colour in letter or figure	..	⅝ in.
Spacing between each letter or figure	..	⅜ in.

(iii) Minor markings or instructions may be painted in any distinctive colour other than red. Red is not to be used for any purpose other than in the national marking for the appropriate area (paragraph 1).

(C.A.F.O. 1901/44.)

(C.A.F.O.s 1950/43 and 1951/43 are cancelled.)

C.A.F.O. 1099.—Aircraft Distinguishing Symbols

(A/A.W.D. 670/45.—21 Jun. 1945.)

The distinguishing symbols carried by naval aircraft are designed as a visual aid in air-to-air and ship-to-air identification, and for use in visual signalling. The following system is to be used for marking operational and non-operational aircraft. The term "Tactical Unit" is employed to denote any number of air squadrons for which a common identity prefix may be required.

2. *Form of Symbol.*—(a) Air squadrons employed in fleet, light fleet and assault carriers.—A letter-figure-letter symbol in which the initial letter denotes the tactical unit, the figure denotes the air squadron, and the terminal letter denotes the individual aircraft.

(b) Aircraft permanently shore based.—A symbol similar to (a). The initial letter (in certain cases two letters) denotes the parent air station.

(c) Aircraft employed in G.P. escort carriers.—A letter-letter symbol in which the initial letter is the parent ship letter and the second letter denotes the individual aircraft.

(d) Aircraft not included above.—A figure-letter or single letter symbol denotes the air squadron and/or individual aircraft. This symbol is for use by newly formed or detached squadrons.

3. *Assignment of Figures and Letters.*—(a) Tactical Unit Letters.—Blocks of letters are provided for operational areas as shown in Table I. These should be assigned by Commanders-in-Chief as necessary to meet operational requirements. Periodical changes should be made if extra security is required.

(b) Air Station Letters.—The list of air station letters is shown in Table II. Additions or amendments may be made by the flag officers concerned, details being reported to the Admiralty.

(c) Air Squadron Figures.—These are to be assigned by the parent ship or air station in accordance with the system shown in Table III. When squadrons of a tactical unit are distributed between two or more ships the flag or senior officer is to assign the figures.

(d) Terminal Letters.—These are to be allotted by squadron commanders. A squadron of more than 26 aircraft is to be considered for this purpose to consist of two or more flights, distinguished by separate figures from Table III.

4. *Method of Marking.*—(a) Symbols are to be carried on both sides of the fuselage and are to be as large as possible consistent with the type of aircraft.

(b) Tactical unit, station or parent ship letters are to be on the left of the national roundel; squadron figure and/or aircraft letter on the right of the roundel.

(c) Symbols are to be painted in the following colours:—
(i) Operational aircraft (except A/S aircraft)—sky.
(ii) A/S aircraft—medium sea grey.
(iii) Training and ancillary aircraft—yellow.

Table I.—Tactical Unit Letters

Home Fleet	A—J
Mediterranean Fleet	N—Z
East Indies Fleet	A—J
British Pacific Fleet	N—Z

Letters K, L, M are spares.

Table II.—Air Station Letters

Station	Letter	
Arbroath	A	
Donibristle	B	Brisbane.
Crail	C	Bankstown.
Drem	D	Trincomalee.
East Haven	E	Dekheila.
Fearn	F	
Henstridge	G	
Hatston	H	
Crimond	I	Cochin.
Eglinton	J	
Inskip	K	Jervis Bay.
Lee-on-Solent	L	Katukurunda.
Machrihanish	M	Colombo.
Maydown	N	Takali.
Burscough	O	Nowra.
Dale	P	Puttalam; Ponam.
Belfast	Q	Coimbatore.
Ronaldsway	R	Sollur.
St. Merryn	S	Schofield.
Twatt	T	Tambaram.
Hinstock	U	
Woodvale	V	
Worthy Down	W	Wingfield.
Abbotsinch	X	
Yeovilton	Y	
Zeals	Z	
Grimsetter	GM	
Anthorn	AN	
Culham	CM	
Stretton	ST	
Evanton	EV	
Dunino	DO	
Ayr	AR	
Eastleigh	EL	

Table III.—Air Squadron Figures

Operational.		Shore-based.
T.B.R.	1, 2, 3	
S.F.	4	Training squadrons or flights.
	5, 6, 7, 8, 9	
Fighter	0	F.R.Us, communications, trials units, etc.

(C.A.F.O. 1901/44 is cancelled.)

A.413.—Colouring and Marking of Aircraft

(S.59966/VII/Ops. (A.D.) 1(a).—15.5.47.)

1. The following regulations, which take effect immediately, apply to all aircraft of the Royal Air Force in the production line and to those in the Service which require re-doping in the normal course of maintenance.

2. These instructions supersede those contained in all Air Ministry orders previously promulgated on this subject.

3. *Wood and fabric aircraft.*—Wood and fabric types of aircraft, *e.g.,* Mosquito and Wellington are to be painted with a silver finish, except—

(a) night fighters,
(b) night bombers,
(c) training aircraft.

4. *Day fighters.*—All day fighters are to be painted with a silver finish and with the smoothest surface possible, to produce the best performance.

5. *Night fighters.*—All night fighters are to be—

(a) *Upper surfaces*—
   unshaded areas—dark green
   shaded areas—medium sea grey.
(b) *Under surfaces*—medium sea grey.
(c) *Boundary between upper and under surfaces.*—In side elevation, the boundary is to follow the centre line of the fuselage, but is to be curved upwards or downwards to meet the leading and trailing edges of the main plane and tail plane roots.
(d) *Fins and rudder*—medium sea grey, with a standard flash on the fin.
(e) *Spinners*—medium sea grey.

6. *Night bombing aircraft.*—All night bombers or aircraft with a day/night rôle, are to be—

(a) *Upper surfaces*—medium sea grey.
(b) *Under surfaces*—anti-searchlight black.   (A.P. 2656A, Vol. I, section 7, chapter 4.)
(c) *Boundary between upper and under surfaces*—pattern No. 2.   (A.P. 2656A, Vol. I, section 6, chapter 1.)
(d) *Spinners*—medium sea grey.

7. *Coastal aircraft.*—Medium and long range anti-shipping, anti-submarine, and G.R. aircraft, are (subject to para. 3 above) to be—

(a) *Upper surfaces*—medium sea grey, except where white is specified in the following sub-para. (b).
(b) *Under surfaces*—under surfaces as defined in pattern No. 1 A.P. 2656A, Vol. I, section 6, chapter 2, including the under surfaces of the wings and tail, are to be glossy white—*see* chapter 2. (c) below for definition for special requirements for flying boats. The under surfaces between the boundaries defined in patterns Nos. 1 and 2 are to be white (*i.e.*, with the standard matt finish) and, in addition—

(i) the standard white is to be extended upwards and merged into the upper surfaces in such a manner that, in front and side elevations the aircraft appears almost entirely white ;

(ii) for the engine nacelles, the standard white is to be extended upwards to cover the whole of the top surface, forward of the boundary of the upper surface colour of the wing near the leading edge.

(c) *Definition of glossy white.*—The glossy finish called for in sub-para. (b) above is to be obtained as follows :—

(i) Where " C " finishing materials are used, A.P. 2656A, Vol. I, section 6, chapter 1, para. 35, sub-para. (i) will apply. Where " C " finishes are to be specification D.T.D. 751-764, the white is to be followed by a final coat of transparent cellulose finish (Stores Ref. 33B/803, 804, 805).

(ii) Where " S " finish materials are used, A.P. 2656A, Vol. I, section 6, chapter 1, para. 35, sub-para. (ii) will apply.

(iii) For flying boats, the under-water surfaces of the hull and wing-tipped floats are to be given two coats white anti-fouling, to specification D.T.D.420B (Stores Ref. 33B/367.)

(d) *Fins and rudder*—white with the standard flash on the fin.

(e) *Spinners*—white.

(f) *Rubber de-icing sheath.*—flexible paint to specification D.T.D.557 (Stores Ref. 33B/505.)

(g) *Engine cowl rings*—white to specification D.T.D.314 (Stores Ref. 33B/176, 177, 343 or 396.)

(h) *Anti-glow shrouds*—anti-glow white (Stores Ref. 33B/528.)

(i) *Identification marking.*—the serial registration numbers on the fuselage by the tail plane are to be in light slate grey instead of night.

8. Other coastal aircraft not covered by para. 7 above are (except aircraft coming under para. 3 above), to be—

(a) *Upper surfaces*—medium sea grey ;
(b) *Under surfaces*—white.
(c) *Boundary between upper and under surfaces*—pattern No. 1.   (A.P. 2656A, Vol. I, Section 6, Chapter 1.)

9. *Training aircraft.*—Training aircraft, other than operational or semi-operational types which may require an operational finish to simulate realistic conditions, are to be painted silver if of wood or fabric construction, or left unpainted with a polished bare metal surface if of metal skin construction. In addition, a band of identification yellow is to be painted round the fuselage and each main-plane :—

(a) *Size of bands.*—yellow bands are of three widths. Small aircraft will have 2 ft. wide bands, medium size aircraft will have 3 ft. wide bands, and large aircraft will have 4 ft. wide bands.

(b) *Position of bands.*—the position for the fuselage band is between the roundel and tail plane. The position for the main-plane band is half-way, approximately, between the roundel and the fuselage. *Note.*—The exact position of each band will vary by aircraft, and is to be decided by commands, so as to present the best appearance.

(c) For economy, where aircraft with an operational finish are allocated for training but require the silver and yellow training scheme, it will be sufficient if the yellow bands only are applied until the complete aircraft requires re-doping in the normal course of maintenance, when a silver finish can be given.

10. Operational and semi-operational training aircraft in operational training units, Central Fighter Establishment, Central Gunnery School, Empire Air Navigation School, Empire Central Flying School, and other advanced training units are to conform to their operational function. This does not affect the authority given for certain specific aircraft at Empire Schools, and other advanced training units, to have a polished metal finish.

A.M.Os. A.388—A.416/1947

11. *Target towing and parachute test dropping aircraft.*—These aircraft are to have superimposed on the training scheme given in para. 9 above, under-surface additional markings of night coloured stripes, 3 ft. wide, running from port forward to starboard aft, and inclined at 60 degrees to the lateral axis of the aircraft. The distance between the centre lines of the stripes is to be 9 ft., and the centre line of one stripe is to intersect the centre of the port roundel. The under surface of the tail plane excluding the elevators is to be night.

12. *Moveable control surfaces.*—Moveable control surfaces are to be kept free from identification markings, including the yellow bands applied to training aircraft.

13. *Communication aircraft.*—Communication aircraft with a metal skin are to be paint free, *i.e.*, in bare metal—polished bright.

14. *Photographic reconnaissance aircraft.*—Photographic reconnaissance aircraft are to be painted with a silver finish and with the smoothest surface possible, to produce the best performance.

15. *Air observation post aircraft.*—Air observation post aircraft are to be—

(a) *Upper surfaces*—
    unshaded areas—dark green
    shaded areas—dark earth

(b) *Under surfaces*—as upper surfaces.

(c) *Spinners*—dark green or dark earth.

16. *Other aircraft.*—Aircraft not specified in the foregoing paragraphs are to be uncamouflaged and unpainted, except for certain specific parts of some aircraft which may require a protective covering of paint (those parts requiring paint are to be decided upon after consideration is given to them by the Ministry of Supply—the colour of any such painted areas is to be silver), where, however, aircraft require certain surfaces filled to provide a smooth surface, the complete aircraft should be painted to obtain uniformity of colour.

17. *Patterns.*—Where aircraft require a disruptive pattern camouflage, appropriate diagrams of A.P.2656A, Vol. I, section 6, chapter 1, will apply.

18. *Roundels.*—A decision has been made to revert to the pre-war roundel on all aircraft. Unfortunately it has proved impossible to obtain the requisite bright red and bright blue paints on account of the acute shortage of the necessary raw materials. It is hoped, however, that supplies will be available in the not distant future, and modest demands for supplies should be submitted in the usual way. Stores reference numbers are contained in A.P. 1086.

Details of the roundels which are to replace existing roundels when supplies of paint are available are as follows :—

(a) *Position and dimensions.*—Position and outside dimensions of roundels are to remain as they are at present.

(b) *Proportions.*—The proportions of the colour bands are to be as follows :—

Where R is the radius of the roundel.
The radius of the red inner = $\frac{1}{3}$ of R.
Radius of the outside of white band = $\frac{2}{3}$ of R.
Radius of outside of blue band = R.

In the interests of economy, new roundels should be applied only when the repainting of existing roundels becomes necessary.

19. *Tail fin flashes.*—Tail fin flashes will be painted with the new red and blue colours when paints are available and when repainting of flashes becomes necessary. The overall size of flashes will remain the same, but the colour proportions are to be changed so that the width of the red, white and blue stripes are all equal.

(A.M.Os. A.864/44 and A.1035/45 cancelled.)

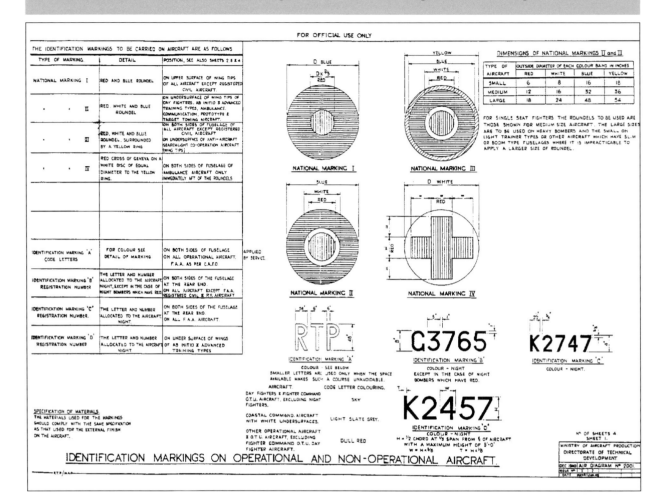

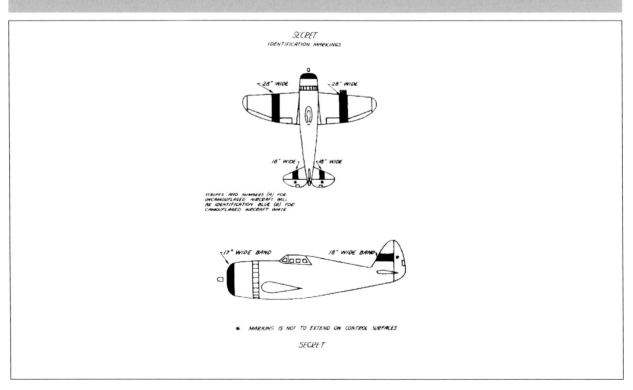

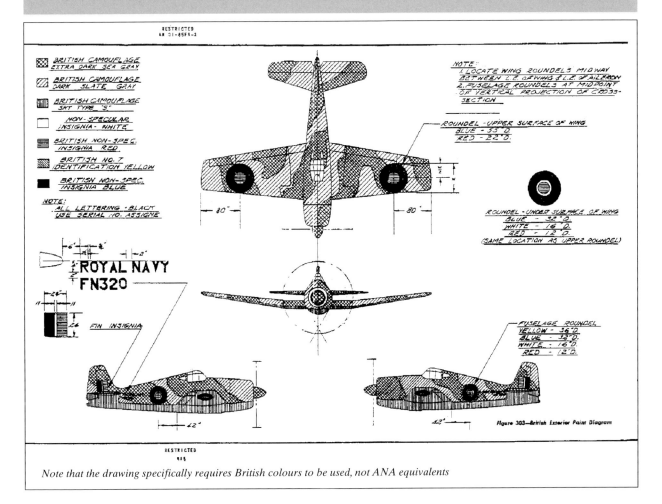

Note that the drawing specifically requires British colours to be used, not ANA equivalents

APPENDIX XII: Facsimile of Report to Air Ministry regarding Aircraft Finishing, December 1944

Report on tour of SEAC, Sept - Dec 1944 by J G Fisher of ICI acting on behalf of Air Ministry DSM.

'Aircraft Finishing'

———————

'Colour schemes in this Command were controlled by an Air Force Order India, of March 1944, consolidating various other orders on the subject. The main difference from UK practice was the combination on upper surfaces of day fighters and bombers of Dark Green and Dark Earth in place of Dark Green and Ocean Grey.
This led, in most cases, to complete re-camouflage of upper surfaces, and so long as this colour scheme is operationally necessary there is no avoiding at least overspraying the Ocean Grey with Dark Earth. A more serious general observation arises from the many Grey colours. In some instances it was felt necessary to re-camouflage the undersurface of an aircraft because the shade of Grey was incorrect or had faded.

Almost all the (Spitfire) VIII had arrived in SEAC in Middle East colour scheme and had been refinished.'

–––––

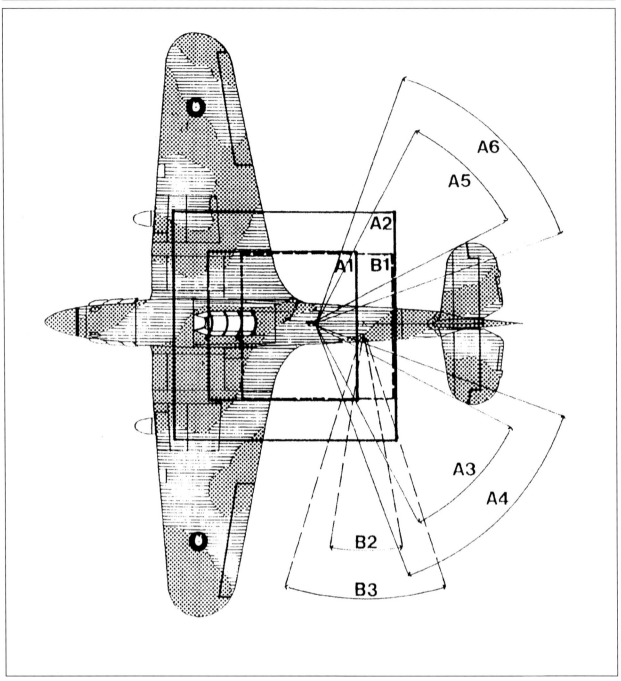

The alternative fields of view obtainable with the locally-produced camera mountings fitted to the Tac/R Hurricanes:

A-position (forward) mounting:

A1   F.24/8inch vertical camera

A2   F.24/5 inch vertical camera

A3   F.24/8 inch vertical camera with angled mirror

A4   F.24/5 inch vertical camera with angled mirror

A5   F.24/8 inch vertical camera with angled mirror

A6   F.24/5 inch vertical camera with angled mirror

B-position (rear) mounting:

B1   F.24/8 inch vertical camera

B2   F.24/14 inch oblique camera

B3   F.24/8 inch oblique camera

888 R.N. Air Squadron,

7th December, 1945.

RE. Recommendation of suitable aircraft for photographic reconnaissance.

There appear to be two different types of P.R. aircraft in existence.

The first and most suitable type is somewhat different internally, and has the camera installation than the standard Fighter Hellcat, the main difference being the position of the flying and tethering tab, and aviator lock lever which are situated much higher in the fuselage will clear of the cameras and mounting. In the aircraft all types of English and American cameras may be installed and a combination of two at one time.

The second type would appear to be a standard Fighter Hellcat which has been modified to carry cameras, the flying wires being in the usual position. In this second type of aircraft it is impossible to mount the K 17 or K 18 camera, and in addition only one camera can be installed at a time.

The camera mounting in the first type of aircraft consists of a tubular cradle mounted on shock absorbers as fitted in the fuselage. In the second type of aircraft the mounting consists of two wooden beams mounted athwartships at stations F7 1/2 and F8 1/2. These although proving adequate strength only permit the mounting of the F 52 camera. When other types are fitted, either the camera fouls the flying wires or "cut-off" occurs on the photographic prints due to the camera lens being too far away from the open hatch. The hatch as fitted consists of two sheet of perspex windows which have to be cut out leaving one large open hole. An oil scoop has been fitted on the forward face of this hole and no trouble has been experienced with oiling up of camera lenses.

In order to allow the installation of other cameras a fitting has been designed by the squadron consisting of a steel frame bolted to the wooden beams and having two camera mounting points at such positions that all types of camera except the K 18 may be fitted without fouling either the flying cables or "cut-off" occurring. But still only one camera can be carried at a time.

It is suggested that the frame mounting be regarded as a temporary measure only and it is proposed to design a more suitable mounting later. A report with diagrams will be submitted.

Disposition of P.R. Aircraft. The squadron is equipped with four of each type of aircraft.

Type 1. Hellcat II JV 93?   Type 2. Hellcat II JW 70?
                  JW 72?   JX 69?
                  JX 676   JX 85?
                  JX 607   JX 932.

In addition to the aircraft in the squadron the following aircraft are known or thought to be in this Theatre.

Hellcat	II	JV	247	At Cochin	1st type camera mounting			
"	II	JV	22?	" "	"	"	"	"
"	II	JV	22?	H.K.	"	"	"	"
"	II	JV	22?	Storage RED	"	"	"	"
"	II	JV	22?	At Cochin	"	"	"	"
"	II	JV	230	" "	"	"	"	"
"	II	JX	50?	" "	"	"	"	"
"	II	JV	72?	" "	"	"	"	"
"	II	JX	65?	Storage RED	Mod	"	"	"
"	II	JV	22?	A.R.?? RED	"	"	"	"

Thus. R. aircraft are not suitable for P.R. work.

263

Aircraft	Maximum Speed/Altitude (miles per hour/feet)	Service Ceiling (feet)	Range (miles)
AIRCRAFT OF THE BRITISH COMMONWEALTH AIR FORCES			
Bristol Blenheim Mk.I	275 @ 13,000	26,000	1,150
Bristol Blenheim Mk.IV	265 @ 15,000	31,500	1,950
Bristol Beaufort Mk.V	260 @ 14,400	22,600	1,600
Brewster Buffalo Mk.I	295 @ 18,700	31,800	950
Lockheed Hudson Mk.III	280 @ 15,000	24,500	2,150
Westland Lysander Mk.II	215 @ 6,500	21,400	600
Hawker Hurricane Mk.II Trop A/B/C	340 @ 22,000	36,500	980
North American B-25C	295 @ 15,000	28,000	2,000
Supermarine Spitfire PR.IV (Trop)	375 @ 13,000	37,000	1,200
Supermarine Spitfire PR.XI	420 @ 27,500	43,000	2,000
Supermarine Spitfire FR.XIVE	445 @ 25,900	44,000	1,320
Consolidated Liberator GR.III	270 @ 20,000	32,000	2,300
De Havilland Mosquito F.II	375 @ 21,800	37,000	1,880
De Havilland Mosquito FB.VI	380 @ 13,000	30,400	2,400
De Havilland Mosquito PR.IX	405 @ 25,700	37,000	1,800
De Havilland Mosquito PR.XVI	395 @ 23,500	33,300	3,600
De Havilland Mosquito PR.34	425 @ 30,500	37,500	3,600
Vought Corsair II	385 @ 22,600	33,200	1,400
Grumman Hellcat Mk.I (P)	375 @ 23,600	38,400	1,100
Grumman Hellcat Mk.II (P)	380 @ 28,000	34,000	1,350
AMERICAN VOLUNTEER GROUP			
Curtiss H81-A3 Hawk (P-40C)	375 @ 15,500	31,400	730
AIRCRAFT OF THE US ARMY AIR FORCE AND US NAVY			
Curtiss P-40N Warhawk	380 @ 10,000	38,000	750
North American B-25C	285 @ 15,000	25,000	1,800
Consolidated F-7 (B-24)	300 @ 28,000	28,000	2,300
Lockheed F-4 (P-38E)	390 @ 24,500	38,000	500
Lockheed F-5 (P-38G/H)	415 @ 25,000	40,000	2,000
North American F-6 (P-51)	450 @ 28,000	42,800	750
Grumman F6F-3P Hellcat	370 @ 22,500	37,500	1,100
Boeing F-13 (B-29)	360 @ 30,000	38,000	3,600

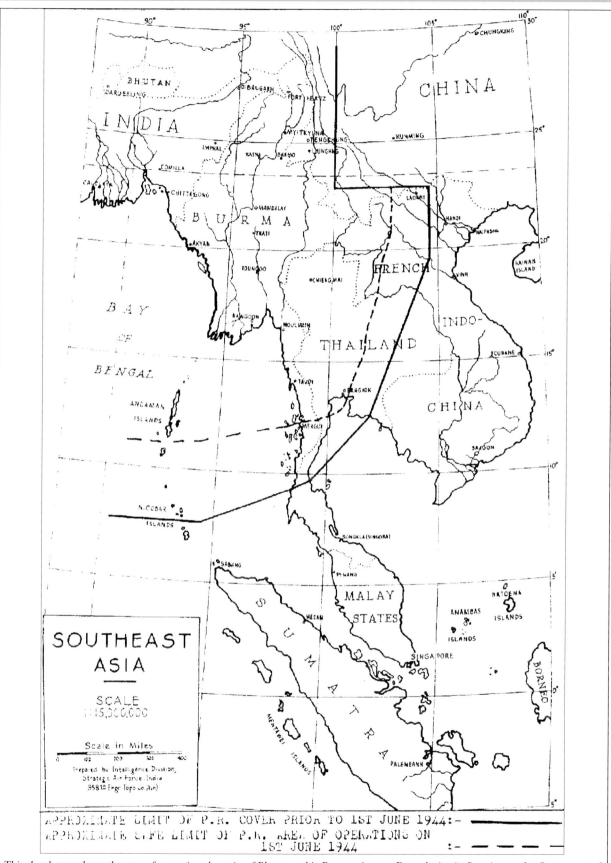

This sketch map shows the area of operations by units of Photographic Reconnaissance Force during its first six months. On account of monsoon conditions the limits of the operational area were reduced to allow sufficient safety margins in case diversions were necessary on the return of aircraft from sorties, restricting almost all long-range reconnaissance

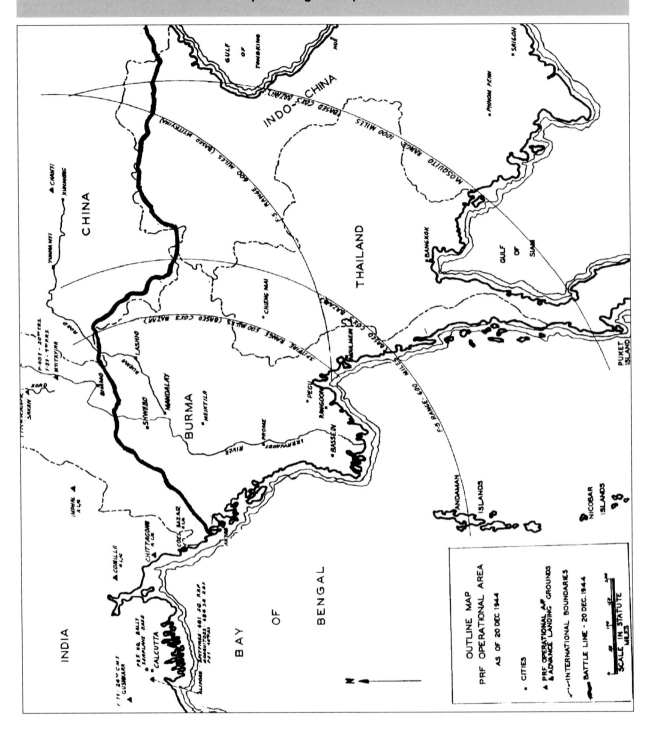

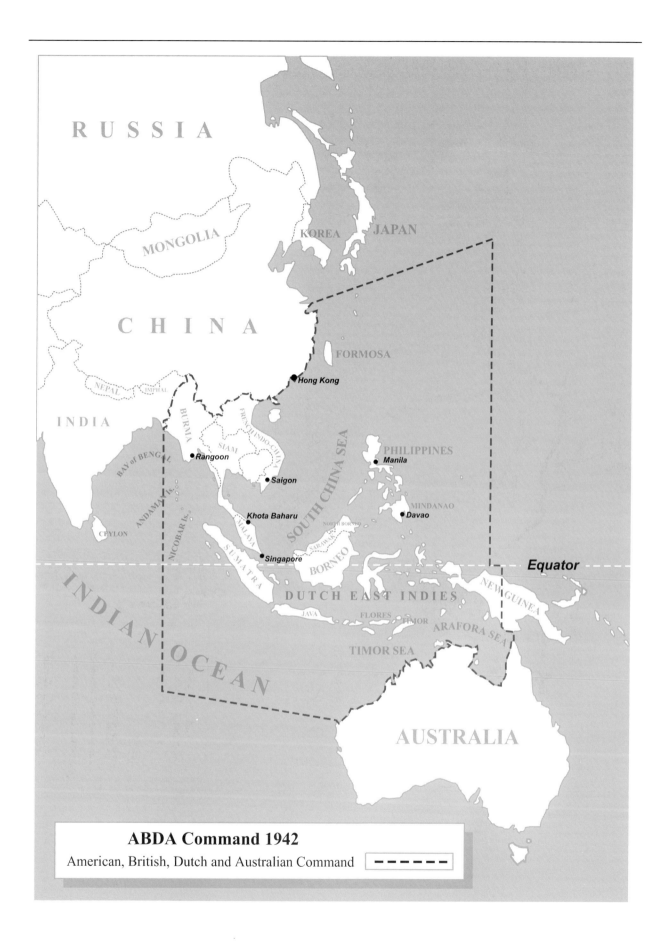

RUSSIA

MONGOLIA

CHINA

KOREA JAPAN

NEPAL IMPHAL

INDIA

BURMA

SIAM

FRENCH INDO-CHINA

FORMOSA

Hong Kong

BAY OF BENGAL

Rangoon

Saigon

SOUTH CHINA SEA

PHILIPPINES

Manila

ANDAMAN Is.

NICOBAR Is.

CEYLON

MALAYA

Khota Baharu

NORTH BORNEO

SARAWAK

MINDANAO

Davao

SUMATRA

Singapore

BORNEO

DUTCH EAST INDIES

Equator

NEW GUINEA

INDIAN OCEAN

JAVA

FLORES

TIMOR

ARAFORA SEA

TIMOR SEA

AUSTRALIA

ABDA Command 1942

American, British, Dutch and Australian Command ‒ ‒ ‒ ‒ ‒

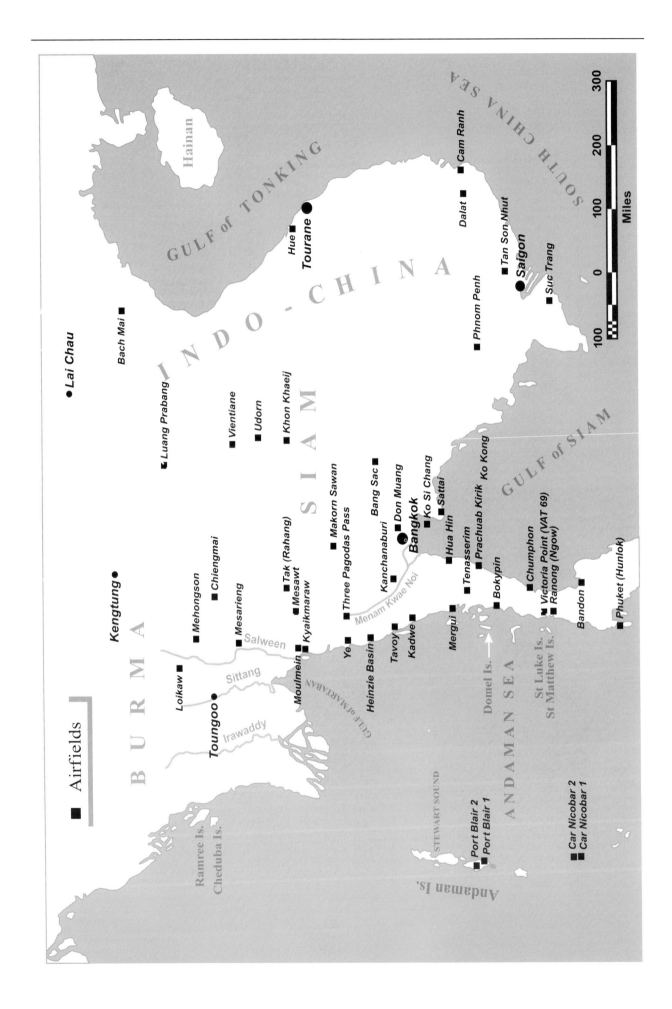

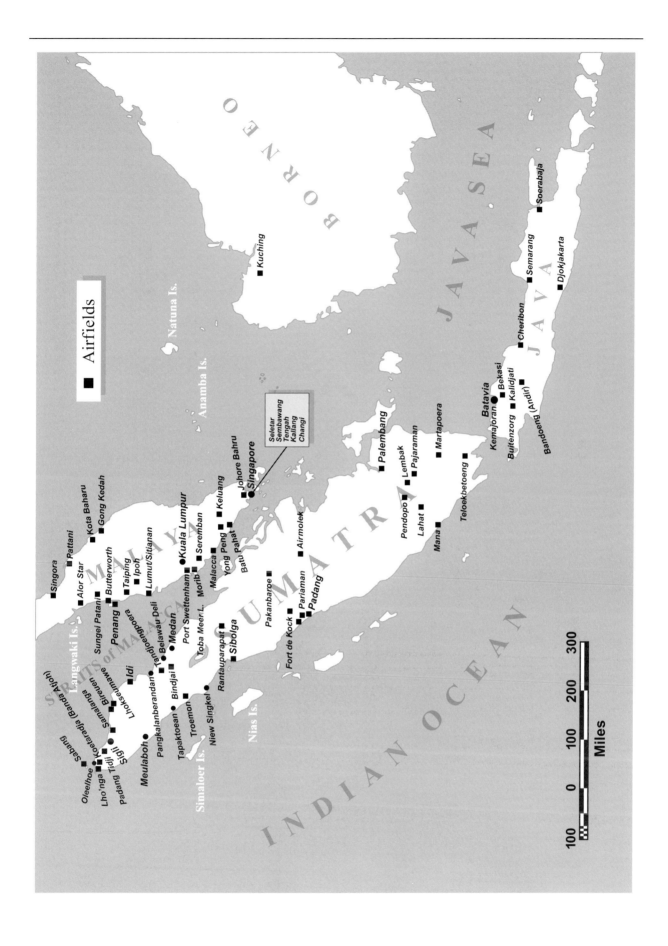

Airfields

BORNEO

JAVA SEA

JAVA

SUMATRA

MALAYA

STRAITS of MALACCA

INDIAN OCEAN

Natuna Is.

Anamba Is.

Langwaki Is.

Sinaloer Is.

Nias Is.

Kuching

Semarang
Soerabaja

Cheribon
Djokjakarta

Batavia
Kemajoran
Bekasi
Buitenzorg
Kalidjati
Bandoeng (Andir)

Palembang

Pendopo
Lembak
Pajaraman
Lahat
Martapoera
Mana
Teloekbetoeng

Seletar
Sembawang
Tengah
Kallang
Changi

Johore Bahru
Singapore

Keluang

Kuala Lumpur
Seremban
Malacca
Yong Peng
Batu Pahat
Morib
Port Swettenham
Airmolek
Pariaman
Padang
Pakanbaroe
Fort de Kock
Sibolga
Rantauparapat
Niew Singkel
Troemon
Tapaktoean
Bindjai
Pangkalanberandan
Medan
Belawan-Deli
Tandjoeng
Toba Meer L.
Lhokseumawe
Idi
Bireuen
Samalanga
Koetaradja (Bandah Atjeh)
Sigli
Lho'nga
Padang Tidji
Meulaboh
Oeleelhoe
Sabang

Singora
Pattani
Kota Baharu
Gong Kedah
Alor Star
Butterworth
Sungei Patani
Taiping
Penang
Ipoh
Lumut/Sitiawan

Miles
100   0   100   200   300

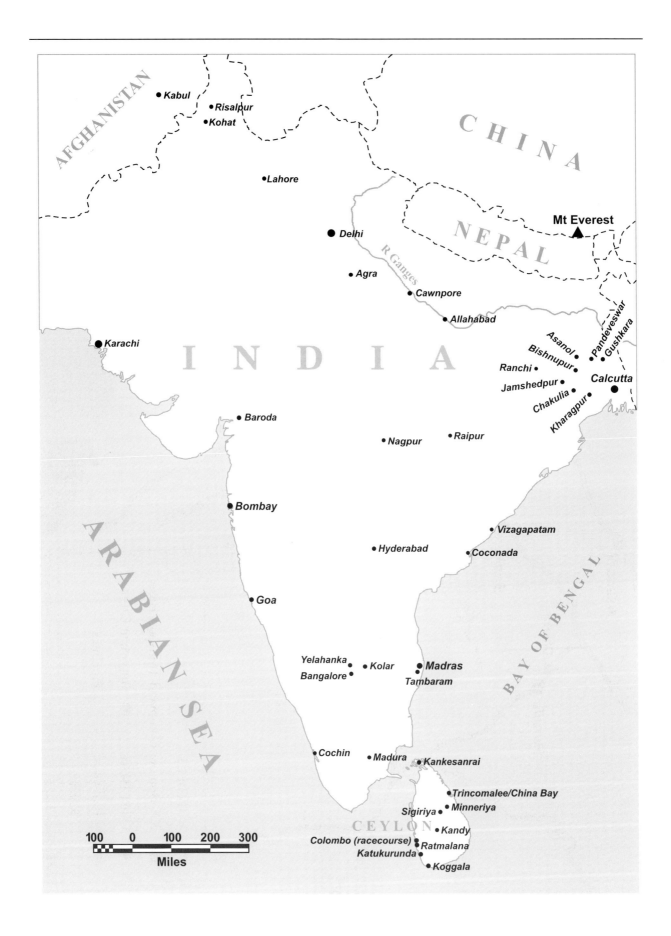

AFGHANISTAN

CHINA

NEPAL

Mt Everest

Kabul

Risalpur

Kohat

Lahore

Delhi

R Ganges

Agra

Cawnpore

Allahabad

Karachi

INDIA

Asanol

Bishnupur

Pandeveswar

Gushkara

Ranchi

Jamshedpur

Calcutta

Chakulia

Kharagpur

Baroda

Nagpur

Raipur

Bombay

Vizagapatam

Hyderabad

Coconada

Goa

ARABIAN SEA

BAY OF BENGAL

Yelahanka

Kolar

Madras

Bangalore

Tambaram

Cochin

Madura

Kankesanrai

Trincomalee/China Bay

Minneriya

Sigiriya

CEYLON

Kandy

Colombo (racecourse)

Ratmalana

Katukurunda

Koggala

100   0   100   200   300

Miles

270

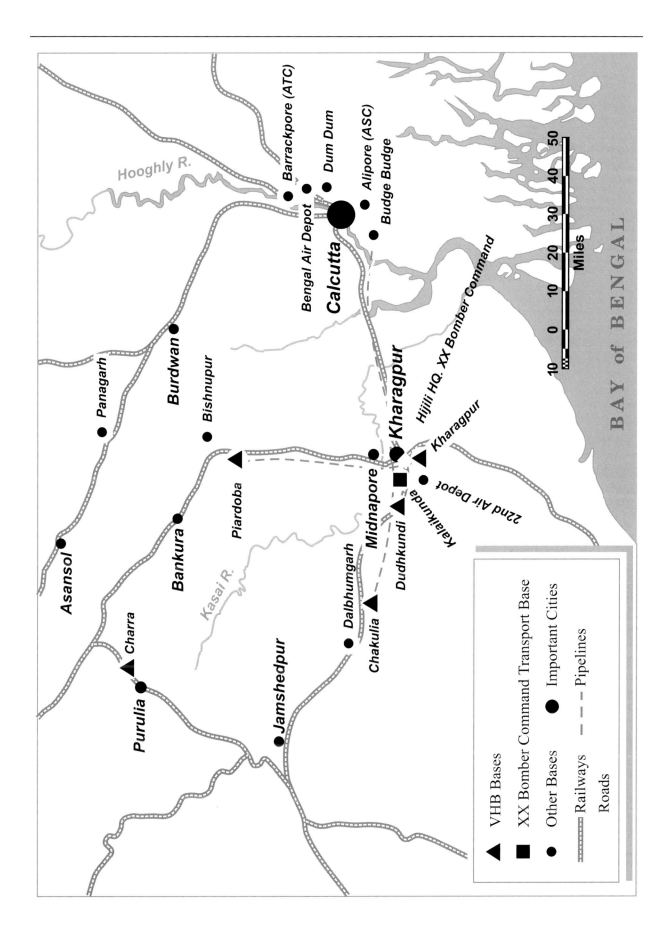

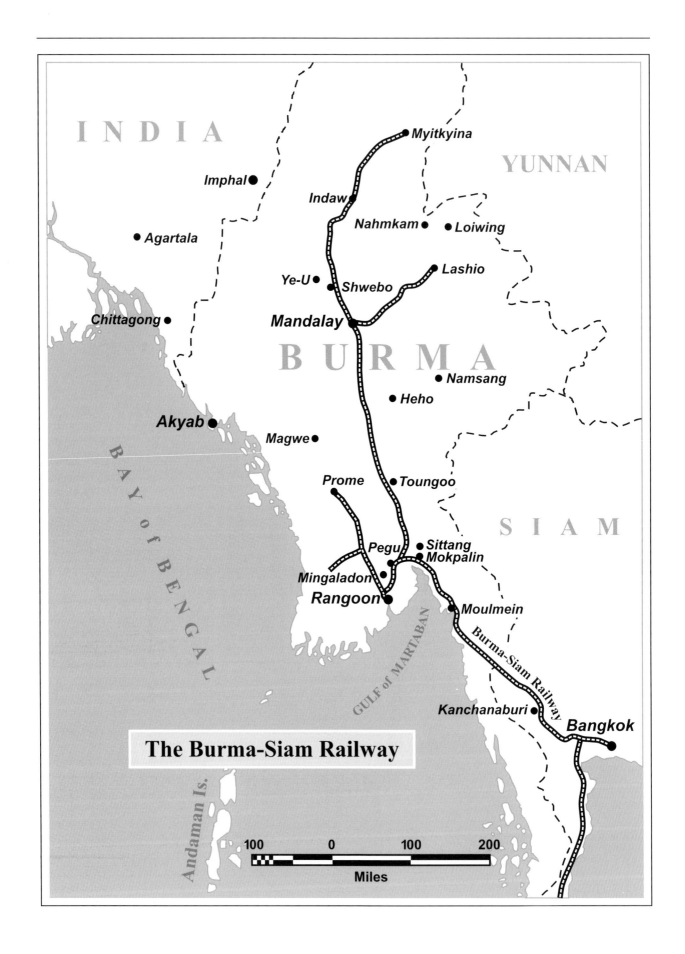

The Burma-Siam Railway